# Capitalism and Capitalisms in Asia:

## Origin, Commonality and Diversity

SNUAC SERIES in Asian Studies ❼

# Capitalism and Capitalisms in Asia:
## Origin, Commonality and Diversity


Printed in Seoul, Republic of Korea



Seoul National University Press
1 Gwanak-ro, Gwanak-gu, Seoul 08826, Republic of Korea

E-mail: snubook@snu.ac.kr
Home-page: http://www.snupress.com

First Printing: Aug. 20, 2018
ISBN 978 - 89 - 521 - 2009 - 0 94330
ISBN 978 - 89 - 521 - 1125 - 8 (set)

# Capitalism and Capitalisms in Asia:

## Origin, Commonality and Diversity

Edited by

Hyun-Chin Lim,

Jan Nederveen Pieterse,

and Suk-Man Hwang

**Seoul National University Press**

# CONTENTS

## PART III Asia Capitalism in Global Context

# *Tables and Figures*

## Tables

## Figures

Introduction

# *Capitalism in Asia*

Jan Nederveen Pieterse, Hyun-Chin Lim
and Suk-Man Hwang

Asia is on rise. It has shown remarkable developmental dynamism as compared to Europe and North America. Despite as late- or late-late-developers in terms of economic growth and democracy, Asia now spearheads the world's most rapid transformation into the 21st capitalism.

Then, we are tempted to find out the underlying nature of Asian capitalism. In what ways does Asian capitalism converge on or diverge from the original models of Western and American capitalism? How can we define the regional and national commonality and diversity of capitalism among Asian countries? Can Asian capitalism provide an alternative model to Western capitalism? These were some of the main questions we were going to ask in the conference held jointly by Seoul National University Asia Center and Korean Social Science Research Council, in Fall, 2015.

This book is an outcome of the 2015 conference in that an excellent group of scholars and researchers from different countries had participated with their knowledge and expertise to discuss a wide range of issues on Asian capitalism in terms of development policy, state-society relations, government-business nexus, labor market structure, industrial relations, corporate governance system, innovative entrepreneurship, and so on.

It would be tempting to say that the global center has moved from the Atlantic, between Europe and the US, to the Pacific, linking the US and China. Simply put, the world is witnessing a power and wealth shift from Europe to Asia. In particular, China's rise and Europe's downfall provide a vivid portrayal of hegemonic shift. China takes the place of Europe within G2 to stand abreast with the US. The size of Chinese economy already surpassed Japan and Germany, and is closing into the US. Its economic volume is projected to surpass the US in 2020. The records of other Asian countries, such as Japan, South Korea, Taiwan, Singapore, India, Malaysia, Vietnam, and Indonesia are also remarkable. Some of the Asian countries have overtaken other regional economies in computer and internet access, progress of the digital industry, mobile phone penetration, and the use of social service networks (SNSs).

These changes usher in the advent of the "Asian Century" which was initially mentioned in the mid-1970s during the encounter between the Deng Xiaoping and Rajiv Gandhi. Asia bears the hallmark of commonality within diversity, and this is clearly embodied in the following concepts: the "Asian Way," "Asian Values," the "Asian View" or "Neo-Asianism." However, we do not know as to whether Asia could be really nicknamed "the second modernity," an alternative for Western modernity. Even if Asia has shown remarkable development dynamism, it has been plagued by widening economic equality, social conflict, political instability, environmental degradation, and so on.

## Theoretical Contexts and Analytical Framework

Is the appropriate terminology capitalism or capitalisms? An early source of thinking in terms of capitalism in the plural is Michel Albert's book *Capitalism versus Capitalism*. His key argument is the contrast between Anglo-Saxon capitalism and Rhineland capitalism, for which he uses the metaphor of the hare and the tortoise. Rhineland capitalism is slower in growth, profits are lower, but growth is more stable, less crisis prone, inequality is lower and social protection is stronger. Thus, the tortoise wins the race. In France, Albert's argument is a sequel and counterpoint to Jacques Servan-Schreiber's 1960s book in praise of American dynamism, *The American Challenge*. The context is also the end of the cold war. In Abert's words, the cold war was an era of capitalism versus socialism; the post-cold war era ushers in an era of capitalism versus capitalism.

Will Hutton in England also draws a contrast between Anglo-American and continental European capitalism, and the UK as a mixed economy. Here the subtext is criticism of Thatcherism and the drift is that the UK should not veer towards the American model. Hutton includes Japan in his comparison as a bureaucratically coordinated market economy, in some ways similar to the German approach. Ronald Dore contrasts Anglo-American capitalism organized around the stock exchange and Japanese and German corporations that rely more on bank credit.

In the nineties, the Third Way with New Labor (Blair) and New Democrats (Bill Clinton) seeks to 'triangulate' both approaches and in effect embrace liberalization and flexibilization of the labor market in order to be more dynamic and competitive, at a time when American capitalism seems to be more innovative, dynamic and better at creating jobs than Europe. In the 2000s Gerhard Schröder's SDP implemented similar policies in Germany. The 'rigidities of the labor market' have been a constant American criticism of European capitalism. Europeans save too much, spend too little and welfare capitalism is a drag on growth. Japan has been criticized for similar reasons.

The varieties of capitalism perspective (VoC) of Hall and Soskice takes the analysis further. Their approach has been criticized as too state-centric a perspective and for identifying different capitalisms with nation states, yet the distinction they draw between liberal, coordinated and state-led market economies remains insightful and influential. Subsequent approaches such as comparative capitalisms (CC) are more flexible, wide-angle and less preoccupied with Europe (Redding and Witt, 2010). CC also identifies multiple capitalisms *within* and *across* countries. Institutional analysis, thick business studies and comparative sociology, more fine-grained than comparative political economy, contribute to this approach. At issue in all these approaches are the institutions and principles that coordinate economies.

The big three in social science are the *state, market and society*. The varieties of capitalism, liberal market economies (LME), coordinated market economies (CME) and state-led market economies (SME), each refer to a different balance of the big three. In LME markets and corporations come first, in SME the state leads and in CME all three are represented. An overlapping terminology is shareholder capitalism for LME and stakeholder capitalism for CME (in which stakeholders include not just owners and managers of enterprises but also employees, consumers, communities and government).

That Europe is a collage of capitalisms is widely acknowledged. The LME dominates in the UK, CME in Nordic Europe, SME in France (dirigisme, but over time France has become a CME) and patronage capitalism of various stripes in southern Europe. In eastern Europe SME have over time transformed to CME. The interplay of diverse capitalisms has made the European Union a difficult compromise to navigate, often with Britain as an outlier, which has now led to Brexit. LME standards have often prevailed such as the Maastricht Treaty (1992) criteria for the Eurozone, balanced budget principles and austerity policies (imposed at the instigation of Germany), all of which, according to Wolfgang Streeck, represent a 'creeping liberalization' of Europe.

How does Asia enter the conversation? First, Asia is a much larger region than any other, about four times the size in terms of population and including the world's two most populous countries. Second, of all regions Asia has lived longer under the shadow of the cold war than any other, as a theater of war and as a frontier between capitalism and socialism. In Southeast Asia the cold war divide has only recently been overcome in ASEAN and the ASEAN Economic Community (2015). In Northeast Asia, the cold war lives on in the division that runs through Korea. If Europe, a small region by comparison, hosts diverse capitalisms, we would surely expect Asia to hold diverse types of market economies as well. Yet because capitalisms in the plural is a post-cold war perspective, we would also expect it to be less salient in Asia. In Asia capitalism has mostly figured as a category in the singular with variations in the margins — market economies with variations in degrees and styles of state guidance, in historical trajectories and institutional makeup, and in rent seeking and crony capitalism. Proponents as well as critics of capitalism in Asia generally speak of capitalism in the singular. Empirically, diverse and mixed economies are clearly mapped but analytically the singular perspective prevails (e.g., Bello, 1992). Third, although Asian experience with newly industrializing economies is recent, Asia's experience with market economies and openness to trade, also long-distance trade, may well be the world's oldest and longest, as old as the Silk Roads. The rise of Asia is a comeback, a resurgence.

Japan's Meiji revolution followed the Prussian and German example and succeeded in this course where others failed (the Habsburgs, the Ottomans, the Qing failed; Russia achieved limited success and was defeated by Japan). It followed the mold of nineteenth-century European industrializing economies and their state-supported industries. Chalmers Johnson attributed Japan's postwar economic success to the developmental state. The Asian tiger economies followed this path but without the military-industrial complex. They have become the most successful experience in the annals of postwar development. The model of the East Asian developmental state (EADS) continues to have ramifications worldwide.

The quality and caliber of states and institutions shapes differences among SME — is the state developmental or predatory, efficient or inept, weak or strong in terms of institutions? There is a tendency for SME to evolve over time towards CME or LME because these are more responsive to market and social dynamics. In Asia this has occurred in Japan, South Korea, Taiwan and to some extent in China (Deng Xiao Ping), India (1991 liberalization), Vietnam and other countries. The countertrends are several. They include the EADS, autocratic and technocratic governments, socialist economies (China, Vietnam, Laos, North Korea), economies under military rule or steeped in military influence (Pakistan, Myanmar, Indonesia, Thailand), feudal societies (Brunei) and countries under de facto one-party rule (Singapore). At times of crisis, emergency and war, state-led policies, and sometimes also institutions, make a comeback (such as the New Deal in US during the Great Depression). The state must usually clean up after the market.

When South Korea changed from a developmental state to a post-developmental economy it morphed from a SME to a CME. After IMF intervention in the Asian crisis (1997/98), South Korea adopted elements of the liberal market economy, notably the flexibilization of the labor market (Lim and Jang, 2006). Korean trade unions continue to protest against the growth of contract labor. A further rebalancing has been the growth of welfare spending (Teichman, 2014; Hwang and Lim, 2016). At the time Germany and Japan adopted parallel changes. The flexibilization of the labor market — in effect, depressing wages — is now being implemented in Spain, Italy and in France it is on the agenda in the 2017 elections.

The state sector is large across Asia: "state-run firms make up 40% of Asia's total and family-run firms, often conglomerates or 'business houses,' account for 27%," with some variation across countries (The Economist, 2014).

Thus, in Asian countries the state sector is the largest and comprises state-owned enterprises (SOEs), the government-linked corporations (GLC) of Singapore and Malaysia and sovereign wealth funds. The second largest sector in most countries are the family-run conglomerates, such as the *chaebol* in South Korea (Daewoo, Samsung). In China, SOEs occupy this terrain. The third segment are the private sector of small family-owned and managed enterprises, notably in Southeast Asia. In China this sector is characterized as 'network capitalism'. A fourth domain is the informal sector, which is large in South Asia India, Pakistan and Southeast Asia. In China three market economies coexist: the state-owned enterprises, the small family-owned enterprises, and the public-private partnership corporations of local governments, all of which compete with one another (Redding and Witt, 2010).

Do these represent multiple capitalisms within countries? Yes, in that each sector responds to different rules and institutions of economic coordination; no or up to a point, in that there are also overarching institutions of economic coordination. Thus, we can broadly characterize an overall pattern and at the same time recognize mixed economies of diverse strands. Thus, most Southeast Asian economies are hybrid CME that combine state control (macroeconomic policy, GLC, sovereign wealth funds), liberal market strands, foreign companies and joint ventures and the network capitalism of family-owned enterprises.

Meanwhile a series of crises in the US, the headmaster of the LME has changed the global landscape. The dotcom bubble burst (2000), the Enron series of corporate scandals (2001), the collapse of subprime mortgages (2007), the fall of Lehman Brothers (2008) and a full-fledged Wall Street crash that spread to the UK and Europe and triggered a global slowdown, also in Asia. These crises signal that following the American model is no longer on. Political crisis follows economic crisis, with a surge of populism, producing Brexit and the election of Trump and 'a bonfire of certainties'. The implosion occurs in the two countries that have led the way to neoliberalism, societies where inequality is highest, financialization most advanced and social protection most eroded. In LME growing inequality is built in, which undercuts demand, hampers recovery, erodes hope and fuels populism and division. Financialization is politically embedded, out of control and crisis prone. Because of structures and institutions built over decades, major course changes in LME are not likely. The spread of options is narrow.

If LME are unstable and European CME are in a rut of stagnation, the radar pivots to rising Asia. Several challenges are familiar: are state institutions nimble enough to engage innovation and competition? Can Asian countries deal with aging populations? With rising protectionism in advanced economies, and emerging economies in Asia dependent on trade can regional and global South demand take up the slack? Asia is becoming increasingly part of a China-centric networks, but what if China's growth falters?

The above is a rudimentary sketch towards an analysis of capitalism(s) in Asia, an outline towards a research agenda. Is this diagnosis productive, do the analytics measure up, how should they be adjusted to fit Asian trends, and down the road, what ramifications for institutions and policies would follow? Discussions in Asia join wider comparative political economy and analysis of comparative capitalisms, which is part of the backdrop to the themes in this volume.

## Organization of the Argument

This is the backdrop to the emergence of the theme of capitalisms in Asia. This theme means that Asian discussions join wider comparative political economy and analysis of comparative capitalisms and that analytics take on a more reflexive and critical character.

We really expect that this book can provide a platform for those who are interested in comparative political economy to work together more actively for developing new ideas and insights on Asian capitalism in the future.

Part I, "Recent Changes in Asian Capitalism," includes four papers presenting the process of development and recent changes in Asian capitalism throughout the various industrial sectors and countries. Kyong Dong Kim attempts to explicate the emergence and evolution of capitalism in three East Asian nations in "Formation and Development of Capitalism in the Modernization of East Asia: An Alternative Theoretical Explication." He utilizes the concepts of international acculturation and adaptive change that are defined by selectivity of both political and cultural sources. The analysis focuses on the issue of the convergent and divergent patterns of change resulting from modernization in two separate waves of modernization in the nineteenth century and the post-World War II period. Jan Nederveen Pieterse discusses varieties of capitalism in relation to regions and countries and types of social formations in "Comparing Capitalisms, East and West." He asks what the relationship between conceptualizations of singular (capitalism) and plural (capitalisms) is and suggests a layered analysis to accommodate common as well as variant components. He notices that liberal, coordinated and state-led market economies are all market economies, though the way the market economy is understood differs in each setting. Wolf Schäfer examines capitalism and technoscience as they are and explores how they should be in the light of pressing global problems in his article, "Regional Capitalisms and Global Technoscience: Controllable or Uncontrollable Forces of Planetary Change?" Considering Chinese, Nordic, German, and American models of capitalism as regional capitalisms and distinguishing the formations of state, welfare state, and free market capitalisms, the two-pronged question is tackled: Can capitalism deliver material wealth to all people and serve the commonweal? The article concludes that the contemporary human predicament is dire but not hopeless. "A New "Spirit" of Capitalism?: Globalization and Its Impact on the Diffusion of Neoliberal Management Thinking in Germany and the East Asian Economies" by Markus Pohlmann and Hyun-Chin Lim questions mainstream globalization literature's assumptions about how globalization affects industrial enterprise. It is presumed to give rise to transnational companies and subsequently, to a transnational class of managers, who use neoliberal management thinking to accelerate the neoliberal transformation of the economy. The article puts these engrained assumptions to a strong empirical test by analyzing how transnational the life courses of 475 CEOs of the Top 100 industrial company groups in Germany as well as in Korea, Japan, and China are. The findings indicate that neoliberal management thinking is not emerging and that top managers are not the switchmen leading toward a financial market-driven economy.

Part II, "Diversity of Asian Capitalism: China, Japan and Indonesia," deals with growing interest in Asian capitalism triggered by the rapid and prolonged growth in China and other countries in this region. Nan Lin wrote the article "Capitalism in China: A Centrally Managed Capitalism (CMC) and Its Future." According to him, under centrally managed capitalism, the party-state commands the economy by controlling personnel, organizations, and capital in both political and economic arenas. At the same time, it delegates fiscal and administrative authorities to multiple and diversely formed corporations to compete in the marketplace. He also explores feasibility and paths toward an indigenous ideology of democracy. "State Neoliberalism: The Chinese Road to Capitalism in Comparative Perspective," by Alvin Y. So and Yin Wah Chu aims to identify the main elements of a new variety of capitalism in China within the context of Chinese domestic political economy, thus providing the first step toward examining China's emergent capitalism since 1978, what we label as "state neoliberalism." This paper compares the similarities and differences between state neoliberalism in China with other varieties of capitalism. After identifying the distinctive characteristics of state neoliberalism, the authors argue that state neoliberalism has engendered a ceaseless drive of capitalist accumulation in China, propelling China from a poor third world country to an economic powerhouse of the capitalist world-economy. In "The End of the Long Boom?: A Comparative Institutional Analysis of Long-term Growth in China," Tobias ten Brink identifies the institutional foundations of long-term growth in the People's Republic of China. The peculiarities of the Chinese system include a selective integration into the world economy; the stabilizing role of private-public growth alliances mostly at the local level; strong state permeation in corporate governance and corporate finance; company access to large domestic markets; segmented systems of low cost, yet comparably well-educated labor; and increasing innovation capacities. Yet, this variegated state-permeated capitalism is currently confronted with serious challenges that are addressed in order to tackle the question of whether the long boom is about to come to an end. "Beyond Predatory Productivism?:

The Political Economy of Welfare Capitalism in Post-New Order Indonesia," by Andrew Rosser and Maryke van Diermen examines the evolution of welfare capitalism in Indonesia in recent decades and the political dynamics that have shaped this process using an analytical framework that understands the nature of welfare capitalism in terms of a contestation between competing political and social forces and the balance of power between them.

Part III, "Asian Capitalism in Global Context," explores how Asian capitalism has interacted with other capitalisms. Hyungkee Kim aims to clarify how financial liberalization has transformed the East Asian development model in his paper, "How Financial Liberalization Transformed the East Asian Development Model," which argues that the East Asian development model has transformed into a hybrid model in which the elements of the Anglo-American model were grafted onto the East Asian development model. Financial liberalization was followed by labor market flexibilization. The result of the transformation has been hybridization rather than transition. "The "Renminbi Swap Lines" and the Emergent Role of China as an Emergency Lender: Evidence from Argentina" is written by Rodrigo Luiz Medeiros da Silva. He evaluates the current internationalization state of China's domestic currency, the yuan-renminbi and then discusses the motivations behind the Chinese aim to achieve a global status for its currency. He also reviews the official initiatives to internationalize it. Joonkoo Lee and Hyun-Chin Lim examine the changing patterns of international trade in the mobile phone global value chains (GVCs), specifically the growing role of East Asia in inter- and intra-regional trade networks, and the divergent positions of East Asian countries in the GVCs in the article "East Asia's Inter- and Intra-Regional Trade Networks and

Changing Roles in Global Mobile Phone Value Chains." Building on a framework of differing positions in GVCs and using international trade statistics, the paper finds that major exporting and importing countries were located in different positions in GVCs and a significant shift occurred for some of the countries in the post-crisis period of 2007-2013. Thomas Kalinowski and Minjoung Park participated in the volume with the article "Development Cooperation and the Legacy of the Developmental State: Government Initiative and State-Business Partnership in Korean Development Cooperation with Mozambique and Rwanda." Building on concepts of path dependence, it attempts to understand recent changes in Korean state-led capitalism. Unlike most studies of comparative capitalism, it intends to find out how much of the Korean state-led capitalism can be found in a new policy field of development cooperation with many countries.

Finally, Glenn Morgan makes a cautious forecast on the future of Asian capitalism in his paper, "Exploring 21st Century Capitalisms and Asia: The Impact of Financialization." He explores the connection of financialization of Western form of Capitalism with the developments in Asian capitalisms and attempts to answer whether Asian capitalisms were becoming more financialized. He demonstrates the strength of China's manufacturing sector has effectively destroyed the US one, resulting in weakened the power of US labour to resist the development of shareholder value ideology, a key part of financialization. Regarding financialization in East Asia, he doesn't seem to believe to be the case. He, however, reports the expansion of credit and debt to the population as a whole and possible financialization from below.

## References

Albert, Michel. 1993. *Capitalism against Capitalism*. London: Whurr (orig. French ed. 1991).

Bello, Walden. 1992. *People and Power in the Pacific*. London: Pluto.

Dore, Ronald P. 2000. *Stock Market Capitalism/Welfare Capitalism: Japan and Germany versus the Anglo-Saxons*. Oxford: Oxford University Press.

Hall, Peter A. and David Soskice, eds. 2001. *Varieties of Capitalism: The Institutional Foundations of Comparative Advantage*. Oxford: Oxford University Press.

Hutton, Will. 1995. *The State We're in*. London, Jonathan Cape.

Hwang, Suk-Man and Hyun-Chin Lim. 2016. "Legacy of the developmental state: Globalization, income polarization and welfare spending in Korea." Society for the Advancement of Socio-Economics conference paper.

Johnson, Chalmers. 1982. *MITI and the Japanese Miracle*. Stanford, CA: Stanford University Press.

________. 1998. "Economic crisis in East Asia: The clash of capitalisms." *Cambridge Journal of Economics* 22(6): 653-661.

Lim, Hyun-Chin and Jin-Ho Jang. 2006. "Neoliberalism in post-crisis South Korea." *Journal of Contemporary Asia* 36(4): 442-463.

Morgan, Glenn and Richard Whitley, eds. 2012. *Capitalisms and Capitalism in the Twenty-First Century*. Oxford: Oxford University Press.

Redding, Gordon and Michael A. Witt. 2010. *The Future of Chinese Capitalism: Choices and Chances*. Oxford: Oxford University Press.

Servan-Schreiber, Jacques. 1967. *Le défi Américain*. Paris.

Streeck, Wolfgang. 2011. "The crises of democratic capitalism." *New Left Review* 71: 5-29.

Teichman, Judith. 2014. "Struggling with the social challenges of globalization: Mexico, Chile and South Korea." pp. 63-75 in *Civilizing Globalization: A Survival Guide*, edited by R. Sandbrook and A. Burak Güven. 2nd edition. Albany, NY: SUNY Press.

The Economist. 2014. "Business in Asia." May 31.

# PART I

## Recent Changes in Asian Capitalism

Chapter 1

# *Formation and Development of Capitalism in the Modernization of East Asia: An Alternative Theoretical Explication*

Kyong-Dong Kim

## Introduction

The main objective of this work is not to offer a detailed descriptive account of how capitalism in East Asia has historically emerged and unfolded in its modern era. Rather, it is to examine the theoretical implications of the experience of the formation and development of the modern capitalism in this region. The theoretical framework to be used for this particular purpose is an alternative theory of modernization propounded by the author. It is 'alternative' in a specific sense that it purports to provide a set of theoretical ideas from the 'other side of the track,' so to say, a vantage point of late-modernizing societies in the modern world, enabling us to identify and explicate more effectively both the convergent and divergent trajectories and substantive consequences of changes, including the emergence and evolution of capitalist economy, occurring in the historical process of modernization in various world regions and societies.

The region of Asia to be considered for this task is confined to East Asia (variably labeled as Northeast Asia or the Far East), consisting of China, Japan, and Korea.[1] This option is deliberate with cultural implications, manifested in their commonalities and differentials in their historical unfolding of the capitalist economy. In this study, the term capitalism is not going to be defined anew. Instead, it is taken to be a given as an inherent or almost an ineluctable socioeconomic component in the very dynamic of modernization. In this sense, a theory of modernization is not merely a useful frame of reference for a more adequate understanding of the meaning and significance of capitalism in these societies. Any social science discourse on capitalist development without reference to modernization may also be considered to be insufficient or at least leaving out the relatively more important contextual ingredients of the whole phenomena under study. The present work focuses on this usually missing part of such discourses, to fill the gap in the existing literature. And the first section of this paper presents a brief synopsis of the alternative theory of modernization which will aid us to characterize the evolution of the capitalist system in East Asia. Of necessity for the sake of parsimony, I can only offer the minimum gist of my own views on modernization.[2]

## A Theory of Selective Modernization and Alternative Modernities: A Synopsis

### The Basic Premises

The basic premises of this theory are twofold: (1) modernization is a *historically particular* case of grand societal transformations that has occurred in a specific time period of human civilization; and (2) it is important for a theory of modernization to identify and explicate the characteristic nature of the *process* of change entailed in this historical experience.[3] In short, our central concern here is the historically delimited changes and the nature of the processes of those changes. The concrete substances resulting from such changes are then taken to be 'modernities.'

## The Historical Meaning of Modernization

In this theory, modernization is defined strictly in terms of its historical meaning as the broad transformations of societies that were initiated in the western part of Europe ushering in the modern era in the history of human civilization. The modern era in this scheme refers to the period beginning around the turn of the sixteenth century when Europe went through the significant civilizational shifts (Black, 1966: 5-6; McNeil, 1986: 372 ff; Hall *et al.*, 1996: 3-18). What is important for our discussion is to acknowledge with Chirot (1994: 57) that "it was in a part of western Europe the modern world was invented, and it was from there that modernity was spread around the world."[4]

## The Major Characteristics of the Processes

'Spread' is one of the key words to depict the distinctive characteristics of modernization as a process. This tendency of expansionism innate to it was an inherent feature of the modern capitalism which almost by nature required as large a market as possible. International expedition naturally ensued, with the aid of the capital and technologies needed for maritime journey, business, and warfare. Later in the nineteenth century, the imperialistic encroachment on other nations further pushed the process of global modernization. Having originated in Europe, it automatically caused 'international acculturation,' or changes in the cultures coming into contact. Once exposed to this acculturation, each society made some form of selective adaptation to this external challenge, but eventually the modernization process itself was indigenized, with the final product emerging as 'alternative modernity' unique to each country. In short, modernization entails by nature a delicate dialectical interaction of two central processes of change: (1) international acculturation and (2) selective adoption of foreign cultures brought from the West resulting in the eventual indigenization of them as part of their own.

### *International Acculturation*

In its generic sense, acculturation is supposed to result in some changes in the cultures of the both sides coming into contact. However, one unique feature of the actual form of international acculturation in the historical modernization, which has eluded serious attention by most observers, is that it's influence has been unusually tilted, the cultures of the early modernizer societies of the West flowing 'down' one-sidedly into the late modernizers. This was due chiefly to the asymmetry between them in their relative power in the economic, military, and scientific-technological spheres. Theoretically then, most of the scholars in the field came to believe that this process would eventually result in the convergence of the social and cultural patterns of all societies affected by modernization (Moore, 1965), thus, modernization was seen as identical to westernization or even flatly Americanization (Levy, 1955; Eisenstadt, 1964).

The actual unfolding of international acculturation, however, turned out to have deviated from that assumption of general convergence. Some new frame of reference became required to explain these very diverse results. A dominant strain of this endeavor is found in the discourses on multiple modernities, acknowledging the different paths of modernization taken by various regions and nations, yielding a variety of alternative modernities (Eisenstadt, 2002a; 2002b; 2003; Sachsenmaier *et al.*, 2002). This new scholarly movement suggests that the field has finally accepted the idea of modernization yielding divergent consequences.

### *The Principles of Selectivity and the Dynamics of Interactions among Societal Forces*

Viewing from the vantage point of the later-modernizer society at the receiving end of international acculturation, perhaps it may be more feasible to identify the kinds of processes that produce such divergent changes. And for this purpose a different analytic scheme is needed and this entails the two-fold principles of selectivity in the political arena and cultural resources. In the face of the surging tide of modernization, each society must make decisions regarding its response to it with regard to how and what kind of reactions should be made. In this context the political decisions have to be made and this is the political selectivity that intervenes here. The actual characteristics of the process is largely determined or affected by the degree of structural flexibility influencing the extent and nature of the participation of various sectors and strata of the society in the selective processes. But at the same time, those who are engaged in the dynamics of decision-making for the selective adaptation are of necessity operating under the guidance of the cultural factors. In a sense, it is culture that makes the selection behind and beneath the political decision. And such features as the degree of cultural flexibility and openness, cultural preparedness, and cultural affinity or compatibility can influence the selective decisions and shape the adaptive processes required.

In addition, the scheme also deals with the societal dynamics of interaction among the various societal forces with some stake at these processes of selective adaptation. They would be different social strata, various social sectors and segments, groupings and organizations with diverse ideological orientations, beliefs, interests, and so on. And with the variable relative prowess, they would be engaged in competition and conflicts vying for influence, privileges, and power to make the final say. Finally, in consequence of all such dynamic interplays, alternative modernities in each society emerge as the product of indigenization of modernization by means of the selective adaptation.

About this much of a skeleton sketch of the general tenet of my theory of selective modernization surely does not do justice to the theory itself. But some of the essential ingredients of the theoretical scheme will be duly introduced by way of illustrations of the historical dynamics of the formation and development of the modern capitalism in the process of East Asian modernization.[5] I just wanted to make sure that this work is looking into the issue of how the modern version of capitalism has emerged and evolved in East Asia with the result of yielding unique modes of capitalist economy in the three countries of this part of the global community in question. This will be done by dividing the history of modernization in East Asia into two 'waves': the First Wave in the nineteenth and early twentieth century, and the Second Wave since the end of the Second World War or the Pacific War in the mid-twentieth century.[6]

## The Birth of Capitalism in the First-Wave Modernization in East Asia

### Commonalities in the Initial Reaction to International Acculturation

Although Europeans seeking diplomatic recognition or trade with the three East Asian nations made sporadic visits and voyages to this region even in the sixteenth century, the beginning of the international acculturation ushering in modernization in the region can be set around the time when they signed official treaties with the European nations. And the sign of 'tilted' acculturation was already manifested in that they were all unequal treaties between the Western imperial powers and their Asian counterparts. Facing this surge of a new tide, all the three nations shared a common response, reflecting their shared cultural heritages, with the political and cultural selectivity working in combination.

The first reaction by them was the posture of 'closure,' a stance of seclusion, isolation, or closed-door toward the world outside except among themselves. This apparently simplistic xenophobia was based on the Confucian worldview which designated China as the 'Central or Middle Kingdom of High Civilization (*Zhongguo* or *Chung-kuo*, and *Zhonghua*) surrounded by barbarians' and the Doctrine of Distinction between the Civilized China (ruled by the Confucian virtues) and the barbarians (Ebrey *et al.*, 2009; Ringmar, 2005; Stockman, 2004; Vohra, 2000; Yao, 2010). Apparently backed by the geographical setting making for a sense of self-sufficiency, China came to harbor this notion of exclusiveness and cultural superiority, "which they have not lost to this day" (Vohra, 2000: 3). Japan's isolationist policy of *sakoku,* the closing of the country, also was predicated on an amalgam of ideological credos of both the neo-Confucian principles of separation of the civilized from the barbarians after China and the indigenous nationalist belief that Japan was superior to all other nations including China because the emperor was descended from the sun goddess (Ebrey *et al.,* 2009: 328-330; Gordon, 2003: 46-48; Morishima, 1982: 57). For Joseon Korea, the more staunchly xenophobic policy of seclusion called *swaeguk jeongchaek* was a bit more complicated. Based on the tenacious adherence to the Doctrine of Zhonghua or centrality of China, and the honorable title bestowed by China as 'Little China' or 'Little Middle Kingdom' of superior men faithfully upholding the Confucian orthodoxy, the conservative Confucian ruling forces stood firm on the principle of 'Uphold Orthodoxy and Reject Heterodoxy' (*wijeong cheoksa*) and the ideology to 'Honor China and Repel Barbarians' (*jonhwa yangi*), with the core idea of "Defend Confucian correctness against foreign perversity" (Ebrey *et al.,* 2009: 359). And this was explicitly expressed in the form of warning that "Western barbarians are invading. Failure to fight amounts to appeasement. Appeasement is treason" (Hwang, 2010: 125).

When this posture common to all three nations proved nonsensically outdated, they eventually succumbed to the external pressures only to sign a series of treaties to open ports which turned out to be 'unequal' by their provisions and to embark on various reform movements in the internal institutional infrastructures and arrangements. Once again, an interestingly common approach was taken by the three nations in their mode of political and cultural selectivity. While they would not hesitate adopting certain tangible frameworks of the modern Western institutions, they were adamant in preserving their own cultural traditions in spirit. And this was expressed differently by each of the three: China with the catchphrase of 'Chinese Substance of Culture complemented with Western Technologies' (*zhongti xiyong or chungt'ihsiyung*) (Yao, 2010: 249), Japan, with the slogan of *wakon yōsai* (Japanese spirit with Western ability) (Morishima, 1982: 63), and in Korea, the so-called Doctrine of 'Eastern Ways, Western Technology,' (*dongdo seogi*) (Yi, 2007: 316-317). Despite the shining pretext of a balanced stance on the surface, those catchphrases in fact were merely reflecting the perplexing ambivalence of the attitudes of the authorities and intellectuals of these countries toward the West and modernization. And this ambivalence turned into the source of serious divisions and factional strife vying for the upper hand in the ensuing attempts at their selective modernization. One can notice the delicate operation of the political and cultural selectivity in combination in this case, with the reform-minded modernizers and more conservative traditionalists clashing over different issues involved in the early modernization of this period. The budding of the modern capitalism in the region needs to be understood within such contexts.

## China: Capitalism without the Strong Hand of the State

One of the most commonly raised issues in the studies of capitalism has to do with the role of the state in the evolution of the modern version of capitalism. This is apparently based on the historical experience of the West where, for example, key economic institutions such as property rights, contracts, standardization of weights and measures, banking, and insurance were maintained by the state regulatory apparatus, and the state resting on a legal system has created the conditions for and established the legitimacy of the economic order that spawned capitalism (Hamilton, 1996: 339). This study is also going to look into the role of the state and its relationship with the private sector in analyzing the divergent paths of capitalist development in East Asia.

As far as the history of the emergence of a modern capitalist economy in China in the first wave modernization is concerned, it was not the strong and autonomous state that had a big hand in initiating or promoting this development. Relative to the capitalist development, in fact, during the modern era when Europe was embarking on its grandiose projects of global modernization, China was more thoroughly commercialized than Europe with private economic entrepreneurs continued to be active, some even making great profits. In short, because as the well known adage goes, the Chinese are born capitalists with natural propensity to making money whenever and wherever the opportunities arise, they were already 'capitalistic' in the profit-orientation in the private sector, the groundwork for the capitalist development had been laid long in advance (Hamilton, 1996: 331). In its early phase of modernization, China was relatively free from the scarcity of physical resources, with more social mobility, and even better integrated markets and better protection of private property. But it was the political sphere that China had its Achilles heel. The Chinese state as the political center was too powerful with not enough non-state actors with a capacity for independent action and the regional powers largely in the form of local warlords with little experience of self-governance or the military capability. Ironically, it was too weak, too, to carry out successful reforms due to the fierce resistance by the various political forces within the society and the growing pressures from outside, undermining the political order. But because there was nothing that could take its place, China simply disintegrated (Ringmar, 2005: 198-200).

The characteristics of capitalism in China in its formative phase was virtually defined by this kind of historical background. It rested on very different political, economic, and social foundations; it was not an elite-based capitalism, and nor did it rely on an explicit political system. The carriers of Chinese capitalism were peasants, merchants, artisans, or scholars, not organized as distinct classes but instead were "family heads who moved into and out of these ambiguously defined political and economic roles ... In other words, it is not an economy organized through institutions controlled directly by the state ... In sum, ... the formation of Chinese business networks was linked nor to government patronage nor to government planning and supervision" (Hamilton, 1996: 334; 341). It constituted, and still does so even today, of family enterprises, using consanguineous relationships as the organizational medium for the economy, not an economy organized through institutions controlled directly by the state (Hamilton, 1996: 332; 339).[7] From the perspective of the typology of capitalism, "Chinese capitalism followed Smithian rather than Schumpeterian prescriptions: things were becoming ever more efficiently allocated but markets were not adapting to new technologies or opportunities" (Ringmar, 2005: 178).

The continued development of commercial activities in China even through the turbulent modernization periods was largely due to the 'cultural selectivity' intervening in the process of interactions between the state and the private business sectors. On the surface, it was 'benign neglect' of the imperial bureaucracy that had done more good than harm, leaving economic entrepreneurs to their own devices to pursue their goal of making money. Culturally, however, this was partly reflecting the Confucian disdain of commercial activity as involving profit-seeking without regard to moral righteousness and under this principle merchants were officially considered as an unproductive class. On this cultural ground, the central concern of the Confucian ruling elite was not the commercial development but political, social, and moral matters. The benign neglect sprang from this cultural source (Ringmar, 2005: 174-177). In the face of chaotic circumstances surrounding the crumbling empire, though, the state was not simply prepared to meet the challenge of times effectively (Ebrey *et al.*, 2009: 304; Worden *et al.*, 1988: 21).

One may still wonder about how economic activities of these business entrepreneurs could continue to flourish even when the empire was going down the drain and the public institutions were beginning to decay. Initially, the opportunities were limited both sectorally and spatially for those entrepreneurial individuals to engage in genuine capitalistic activities directly conducive to industrial development, with agriculture as the predominant industry which could not be the basis for economic fortune-making compared to industrialization. Thus those entrepreneurial individuals had to seek fortune in the commercial, service, and industrial sectors centered primarily in the urban areas, especially the coastal cities under the direct or indirect influence of the Western capitalists. The Chinese also sought the opportunities for making money outside China, including Hong Kong, Singapore, plus other Southeastern Asian countries, the Philippines, Indonesia, the US, and even Latin America. This was the beginning of the Chinese Diaspora eventually creating a global network of overseas Chinese communities which would determine the nature of Chinese capitalism in the 20th century and on (Ebrey *et al.*, 2009: 300). In short, the development of the early form of Chinese capitalism was possible "without the support and coordination of a strong state" for this was a time of tumultuous confusions and conflicts in the state sector or in the political arena (Hamilton, 1996: 336).

In fact, a modern economy was beginning to take off despite the severe political and cultural turmoil of the first two decades of the twentieth century. World War I had a great impact on the emergence of bourgeoisie made up of merchants, bankers, industrialists, even compradors working for foreign firms, while overseas Chinese were actively engaged in import-export. Even though those Chinese enterprises were of small-medium scale, they were flourishing with the increasing foreign investment especially from Japan and the declining imports from Europe where the major powers were preoccupied with their own affairs. Now, the urban businessmen started to buttress their voice in politics by forming chambers of commerce and as the national government was deteriorating in the wake of WWI, they even took over running cities, looking after the business of sanitation, education, and police. In short, such was the general historical root of the unique type of capitalism developed in China later on (Ebrey *et al.*, 2009: 409).

It was largely thanks to the presence of private alternatives to the public institutions. When the public space was not available for their pursuit of economic profit, they still could fall back on their families, lineage organizations, guilds and secret societies. When the public institutions were faltering and uncertainty was high, personalized networks such as these provided the social capital for predictability and trust (Ringmar, 2005: 177-178). Thus, this version of Chinese capitalism taking on a household-based economy nurtured a distinctive form of enterprise structure of small and medium-sized firms. Some successful family businesses grew larger with the inclusion of more relatives and employees in the expanding circle of household members, but really large corporations were the exception. This phenomenon had its cultural root in China's inheritance system which basically divided up the father's estate among the sons in contrast with the case of the straight primogeniture where a single heir inherits the entire asset. A more reasonable strategy under this system would then be to create economies of scale from networks of smaller firms that are interconnected by special relationships or connections (*guanxi*).[8]

As such the *guanxi* networks could serve as the basis for creating production, distribution, or even investment networks. This phenomenon also represents an instance of cultural selectivity providing the socially formed cultural basis or social capital for a certain specific type of economy. While this form of economy may not be conducive to developing heavy industries, it has the advantage of being a non-politically based form of capitalism that is more flexible and easily adaptable to external opportunities. In short, the Chinese businesses monopolized segments or niches of the service sector in the global economy in the formative period of capitalist development in the nineteenth and early twentieth century (Hamilton, 1996: 335-336; 340).

In general, the distinct feature of the Chinese version of capitalism in the first-wave modernization phase was not so much a work of the political selectivity as that of cultural selectivity on the part of the network of family-centered entrepreneurs in the private sector.

## Japan: Capitalism with the Strong Corporate-Oriented Political Economy

In contrast with China, the Japanese strategy of political selectivity was largely based on political economy steered by the elite in the state sector. By the turn of the nineteenth century, Japan was facing widespread symptoms of distress and decline. Beset on all sides, the Shogunate failed to deal with them effectually, which weakened its position in the eyes of the military ruling class, and some minor *samurai* elite groups challenged the authority of the Shogunate, toppling it in a coup d'état in 1868. They restored Emperor Meiji as the sole legitimate ruler and head of state (Ebrey *et al.*, 2009: 324-337; Gordon, 2003: 33-34; 56-59).

The Meiji Restoration marked the beginning of profound and breathtaking changes in politics, economy, society, and culture, which fully deserved to be called 'revolution.' Such transformations were indeed the result of successful adaptive effort on the part of Japanese society to study, emulate, adopt and graft the Western modernity on to the existing conditions. And amazingly enough, this formidable task was carried out by a small group of self-selected ex-*samurai* men, who led the political and military drive to overthrow the *shogun*. This group of leaders of Japanese modernization project, often referred to as Oligarchs, set out to construct new institutions to pursue this task. Aware and fearful of the power of the West, they promoted what their slogan would pursue, the national goal of *fukoku kyōhei* (rich country, strong army) which was taken from a line in the Chinese classic. This awareness led them to acknowledge the necessity to import Western military technology, industry, legal norms, constitutional thought, science, and whatever institutional models needed for the reform. No sooner than they consolidated power, the revolutionary leaders themselves took off on a lengthy study trip to Europe and North America, which was followed by other specialized missions and the invitation of foreign experts as teachers and advisors. In a few decades they issued some 11,000 passports for overseas travel. Such was the way political and cultural selectivity played in the initial modernization process of Japan. Of course, there were opposition forces resisting reforms mainly from the old groups of *daimyo* and different segments of the general populace, and oligarchs quarreled among themselves, too. But with the emperor untarnished by the past at the helm, they were able to invoke the imperial institutions as symbols of national unity, and in due course, nationalism blended with Shinto, the indigenous religion, and Confucianism, helped bring and keep Japanese society together (Ebrey *et al.*, 2009: 337-343; Gordon, 2003: 33-34; 56-59; Ringmar, 2005: 201).

These Meiji leaders, especially those who traveled abroad, were tremendously impressed with the impact of industrial capitalism, with manufacturing and trade as the important source of national power in the Western societies. Motivated by this experience, they undertook the task of realizing the foremost Meiji slogan of 'rich country, strong army' by engaging in necessary economic reforms. This was to be the background of the birth of modern Japanese capitalism. Without going into the detailed account of the major economic reform programs, let me simply summarize the characteristics of this new version of capitalism emerged in Japan in the incipient stage of modernization (Ebrey *et al.*, 2009: 345-347; 373-374; Gordon, 2003: 70-73; 96-108; Hamilton, 1996: 333-334; Ringmar, 2005: 193-198).

Once again, focusing on the role of government in the development of the modern capitalism, contrary to China, the Japanese state took a rather active part in orchestrating economic development. In principle, Japanese capitalism was a product of political economy. By borrowing industrial technology and economic organization from the West and adapting and refining them to the existing social and economic conditions, the state and the elite forces in society in combination consciously designed and implemented the capitalist economy to achieve industrialization. It was not a completely state controlled strategy but a hands-on stance that sponsored and promoted economic development. This posture was partly a heritage of the experience of running domain monopolies during the Tokugawa era when both the Tokugawa and Meiji regimes did not serve as strong, authoritarian states. It was the elite group which actually ran the government using the state apparatus. The Meiji elite also turned to a German philosophy of state-led development, such as the economic thought of Frederick List, in particular (Hamilton, 1996: 335; Gordon, 2003: 72-73). In essence, therefore, we may summarize this development pattern as follows (Hamilton, 1996: 336):

> the primary carriers of capitalist development came to be co-operating coalitions of political and economic elite. Japanese capitalism was not a creation of the merchant class, although a few merchants participated in the elite coalition. Nor was Japanese capitalism a creation of the peasants, although peasants certainly changed their productive and labor output drastically ... [it] was a creation of a ... mutually reinforcing system of governmental controls and elite privileges.

The fact that the elite played the crucial role in this whole process is to be noted. During the volatile period of transition, there was no doubt a rather rapid turnover in the elite groups, especially in the early part of industrialization, basically mobility occurring from the traditional privilege based on ascribed heredity to the one based on educational achievement under the new system of modern education. Nevertheless, "Japanese society was and continues to be fundamentally a society dominated by such elite groups" (Hamilton, 1996: 334). Now with industrialization which was launched by the active initiative of the elite in the government sector, a new elite group emerged within the economic sector as well, forming an elitist economy. This is well represented by the powerful business networks of *zaibatsu* (literally translates as 'financial clique') even today. In a sense, therefore, from the beginning Japanese capitalism was a powerful politically bounded form of capitalism and it still remains so today (Hamilton, 1996: 334).

Guided by such strategies, the Japanese economy was "able to shift from small-scale production of handicraft goods to large-scale production of industrial products, and from small factories to a hierarchy of bureaucratic corporations organized into conglomerate networks known as *zaibatsu*" (Hamilton, 1996: 334). In this endeavor to create an industrialized capitalist economy, the Meiji government basically started to reform the tax system with a view to stabilizing state revenues sufficient to sustain the now centralized administrative functions of a newly unified nation. Then, the new government used parts of these tax revenues for public works and institution-building projects to create the infrastructure of a capitalist industrial economy in such basic areas of communication, transportation, financial systems, and the like. This was followed by direct government investment in establishing and operating industrial enterprises. Government leaders were not convinced that private investors were prepared for such undertakings in their initiative as well as know-how, and they were weary of foreign investment, too. As a matter of fact, the government initially wanted to encourage private investment but the Edo era merchants, landlords, and others with means were reluctant to take part in the risky new businesses. Although not all the government ventures were profitable and some had to be sold out in due course, through such ventures, a first generation of managers and engineers of large-scale enterprises had been trained and a small industrial labor force had been created. In short, these state enterprises did constitute an important launching pad for further growth (Gordon, 2003: 70-73).

Rapid industrialization started with the government initiative now provided enough motivation as well as the social and economic ground on which the entrepreneurship on the part of the private sector could flourish. And the economic growth of Japan in this early modernization stage largely depended on a "dynamic mix of state and private initiative" but it was paralleled by a mix of ideals on the part of the business elite of service to the nation with a drive for personal wealth. Put in other words, "Japanese capitalists, like state bureaucrats, drew on Confucian language to put forward a philosophy of what might be called 'selfless' profit-seeking" (Gordon, 2003: 99). Another distinctive element of Japanese capitalist development is the central role played by monopolies in the name of *zaibatsu*. By origin, there are two groups of *zaibatsu*, one with their roots in merchant houses of the Tokugawa era, most notably Mitsui and Sumitomo, and the other founded from scratch by entrepreneurs in the Meiji era, like the famous Mitsubishi. The founders of these monopoly enterprises took advantage of the longstanding close ties with the government and synergetic links with other key industries to create these business enterprises. It is remarkable that these *zaibatsu* organizations adopted the practice of the separation of ownership from management at a relatively early stage of modern capitalist development by recruiting able young men from outside the family and delegating important managerial responsibilities to them (Gordon, 2003: 97-98).

Some of the main reasons for this phenomenon of prominent rise of *zaibatsu* type of monopolies are as follows: First, it was a general tendency of all capitalist economies toward concentration but in the case of Japanese monopolies they also spanned the range of business endeavor covering diverse industries under the umbrella of the conglomerate. Second, late-modernizer countries such as Germany and Russia also developed large-scale corporations to swiftly mobilize scarce resources for modern industrial development. In some of such countries, the state played the mobilizing role, but in Japan it was a combination of government and large private enterprises that led this development. In addition, Japanese capitalism of the Meiji era enjoyed the legacy of the Tokugawa era in terms of rather widespread entrepreneurial and manufacturing skills and a sophisticated network of commercial finance and coastal transport. On this basis, the Japanese producers were able to utilize a pool of relatively inexpensive labor (Gordon, 2003: 98-100).

On top of that, what is more impressive was the spirit of newly arising capitalism unique to Japan. In the words of a Meiji-era trade, "the secret to succeed in business is the determination to work for the sake of society and mankind as well as for the future of the nation, even if it means sacrificing oneself" (Gordon, 2003: 99-100). Indeed such sacrifice was imposed chiefly on the work force, especially heavy burdens placed on female laborers, many of who were the teenage daughters of the farm families. They had to work long hours, for punitive incentive wages, in physically poor working conditions, and under harsh discipline. On occasion, therefore, these female workers engaged in collective act of protest. The emerging communities of skilled male factory workers harbored a mixed sense of humiliation at the condition of their lives, on the one hand, with pride, assertiveness, and commitment to self-help. The famous 'lifetime employment' which only came into being after World War II was not available and they "typically aspired to save money and start up their own small factory" (Gordon, 2003: 100-103). They also organized strikes and tried to organize unions. But the government suppressed such movement by law. The cultural image of skilled factory workers was rather negative compared to clerks and other white-collar workers and they were viewed by their bosses as notoriously unreliable. Nonetheless, such negative view was countered in reality where workers themselves expressed "their determination to study, improve their skills, and one day open their own small workshop. The managerial view that employees were stubborn and poorly disciplined did not reflect a genuine deficit of talent or energy among laborers. It reflected the unwillingness of these workers to devote themselves to bosses who offered unreliable treatments" (Gordon, 2003: 103-105).

Compared with the case of early capitalism of China, Japanese capitalism of the first-wave modernization was a product of the conscious political selectivity with the aid of cultural selectivity, largely led by the political elite in the state sector and the participation of the entrepreneurial elite of the private economic sector.

## Korea: The Budding of Capitalism under Colonial Rule

The case of Korea presents another unique type of early capitalism of the first-wave modernization in East Asia. The incipient emergence of a capitalist economy in Korea is more complicated mainly due to the intricate intermixture of both internal and external forces involved in the process. As was the usual case in any late-modernizer society, modernization was triggered by external forces in the form of international acculturation. But the root cause of troubles experienced by the Joseon Dynasty of the late nineteenth century was the internal factor of the ineptitude of the state in adapting to the changing situation. Under the stressful threat to national survival by foreign imperialism, the state failed to solve long-standing institutional and economic problems, especially the pervasive corruption in the government all over the country from the center down to the lowest level of administration in the localities.

This does not necessarily mean that the state did not attempt to meet the challenge by selective adaptation of various forms under the cultural banner of 'Eastern Ways, Western Technology,' as was indicated above. In fact, the ruler of the already quickly declining Joseon Dynasty made some efforts at introducing the modern capitalist industrialization projects albeit in a rather elementary form (Yi, 2007). Nevertheless, swamped by the vicissitudes marked by the most severe disruptions of political stability and social order brought about by the incessant rebellions and insurgencies of large and small scale, which in turn inadvertently solicited invasions and international conflicts between China and Japan and Russia and Japan, with the result of Japanese triumph assuring the upper hand on the part of the latter in the Korean affairs, the newly inaugurated Empire of the Great Han Empire (*Daehan jeguk*) finally succumbed to the colonial ambition of the rising Asian empire of Japan in 1910 (Ebrey *et al.*, 2009: 353; Hwang, 2010).

Emperor Gojong embarked on his own programs of modernization which if succeeded would have laid the groundwork for the emergence of Korean capitalism. Unfortunately, his scheme was interrupted by the Japanese take-over. And it is now generally acknowledged that the Korean version of capitalism was actually undertaken under the colonial policies of Korean economic transformation within the larger framework of Japanese capitalist expansion into her Asian neighbors. Even though authors have advanced different views and interpretations of the characteristic of the formative processes of early Korean capitalism, basically relative to the nature of the role of Japan and the national capital, the theoretical approach introduced in this work adheres to the view that the emergence and development of Korean capitalism under colonial rule was very much an integral part of Korean modernization.[9]

In this view, the crucial difference in comparison with other late-modernizing societies without colonial history was that it entailed dual paths of modernization, one undertaken by the Korean people and the other by the Japanese. From the perspective of the Korean nation, it was heteronomous modernization enforced by the Japanese colonialists strictly from the stand point of their own national interest and as such it was unnecessarily distorted, inflicting a great deal of suffering on the part of the Korean people as a consequence. According to this interpretation, Korean colonial capitalism also was a dual process. On the one hand, it was a model of state-led industrialization which much smack of an early model of the so-called developmentalism, a far cry from the free-market capitalism of Britain and the US. On the other hand, even under severely restricted conditions, some entrepreneurial Korean landowner and merchant families also began to participate in this process of early industrialization as the incipient 'national capitalists' or entrepreneurs (Ebrey *et al.*, 2009: 391).

By the last decades of the nineteenth century when Korea had to open ports to the Western imperial powers for trade, which marked the beginning of modernization in this country, Korea was a relatively poor agrarian society. Immediately after the opening of the ports, more entrepreneurial merchants and landowners made fortunes by exporting grains (rice) and importing manufactured goods. But the capitalist industrialization in Korea only started when the Japanese colonialists started building the infrastructure to facilitate their control over the modernization of Korea's economy, as part of Japan's own industrialization program which was aimed at exploiting the Korean economy for the raw materials and agricultural products and then build industries later to lay the ground for their preparation for the military expedition in the region and eventually leading to the Pacific War in the 1940s. At any rate, it is important to note that the Japanese government played a more active role in the development of the Korean economy than it had in Japan's own in the late nineteenth century. While much of the basic approach was borrowed from the Meiji period, colonial economic growth was implemented through powerful government efforts with the strong authoritarian government that combined civilian and military administration to govern the colony with strict discipline, fostering and implementing comprehensive economic programs, controlling the huge national bureaucracy, and collaborating with the major *zaibatsu* networks. As the colonial economy was growing, many Japanese looking for opportunities of making fortunes also increased their investment in the Japanese businesses in Korea (Kim, 2006: 103-105; Savada and Shaw, 1992: 139-140).

As for the rise of the Korean national capitalists, the pivotal interests of the colonial authorities were to meet the needs of the Japanese colonists, not the Koreans. Of course, there were entrepreneurial elements among the Korean landowner and merchant classes trying to pursue their fortune in the commercial and industrial sectors open to them under the constraints of the suppressive colonial rule. Even if Korean entrepreneurship was not totally blocked, Korean business activity was restricted by various means including such legal provisions as the Company Act. After the first decade of colonial suppression, which eventually instigated the nationwide uprising in the March First Independence Movement in 1910, the colonial policies have shifted to a more open stance toward the Koreans and during the 1930 and 1940s not only Japan invested huge amounts of capital in industries but the more opportunities was also rendered to Korean entrepreneurs for participation in trade and manufacturing, mostly in the areas of war supplies. For most Koreans, however, the scale and gains were modest at most. And except for some leading industries flourishing with a certain amount of collaboration with the Japanese businesses, Koreans continued to develop small-scale businesses on their own (Baek *et al.*, 2011; Ebrey *et al.*, 2009: 393-394; Eckert, 1993: 98-99; Hwang, 2010).

Such constraints notwithstanding, "by the end of the colonial period, Korea had clearly seen the emergence of a true 'sprout' of capitalism, a nascent bourgeoisie, a number of whose members, went on to become major business figures in South Korea" (Eckert, 1993: 99). Among those are the founders of such leading business groups as Samsung, Hyundai, and Lucky-Gold Star (LG for short).

## The Development of the Modern Capitalism in the Second-Wave Modernization in East Asia

The second-wave modernization in this region was to begin after the end of World War II. One justification for this approach to distinguish with the first-wave rests on the historically meaningful discontinuities between the two periods, detected in all three East Asian countries. Interestingly, such disjunctions were not the result of any deliberately schemed incidents in their histories. They were only historical accidents of the process of global modernization occurring in this part of the world. All three nations had been embroiled in warfare of internal or external origins and suddenly found themselves encountering an entirely new international order with the abrupt termination of the Pacific War. Japan was the villain in this drama, responsible for waging war with China and the US in the 1930s and 1940s only to be defeated in 1945. China had conflicts on two fronts, the civil war between the Nationalists and Communists internally and the war against Japan externally. Because Korea was a colony of Japan, she also had been involved in the war caused by Japan. With the end of the war in 1945, they were put in a new place in the process of global modernization. After the departure of the Japanese armed forces from its land, China was finally reunited under the rule of communists headed by Mao Zedong, Japan was placed under the supervision of the Supreme Commander for the Allied Powers (SCAP), in the person of General Douglas MacArthur, as the leader of the US occupation army, and Korea was liberated from the shackles of colonial domination but divided into two parts with the southern half governed by the US Army Military Government in Korea (USAMGIK). These incidents clearly indicate the temporary interruption of the stream of history in all three countries in this particular period. The process of modernization now was to start anew and the similarities and variations of capitalist development among them are to be discovered in this dynamic context.

## The Mode of Selective Adaptation in the Immediate Post-War Era

To begin with, our subject matter being capitalism, we could readily dismiss China from our discussion because it selected the path of socialism. However, China in the post-Mao era turned to a different direction of economic development under the ideology of 'socialist market economy' advocated by Deng Xiaoping, thus often referred to as 'Deng Xiaoping Theory.' This choice of terms was merely to avoid the arousal of the stigma attached to the word capitalism. We could, therefore, examine this Chinese version of capitalism (Vohra, 2000: 289). Since the Pacific War destroyed about 40% of the industrial plants and infrastructure, with production reverting to levels of about 15 years earlier around the end of the 1930s, Japan also had to start almost from scratch in the immediate aftermath of the defeat in the war (Dolan and Worden, 1992: 199-200). In the case of Korea, the situation was much more complicated and difficult. The nation was divided by the decision of the two superpowers occupying the peninsula, the US in the South and the Soviet Union in the North. Since most of the mines and industrial plants existing in the South had been owned and operated by the Japanese, when they repatriated to Japan, almost all of those facilities were without manages, technicians, and capital resources. On top of that, administered by the US military government which was unprepared for the job of running a national government, South Korea was in a severe confusion amidst violent conflicts among different political and ideological factions vying for power. Then came the 6.25 War (usually known as the Korean War) which almost completely devastated the entire nation. It was under such circumstances of uncertainty and hardships that the three nations embarked on their respective versions of modernization including capitalist economic development.

## China: In Pursuit of the Socialist Market Economy

The importance of political selectivity in the pursuit of modernization may not be more starkly demonstrated than in the experience of China after Mao. It becomes much more so when the subject of discourse is capitalism because China officially is a 'socialist' nation. To follow the usual common-sense logic, examination of the emergence and unfolding of a capitalist economic system in a socialist society would quickly fall into a deadlock of contradictions by definition. In China, however, they have found a wise leeway of avoiding such contradictions by the clever strategy of political selectivity. We are dealing with a society ruled by a strong party apparatus with almost omnipotent, if not totalitarian, power over the society and people. If the power center claims that they pose no contradictions, then there are no such problems.

Even so, China prior to the end of civil war and establishment of the People's Republic was transforming itself toward a modern capitalist economy, with a dual structure consisting of big capital and small-medium domestic capital. The Nationalist regime was maintained by the support of the famous 'Four Big Families' as the representative big capitalists, with small-medium capital in a subordinate status. When Mao Zedong came to power, the Chinese Communist Party (CCP) designated the big capital as bureaucratic capital considered as an enemy of the revolution and confiscated them, whereas small-medium capital called national capital was regarded as an ally of the revolution becoming the object of controlled development. Ever since the initial period of planned economic development of the 1953-1957, capitalist entrepreneurs disappeared from the economic arena (Baek, 2007: 176-177).

Deng Xiaoping was basically a pragmatist and after consolidating his power he came out and pronounced his catchword of 'Four Modernizations' (of agriculture, industry, science and technology, and defense) for China's development. His philosophic guidelines for China's reform and modernization came to be known as Deng Xiaoping Theory as mentioned above in passing, and this legitimized the capitalist economy by naming it anew as the 'socialist market economy' as an essential part of his larger vision of 'Building Socialism with Chinese Characteristics' (Vohra, 2000: 289). Of course, critical voices were raised not only as to the feasibility of policies with that sort of philosophy, and some doubted that it was only a pretext for capitalism. Deng's answer to such criticisms was as follows (Vohra, 2000: 289):

> The reason some people hesitate to carry out the reform and the open policy and dare not break new ground is, in essence, that they are afraid it would mean introducing ... capitalism and, indeed, taking the capitalist road. The crux of the matter is whether the road is capitalist or socialist. The chief criterion for making that judgment should be whether it promotes the growth of the productive forces in a socialist society, increases the overall strength of the socialist state and raises living standards ... [We should not be afraid of the foreign invested sector because we control] the large and medium-sized state-owned enterprises and the rural enterprises. More important, political power is in our hands.

The inherent contradictions in this proposition are apparent, yet the Chinese Communist Party (CCP) had to support this theory for the sake of its continued hold on to political power while vigorously pursuing urgent economic growth. And these contradictory ideas put in practice created a rather incredible mixture of a system with the state control of the economy or business retained yet attenuated by necessity. While it is true that even the State Constitution of 1982 specifically pronounces that the "state is to guide the country's economic development and that the State Council is to direct its subordinate bodies in drawing up and carrying out the national economic plan and the state budget, ... A major objective of the reform program was to reduce the use of direct controls and to increase the role of indirect economic levers" (Worden *et al.*, 1988: 228-229).

Note that in the above quote, Deng not only offers the goal pursued with that philosophy but also emphasizes that 'political' power is in their hands. Supporting this faith in the importance of political selectivity is the culture of nationalism. For a market economy is to be realized you are most likely to have to accommodate a situation where differentiation and autonomy is also demanded. If left unchecked, differentiation and autonomy could lead to social disorder and disintegration. What other cultural options would you take than nationalism calling for cohesion, cooperation, and sacrifice? And a brief review of the actual processes of implementing various reform programs should reveal that such problems have really been irritating. To make long story short, we may take a summarized view of the development of the socialist market economy in China in the period after the death of Deng in 1997 and of subsequent regimes since then.[10]

One of the most remarkable tendencies of the recent decades may be the loosening of the actual control of the central party-state, especially in the economic sphere, and interestingly this basically has to do with the pursuit of the very ideology of the socialist market economy, or capitalist economy in short. A series of economic reforms has caused the emergence of sort of a new class which came to gain some autonomy in economic action, either individually or collectively. Of course, this autonomy still may be partial, because the CCP continues to hold a formal monopoly of political power in the state sector with the control over the means of coercion, and economic power remains to be intertwined with political power one way or another. Moreover, in this process of shifting power relationships, greater autonomy has also been gained by the lower echelons of the state apparatuses themselves. And the social consequences of these changes have significant implications for the future development of not only the capitalist economy but also the Chinese society as a whole.

The transformation started in agriculture which was decollectivized, discarding the collective system of planned production, so that the household responsibility system emerged. While this has differentiated agriculture and fragmented peasantry without land-ownership, larger land-holdings of specialized households fulfilling state contracts or voluntary agricultural co-operatives were permitted. Under such new arrangements, party cadres and former cadres came to find new roles with new advantages in mediating between peasant households and their wider environment. In addition, members of farming families can enjoy freedom to seek alternative non-farming jobs, providing labor force for rapid expansion of rural industry. At the same time, communes and brigade enterprises also were decollectivized and their management was contracted out to private individuals, while their public ownership was still retained. And with their administrative responsibilities transferred to township (*xiang*) and village (*cun*) governments, these enterprises came to be called 'township and village enterprises' (TVEs). They continued to grow in number to over one million accounting for nearly one quarter of all industrial employment in China by the early 1990s.

These TVEs with the functions of buying their inputs, hiring labor, and selling their outputs in markets that stretch beyond their localities, are said to have created what is called 'local state corporatism' or 'local market socialism' in the sense that local governments now have property rights and function as complex industrial firms playing the role of employer vis-a-vis the managers. Cadres have been encouraged to take this role as directors. But one interesting phenomenon has emerged in this process that this system of local corporatism is embedded in local kinship networks with members of powerful families occupying key positions in these organizations.

Then came the reintroduction of private enterprise. In terms of ownership and actual management, there are public and private enterprises, including (1) state-owned enterprises (SOEs), (2) semi-private enterprises such as foreign-invested enterprises (FIEs) and township and village enterprises (TVEs), (3) private enterprises of larger scale in the manufacturing sector, and (4) private firms of self-employed entrepreneurs, usually called *getihu* (self-employed firms) which flourished in businesses like retail, food, repair, and other services requiring little fixed capital (Baek, 2007: 175-178). The first type of private enterprises reinstated was *getihu* which did not impose fiscal burdens on the government, channeled capital to productive activities in rural areas, was expected to solve urban unemployment, encouraged the development of tertiary industries lagging behind heavy industries, and was not expected to be harmful to the public ownership sector. Some of them grew to become large enterprises. By the early 1990s, there were several millions of private enterprises but the vast majority were still individual household businesses of *getihu* type, though several hundred thousand larger private enterprises also had come into existence (Stockman, 2000: 139).

As may be expected of any public corporations, the SOEs soon manifested serious inefficiency and many of them ended up in the red, losing money not making money. And efforts to remedy this trouble was expressed by Jaing Ze-min who while emphasizing that "the state-owned sector must be in a dominant position in major industries and key areas that concern the life-blood of the national economy," he had this to say (Vohra, 2000: 292):

> We should convert large and medium-sized SOEs into standard corporations according to the requirements of clearly established ownership, well defined power responsibilities, separation of [management] from administration, and scientific management so that they will become corporate entities and competitors adaptable to the market.

In spite of such efforts to reform the SOEs, after Deng's death, the conditions did not improve so that the leaders in the party and government had to take a harder look at them and came out with recommendations to restructure them in the direction of the state releasing its hold on the ownership of the SOEs. The relationship between state officials and private entrepreneurs also comes into the scene. The *getihu* type household enterprises are very much at the mercy of the state bureaucracy, whereas larger entrepreneurs have developed more symbiotic relationships with cadres because they need to cultivate good connections or *guanxi* with officials who can meddle in the various aspects of business affairs of the private firms. The dependency, however, is not one-sided because both parties can benefit from such patron-client relationships in which officials protect and favor their clients who in return can offer pay-offs, kickbacks, employment or partnerships (Stockman, 2000: 140).

In that sort of close interdependent and particularistic relationships, the problem of depravity cannot be readily avoided. Thus, the issue of corruption plagued the Chinese leadership. Ironically, the issue of corruption is also a consequence of the contradiction of the system that "concentrates political power in the hands of a supposedly selfless and self-sacrificing socialist party while decentralizing, and making more autonomous, profit-oriented economic and administrative establishments" (Vohra, 2000: 295). And an attending phenomenon occurred relative to this very "autonomous and profit-oriented" market sector, eroding the ethical standards of the system. Quite interestingly, this was also an expression of the culturally in-born 'capitalistic' inclinations of the Chinese people who unhesitantly responded to the enticing call to "plunge into the sea [of business]" and make money so that "tens of millions of Government and Community Party officials" left their jobs to take the drive. In addition, some of them who decided to retain their jobs neglected their official work for private business activities, thus creating shortages of staff in schools and offices. The list of such cases is astonishing as shown in the following paragraph (Vohra, 2000: 294).

"Policemen moonlight as pimps. Factory workers wave rags

> on the street corners as an offer to wash cars. University students sell photocopiers and X-ray machines on commission. Professors become corporate consultants, working with such enthusiasm that The Economic Daily complained recently about faculty members who rush out of class when their beepers go off" ... The military, not to be left behind, established 20,000 economic enterprises of its own. This frenzied activity for quick gains led naturally to a watering down of socialist ideology and to a huge growth in corruption and criminal scams.

These examples are introduced here to show albeit indirectly and in piecemeal that the general characteristics of the Chinese capitalism is such that although the government dominated the economy, the extent of its control was limited by the sheer volume of economic activity. Furthermore, the concept of government supervision of the economy had changed — at least in the minds of the advocates of reform — from one of direct but stifling state control to one of indirect guidance of a more dynamic economy (Worden *et al.*, 1988: 230-231; Baek, 2007: 181).

In more recent years, China has been experiencing the steady decline of state power especially relative to the economic sphere. From the vantage point of the economic actors, the development of private business, the growth of TVEs, devolution of authority in state enterprise, joint ventures and foreign direct investment, marketization of conditions facing them, all have caused the release or escape of more and more economic activity from the reach of the central state authorities. There also have emerged more sources of economic and social reward for subordinates in party and state over which their superiors have little leverage. Officials and cadres have more opportunities to form fruitful relationships with economic organizations on the local levels, and the younger and more able cadres may take off for benefits in those areas. Under the circumstances, the organizational capacity of the party-state has been significantly weakened. And the decline of state power also has been self-reinforcing through various cumulative effects (Stockman, 2000: 145).

Even in the market sector, in those enterprises which introduced the stock system in the early 1990s, the major part of the shares is still often held by state firms and agencies. Or in some cases, share have been issued to managers and workers, but they are 'internal' shares that cannot be transferred. Only a small number of firms are allowed to issue share for trading at the stock exchanges. Although the growing capital market would have some impact on the direction of investment, the relatively limited shift in ownership of large-scale industry implies only a partial diffusion of state power over the economic sector. On the internal management side, however, increased autonomy of managers in their decisions regarding day-to-day operations including substantial retention of profits for reinvestment, for example, is allowed. Increased labor market flexibility within limit also partially releases workforce to be able to sell their labor power on the market. Even the possibility of bankruptcy for state enterprises has been admitted. Overall, the trend of weakening of state power is evident, and yet, practically speaking, "the continued involvement of state organs as owners, and state officials as regulators, means that authoritative political power has not by any means fully withdrawn from the economic sphere" (Stockman, 2000: 140-141).

It is interesting to observe in the historical unfolding of capitalism in a socialist China where the power of political selectivity originally supported by cultural selectivity of the official ideological orientations seems to start rocking under the influence of cultural selectivity of the newly emerging capitalistic economic systems and mechanisms. We could hardly be indifferent to the nature of change in the political economy of this country as China proceeds further in the current paths of modernization continuously attempting to make necessarily selective adaptive change on the way. It is surely going to be tough for the regime and the party to meet the mounting challenges of the growing inequality in resource distribution, the increased desire for a more democratic open society and politics among the general populace attending the rise of living standards, and the looming societal conflicts brewing underneath the seemingly peaceful social change. And in this picture, the role of capitalism unique to China could be a most potent force defining the future of this society to a significant extent.

## Japan: The Rise of a Capitalist Powerhouse in the Post-WWII Era

For our purpose here, it is not necessary to describe in any detail the pathetic conditions of life for the people of Japan in the immediate aftermath of the Pacific War. The discussion focuses on the dynamics of capitalist development in the post-war Japan. The original goals of SCAP (also shorthand for the occupation bureaucracy) were to demilitarize Japan and to install democracy. The reform programs included the revision of the constitution, land reforms, educational reform, and economic development.

Our main concern here is with the major economic reforms

undertaken by SCAP until it was dismantled in 1952, which included (1) the sweeping land reform eventuating in 90% of Japan's agricultural land cultivated by farmer-owners by 1950, (2) the dissolution of *zaibatsu* because of their contribution to war effort and their inherently undemocratic economic dominance, (3) the promulgation of the Trade Union Law allowing unions to be organized and to participate in politics, and (4) rendering the government bureaucracy greater control over trade and investment than before. Of course, mainly because of the Cold War and the violent collective actions of unions, SCAP had the Japanese government issue regulations forbidding public employees to strike and halt the disbanding of *zaibatsu* in 1948. Because rebuilding lost industries was most urgent in the early postwar years, major investments had to be made in the industrial sector, the Ministry of International Trade and Industry (MITI) had the Japan Development Bank lend money from the government's postal service system to private companies and also advised the Bank of Japan on its loans to private banks (Dolan and Worden, 1992: 200; Ebrey *et al.*, 2009: 449-450).

The story of Japan's postwar 'economic miracle' reaping a growth of more than 10% an average annual rate between 1950 and 1973 is history by now. Our interest at this juncture is in examining the role of the government and its relationship with the private business sector in this process of Japan's post-war capitalist development. No doubt, there were a few other internal and external factors that contributed to the growth. The Tokugawa period already bequeathed a commercial sector in urban centers, a sophisticated government bureaucracy, a relatively well-educated elite and literate populace, productive agriculture, a unified nation with well-developed financial and market systems, and a national infrastructure of roads. The Meiji era renovated much of those systems after the models of the West and built up some heavy industries leading the surge of the militarized economy of the pre-war decades. Japan's work force was not only highly qualified but committed and disciplined. And the international environment was unusually favorable to the growth of various industries of the times, with new technologies available to use in Japan's industrial growth. Most of all, international conflicts in fact were conducive to stimulating the Japanese economy, including Russo-Japan War (1904-1905), World War I (1914-1918), the 6.25 War in Korea (1950-1953), and the Second Indochina war (1954-1975). It is especially remarkable that the war in Korea actually made a crucial contribution to the immediate post-war rehabilitation of the Japanese economy in the early 1950s under the SCAP administration (Dolan and Worden, 1992: 199-202; Gordon, 2003: 246-249). In addition, Japan also benefited from the economies of scale, especially the large corporations like *zaibatsu*. They were wealth groups of large holding companies which dominated most industries. After they were dissolved by SCAP, large and modern industrial enterprises newly emerged to form *keiretsu* which is a new form of corporate groupings cooperating with one another under the major banking institutions. By coordinating activities of enterprises within these groupings and integrating smaller subcontractors into them, Japanese industries were able to enhance their efficiency. In other words, these subcontractors supported corporate growth by producing quality components for finished products (Dolan and Worden, 1992: 203; Ebrey *et al.*, 2009: 452-453; Sugimoto, 2010: 89-91).

Still controversial is the relative role of the state in this whole process. 'Japan Incorporated' (Japan Inc.) is a relatively popular term when the economic miracle of Japan is referred to. And it implies the nature of alliance between business and government interests. Some may describe the relationship as follows (Dolan and Worden, 1992: 204):

> Although Japan's economic development was primarily the product of private entrepreneurship, the government has directly contributed to the nation's prosperity. Its actions have helped initiate new industries, cushion the effects of economic depression, create a sound economic infrastructure, and protect the living standards of the citizenry.

The root of this posture of government is then traced back to Confucianism. The Japanese version of Confucianism stresses loyalty and business would look to government for guidance for leadership and authority stem from it. Such attitudes and the notion that the nation is a family allow government to influence business which in turn work hard not for the sake of its own profit alone but for national well-being, too. For Japan to become an economic power, the national consensus calls for the self-sacrifice of all Japanese for this national goal (Dolan and Worden, 1992: 205).

Before we proceed further with the analysis of the role of government, a look into the nature of private entrepreneurship is needed. The seed of entrepreneurship already had begun to bud under the long-lasting peace of the Tokugawa era among the element of samurai out of job, urban merchants, and wealthy farmers, and the Meiji industrialization bred strong entrepreneurial force in the private business sector, especially the *zaibatsu* groups. In the immediate postwar period under the SCAP administration, there were purges of many top managers of the wartime economy and when *zaibatsu* were disbanded, thousands of executives were fired on the charge of aiding war machine. Facing the threat of the communist influence from China and North Korea under the Soviet rule, SCAP later decided to reverse such measures and stopped the dismantling of *zaibatsu* and rehabilitated previously purged politicians, bureaucrats, and business leaders. However, when these top managers and entrepreneurs were forced to retire earlier, a new generation of daring younger managers and entrepreneurs came to fill the gap and take charge of established business organizations and some even found their own new companies. Not only that, some of such entrepreneurial individuals even took advantage of purchasing or taking hold of some of the government assets including construction materials and machinery that Japanese bureaucrats allowed to disappear into the black market or the hands of business cronies. As a matter of fact, some of those entrepreneurial individuals defied the cautious warnings of government bureaucrats in investing in new fields and new technologies. At any rate, it is true that Japanese private companies expanded quickly and fearlessly, borrowing massive amounts from banks and taking on large debts (Ebrey *et al.*, 2009: 450; Gordon, 2003: 248). It was with this kind of people in the private business sector that Japanese government had to pursue their national goal of economic recovery and development in the post-WWII era.

Now as for the role of the state, a general observation has that (Gordon, 2003: 249):

> The government did not run a 'command economy' on the Soviet model. Private businesses took significant initiatives, sometimes against official advice. But even so, Japan's postwar

> economic story is not a simple tale of a free market miracle. State management, which grew out of practices improvised in the prewar and war years, was extensive. These practices are summed up by the term, *industrial policy* and they made a difference.

How did then government make a difference? During the occupation era, the Japanese government aided by SCAP retained important wartime powers over access to key resources like foreign exchange and technology licenses, using them as levers to support or discourage private business ventures. Whereas this formal authority played a major role in the immediate postwar years, the weight of state intervention shifted later to more informal practices not officially stipulated in law and this was called 'administrative guidance.' And the most important guiding agency came to be none other than the famous MITI. On a more general level, the government acted as economic 'cheerleader' and 'sign-painter.' A series of Five-Year Plans were issued, for example, and in implementing them, it stood ready to step in as lender, as facilitator of access to foreign exchange, raw materials, or technology licenses, and rescuer in cases of problems. On a more intimate level, state bureaus protected and nurtured nascent industries, by processing the conversion of yen to dollars for import, obstructing import of certain items, offering low-interest loans, giving tax breaks, and so on. This informal mechanism of *administrative guidance* was a cornerstone of the transwar political economy but it was further developed later in the postwar era as practices of 'managed capitalism' as less coercive forms of persuasion (Dolan and Worden, 1992: 204-207; Gordon, 2003: 249-250). As such, "They left more room for the market to reward those who used government help effectively, and their interaction with businessmen proved considerably more constructive" (Gordon, 2003: 251).

Unlike China where the twentieth-century was pretty much severed from the traditional period and the second-wave modernization did not retain the main ingredients of the transformations of the first-wave modernization, Japanese modernization in the second-wave period seems to have maintained a degree of continuity from not only the first-wave of modernization but even from the pre-modern culture of the Tokugawa era. This is so despite the ruptures of the Meiji revolutions, World War II ending in Japan's defeat, and a few years of direct rule by the occupation forces of the allied powers. Such tenacity of historical continuity suddenly reminds us of the unceasing resilience of the ultra-nationalistic tendency of the Japanese nation, the ghost of which seems to be resurrected in the recent move by the conservative Japanese politicians to concoct the return to the militaristic past of the early twentieth century. The power of cultural selectivity overriding political selectivity is distinctly manifested in this case of Japan's modernization.

## Korea: Building a Mixed Version of Capitalism

As was indicated earlier, the situation in Korea was much more compounded and complex. There is no need to go into the detail of historical unfolding in Korea in the second phase of modernization. A synoptic review would suffice. Upon liberation from the colonial bondage in 1945, the Korean peninsula was divided into two parts, with the North occupied by the Soviet forces and the South ruled by the US Army Military Government in Korea

(USAMGIK). We are dealing only with South Korea here to be designated as 'Korea.' When Japan left Korea after its defeat in the Second World War, Korea was almost deserted, with almost no industrial base, and a lack of well-trained managerial and engineering-technical manpower. While struggling to rebuild the national economy from scratch, under the dark clouds of the extremely confusing and often violent conflicts among a myriad of political factions, a new Republic of Korea was inaugurated in the southern part in 1948. Only two years elapsed before North Korea invaded the South at the dawn of Sunday, June 25, 1950. We in Korea call it the 6.25 War. Three years of war on the peninsula virtually obliterated the industrial base of the country. In the process of rehabilitation, primarily under the aid program of the US, a batch of entrepreneurs emerged. They played on various political connections and special favors from the government in their growth (Kim, 1976). Tainted by corruption, abuse of power, election rigging, and other attending malaises, the regime of President Syngman Rhee crumbled in the face of nationwide student protests in 1960. The ensuing Chang Myun government did not even have enough time to settle down when General Park Chung Hee and his junta took power through a bloodless coup in May 1961.

The benchmark for our discussion of the nature of the second-wave modernization is set for this period. The first Five-Year Economic Development Plan came into effect in 1962. The initial attempts to draw up such plans were made by the Syngman Rhee regime and the short-lived Chang government, both of which did not survive to materialize the plans. Drawing upon these earlier aborted plans then, the new junta regime finalized the program and actually embarked on active economic growth policies. Typically, the growth was attained by industrialization, and the industrial sector was led by manufacturing, and manufacturing by exports.[11] And in the whole process of modernization concentrated on economic development the workings of political selectivity are apparent, as is clearly described by Kim (2006: 108) in the following fashion:

> South Korea's selective imitation and export-oriented strategies have helped to achieve relatively successful economic growth over the last four decades. However, the prevailing social structures as the legacies of her past prevented South Korea from following the same patterns of industrialization and development experienced in other more early industrialized countries. The choice of development strategy is a political choice.

When Park Chung Hee regime embarked on the economic development programs, he actually benefited from the Syngman Rhee administration's decision to use foreign aid from the US during the 1950s in the aftermath of the 6.25 War to build an infrastructure that included a nation-wide network of primary and secondary schools, modern roads, and a modern communications network. As a result, by 1961, Korea could enjoy the well-educated young work force and a relatively modernized infrastructure that provided Park's regime with a minimum foundation for economic take-off. But the crucial decision on the part of the Park administration had to do with the role of the central government in this project of national economic development. And here we now could apply the theory of selective modernization suggested earlier to the explication of the formation and development of the Korean version of capitalism in the process of modernization.

The first item on the agenda for discussion would be the external factor of international acculturation. To begin with, it was a very much tilted acculturation from the advanced industrial nations of the world, the US and Japan as the most influential ones. Especially, the US provided a variety of material and financial resources, technical and managerial know-how, personnel training in the areas of government bureaucracy, business management, university professors, graduate students, and even the military, on top of which of course the national security protection (Kim and Lee, 1983; 1987; Kim *et al.*, 1985). In addition, the international economic environment was favorable to Korea in general. With the growth of the advanced industrial nations of the West and Japan, a new system of international division of labor has been formed in terms of manufacturing functions and markets for different types of products. Korea and, in fact, countries like Taiwan and other newly industrializing nations in Asia and Latin America, came to put out low-priced, low quality goods to compete in the global market (Kambhampati, 2004).

Under the circumstances, Korea had to make selective adaptation of the institutional framework for the task of pursuing modernization and a philosophy or ideology to justify it. As implied in the discussion made above, the state decided to direct the whole program of national development mainly owing to the absence of other institutions with the capacity or resources to plan and implement such drastic changes never tried before in this country and accomplish the goals in such a short time. In short, the "economic system" in essence "incorporated elements of both state capitalism and free enterprise" (Savada and Shaw, 1992: 141).

When President Park Chung Hee initiated the series of five-year economic development plans, his utmost motto was 'Modernization of the Motherland' (Shin, 1965). Although the idea of modernization of the nation was already the essential concern of the leaders of the first wave modernization of the turn of the 20th century, this particular term appeared in the public discourse only in the second wave period of the 1960s on. And this ideology has become the magic wand enchanting the mind and heart of the Korean people in their pursuit of happiness in the ensuing decades of rapid growth (Kim *et al.*, 1985:169-185). This ideology of modernization was originally introduced from the West, or the US, in particular, with the central goal of achieving economic development in the less well-to-do nations around the world. No doubt, this orientation was directly adopted by President Park and his men.

Initially, in a book published in 1962, entitled *The Road Forward for Our Nation*, Park Chung Hee (1962) declared that "Our nation is facing the task of modernization in front of us. To complete the task of modernization which had been left unfulfilled since the eastward surge of the western powers at the end of the 19th century" and laid out three major tasks of 'Korean Modernization' (as quoted in Shin, 1965: 5-49) as follows: (1) nationalistic modernization to emancipate the nation from the semi-feudal, semi-colonial legacy; (2) achievement of the self-reliant national economy to emancipate the nation from poverty; and (3) reconstruction of healthy democracy. In connection with democracy, however, he argued that since we cannot absorb everything down to the root of democracy, even if we imported it from the outside, we should endeavor to create 'Koreanized democracy' by grafting it on to our self-identity based on traditional Korean thoughts and materialize it by the leadership of a newly formed modern democratic force. In short, a strong nationalistic tenet was apparent (Shin, 1965: 5-49). Then, in another book with a title, *The State, Revolution, and I*, put out in 1963 after he officially became President and embarked on the first five-year plan, Park Chung Hee (1963) proposed what is known as the philosophy of the 'Economy First' policy with which he pleaded to the people "Let us shed our blood, sweat, and tears!" to pursue three action platforms of (1) supremacy of the economy, (2) priority of construction, and (3) utmost value of labor (Shin, 1965: 60-70).

And this line of thinking emphasizing the economic element of national development remained intact until the early 1980s and this period is often identified as the 'generation of modernization.' Nonetheless, as time changed with some remarkable success in economic growth, there were attempts to upgrade the political platforms. For example, in 1981 the new government of President Chun Doo Hwan who took over power in 1980 through a second coup after the assassination of President Park altered the title of the five-year plan from the 'Five-Year Economic Development Plan' to the Five-Year Economic and Social Development Plan.' Then, despite the fact that the ensuing regimes from 1980 to 1987 when democratic transition took place inherited the basic tenet of stressing the importance of economic growth, the political rhetoric also changed so that terms like 'modernization of the motherland' or 'the economy first' quietly disappeared from the scene. Ironically, however, this phrase of 'the economy first' was resurrected during the Kim Dae Jung regime when he had to struggle with the guidelines supplied by the IMF to clean the mess of the notorious and shameful foreign exchange crisis of 1997. Recall that Kim was one of the leading anti-Park democracy fighters under the rule of Park Chung Hee.

The strategy for economic development selected by the Park regime was known as the 'Guided Capitalism' aiming at the 'export-led industrialization' as the concrete program of economic plans. While the economy was planned by the state, the principle was a market economy; government assumed primary responsibility for capital formation, resource allocation, project selection etc, and the private sector was mobilized to materialize the plans and projects that government decided to pursue. In short, the will of government to undertake economic development played a crucial role, but it was not confined to such measures as mobilizing capital and allocating investments. It stretched its hand into the areas of restructuring of industries, especially defense and construction, or it would sometimes stimulate competition in the market but other times suppress or eliminate it. Government set export targets and provided additional government-subsidized credit and further access to the growing domestic market, if those firms in this area of business succeeded to meet the targets. Failure to meet them, however, resulted in the withdrawal of credit etc. The central government agency in charge of all these tasks was the newly created Economic Planning Board (Savada and Shaw, 1992: 143-144; Steinberg, 1988a).

In a sense, this was a form of mixed economy of both the public and private sectors in action. But it was also mixed in the sense that both the modern formal bureaucratic organized and the traditional informal private bur less well-organized sectors, equally contributed to the overall national development. The general goals of export-led industrialization were to attain quick capital accumulation and fast eradication of chronic poverty. And the basic approach involved was to shift the industrial policies step by step from (1) the development of import substitute consumer goods industries, (2) through export-oriented consumer goods industries producing cheap stuff, price competitive in the world market, and to (3) heavy-chemical industries around the mid-70s, putting out capital as well as consumer goods, now to (4) hi-tech industries in the information-communications technology (ICT), biotechnology (BT), nanotechnology (NT) and so on since the 1990s. Foreign loans and high domestic savings supplied needed capital, while long hours with low wages in poor conditions made it possible to sustain low-price competitiveness, in the earlier phase of economic development (Savada and Shaw, 1992: 143-145).

To push for quick take-off and sustained growth, large business organizations or corporations, especially *chaebol,* the conglomerates, were favored over against small-medium firms, despite the significant contributions made by the latter. During the colonial period, very few large firms had been owned or managed by Koreans. It was after the departure of the Japanese that some Korean businessmen maneuvered to obtain the so-called vested properties of former Japanese ownership and many of them grew into the *chaebol* of later decades. Those who gained this right were people who used to have some special connections with officials in the USAMGIK or the Syngman Rhee regime. And they were alleged to have received some special favors from the government in return for kickbacks and other gifts. Park Chung Hee's junta initially charged for corruption and jailed many of the leading *chaebol* and other wealthy businessmen in accordance with their slogan of eradicating corruption in government and businesses, but they soon came to realize that without the cooperation from these leading entrepreneurial elite corps they could not proceed with their ambitious economic development plans and compromise was inevitable. The accused corporate leaders had to pay a huge amount of fines and were released, and then they were summoned to cooperate and take active part in the national task of economic development. Basically, the typical *modus operandi* under the guise of 'guided capitalism' entailed the government's selection of companies to undertake some planned projects and channeled funds from foreign loans, with the state guarantee of repayment. If needed, additional loans were made available from domestic banks (Eckert, 1993; Kim, 1976; Lie, 2006; Savada and Shaw, 1992: 147-148). In short, "state patronage and social networks shaped *chaebol* growth. It would be misleading to highlight the individual initiative of the founder-entrepreneurs of major South Korea *chaebol* in explaining conglomerate growth. They were undoubtedly bright and diligent, but their entrance to the ranks of the *chaebol* during the 1960s and 1970s depended on their ability to cultivate political favors" (Lie, 2006: 143).

Often, the Korean *chaebol* is compared with the Japanese *zaibatsu*. In fact, these two words are written in identical Chinese characters (財閥). There are, however, some important differences. First of all, the Japanese *zaibatsu* were replaced by *keiretsu* — large and modern industrial enterprise groupings. Second, while the *chaebol* were family dominated corporations, *keiretsu* were controlled by professional corporate management. Third, individual *chaebol* were prevented from buying controlling shares of banks, with regulations making it difficult to develop an exclusive banking relationship, but usually worked with an affiliated bank and had almost unlimited access to credits. Finally, the *chaebol* often formed subsidiaries to produce components for exports, while large Japanese corporations often employed outside contractors (Dolan and Worden, 1992: 202; Savada and Shaw, 1992: 148; Steinberg, 1988b).

Many argue that this sort of developmental state is a legacy of the Japanese colonial industrial policy, even the post-war Japanese development model, or some characterize Korea as a bureaucratic capitalist society (Chang and Lee, 2006; Ebrey *et al.*, 2009: 391; Kim, 2006). No matter how it is labeled, the significance of the role of government in the decision-making and policy implementing processes relative to the capitalist economic development is undeniable. And it is also true that not unlike in the case both of China and Japan, though in different historical and cultural contexts, a very complex dynamic interplay between the state and business sectors, together with the relative posture of changing civil society would define the future unfolding of the political economy of capitalism in Korea and the region. In other words, it may be envisioned that in the future transformations of these societies the intervention of political selectivity is ineluctable in this whole dynamic process and yet there is also a likelihood that the injection of cultural selectivity may be enhanced. Social science research may want to pay due attention to this form of transformation in order to improve our understanding of the subject matter under consideration here.

## In Closing

As was indicated in the opening remarks, this was intended as a case of intellectual exercise to illustrate the application of a newly formulated general theoretical scheme on modernization to the examination of the historical unfolding of the modern capitalism in the three nations of East Asia, China, Japan, and Korea (South Korea) from the times of its formative stage to the more recent generations since the end of the Second World War. The main interest of my study was to look into the nature of the operation of political selectivity involved in the process of modernization affecting the emergence and evolution of the modern version of capitalism in this region, with some minor observations on the relative role of cultural selectivity. As such, the focus of analysis of necessity was placed on the role of the state and its relationship with the private business sector in the process of developing capitalism. Parsimony was of course the first pretext for such a restrained approach. It was necessary above all to concentrate on this limited aspect of the extremely complex transformations entailed to figure out how a theoretical explication of the type introduced here can be useful to our understanding of the meaning of the phenomena under scrutiny.

This approach has shown that the nature of capitalism or capitalistic economy emerged and evolved in the three nations when the region encountered the surge of modernization emanating from the West in the form of imperial encroachment in mainly the nineteenth century under distinctly different internal conditions of each society. Interestingly, the initial response was similar under the commonly shared ideological influence of Confucian world view originated in China. Soon, however, each took divergent trajectories by making their own selective adaptation under the given circumstances. It was here that political selectivity aided by cultural selectivity operated to yield the divergent responses and paths of modernization. In this context of modernization the modern version of capitalism sprouted and evolved in the subsequent decades. After experiencing certain disruptions of different nature caused by both internal and external factors, they embarked on the path to the second wave of modernization in the post-WWII era and each took divergent roads toward establishing their own versions of capitalism. In this process certain variations as well as commonalities in the role of the state and its relationship with the private entrepreneurial sector also were manifested and one common element was that all three countries were able to achieve impressive economic growth in this period.

If I was allowed to spend more space and time, I would certainly have additionally delved into such issues as the internal principles of organization of business enterprises evolved in the process of capitalist development of the economy, the nature of industrial relations system formed and established in each society in this process, and even the question of the so called 'Confucian capitalism' in East Asia. I decided to reserve them for further research probably sometime in the future. It would be nice if someone else took up this task. At the moment, I should be content with what I have been able to handle. Anyhow, I should like to stress at this closing sentence that we may want to watch out closely to see if the relative clout of the state and political selectivity may gradually wane in the future even in this region with relatively conservative cultural heritages, partly due to the further evolution of capitalism itself, that is. My gut reaction is that either way the prospect does not seem to be too comfortable to me at least unless the relative power of civil society is substantially enhanced.

## *Notes*

1. The reason for this ordering of the three countries is based on the timing of their official signing of treaties with Western nations. Also note that Korea in this paper refers to the Republic of Korea (South Korea) unless otherwise indicated.

2. For this summary, refer to the following works by the author: Kim (1977; 1981; 1985; 1993; 2002; 2005a; 2005b; 2008).

3. These two propositions imply that any change that took place outside the confine of this specific historical time period, namely, the modern era, is not to be considered as 'modernization,' as this specific temporal designation has to do with the periodization undertaken by European intellectuals to divide their history into three eras of Ancient, Medieval, and Modern in the 14th century and on (Kumar, 1995: 66-100).

4. Suchshiftsinclude the Renaissance, the fall of Constantinople,the discovery of the New World, the Copernican Revolution in science and technology, the Reformation, and the ensuing changes of revolutionary scale in various spheres of life, especially the modern capitalism. Authors do not necessarily agree on the exact timing of the beginning of the modern era. Some view modernization as a process started around the mid-18th century with industrialization (for example, Martinelli, 2005: 9), while still others like Eisenstadt (1966) think it started in the 17th century.

5. As a matter of fact, part of this issue is dealt with in two chapters of my book, *Alternative Discourses on Modernization and Development: East Asian Perspective.*

6. Modernization in this region was initiated in the nineteenth century but this was interrupted by historical circumstances and a new effort was exerted in the aftermath of the Second World War, and it is obvious that the nature of the international contexts and internal dynamics was different significantly between the two periods.

7. Of course, one should not ignore that even in China they developed some state-owned and merchant-run heavy industry in the nineteenth century, but they were not particularly successful (Hamilton, 1996: 332; 339).

8. These *guanxi* connections included those ties based not only on the blood relations but also the locality or area of origin often sharing dialects, schools attended, and other cohort experiences, that represented important linkages used to build extensive networks of those family-centered firms.

9. Detailed discussion on this issue may be spared here but some works dealing with it are introduced for references: Eckert (1991); Kim (2006); McNamara (1990); Shin and Robinson (1999); and Suh (1996).

10. The discussion that follows mainly draws upon the analysis offered in Baek (2007); Ebrey *et al.* (2009: 474-482); Stockman (2000: 136-137); Vohra (2000: chapter 288-314); Worden *et al.* (1988: 210-263); and otherwise indicated.

11. In this work, no detailed description of concrete economic development programs and measures is provided here. Instead, brief discussion of major goals and strategies will be made later. For a general account of the nature of economic policies, one may want to refer to the following: Amsden (1989); Kim (1993); Kim (2006); Korea Development Institute (KDI) (2010); and Kwack (1994).

## *References*

[Works in English]

Baek, Okkyoung, Jihyun Cho, Dongju Ham, Byungjoo Jung, Hynsook Lee, and Jungsook Sohn. 2011. *Understanding Korean History*. Edison, NJ: Jimoondang.

Baek, Seung-Wook. 2007. "The Emerging Capitalist Spirit of Private Enterprises in China: Capitalism with Chinese Characteristics." pp. 175-191 in *East Meets West: Civilizational Encounters and the Spirit of Capitalism in East Asia*, edited by Kyong-Dong Kim and Hyun-Chin Lim. Leiden and Boston: Brill.

Black, Cyril E. 1966. *The Dynamics of Modernization: A Study in Comparative History*. New York: Harper & Row.

Chang, Yun-Shik and Steven Hugh Lee. 2006. *Transformations in Twentieth Century Korea*. London and New York: Routledge.

Chirot, Daniel. 1994. *How Societies Change*. Thousand Oaks, CA: Pine Forge Press.

Dolan, Ronald E. and Robert L. Worden. 1992. *Japan: A Country Study*. 5th edition. Washington, DC: Library of Congress.

Ebrey, Patricia, Anne Walthall, and James Palais. 2009. *East Asia: A Cultural, Social, and Political History*. 2nd edition. Belmont, CA: Wadsworth.

Eckert, Carter J. 1991. *Offspring of Empire: The Koch'ang Kims and the Colonial Origins of Korean Capitalism: 1876-1845*. Seattle: University of Washington Press.

_______. 1993. "The South Korean Bourgeoisie: A Class in Search of Hegemony." pp. 95-130 in *State and Society in Contemporary Korea*, edited by Hagen Koo. Ithaca, NY: Cornell University Press.

Eisenstadt, Shmuel N. 1964. "Breakdowns of Modernization." *Economic Development and Cultural Change* 12(4): 345-367.

_______. 1966. *Modernization: Protest and Change*. Englewood Cliffs, NJ: Prentice-Hall.

_______. 2002a. *Multiple Modernities*. New Brunswick, NJ: Transaction Publishers.

_______. 2002b. "Some Observations on Multiple Modernities." pp.

27-41 in *Reflections on Multiple Modernities: European, Chinese and Other Interpretations*, edited by Dominic Sachsenmaier, Jens Riedel, with S. N. Eisenstadt. Leiden: Brill.

_______. 2003. *Comparative Civilizations and Multiple Modernities*. Leiden: Brill.

Gordon, Andrew. 2003. *A Modern History of Japan*. Oxford: Oxford University Press.

Hall, Stuart, David Held, Don Hubert, and Kenneth Thompson. 1996. *Modernity: An Introduction to Modern Societies*. Malden, MA: Blackwell Publishing.

Hamilton, Gary G. 1996. "Overseas Chinese Capitalism." pp. 328-342 in *Confucian Traditions in East Asian Modernity: Moral Education and Economic Culture in Japan and the Four Mini-Dragons*, edited by Tu Wei-ming. Cambridge, MA: Harvard University Press.

Hwang, Kyung Moon. 2010. *A History of Korea*. New York: Palgrave Macmillan.

Kambhampati, Uma. 2004. *Development and the Developing World*. Cambridge, UK: Polity.

Kim, Kyong-Dong. 1976. "Political Factors in the Formation of the Entrepreneurial Elite in South Korea." *Asian Survey* 16(5): 465-477.

_______. 1977. "The International Dynamics of Modernization: Some Theoretical Issues and Humanistic Concerns." *Journal of the National Academy of Sciences of the Republic of Korea , Humanities and Social Sciences Series* 16: 277-306.

_______. 1981. "The Principle of Political Selectivity in Asian Development: A Conceptual Framework." Paper presented to the Third Conference of Asian Sociologists. Tokyo: October 11-13.

_______. 1985. *Rethinking Development: Theories and Experiences*. Seoul: Seoul National University Press.

_______. 2005a. "Modernization as a Politico-Cultural Response and Modernity as a Cultural Mixture: An Alternative View of Korean Modernization." *Development and Society* 34(1): 1-24.

_______. 2005b. "Alternative Modernities Emerging via Selective Modernization: The Case of the Two Koreas." Paper presented at the Workshop on "History of Modernity Reconsidered: East Asian Paths and Patterns" of the 20th International Congress of Historians. July 3-9, University of New South Wales, Sydney, Australia.

_______. 2008. "Selective Modernization and Alternative Modernities: In Search of an Alternative Theory." *National Academy of Sciences Journal of Humanities and Social Sciences* 47(2): 105-161.

Kim, Kyong-Dong and Lee On-Jook. 1983. "The U.S. Educated among the Korean Politico-Bureaucratic Elite: An Aspect of American Socio-Cultural Influence." *American Studies* 6: 53-69.

_______. 1987. "Educational Background of the Korean Elite: The Influence of the United States and Japan." pp. 434-458 in *Dependency Issues in Korean Development: Comparative Perspectives,* edited by Kyong-Dong Kim. Seoul: Seoul National University Press.

Kim, Kyong Ju. 2006. *The Development of Modern South Korea: State Formation, Capitalist Development and National Identity*. New York: Routledge.

Kumar, Krishan. 1995. *From Post-Industrial to Post-Modern Society: New Theories of the Contemporary World*. Oxford, UK; Cambridge, MA: Blackwell Publishers.

Levy, Marion J. Jr. 1955. "Some Social Obstacles to Capital Formation in Underdeveloped Areas." In *Capital Formation and Economic Growth,* edited by M. Abraomovitz. Princeton, NJ: National Bureau of Economic Research.

Lie, John. 2006. "What Makes Us Great: ChaebŏlDevelopment, Labor Practices, and Managerial Ideology." pp. 138-152 in *Transformations in Twentieth Century Korea,* edited by Chang Yun-Shik and Steven Hugh Lee. London; New York: Routledge.

Martinelli, Alberto. 2005. *Global Modernization: Rethinking the Project of Modernity*. London: Sage Publications.

McNamara, Dennis. 1990. *The Colonial Origins of Korean Enterprise, 1910-1945*. Cambridge: Cambridge University Press.

McNeil, William H. 1986. *History of Western Civilization: A Handbook*. 6th edition. Chicago: The University of Chicago Press.

Moore, Wilbert E. 1965. *The Impact of Industry*. Englewood Cliffs, NJ:

Prentice-Hall.

Morishima, Michio. 1982. *Why Has Japan "Succeeded"?: Western Technology and the Japanese Ethos*. Cambridge: Cambridge University Press.

Ringmar, Erik. 2005. *The Mechanics of Modernity in Europe and East Asia: The Institutional Origins of Social Change and Stagnation*. London: Routledge.

Sachsenmaier, Dominic. 2002. "Multiple Modernities: The Concept and Its Potential." pp. 42-67 in *Reflections on Multiple Modernities: European, Chinese and Other Interpretations*, edited by D. Sachsenmaier, J. Riedel, with S. N. Eisenstadt. Leiden: Brill.

Sachsenmaier, Dominic, Jens Riedel with Shmuel N. Eisenstadt, eds. 2002. *Reflections on Multiple Modernities: European, Chinese and Other Interpretations*. Leiden: Brill.

Savada, Andrea M. and William Shaw. 1992. *South Korea: A Country Study*. Washington, DC: Library of Congress.

Shin, Gi-Wook and Michael Robinson. 1999. *Colonial Modernity in Korea*. Cambridge; London: Harvard University Asia Center.

Steinberg, David I. 1988a. *South Korea's Economy: Past Successes, Future Prospects: A Background Report*. New York: Asia Society.

_______. 1988b. *Chaebŏl: Engine of South Korea's Growth: A Background Report*. New York: Asia Society.

Stockman, Norman. 2000. *Understanding Chinese Society*. Cambridge: Polity.

_______. 2004. *Understanding Chinese Society*. Cambridge: Polity.

Sugimoto, Yoshio. 2010. *An Introduction to Japanese Society*. 3rd edition. New York: Cambridge University Press.

Suh, Yong-Sug. 1996. "The Transformation of Historical Perspectives on Postliberation Capitalism". Translated by Eun-Hee Chae and W. A. Hays. *Korean Studies* 20: 161-188.

Vohra, Ranbir. 2000. *China's Path to Modernization: A Historical Review from 1800 to the Present*. 3rd edition. Upper Saddle River, NJ: Prentice Hall.

Worden, Robert L., Andrea M. Savada, and Ronald E. Dolan. 1988. *China: A Country Study*. Washington, DC: Library of Congress.

Yao, Xinzhong. 2010. *Chinese Religion: A Contextual Approach*. A&C Black.

Yi Tae-jin. 2007. *The Dynamics of Confucianism and Modernization in Korean History*. Translated by Edward Park, Milan Hejtmanek, Todd A. Henry, Hong Soon-kwon, and Scott Swaner. Ithaca, NY: Cornell University East Asia Program.

[Works in Korean]

Kim, Kyong-Dong. 1993. *Han-guk Sahoe Pyeongdeungnon* (Theories of Korean Social Change). Seoul: Nanam.

Kim, Kyong-Dong. 2002. *Han-guk Sahoe Baljeonnon* (On Korean Societal Development). Seoul: Jipmoondang.

Kim, Kyong-Dong *et al.* 1985. *Han-guk Sahoe Han Sedae* (One Generation of Change in Korean Society). Seoul: Seoul National University Press.

Park, Chung Hee. 1962. *Urinaraga Naagal Gil* (The Road Forward for Our Nation). Seoul: Dong-A Publishers.

_______. 1963. *Gukga, Hyeokmyeong, guerigo Na* (The Nation-State, Revolution, and I). Seoul: Hyangmunsa.

Shin, Pŏm-Shik. 1965. *Joguk Guendaehwa* (Modernization of Motherland). Seoul: Dong-A Publishers.

Chapter 2

# *Comparing Capitalisms, East and West*

Jan Nederveen Pieterse

## Introduction

Major, widely recognized families of capitalism are Nordic capitalism, Anglo-American capitalism, East Asian capitalism and in addition, China and many variations such as Mediterranean capitalism. Major literatures on this theme are varieties of capitalism (VoC), comparative capitalisms (CC), thick business studies and comparative political economy. The VoC literature has contributed the widely recognized categories of liberal market economies (LME), coordinated market economies (CME) and state-led market economies (SME); distinctions that essentially concern how, according to which institutions and rules economies are coordinated.

If we plot these varieties of capitalism by regions and countries, a schematic overview is as follows (Table 2.1).

From this overview it is readily apparent that LME are a minority and most countries are CME. Second, LME predominate in settler immigrant societies. Third, there are crossover countries such as the UK, which can be placed in both LME and CME cat-

**Table 2.1** Varieties of Capitalism by Region/Country

| Capitalism | Region |
|---|---|
| LME | US, Australia, New Zealand, UK |
| CME | Europe, UK, Canada, Japan, Northeast Asia, Southeast Asia, South and West Asia, Middle East, Brazil, Argentina, Chile, Mexico, etc. |
| SME | Singapore, China, Vietnam, Laos, North Korea, Russia, Cuba, Venezuela, Iran, Saudi Arabia, Emirates |
| Mixed | All |

**Table 2.2** Varieties of Capitalism and Social Formations

| Social formations | Varieties of capitalism |
|---|---|
| Settler immigrant societies | LME |
| Post feudal societies | CME, SME |
| Post-revolutionary societies, post war and crisis | SME |

egories. This also applies to Canada among immigrant societies. As Polanyi and many others point out, markets are embedded in society. Let us consider then, taking a step further from the overview above, the type of social formations that are typically associated with types of capitalism. An overview is in Table 2.2.

Settler immigrant societies which are highly individualized typically tend towards LME or have, borrowing Goethe's language, 'elective affinity' with LME. Contracts are a central coordinating mechanism in LME, which are appropriate to this type of social formation. Law, property rights and contracts are key components of this kind of social formation; more precisely, they are key social components in most social formations but in LME there are virtually no other sources of social organization. Liberal democracy and its inherent strain of possessive individualism (Macpherson, 1962) resonate well with LME. LME also combines well with post democracy (Crouch, 2004), which we may also term neoliberal democracy.

Post-feudal societies are societies with much deeper, longer histories than immigrant societies so they feature multiple sources and principles of social organization and cohesion, such as legacies of feudalism, aristocracy and monarchy, which establish deep canons of social behavior, traditions of noblesse oblige and classical cultural traditions, all of which are overlaid by and interspersed with later forms of governance and democracy. Political economies of post feudal societies tend toward CME or, in brief, round tables of government, capital, labor and diverse stakeholders (such as farmers, consumers, regional and religious groups, and minorities). Forms of democracy that resonate with these formations are social democracy and, in Europe, Christian democracy (Nederveen Pieterse, 2016).

Immigrant societies are recent formations and LME (or the actual implementation of LME) is more recent still. The historical norm for many societies is to be state-led. Nineteenth century industrialization was, without exception, state led. SME are a historical normal and LME are a historical newcomer. In addition, in times of war and crisis, for a period the state in all social formations leads economies.

Statism (étatisme) or the idea that the state should lead is a further step. There are various kinds of statism, from absolutist monarchy onward. The French revolutionary era centralized state power to counteract nobilities in the countryside and the Church. The two types of revolution, political and social, have both given rise to state-led economies. Social revolution led to centrally planned economies in Russia, Eastern Europe, China and Cuba, which have over time transformed to SME. Political revolutions gave rise to SME such as Ataturk in Turkey, fascism in Italy, Germany and Spain and in most postcolonial newly independent countries such as India (Nehru), Indonesia (Sukarno), Iran (Mosadeq), Ghana (Nkrumah), Tunisia (Bourguiba), and so forth. Another variant have been 'socialist-oriented' states in Egypt (Nasser), Algeria, Ethiopia, North Korea, Guinea, and so forth. Venezuela, Bolivia and Ecuador recently adopted SME or hybrid (CME/SME) institutions.

This schematic account needs further refinement by time and place. Time series should accommodate variations over time. Thus, after the 1929 crash and the Great Depression, the US turned to state intervention with the New Deal and Fordism. In the wake of the Second World War came Keynesian elements such as the GI bill and 'military Keynesianism'. The postwar boom ('the golden years of capitalism') was a period of Keynesian consensus in advanced economies and developing countries. The cold war and subsequent wars of hegemony continued profound strands of SME in key sectors of the American economy, particularly the military-industrial complex and related sectors of technology, finance and foreign policy.

As to variation across space, the title of this paper mentions East and West,[1] a framework that is reminiscent of the colonial era. We must, of course, unbundle 'the West'. Europe is profoundly different from the US and within Europe, Mediterranean Europe is quite different from Nordic Europe, Greece is different from Sweden, and so forth. In addition, there is differentiation within countries. For instance, the plantation economy of the American South (Dixie, the former Confederacy) differs from the industrial Northeast, a pattern of difference that goes back to the American civil war and that overlaps with the later so-called rustbelt and Sunbelt. Data over time show a 'regional clustering of disadvantage' in which regions with 'cumulative disadvantage' (in education, labor market, health, safety net, etc.) are clustered in the South up to present times (Grusky *et al.*, 2015: 8).

Likewise, we must unbundle 'the East'. Varieties of capitalism also play a part in Asia, as in the gap between Northeast Asia and Southeast Asia. Can tiger cubs (in Southeast Asia) become tigers? Southeast Asia does not match the main achievements of South Korea and Taiwan — advanced industrialization, low Gini indices and consolidation of democracy — and may not catchup anytime soon. The elephant in the room, as it is discussed in the region, is institutions, which follow from social formations as well as external influences. While the tiger economies of Northeast Asia followed the model of Japan (and Germany) and underwent land reform, most Southeast Asian countries leaned towards American influence and did not experience land reform (discussed in Nederveen Pieterse, 2015a; 2015b).

The key role of the state has given rise to the notion of the East Asian developmental state (EADS). The coordinated market economies of Northeast Asia are quite different from Anglo-American capitalism and rather match the profile of Northwestern Europe (while Southeast Asia in some respects matches Latin America). Northeast Asia followed the model of Japan in terms of the role of state, labor unions and social policies (even after the Asian crisis and the neoliberal turn; Teichman, 2014). This includes institutions and policies but it goes deeper too; as post-feudal societies they share multiple sources of social cohesion, which more easily give rise to social market capitalism than immigrant societies can.

Thus Northeast Asia matches Nordic Europe in several respects. Both are post-feudal social formations. Both have experienced major episodes of war. Gini indices in Nordic Europe range from .25 (Norway) to .30 (Germany) while in Northeast Asia are in the low .30s.

## Why Totalize Capitalism?: 'The Map is Not the Same as the Territory'—Borges

Why would we uphold the idea of a single, normative capitalism and, implicitly or explicitly, expect convergence to take place towards this dominant or ideal-type form? Why would we totalize capitalism?

Let's take a step back and, instead of capitalism, take 'culture' as a theme. Here we can usually easily recognize multiple strands and levels of culture such as transnational culture and the 'global cultural supermarket' (and its identity confetti) along with Hollywood, Disney, CNN, McDonald's, Barbie, etc. AND we recognize Bollywood, Hallyu, Japanese design, Turkish soaps, Brazilian samba, flamenco, etc., AND micro-regional variations as well as diverse subcultures, along with new hybrids and ongoing bricolage across popular and high culture.

Thus we fairly easily recognize multiple layers of culture. It is relatively easy to keep multiple culture balls in the air and juggle them — probably because about culture there are no compelling, overarching narratives. Or, the grand narratives that did exist have lost appeal — such as the romantic notions of Herder and Carlyle; notions of 'race'; nineteenth-century orientalism; and rigid civilizational categories, from Toynbee to Bernard Lewis, Samuel Huntington, etc.

In contrast, in relation to capitalism there are not just powerful drives but also powerful narratives. The narratives include theories from the nineteenth to the twenty-first century (such as Capital in the twenty-first century; Piketty, 2013). In addition, there is hegemonic pressure such as Washington institutions, the Washington consensus, ongoing projects such as the Trans Pacific Partnership (TPP) and the Transatlantic Trade and Investment Partnership (TTIP), as well as agencies such as McKinsey, PricewaterhouseCoopers and international law firms. Financialization, Wall Street, international banks and credit rating agencies are another driver of convergence. Goldman Sachs coined the notion of the BRICS. Another driver is technological change — with ICT, global value chains and Silicon Valley. Although technological change is multicentric with diverse sources of innovation, ownership tends to be associated with major centers of capitalism.

Thus, while in relation to culture notions of convergence are thoroughly outmoded, when it comes to capitalism they continue to be prominent. Familiar notions of convergence are global capitalism, global plutocracy, the transnational capitalist class, and ideas such as 'neoliberalism everywhere' (Peck and Tickell, 2002) and 'Davos man.' Recent notions of 'variegated neoliberalization' (Peck and Theodore, 2007) add differentiation and yet retain the idea of an overall momentum.

Settler immigrant societies are outliers and post-feudal societies are far more numerous and the world majority. How is it then that an anomalous social formation, the US, could set the terms of capitalism — as if its form of capitalism represents 'real' capitalism? While there are several strands to the answer, the main point is postwar American hegemony and its influence in international institutions and regimes. The 'American century' also coincided with major technological advances from mass production to ICT, flexible production and transformations such as financialization.

Yet, because American society is an outlier, even as the US attempts to set global standards and rules — such as the Washington consensus and the Wall Street-Treasury-IMF complex of the 1990s — because they are out of sync with most of the world's social formations, these attempts have often been doomed to fail. This is the background of the 'lost decades' of development in Africa and Latin America as they followed Washington economic prescriptions. It is significant that societies that have been successful in terms of development, in particular Northeast Asia and later China, have largely developed outside the orbit of American capitalism. The EADS is in many ways the polar opposite of the Washington consensus.

Another way to gauge whether convergence is in fact taking place is to look at learning processes. The classic convergence thesis implies that learning is vertical, i.e. follows the dominant and most dynamic form of capitalism. However, learning isn't just from dominant capitalism; learning occurs just as much lateral and horizontal. Developing countries look to other developing countries. For most developing countries the East Asian tiger economies and EADS have long been a model, as in Malaysia's 'Look East' perspective. SME look to other SME. A report notes 'Beijing hopes to learn from Temasek', 'Good role model: China wants to boost private ownership while avoiding mass privatization pitfall that cripples Russia' (*New Straits Times*, October 5, 2015: B11).

Emerging economies' sovereign wealth funds also share learning curves.

One way of understanding the variety of perspectives on capitalism is to distinguish between low resolution and high resolution perspectives. Perception follows resolution and paradigms function in tandem with levels of resolution. Low-resolution perspectives are coarse grain and broad stroke. Part of sociology, world system analysis and TCC tend to function at a high level of abstraction. For instance, by using the broad and sweeping category 'OECD capitalism,' Wolfgang Streeck (2011) implies in effect that all advanced economies are alike. In contrast, anthropology, thick business studies and much geography typically adopt high-resolution, fine-grain perspectives. Thick description implies finer analytics and thus yields finer analyses than work at high levels of abstraction (Redding, 2005). This perspective is taken up further below under the heading of layered analysis.

A further dimension is hybridity. Several economies are hybrids in which multiple capitalist formations and institutions coexist — such as in China the state sector of SOEs, the fast growing sector of private SMEs and local state corporates, while foreign direct investment is interspersed with all sectors (Redding and Witt, 2010). Countries such as China, East Asian development states and emerging market developing countries (EMDC) embrace markets, but their embrace tends to be partial and instrumental — markets are welcome to the extent that they contribute to overall development ('the market is a good servant and a bad master') — and is of a different nature than the 'market fundamentalism' of immigrant societies and LME, where individual objectives prevail over social objectives ('private wealth and public squalor') and where there are no or few other societal values and organizing principles.[2] Low-resolution approaches often lack the perceptual and analytical tools to deal with hybrid capitalisms and simply place them in a single box. A further distinction runs between passive (being hybridized) and active hybridization (agency). Of course, active hybridization has played a major role, for instance in the selective borrowing of Meiji Japan, of the Asian tiger economies and now China.

## Plurality and Layered Analysis

In each plurality, such as modernities and capitalisms, there are common elements. The variants imply an invariant component. Yet the meaning of the common element is contextual; thus while state-led, coordinated and liberal market economies are all market economies, the way the market economy is understood differs in each setting. The invariant or common element among the variants is itself variable in meaning. A layered analysis means that we can see convergence occurring at one level, divergence of institutions and practices at another level, and at yet another level, mixing and new combinations of institutions and policies, all occurring simultaneously. Applying one theory or generalization across levels (which classical theories have often done) is scale inflation. Marx's 'iron laws of social change' and Weber's rationalization apply but not necessarily at all levels and across the board.

A further aspect of layered analysis is differentiation across space such as the recognition that conditions are different in Mumbai than in Delhi, different in old Delhi than in New Delhi, different in Mumbai slums than in the Mumbai Four Seasons, and different again in Chennai, different in Bihar, in Orissa, different in Assam, and so forth.

To Douglas North's perspective of path dependence we may add path disobedience. As we go up the level of reflexivity, there is greater room for choice and agency and hence outcomes are contingent.

## Capitalism, Capitalisms

Both critics and advocates of ongoing changes often use the category of capitalism in the singular, as in 'global capitalism' and 'the capitalist world-system.' Some accounts cast the 'Davos class' as a de facto world ruling class and, minor deviations notwithstanding, everything is falling or will fall under its sway. That it is only a matter of time for global capitalist convergence to take hold is a view that is shared by many advocates as well as critics of capitalist expansion.

This kind of capitalist teleology short circuits the question where the new emerging economies are on the spectrum of the diversity of institutions that coordinate economies. A fundamental dimension to assessing current trends is whether they are viewed through the lens of capitalism or capitalisms. The rise of emerging economies could in principle be understood in terms of the 'rise and decline of nations within the world-system' (Friedman, 1982), or as a reshuffling within the bounds of western capitalism. Yet, whether or not they unfold within the sphere of western capitalism is not a given but part of the problem to be examined.

The 2008 crisis highlights the variation in capitalisms. While the impact of crisis is global it is not uniform. Societies across the world are affected but are affected in markedly different ways. Crisis is a threat for some and an opportunity for others. Some institutions are crisis-prone and others are crisis-resistant (for instance, consider the difference between Wall Street banks and Canadian banks in relation to the 2008 crisis).

During the previous major crisis, the 1997-1998 Asian crisis, Anglo-American capitalism was upheld as the sole viable model. The 2008 crash, however, shattered the headquarters of the erstwhile exemplar. Several after-crisis assessments seek to reclaim the paradigm of a single standard-bearing capitalism — in relation to which also Western Europe is an outlier. However, the 2008 crisis exposed the frailties of Anglo-American capitalism on all levels — as ideology (laissez-faire), as paradigm (efficient market theory), as economics (shareholder short-termism, financialization), as policy (deregulation, liberalization), as institutions (accounting, rating agencies, regulators, market analysts), as methodology (financial mathematics, quantitative investments) and as culture (bonus culture, predatory CEOs). The 2008 crisis is part of a series of the American bank crises (Savings and Loans) in the early nineties, the bailout of LTCM, the dotcom crash, the collapse of Enron and other corporations, the subprime mortgage crisis and the Goldman episode (Nederveen Pieterse, 2004; 2008). The shareholder principle fosters short-termism (boost quarterly earnings numbers to ensure high stock ratings and dividends) and financialization fosters disconnect between finance and economics (Dore, 2000).

For decades the Washington consensus lorded over the developing world; in recent years lecturing has changed direction and emerging economies 'talk back.' From Europe to China, critical comments about American capitalism have come not just from backrooms but from official podiums. The tables have turned and a different refrain is in the air: the west must learn from the Asian crisis and must learn economic prudence from Asia (e.g., Mahbubani, 2009).

Indexes such as the 'economic freedom' and 'competitiveness index' typically assume a single model of capitalism. However, the question the 2008 crash poses anew is the absence of a general growth model or script for the relations between state, capital and civil society (Hall and Soskice, 2001; Stiglitz, 2006).

This variation is central to rebalancing processes. Institutions matter as part of economic imbalances and as part of rebalancing. Certain institutions prove to be crisis-prone and others crisis-resistant. Since institutions are political formations, analyzing this involves, besides institutional economics, politics and ideology. There is no general benchmark against which to measure and evaluate institutional change. Yet most perspectives, explicitly or implicitly, treat capitalism in the aggregate. This holds for mainstream views in media and economics as well as for neo-Marxist views such as world-system analysis and transnational capitalist class perspectives. Crisis, then, becomes a crisis of capitalism tout court, rather than of a particular type and strand of capitalism.

The main variation this view acknowledges is temporal or historical, between stages of accumulation and phases of capitalism, between early and latecomers to industrialization and modernity. In treating capitalism in the singular, unilinear theories of capitalism from Marx to world-system analysis view variation mainly as variation over time (with 'dependent capitalism' as a major outlier). This perspective is unsuited to examining regional variation because, like postwar modernization theory, it tends to assimilate regional variation into historical patterns (such as 'lagging behind' or 'catching up'). Thus while much post-crisis discussion focuses on the 'future of capitalism,' a more productive question is 'the future of capitalisms.' Capitalism survives thanks to the diversity of capitalisms: 'the flexibility of capitalism derives from capitalisms and regional variation' (Nederveen Pieterse, 2004: 146).

Diversity is not disappearing but the terms of diversity are changing and what is at issue is a reshuffling and realignment of capitalisms. Now, far more than in the past, this involves regions outside the old metropoles, the emerging economies from Asia to Latin America and the Middle East.

The idea that emerging economies will be incorporated in Anglo-American capitalism underestimates their different ways of organizing capitalism given different social structures and the political and social pressures they face. With the lead model imploding under corporate scandals, toxic finance, feeble institutions, inept governance, outdated infrastructure, aging populations, mammoth fiscal debt, massive sovereign debt and government eviscerated by tax cuts, several developmental state capitalisms in the east and south emerge as equally or as more dynamic. Whether they are also more sustainable is a different question, which the aftermath of the 2008 crisis makes apparent.

The Asian crisis was attributed to 'crony capitalism'; in 2008, 'permissive capitalism' turned out to be a much greater weakness and the robust public sector in many emerging economies emerges as a source of strength as long as it is accompanied by competent policies. This isn't just a matter of state or market; what matters is what kind of state. In the US, the concentration of wealth and power combined with free market ideology has contributed to an 'anti-state state' (MacLennan, 1997). In an earlier discussion of 'thinking in the plural', I argued (Nederveen Pieterse, 2014):

> Part of social science is the recurrent tension between the universal and the particular, between structures and adaptations, etc. Structural trends are often typecast as invariants and imperatives — accumulation, rationalization, modernization, rational choice, neoliberalism — that override differentiation, and much social science is concerned with calibrating the relationship between the universal and the particular. The macro theories of modernity and capitalism are both wedded to universalist approaches. The classic script of modernity is disembedding from social institutions (Giddens, 1990), a premise that runs through Weber (rationalization), Tönnies (shift from Gemeinschaft to Gesellschaft) and Parsons (pattern variables), or rather, to the schematic understanding that social theory retains from the classics, which are more subtle than their handbook versions. The plural approach, modernities, takes an idiographic turn and re-embeds actual modernities in specific spatiotemporal conditions. Similar considerations apply to capitalism. If capitalism is viewed as 'a foundational category' (Dirlik, 1994), what is it foundational of? If what matters are the 'organizing logics of capitalism' (Harvey, 2005), what do they organize? One of the definitions of ideology is applying general principles outside or regardless of context. The upshot of many perspectives on macro theory is decontextualization. However, if we don't hesitate to reject economism in economics, why would we embrace it, in the guise of macro theory, in sociology? The varieties imply the decentering of the paradigm. Rather than 'organizing logics', there are diverse responses to the question how to coordinate social action in relation to the economy. 'Capitalism' as a category is an approximation, an assemblage. Categorizations of capitalisms are approximations: 'the diversity and complexity of various typologies of capitalism reflects in part the fact that they are "typologies of typologies," i.e., national or "grand" ty-

> pologies are assemblages (syntheses) of institutional domain typologies' (Jackson and Deeg, 2006: 13). ... Fernand Braudel (1984) draws a sharp contrast between capitalism and the market economy. Wallerstein opts for assessing 'degrees of capitalism' (2001: 249). The VoC approach distinguishes between market economies (liberal and coordinated), rather than between capitalisms.

Anglo-American capitalism involves frictions between the US and Europe and between the US and emerging economies. In 2015 the US Congress voted against increasing the IMF vote quota of developing countries including China. With the TPP and the TTIP the US makes a new bid for economic leadership, which may not be successful or if it is successful may not make much of a dent (e.g., Rachman, 2015). The TPP doesn't include China, the world's second largest economy. Trade pacts generally aren't as important as in the past because among many countries tariffs are already low. Yet trade pacts do hold implications for governance. Through trade pacts corporations seek to gain advantages such as the ability to sue governments for changes in regulations that would impair their anticipated future profits. The general question remains, does one size fit all?

## Layered Analysis

Let's be wary of totalizing scripts, whether they come from Davos or Porto Alegre, from the World Economic Forum or the World Social Forum. Part of this is the fallacy of units. We speak of 'China' and 'the US' because that is how economic data pile up, but what matters as much are classes, strata and regions within and across these units. This is a two-way street: because technological, business and communication interweaving is growing, national units are of limited purchase; yet nations are units of political decision making and provide legal frameworks, institutions of economic coordination and forums of public reflexivity.

In each country there is a continuously shifting balance between political factions, also in response to international trends. Thus in China, the New Right (neoliberal), the New Left (social and green), the old left (neo-Maoist), the old right (nationalist and neo-communist) and liberals, vie for influence, and each comes with different shades of nationalism (e.g., Leonard, 2012).

Multilevel approaches are standard fare in several fields, such as multilevel governance in relation to European Union decision making. In social geography, multi-scalar approaches address the different spatial scales at which processes unfold, including processes of globalization at global, national, regional and local scales (e.g., Dicken, 2007). International institutions such as the World Bank and UNDP gather data and analyze processes at multiple scales — global, regional, national and often micro-regional and urban as well. 'New regionalism' approaches combine regional, national and local levels to understand production networks and clustering (Yeung, 2013).

A parallel perspective in cultural studies is that while many expect globalization to produce cultural standardization and 'McDonaldization' (Disneyfication, etc.), this happens, but only in some spheres and to some extent; regional, national and local variations continue with dynamics of their own, combine with transnational cultural assemblages and generate processes of hybridization and new patchworks of difference, which have been described as 'global multiculture' (Nederveen Pieterse, 2007; 2015c).

Totalizing theories produce scale inflation or commit the fallacy of privileging just one scale of analysis. Methodological nationalism means taking nations as the units of analysis. Methodological globalism is taking the global as unit of analysis — as in global capitalism, global crisis, global culture, global modernity, global inequality, global exclusion, global policing, etc. Does paying attention to national variation and dynamics mean that we must therefore ignore or sideline the transnational dimension? Does paying attention to transnational dynamics mean that we have to gloss over national and local processes? Do we have to choose between one or the other? The smarter option is a layered analysis in which multiple levels of analysis are relevant. Thus, not just nations are valid units but also firms, combinations of firms, global value networks, technologies, and so forth. A schematic overview is in Table 2.3.

Different analytics privilege different units and scales of anal-

**Table 2.3** Layered Analysis

| Layers | Dynamics | Analytics |
|---|---|---|
| Transnational | Global value chains, MNCs, banks, international institutions, international covenants, technology, ISO, hegemony, stratification | World-system analysis, transnational capitalist class, international organizations |
| | Banks, consultancies, accounting, law firms, risk analysis | Regional, national differences |
| Regional | Diasporas, civilizations, regional cooperation, regional development banks | New regionalism |
| National | Institutions, legal frameworks, corporate governance, labor relations, trade and innovation policies, currencies | Varieties of capitalism, comparative capitalisms |
| Local | Clustering, institutional densities, learning environments, firms | Economic geography, anthropology, microeconomics |

ysis. The varieties of capitalism approach tends to be state-centric and tends to underplay the role of transnational forces (global value chains, transnational corporations, international institutions, etc.) whereas the transnational capitalist class (TCC) approach and world-system analysis emphasize the transnational level and downplay national differences. Some approaches seek to bridge these levels of analysis (Soederberg *et al.*, 2005).

This is also relevant when it comes to questions of convergence or divergence. When it comes to the bulky question of convergence or divergence, a more sophisticated approach is a layered analysis that unbundles nation states and takes into account that convergence is taking place at one level (such as in technology, logistics, ISO, Special Economic Zones, WTO), divergence at another level (institutions of economic coordination, corporate governance, law) and mixing in yet other spheres (marketing, product mixes, consumption, media) (discussed in Nederveen Pieterse, 2007; 2014).

Layered processes produce layered outcomes — with diverse, uneven and combined patterns of transnational, regional, national and local cooperation; an overview is in Table 2.4. Regional entities such as the European Union, the Gulf Cooperation Council and ASEAN follow dynamics and agendas of their own. In addition, there is local variation, such as between China's Pearl River Delta and Harbin in the north, between Guangdong and Chongqing. Hence capitalist convergence and divergence often occur at the same time. Elites and business classes in different countries cooperate and follow their own ways, which brings us back to the classic theme of combined and uneven development.

This approach combines variables wide apart (in the vein of

**Table 2.4** Layered Dynamics

| Tendencies | Dynamics | Scales |
|---|---|---|
| Convergence | Technology, ISO, communication, production systems, logistics, consumption | Transnational, firms |
| Divergence | National, regional and local cultures; corporate governance; law; consumption | National, regional, local |
| Mixing | New combinations | Across scales |

global studies), examines their interaction from the viewpoint of development studies, sets forth scenarios and discusses their probabilities. While the variables in these probabilities may be fairly straightforward, their interaction is unstable and contentious and outcomes depend to a large extent on political processes and policies. After all, everything is a matter of political struggle. It is a fiction that economic models can script societal change. As Polanyi observed, markets are embedded; they are embedded in institutions and political formations, so markets are ultimately political. In contrast to the principle 'enter economism, exit politics' (Teivanen, 2002), what is at issue is taking economism out of economics and putting politics back in: enter politics, exit economism. While there are overall patterns and trends, changing political tides alter equations. It's impossible to take politics out of the equation and with politics in the equation outcomes are unpredictable.

In Asia, as elsewhere, extreme positions in relation to capitalism are to embrace American-style capitalism or to reject capitalism tout court. Neoliberals in Asia advocate similar forms of privatization, liberalization and deregulation as in the US and UK (e.g., Bhagwati and Panagariya, 2013). Singapore has long advocated liberalization policies, but has combined this with a strong and overall capable state (Fukuyama, 2005). Both the right and the left in Asia tend to think of capitalism in the singular. This works to the advantage of the right because it implies convergence: since we are converging on a liberal model, we might as well adopt policies that anticipate and hasten the inevitable. On the left, this perspective plays a bogeyman role: accept more transnational capitalism and we risk losing our autonomy, our sovereignty, our identity, and more.

The upshot of this discussion is that there is no single model. Universalism belongs to the era of hegemony. Ideological and political battles are fought as if they are about principles, such as state or market; but often the real issues are about identifying the mean, in Aristotle's sense, or the optimalmix of government and market — which depends on circumstances and context. All economies are mixed economies: which roles and which combination of government and market forces are best under which circumstances and in which conjuncture?

Why does this discussion matter? The diversity of capitalisms keeps capitalism going. Global value chains function because economies are at different levels. Multinational corporations practice institutional arbitrage because of the differentiation of institutions across countries. We cannot understand these trends and practices without factoring in the diversity of capitalism.

A further concern is the wide diversity in patterns of inequality across the world. This diversity is largely due to institutions and the degree to which they enable or constrain the political and elite capture of wealth. This informs the agenda of social struggles. However, if all capitalism is the same, does it matter?

## *Notes*

1. The origin of this paper is a keynote to the SNUAC conference on Capitalisms in Asia, October 2015. The title is an assigned title.

2. The two quotes in this sentence derive from the Indian economist Sukhamoi Chakravarty and from J. K. Galbraith.

## *References*

Bhagwati, Jagdish and Arvind Panagariya. 2013. *Why Growth Matters: How Economic Growth in India Reduced Poverty and the Lessons for Other Developing Countries*. New York: Public Affairs.

Bremmer, Ian. 2011. *The End of the Free Market: Who Wins the War Between States and Corporations?* New York: Portfolio Trade.

Crouch, Colin. 2004. *Post-democracy*. Cambridge: Polity.

Dicken, Peter. 2007. *Global Shift: Mapping the Changing Contours of the World Economy*. 5th edition.New York: Guilford.

Dirlik, Arif. 1994. "The postcolonial aura: Third World criticism in the age of global capitalism." *Critical Inquiry* 20(2): 328-356.

Dore, Ronald P. 2000. *Stock Market Capitalism/Welfare Capitalism: Japan and Germany versus the Anglo-Saxons*. Oxford: Oxford University Press.

Friedman, Edward, ed. 1982. *Ascent and Decline in the World-System*. London: Sage.

Fukuyama, Francis. 2005. *State-Building*. London: Profile Books.

Giddens, Anthony. 1990. *The Consequences of Modernity*. Cambridge: Polity.

Grusky, David B., Marybeth J. Mattingly, and Charles E. Varner. 2015. *State of the States: The Poverty and Inequality Report 2015*. Pathways Magazine, Special Issue.

Hall, Peter A. and David Soskice, eds. 2001. *Varieties of Capitalism: The Institutional Foundations of Comparative Advantage*. Oxford: Oxford University Press.

Jackson, Gregory and Richard Deeg. 2006. "How many varieties of capitalism? Comparing the comparative institutional analyses of capitalist diversity." *MPIfG (Max Planck Institute for the Study of Societies) Discussion Paper 06/2*.

Leonard, Mark, ed. 2012. *China 3.0: Understanding the New China*. London: European Council on Foreign Relations.

MacLennan, Carol A. 1997. "Democracy under the influence: cost-benefit analysis in the United States." pp. 195-224 in *Meanings of the Market: The Free Market in Western Culture*, edited by James G.

Carrier. Oxford: Berg.

Macpherson, Crawford B. 1962. *The Political Theory of Possessive Individualism: Hobbes to Locke.* Oxford: Oxford University Press.

Mahbubani, Kishore. 2009. "Lessons for the West from Asian capitalism." *Financial Times,* March 19: 9.

Nederveen Pieterse, Jan. 2004. *Globalization or Empire?* New York: Routledge.

_______. 2007. *Ethnicities and Global Multiculture: Pants for an Octopus.* Lanham, MD: Rowman & Littlefield.

_______. 2008. *Is There Hope for Uncle Sam?: Beyond the American Bubble.* London: Zed Books.

_______. 2014. *Rethinking Modernity and Capitalism: Add Context and Stir.* Sociopedia Colloquium (e-journal).

_______. 2015a. "What happened to the Miracle Eight? Looking East in the twenty-first century." *Canadian Journal of Development Studies* 63(3): 263-282.

_______. 2015b. *Goodbye Miracle Eight.* Bangi: UKM Press.

_______. 2015c. *Globalization and Culture: Global Mélange.* 3rd edition. Lanham, MD: Rowman & Littlefield.

_______. 2016. "Democracy is coming." In C. Wungaeo, B. Rehbein, eds. *Globalization and Democracy in Southeast Asia: Challenges, Responses and Alternative Futures.* London: Palgrave Macmillan (forthcoming).

Peck, Jamie and Adam Tickell. 2002. "Neoliberalizing Space." *Antipode* 34(3): 380-404.

Peck, Jamie and Nik Theodore. 2007. "Variegated Capitalism." *Progress in Human Geography* 31: 731-772.

Piketty, Thomas. 2013. *Capital in the Twenty-First Century.* Cambridge, MA: Harvard University Press.

Rachman, Gideon. 2015. "Obama's Pacific trade deal will not tame China." *Financial Times.* May 19.

Redding, Gordon. 2005. "The thick description and comparison of societal systems of capitalism." *Journal of International Business Studies* 36: 123-155.

Redding, Gordon and Michael A. Witt. 2010. *The Future of Chinese*

*Capitalism: Choices and Chances*. Oxford: Oxford University Press.

Soederberg, Susanne, Georg Menz, and Philip G. Cerny. 2005. *Internalizing Globalization: The Rise of Neoliberalism and the Decline of National Varieties of Capitalism*. London: Palgrave Macmillan.

Stiglitz, Joseph E. 2006. *Making globalization work*. New York: Norton.

Streeck, Wolfgang. 2011. "The crises of democratic capitalism." *New Left Review* 71: 5-29.

Teichman, Judith. 2014. "Struggling with the social challenges of globalization: Mexico, Chile and South Korea." pp. 63-75 in *Civilizing Globalization: A Survival Guide*, edited by Richard Sandbrook and Ali Burak Güven. 2nd edition. Albany, NY: SUNY Press.

Teivanen, Teivo. 2002. *Enter Economism, Exit Politics: Experts, Economic Policy and the Damage to Democracy*. London: Zed Books.

Yeung, Henry Wai-chung, ed. 2013. *Globalizing Regional Development in East Asia: Production Networks, Clusters, and Entrepreneurship*. New York: Routledge.

Chapter 3

# *Regional Capitalisms and Global Technoscience: Controllable or Uncontrollable Forces of Planetary Change?*

Wolf Schäfer

## Introduction

My first contribution to the Seoul National University series in Asian studies discussed questions of global terminology and method with regard to global studies (2010). In my second, I outlined the long-term trajectory of global history with respect to energy transitions and subsequent population growth (2014). Now I would like to consider the contemporary predicament of regional capitalisms and global technoscience.

A predicament is a problematic situation, a dangerous state of affairs without a readily available exit into a place of safety. This is the human condition in the early twenty-first century. I pose that the human species has become a terrestrial superpower that could theoretically "manage itself and Earth's ecosystems collectively, cooperatively, and wisely" (108), however, it is not doing that. The two most formidable sources of human power — capitalism and technoscience — are spinning out of control; they do not provide for the well-being of all people and do not harmonize our planet's nature with the aspirations and capabilities of all societies in the world. To be sure, the wealth of some individuals and some of the 193 countries represented in the UN is increasing dramatically — but so is large-scale economic inequality. Crucial scientific knowledge of global ecology is also growing rapidly — but so is ruinous environmental degradation.

Thus, the possibility of a catastrophic failure of Pangaea II in the next fifty years is a real and present danger. "Planetary governance with historical awareness, global foresight, and institutionalized restraint," which is essential for a successful "domestication of Earth and humankind" (115, 97), is not forthcoming; instead, human power and understanding are advancing like wildfire in a self-destructive way. What prevents us from directing the progress of capitalism and technoscience toward a sustainable state of affairs? Must we assume that capitalism is inherently unable to deliver material wealth to *all people*? Do we have to argue that technoscience is per se incapable of bringing all societies into balance with nature?

Capitalism is certainly very good for some people and technoscience solves many problems. Yet if this is the best they can do, one might as well conclude that capitalism and technoscience do not work for the majority of people and do not preclude fatal environmental degradation. But how can we really know this? Is the combination of capitalism and technoscience ultimately bad for the terrestrial environment? Will capitalism never enrich all people in all societies? Alternatively, is a comprehensive socio-economic and socio-natural orientation of both capitalism and technoscience to the commonweal feasible?

## The Capitalism plus Technoscience Conundrum

The capitalism plus technoscience (CPT) conundrum is about the impact of capitalism and technoscience on humanity's future. The future is of course difficult to know in advance. Historians are wont to say that they can only tell the past, not the future. And Ludwig Wittgenstein has famously concluded, "Whereof one cannot speak, thereof one must be silent."[1] However, the philosopher distinguished between rational and religious speech; he had mystical things in mind, when he recommended silence as appropriate. The historian on the other hand is wary of prediction; he thinks that the future is "unknown in a known manner."[2] So let me clarify: When I invoke the future, I do not seek to predict it. Concerned about the sustainability of our species on planet Earth, I aim to analyze the *observable* present in light of its *potential* futures.[3]

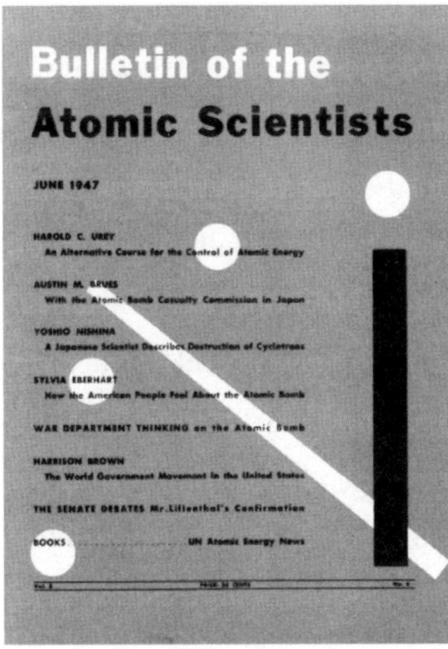

**Figure 3.1** *Bulletin of the Atomic Scientists*, vol. 3, no. 6, June 1947

My model for this present-centric approach to future studies is the 'Doomsday Clock,' which was invented soon after World War II, when atom bombs presented the greatest danger to humanity (they still do among other, newer threats). Designed by Martyl Langsdorf, an artist, whose physicist husband had worked for the Manhattan Project, the clock appeared for the first time on the cover of the June 1947 issue of the *Bulletin of the Atomic Scientists.*[4]

The *Bulletin* had been founded in 1945. The very scientists, who had helped to create the bombs that had devastated Hiroshima and Nagasaki, were now deeply troubled by the unprecedented weapons of mass destruction they had wrought. Going beyond their technoscientific achievement/contribution to winning the Second World War/crime against humanity, they started to refocus and turn to the predicament of their postwar present, then dubbed the 'Atomic Age' by a *New York Times* journalist.[5] Between 1945 and 1947, many American atomic scientists became concerned citizens of the world and pioneered global consciousness. Yet a few years later, they came under suspicion in the period of McCarthyism. Now everybody can see from hindsight that the quest for a sustainable future of human civilization emerged thanks to the responsible turnaround and leadership of brave Manhattan Project scientists.

Alice Kimball Smith has told the history of this momentous professional transformation in her book *A Peril and a Hope* (1965). Quoting a comment about the infamous Oppenheimer hearings (Commission 1954), she noted that the young dissident scientists began "to act into history as they once acted into nature" (v). The *Bulletin,* the educational tool of the new scientist-citizens, has meanwhile reached volume 71 and carries the motto, "70 Years Speaking Knowledge to Power."

> It was conceived amidst the clutter of the local Stineway Drug Store where Hy[man] Goldsmith and Eugene Rabinowitch, drinking coffee with their sociologist friend Edward Shils, held passionate discussions in the autumn of 1945 on how the problems of the atomic age might be adequately discussed and recorded (Smith, 1971: 284).[6]

That drug store coffeehouse was in Chicago, the city where the first controlled nuclear chain reaction had been accomplished in December 1942. Significant is also that Goldsmith and Rabinowitch, two former Manhattan scientists, hit upon the idea of the *Bulletin* not in cool conversations but "passionate discussions" and furthermore, not alone or as fellow physicists, but together with a social scientist. My point here is that the present-centric approach, for which the *Bulletin* with its Doomsday Clock stands, builds on concrete locations, transdisciplinary collaboration, open debate, and political interventions. It combines civic activism with academic analysis.

In 1947, the Doomsday Clock showed 7 minutes to midnight, that is, to nuclear disaster. Since then, the clock has been up and running, sometimes moving forward and sometimes backward. In 2007, considering the nuclear aspirations of North Korea and Iran and for the first time catastrophic climate change, it jumped forward to signal 5 minutes to midnight. In 2010, counting on negotiated environmental progress and strategic arms reduction, it reversed to 6 minutes to midnight. In 2012, the clock indicated again 5 minutes to global doom; and it advanced two additional minutes in 2015: "The clock ticks now at just three minutes to midnight because international leaders are failing to perform their most important duty — ensuring and preserving the health and vitality of human civilization."[7]

The reasons for the clock's advancement ("unchecked climate change, global nuclear weapons modernizations, and outsized nuclear weapons arsenals") are part of the CPT conundrum. If the assessment of the *Bulletin* is correct and our political leaders are guilty of not taking care of the whole of human civilization, the uncontrolled forces of capitalism and technoscience are in charge of humanity's future and the human journey will probably end sooner than later. However, if these forces are untamable — like hippos and zebras, which are not domesticable — our leaders are failing because they simply cannot succeed. So, what are our options? Are the forces of capitalism cum technoscience controllable or uncontrollable?

## Capitalism As It Is and As It Should Be

Looking at capitalism as it actually is, we observe that there is no such thing as a globally uniform capitalism. Speaking about capitalism in the singular appears to be a misnomer. Everybody can see that various forms of capitalism exist competing with each other all around the globe. So, let me adjust our language to that fact and speak about capitalism in the plural. In addition, I will try to catch the distributed ensemble of capitalisms on the ground with a geographic denominator that casts its net neither too narrow nor too wide. For bagging the different varieties of capitalism, I suggest *regional capitalisms,* a term that is intended to grasp all significant national and transnational formations of the economic phenomenon in question.

Sociologist Max Weber famously tried to capture the essence

of complex social phenomena via the construction of "ideal types," i.e., "the analytical accentuation of certain elements of reality."

> An ideal type is formed by the one-sided *accentuation* of one or more points of view and by the synthesis of a great many diffuse, discrete, more or less present and occasionally absent *concreteindividual* phenomena, which are arranged according to those one-sidedly emphasized viewpoints into a unified *analytical* construct. In its conceptual purity, this mental construct (*Gedankenbild*) cannot be found empirically anywhere in reality. It is a *utopia* (Weber, 1949[1904]: 90).

Mindful of this caveat, I will proceed and briefly distinguish four ideal types of regional capitalisms: Nordic, German, American, and Chinese. This is of course a huge simplification. However, since more elaborate classifications like, for instance, Bruno Amable's five types of capitalism (2003), are readily available, I may be allowed to reduce the empirical complexity to think more clearly about the important normative questions I would like to ask.

## The Nordic Model

The ensemble of Nordic capitalisms comprises the economies of Denmark, the Faroe Islands, Finland, Greenland, Iceland, Norway, and Sweden. Nordic capitalism combines a free market economy with state supervised collective bargaining and the benefits of a comprehensive welfare state. The nations of this cluster top the *World Happiness Report 2013*, which has measured 156 countries (Helliwell *et al.*, 2013).[8] The well-being of the populations comprising the Nordic model compares favorably with the capitalisms of Spain, Italy, Greece, and Portugal, which are happiness-ranked 38, 45, 70, and 85, respectively. *The Economist* once called the Nordic countries the "next supermodel" and noted that Nordic capitalism has managed to avoid "southern Europe's economic sclerosis and America's extreme inequality."[9]

## The German Model

Ranked third largest export economy after China and the US, German capitalism radiates outward through global exports. Its export hinterland is worldwide, from European Union countries to America and Asia. In 2013, the top five destinations of German products were France ($120B), the US ($113B), the UK ($88.8B), China ($87.4B), and the Netherlands ($80.5B).[10] However, understanding German capitalism requires a look inside.

The Federal Republic of Germany integrates 16 states (*Bundesländer* or simply *Länder*) of unequal economic strength in a coordinated market economy. The numbers and locations of small and medium enterprises (SME) with global reach mirror this uneven landscape: 337 out of 1,116 are located in Baden-Württemberg, the home state of Mercedes-Benz, 257 in Bavaria, and 208 in North Rhine-Westphalia.[11] Unlike well-known global giants like Mercedes or Siemens, their names are unfamiliar, even in Germany. Yet they are the "hidden champions" of the country (Simon, 1996).[12] Offering unique and specialized products, these SMEs are number one, two, or three in their product line globally (or number one in Europe). Normally family owned and based in small towns, their leadership style is autocratic, yet encourages constructive participation on the operations level; they have high employee loyalty combined with low sickness rates, keep their know-how to themselves, improve their products continuously, and pay detailed attention to their customers' needs.

Additional characteristic features of German capitalism include its strong vocational training tradition (apprenticeship system) that mixes practical work with classroom education and the right of workers to 'co-determine' the management of the companies they work for. Co-determination (*Mitbestimmung*) ranges from the board of directors to the shop floor. It aims to balance the profit motive with the interests of labor by putting trade union representatives on company boards and works councils (*Betriebsräte*). In the tug of war between economic efficiency and social fairness, Germany nurtures a social capitalism that prefers to err on the side of social justice.

## The American Model

If German capitalism supports a coordinated market economy that forces capital and labor to negotiate, US capitalism empowers market self-coordination. An unrestrained market approach based on liberal economic principles drives the capitalisms of the US and UK into the opposite direction of the German and Nordic models. Anglo-Saxon capitalism vilifies the "countervailing power" (Galbraith, 1993[1952]) of non-market coordination;[13] it perceives social commitments as 'socialist' and tries to avoid or eliminate them. However, the US ranks number 17 on the world happiness scale, the UK 22, and Germany 26.

Popular support for the US model is robust and reaches deep down in American society. As a result, the American poor seem to be largely unfazed by the country's inequality, which is, by all measures of income, consumption, and wealth, huge and growing.[14] The wealth of a billionaire running for president is generally viewed without envy or political concern and governmental regulation of the economy is frowned upon. Mechanisms that would help the poor are seen as harmful 'rigidities,' not only by the rich, but also by many of its potential beneficiaries. Handing benefits to unproductive economic agents thus appears to be unreasonable and un-American as well.

One could say the American way of capitalism is a capitalism without tears. Grounded in American culture and attuned to the wants and whims of the markets, US capitalism favors *flexibility*, of capital and labor above all; *untrammeled competition* between everything and everybody, including company staff;[15] and *management autonomy*, especially the ability to hire and fire. Ruthless change and radical innovation are at the root of US corporations, such as Amazon, Apple, Airbnb, eBay, Facebook, Google, Uber, and Twitter — category-busting enterprises that demonstrate the vitality of the American model.

## The Chinese Model

If the Nordic, German, and American models of capitalism can be mapped and distinguished by their relative proximity to free market capitalism on one end and welfare capitalism on the other, Chinese capitalism adds a third dimension and different model: state-sponsored capitalism in a single-party state. This is the Chinese case from a Western point of view, which notes governmental interference with markets, state ownership of enterprises, and the absence of multi-party democracy. The Chinese perspective, however, is focused on attaining the goal of socialism. Given that, China's current economic model is officially called a "socialist market economy" in which market forces play a "decisive role."[16]

Nevertheless, the salient point of the Western view is the *decisive role of the state* in the development of the Chinese economy. This is the understanding of most observers, but not all. Nicholas Lardy, for example, has emphasized the enormous productivity, job creation, and rise of the private Chinese sector since 1978 and questioned the dominant Western storyline in *Markets over Mao* (2014). Lardy's data and findings notwithstanding, and irrespective of the true number of state-owned vs. privately owned businesses, it remains convincing that the Chinese government "has been creating the space for private companies to do their thing."[17] The Chinese state has not relinquished its economic power to the markets; markets may challenge this power, but the buck still stops at the Zhongnanhai gate of the Communist Party of China (CPC).

The economic toolbox of the CPC includes both passive and active state interventions. Passive intervention is evidenced by the present 'Beijing Consensus,' which allows market forces to play an important role in the People's Republic of China, whereas active intervention was on display in the summer of 2015, when Beijing tried to support its crashing stock market with a slew of countermeasures. To be sure, the centrality of the state is not just a Chinese phenomenon, but also a well-known regional feature. The literature abounds with references to "state-led macroeconomic planning in East Asia" and the "East Asian development model," the "hard state" and the "developmental state"; it applies the French example of postwar "dirigism"[18] to economic systems with strong directive

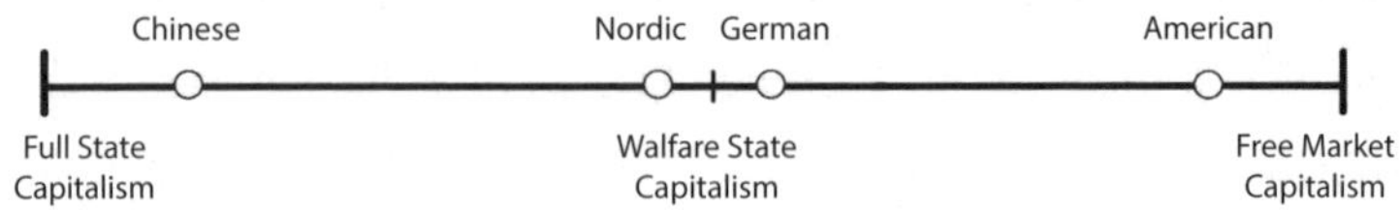


**Figure 3.2** Four Models of Capitalism

influences and government investments in the economy. The state-assisted rise of the 'Four Asian Tigers' — Hong Kong, Singapore, Taiwan, and South Korea — as well as of the socialist market economies of China and Vietnam is still regularly quoted and new 'tigers' are continuously watched out for.

Having sketched the economic models of Nordic, German, American, and Chinese capitalisms, we can now map them on a line from left to right. The extreme left shall indicate a market economy under full-fledged state leadership and the extreme right a market economy free of any external control and direction. Both extremes are *ideal* ideal types with no perfect examples of either one in reality. Yet the four economic models are abstractions from *really existing* economies. Their positions on the line are not determined by any metrics, only by their proximity to one or the other theoretical extreme, and, in the case of the two welfare state models, on their relative equidistance to both ends.[19]

Figure 3.2 shows four regional capitalisms — capitalism as it is, but not capitalism as it should be. This leads to the question: Do we ever have to make do with what is? Yes, but only if there are no alternatives. If alternative models of capitalism exist, and we know they do, humanity does not have to settle for the status quo. The current state of affairs is but a starting point. Humanity is free to aspire boldly from that base and it seems to me that the boldest imaginable goal would beto lift *all* people in *all* societies.

Capitalism is able to enrich some people — why not all people? Capitalism has developed some societies — why not all societies? Given that *wealth inequality* is notoriously difficult to roll back (short of economic catastrophes, revolutionary activities, or the progressive taxation of capital, see below), *income inequality* should be the first target of corrective policies. For proof of concept, one can analyze how welfare capitalisms try to tie private profits to the commonweal. The existing capitalisms are the economic equivalent of biodiversity; they are 'test-driving' capitalistic methods of creating wealth. If humanity wants to make all people and all societies wealthy, it must study and learn from all capitalisms, including the American and the Chinese. The former has astounding creativity and philanthropy on its side and the latter the capacity to make comparatively swift executive decisions for the country that is surpassing the US as the world's no. 1 economy.[20]

China has the largest population in the world with nearly 1.4 billion people and the world's second largest political party with about 88 million members.[21] If humanity resolves to use capitalism for the benefit of all and China has lifted 500 million people out of poverty in less than four decades,[22] its socialist market economy must be doing something right and the country's closed, yet huge, single-party governance laboratory[23] ought to be studied. Of course, it would be naïve to assume that one could simply grab what one wants from the platters of Chinese, American, German, and Nordic capitalisms; they are no buffet arrangement to choose from. However, the very existence of diverse capitalisms betrays malleability; it suggests the possibility of delivering capitalistic gains from the few to the many.

Achieving this goal and transforming the world's antagonistic regional capitalisms into agents for the global common good is a very big task. It will not happen overnight, neither by a stroke of luck, nor through magic or wonder; but it should happen, because "the earth, our home, is beginning to look more and more like an immense pile of filth" (Francis, 2015: 21).[24] These are the words of Pope Francis. His outspoken encyclical on the environment is a full-fledged assessment of our "present imbalance." The authoritative letter is a clarion call to the whole of humanity that reinforces the warnings of the *Bulletin of the Atomic Scientists*; it includes a radical critique of what current capitalisms do with clear indications of what they should be doing instead.

> Doomsday predictions can no longer be met with irony or disdain. We may well be leaving to coming generations debris, desolation and filth. The pace of consumption, waste and environmental change has so stretched the planet's capacity that our contemporary lifestyle, unsustainable as it is, can only precipitate catastrophes, such as those which even now periodically occur in different areas of the world. The effects of the present imbalance can only be reduced by our decisive action, here and now (161).

Facing the third millennium of the Catholic Church as pope number 266, Francis addresses the world from a pulpit with institutional longevity and extensive globality. Unlike most other leaders, he is positioned to take the long view and put the present into historical perspective. Clearly alarmed by our "unprecedented [situation] in the history of humanity" (17), Francis notes the difference between "rapidification" on the one hand — the "continued acceleration of changes affecting humanity and the planet" (18) — and the slowness and unwillingness to learn from history on the other. His analysis of the "roots of our present failures" targets the blind faith in growth for growth's sake.

> The economy accepts every advance in technology with a view to profit, without concern for its potentially negative impact on human beings. Finance overwhelms the real economy. The lessons of the global financial crisis have not been assimilated, and we are learning all too slowly the lessons of environmental deterioration. Some circles maintain that current economics and technology will solve all environmental problems, and argue ... that the problems of global hunger and poverty will be resolved simply by market growth. ... Their behaviour shows that for them maximizing profits is enough. Yet by itself the market cannot guarantee integral human development and social inclusion. At the same time, we have "a sort of 'superdevelopment' of a wasteful and consumerist kind which forms an unacceptable contrast with the ongoing situations of dehumanizing deprivation," while we are all too slow in developing economic institutions and social initiatives which can give the poor regular access to basic resources. We fail to see the deepest roots of our present failures, which have to do with the direction, goals, meaning and social implications of technological and economic growth (109).

Criticizing capitalism but avoiding the term, Francis blasts the "techno-economic paradigm" (203) that has "deified" (56) the markets and threatens to lay waste to "all creation" (221). Speaking as a Christian, he acknowledges "a reality which has previously been given to us" (140). And as head of state, the Pope is familiar with global calls for action — UN resolutions come to mind —

that are rarely followed by actual steps commensurate with the rhetorical urgency. Still, Francis longs for "decisive political action" (179) as a deeply concerned citizen of the world. To save what for him is God's creation, he expresses "the urgent need ... to move forward in a bold cultural revolution" (114). Knowing that radical change cannot come from radical thought alone, Francis seems not to mind the irony of echoing Mao Zedong for a moment. Only embodied passion can achieve revolution. People must ardently want to transform the world. Consequently, the Pope marshals Christian morality for spiritual commitment to the environmental cause. He invokes humanity's ecological "errors, sins, faults and failures," commands "heartfelt repentance," and requests "personal" (218) as well as "community conversion" (219). Francis, who wants to shift the prevalent paradigm, calls for a global "ecological conversion (217).

## Technoscience As It Is and As It Could Be

Pope Francis fears that the CPT conundrum will foreshorten humanity's future with reckless exploitation and mismanagement of the global commons. He has misgivings about the rapidly globalizing industrial civilization and its chaotic megacities, yet he advocates ecological revolution not out of an anti-modern sentiment but for the co-survivability of us with "Mother Earth" and all its creatures — he is not a Luddite.

> Technoscience, when well directed, can produce important means of improving the quality of human life, from useful

> domestic appliances to great transportation systems, bridges, buildings and public spaces. It can also produce art and enable men and women immersed in the material world to "leap" into the world of beauty (Francis, 2015: 103).

According to this papal qualification, good technoscience is "well directed." I fully assent, but not because the Pope says so, rather because technoscience without responsible social direction is prone to be hugely devastating. Washing machines and microwave ovens, for example, are not the only useful products of technoscience; nuclear bombs make the grade, too. Using them would be infinitely more destructive than putting a metal pot in a microwave. However, before concluding this discussion, let me shed some light on the term itself.

## Science

The science in technoscience refers to modern natural science, an activity that was not available before Copernicus, Kepler, Galileo, and Newton. The scholars, who contributed to the European Scientific Revolution in the sixteenth and seventeenth centuries, are credited with the development of modern science. Originally called 'natural philosophers' — the word 'scientist' was coined only later, in the early nineteenth century — the practitioners of this new 'trade' were few at the start and ranked lowly in the Aristotelian universities; their operations were small in the beginning, often self-supported, and in need of powerful patrons. Nonetheless, modern science toppled medieval theology and philosophy and rose from a peripheral origin to a position of dominance in virtually all institutions of higher education today. Now, science, technology, engineering, and mathematics — the STEM fields of our time — dwarf the humanities and all traditional authorities.

Discovering the 'laws' of nature is the business of science. For this, scientists work with an expanding set of universal regularities that are independent of the human will. Early modern science reinforced this understanding by following the interest of Copernicus to find the best (most economical) account of the movement of the planets in the solar system. Human manipulation of heavenly bodies was inconceivable — geometrical (mathematical) ingenuity was the way to grasp their revolutions. Thus, the ideal of universal laws was born and later equally hardened as well as weakened by reaching deeper into outer space and the inner worlds of subatomic particles, where observer effects meet Heisenberg's uncertainty principle. Still, scientists believe that their laws reveal objective truths about nature, something that cannot be determined by democratic voting, the wisdom of crowds, or executive decision. Knowing that the speed of light cannot travel faster than *c* and that no wall can be built to shield against gravity, they are faithful to the observable structures of the cosmos.

## Technology

Here, human will and interest are paramount. From the first tools fashioned by hunters and gatherers to the latest gadgets of postmodern consumer culture, society plays a main role in determining the course and products of technology. Gravity is everywhere and can be 'discovered' but cell phones are nowhere and must be 'invented.' Yet the simplicity of this distinction fades the moment we move away from the ideal types of science and technology and look at the interdependencies between nature and tools. The fact that many have tried to build a perpetual motion machine, but could not do so, shows that nature both restricts and enables what is technologically possible; and the corresponding point that a long predicted particle (the Higgs boson) could only be sought with a unique machine (the Large Hadron Collider) demonstrates that technology equally enables and restricts what humanity can discover about nature.

Technology is capable of creating anything society wants and physics allows. However, it has to navigate an additional context that is also simultaneously restricting and enabling: economics. To quote Pope Francis again, "The alliance between the economy and technology ends up sidelining anything unrelated to its immediate interests" (Francis, 2015: 54). Bluntly put, money making is crucial for the development of technologies. A technology that is promising in this respect will thrive and one that is not will have a hard time surviving. We can think of exceptions to this iron rule of capitalism — the non-profit One Laptop per Child initiative from 2005, for instance — but they are neither numerous nor unproblematic.[25] What may be said about technology in comparison to science in a thought experiment is that science could come to an end by reaching a complete understanding of the physical workings of everything in our universe,[26] whereas technology is an endless endeavor as long as human societies spawn new desires and ways to live.

## Technoscience

Turning from science and technology to technoscience, i.e.,

from components to compound, the combination of the two words indicates that technology modifies science in this case and not the other way round. We can say technoscience is a particular form of science. Going beyond the call of science (to understand nature), technoscience adds value and creates something that satisfies a societal interest. It typically builds upon solid scientific knowledge about a particular part of nature to devise new things, tools, processes, machines, or materials, such as buckyball molecules, electron microscopes, 3D printers, nuclear reactors, or bubble wrap for packing purposes and popping fun.

In Science and Technology Studies (STS), technoscience has been characterized as "finalized" science, a science that is able to deliver useful applications strategically, not via trial and error, but by goal-oriented development (Schäfer, 1983). This attractive feature has fueled science-based industries long before STS caught up with it. Surpassing serendipitous innovation, technoscience enables intentional advancement, which makes it effective and powerful, but also vulnerable. Why? Because anything humans do intentionally, humans could also not do, yet if they do it, the usefulness, desirability, or legitimacy of their action can be challenged. A technoscientific product that looks great from a business perspective may appear harmful from an environmental point of view, or wrong in the light of ethics. For example, reasonable people disagree about genetically engineered (GE) foods and support starkly conflicting attitudes about it.[27] Reflecting the existential ambiguities of technoscience, they cannot but make controversial claims and seek to resolve the impasse in the courts and on the battlefields of politics.

The extraordinary power of technoscience is perhaps best

understood in the aforementioned context of GE foods, or biotechnology in general. According to the UN Convention on Biological Diversity (CBD), biotechnology "means any technological application that uses biological systems, living organisms, or derivatives thereof, to make or modify products or processes for specific use."[28] However, biotechnology is not merely a technology, but a technoscience based on molecular biology. Consequently, the CBD definition would be sharper if it would address "technoscientific" and not just "technological" applications. Technologies have been used for thousands of years to bread animals and modify plants, but only recently have humans begun to do this with the exacting instruments of modern science. Only a technoscience can 'spawn' genetically engineered salmon. The revolutionary import of this is that humanity is taking control of evolution. It is complementing Darwinian evolution with planned evolution. This is what biotechnology means. It is a *technoscientific* intervention that uses biological systems, living organisms, or derivatives thereof to develop nature consciously and deliberately.

The irony of simultaneously reaching a very high level of natural competence and low level of proficient environmental management (in relation to our growing impact) belongs to the predicament of contemporary humanity. And worse, this uncomfortable situation is made even grimmer by the accelerating pace of our civilization. As previously demonstrated, the global energy cum population transitions from fire to agriculture, industry, and nuclear have reduced humanity's adaptation window from hundreds of thousands of years to centuries and decades (Schäfer, 2014) — which leaves little time for course corrections. Nevertheless, facing the perhaps most perilous human condition ever is also invigorating. Temporal foreshortening speeds the delivery of problems up, but, hopefully, the invention of solutions, too.

The rapidly "growing gap" between "the sprinting technologies and the plodding ethical and legal systems that are supposed to be concerned with regulating and recommending policy and procedures to minimize the effects of 'machinery hurtful to commonality'" (Marchant *et al.*, 2011: ix) has been recognized, but the countermeasures under discussion are not nearly bridging the gap. Nobody wants to block useful emerging technologies with regulatory no-votes and everybody is afraid of deploying harmful technologies with yes-votes, hence time-consuming neither-nor-solutions are contemplated, "yellow lights for emerging technologies" (Charo, 2015) for instance. The conclusion that societal oversight and political governance are "not keeping pace with technological and scientific change" (Marchant *et al.*, 2011: xiii) is therefore hard to avoid. What technoscience could and should do for our best and the best of our common habitat remains to be determined.

## Final Remarks

What seems to be true for the heavily interlinked and highly potent new technoscientific fields of nano, bio, robotic, information, and communication technologies — the absence of a holistic control mechanism — is mirrored by the array of regional capitalisms and their core problem of increasing wealth inequality. There, as well, is no enlightened global control. Immense wealth gaps are growing in all market economies and if Thomas Piketty (2014) got it right, they will stay. His massive study on the dynamics of the distribution of wealth since the eighteenth century concluded that despite setbacks caused by wars and revolutions, the rate of return on capital (r) is bound to be higher than the rate of economic growth (g), in short $r > g$. Piercing the illusion that this "fundamental structural contradiction of capitalism" has weakened or disappeared, he noted, "the unlimited growth of global inequality of wealth ... is currently increasing at a rate that cannot be sustained in the long run and ... ought to worry even the most fervent champions of the self-regulated market." Piketty's "right solution" of this contradiction is "a progressive annual tax on capital." He holds, "This will make it possible to avoid an endless inegalitarian spiral while preserving competition and incentives for new instances of primitive accumulation" (Piketty, 2014: 572).

The opinion that great wealth contributes greatly to economic growth has apparently no empirical basis. Recent research based on the first global measure of wealth inequality covering the period from 1987 to 2002 and a representative list of 1,652 individuals around the world owning more than one billion dollars and actively involved in managing their fortunes, found that billionaire wealth impedes economic growth (Bagchi and Svejnar, 2015).[29] In addition, the study also determined that *politically connected* billionaire wealth impedes economic growth significantly.[30] Yet what are the answers to the basic questions of this article?

I have asked, *Is capitalism inherently unable to deliver material wealth to all people*? Piketty's answer is affirmative and I agree. If left to its own devices, capitalism will not enrich all people. I have further asked, is a socio-economic orientation (actually re-orientation) of capitalism to the commonweal feasible? Again, an economist like Piketty, who dares to reclaim "political, normative, and moral purpose" (Piketty, 2014: 574) for his work, would see the possibility and support the proposition provided that adequate measures are not ruled out.

My leading environmental question was, *Is technoscience per se incapable of bringing all societies into balance with nature?* And my answer is twofold. For the fundamental science component of a technoscience, it is negative, that is to say, science can harmonize nature and society. But for all particular technology elements of a technoscience, I am positive that eco-friendliness is not guaranteed "per se." The science in any given technoscience will keep the chimeras of alternate physics, chemistries, and biologies out, because the laws of nature are universal and not Muslim, Christian or Jewish, male or female, American or Chinese,[31] but what kinds of technologies societies want and develop is open-ended and has many degrees of freedom. Putting these two answers together, I would submit that technoscience on its own is *not likely* to bring humanity into balance with nature. The unholy alliance of quick profits linked with the engineer's can-do-temptation (to develop everything that is possible to develop) stands in the way of making tough choices for the benefit of the whole.

Finally, the answer to my overall question — *Are the combined forces of capitalism and technoscience controllable or uncontrollable?* — is a resounding "Yes." Like Yogi Berra ("When you come to a fork in the road, take it!"), I suggest to approach the solution from both ends. By admitting that capitalism cum technoscience are controllable as well as uncontrollable, I am saying, yes, they are controllable — after all, we humans are the primary force that generates and empowers them — and yes once again, both are also uncontrollable. Unsupervised as long as we do not create and empower a responsible global authority to guide them, they will grow wildly. If we continue to allow the twinned forces of capitalism and technoscience to roam as they please, they will drag us deeper and deeper into the destructive planetary change, they have already begun to unleash, and that will almost certainly pull humanity down.

The contemporary human predicament, in which we act as brilliant designers of new forms of nature *and* involuntary destroyers of our natural habitat, is dire but luckily not all bleak. Much good is going on, too, on governmental and civil society levels, in myriad NGOs and countless activities of the UN. All of that is of course material for further study, endlessly promising and perhaps the way for this disparate and fuzzy conglomerate called humanity to move forward and congeal. I have often asked my students: Give me a global problem that has no research institute or think tank working on it. They never found one. So, if we fail, we fail at least knowingly.

## Notes

1. The quote — *Wovon man nicht sprechen kann, darüber muss man schweigen* — is proposition #7, the last sentence of the Tractatus. The online version (see References) presents the German original and two English translations side-by-side.

2. A phrase from Reinhart Koselleck — *DieZukunft ist auf bekannte Weise unbekannt* — quoted from memory.

3. Solving the sustainability problem of the human species is paramount and requires focusing on Earth and not leaving a ruined planet behind. Escapist dreams like the colonization of outer space or imaginary developments toward transhumanity by way of robotics and artificial intelligence strike me as counterproductive at this point.

4. Cf. Wikipedia, Doomsday Clock, en.wikipedia.org/wiki/Doomsday_Clock, accessed 17 Oct. 2015.

5. William L. Laurence (1888-1877). Laurence is credited with coining the term in the summer of 1945; see Greg Mitchell, editorandpublisher.com/Article/At-the-60th-Anniversary-The-Embedded-New-York-Times-Reporter-Who-Brought-Us-the-Atomic-Age-, accessed 18 Nov. 2015.

6. Prompted by the 1968 student movement, the 1971 edition called "attention to the errors and successes of an earlier group of young dissidents, working against time to educate the American public, its political representatives, and above all themselves, in the realities of a new age" (Preface).

7. See thebulletin.org/timeline, accessed 18. Nov. 2015.

8. The list is led by Denmark (#1), followed by Norway (#2), Sweden (#5), Finland (#7), and Iceland (#9). The Faroe Islands and Greenland are not listed.

9. See the print edition leader of *The Economist*, 2 February 2013: "The next supermodel: Politicians from both right and left could learn from the Nordic countries," economist.com/news/leaders/21571136-politicians-both-right-and-left-could-learn-nordic-countries-next-supermodel, accessed 8 Oct. 2015.

10. See the online *Observatory of Economic Complexity* (OEC), atlas.media.mit.edu/en/profile/country/deu/, accessed 18 Nov. 2015.

11. See aktuell.nationalatlas.de/weltmarktfuehrer-11_11-2011-0-html/, accessed 18 Nov. 2015.

12. See also Wikipedia, Hidden Champions, en.wikipedia.org/wiki/Hidden_champions, accessed 18 Nov. 2015.

13. John Kenneth Galbraith found no perfect competition in the US after World War II and argued in 1952 for the "countervailing power" of large unions to "restrain" the economic power of big firms to prevent governmental interference.

14. Cf. Drew DeSilver, "The Many Ways to Measure Economic Inequality." Pew Research Center, pewresearch.org/fact-tank/2015/09/22/the-many-ways-to-measure-economic-inequality/, accessed 18 Nov. 2015.

15. *The New York Times* has published an investigative article by Jodi Kantor and David Streitfeld, "Inside Amazon: Wrestling Big Ideas in a Bruising Workplace" (15 August 2015), which details how white-collar workers are pressed to become "the best Amazonians they can be." Cf. nytimes.com/2015/08/16/technology/inside-amazon-wrestling-big-ideas-in-a-bruising-workplace.html, accessed 4 Oct. 2015.

16. Cf. *China Daily*, 18 Nov. 2013, chinadaily.com.cn/china/2013cpctps/2013-11/18/content_17113583.htm, accessed 8 Oct. 2015.

17. See *The Economist*, 25 Oct. 2014: "Unstated capitalism: Private companies have been hugely underestimated in China," economist.com/news/business-books-quarterly/21627564-private-companies-have-been-hugely-underestimated-china-unstated-capitalism, accessed 8 Oct. 2015.

18. From *dirige*, French, meaning "to direct." *Dirigisme* was exercised in France after World War II; it goes beyond state regulation and indicates strong state directives.

19. My comparison goes beyond capitalist democracies and does not analyze the US as a welfare state like Esping-Andersen (1990). Esping-Andersen famously distinguished three welfare-state regimes: a "social democratic" regime for Sweden, a "conservative" regime for Germany, and a "liberal" one for the US. "We will in this book understand welfare states as clustering into three different types of regime that we have labeled conservative, liberal, and 'social democratic'" (3). But unconvincingly, the author called the Swedish model also "socialist": "each country stands as an 'ideal-typical' representative of the socialist, conservative, and liberal regime-type, respectively" (222).

20. China's current status between no. 1 and 2 is unclear, but not the global influence of its phenomenal growth; see for instance bbc.com/news/magazine-30483762, accessed 17 Oct. 2015.

21. India's fast growing right-wing Bharatiya Janata Party (BJP) is the largest.

22. See the summary of the World Bank at worldbank.org/en/country/china/overview: "Since initiating market reforms in 1978, China has shifted from a centrally planned to a market based economy and experienced rapid economic and social development. GDP growth averaging about 10% a year has lifted more than 500 million people out of poverty. All Millennium Development Goals have been reached or are within reach."

23. China's population is far larger than that of any other single-party state: Vietnam (90m), North Korea (25m), Cuba (11m), Laos and Eritrea (both 6m).

24. Entitled *Laudato Si'* and dated 24 May 2015, this Papal encyclical is available in several languages and online at w2.vatican.va/content/francesco/en/encyclicals/documents/papa-francesco_20150524_enciclica-laudato-si.html. Since each paragraph of the document is numbered in the print editions and online, I will quote the paragraph, not the pagenumbers. The total paragraph count is 246.

25. Cf. Wikipedia, One Laptop per Child, en.wikipedia.org/wiki/One_Lapis uncomfortable top_per_Child, accessed 14 Nov. 2015.

26. The full-understanding-of-nature hypothesis excludes unobservable, parallel universes that may or may not exist.

27. When I was writing this sentence, the *New York Times* headlined on its front page, "Genetically Engineered Salmon Declared Ready for U.S. Plates" (20 Nov. 2015). The article reported the conflict ("The approval of the salmon has been fiercely opposed by some consumer and environmental groups, which have argued that safety studies were inadequate and that wild salmon populations might be affected if the engineered fish were to escape into the oceans and rivers"), that a lawsuit challenging the FDA. approval would be filed, and that "the White House is now reviewing the entire framework for regulating genetically engineered products."

28. See use of terms at cbd.int/convention/articles/default.shtml?a=cbd-02, accessed 20 Nov. 2015.

29. "Our first set of findings suggests that wealth inequality tends to have a negative effect on economic growth, income inequality has no or at most a weak positive effect on growth, and the effect of poverty on growth is insignificant" (524).

30. "Our second key finding is that when we enter politically connected and unconnected wealth as two separate explanatory variables into our regressions, our estimates suggest that it is politically connected wealth inequality that has a significant negative effect on growth, while the effects of politically unconnected wealth inequality, income inequality, and poverty are all insignificant" (524).

31. Cases in point: the failure of creating an 'Aryan' physics for Nazi Germany (Beyerchen, 1977) and a communist genetics for the Soviet Union (Joravsky, 1986).

## References

Amable, Bruno. 2003. *The Diversity of Modern Capitalism*. Oxford; New York: Oxford University Press.

Bagchi, Sutirtha, and Jan Svejnar. 2015. "Does wealth inequality matter for growth? The effect of billionaire wealth, income distribution, and poverty." *Journal of Comparative Economics* 43(3): 505-530. doi: http://dx.doi.org/10.1016/j.jce.2015.04.002.

Beyerchen, Alan D. 1977. *Scientists under Hitler: Politics and the Physics Community in the Third Reich*. New Haven: Yale University Press.

Charo, R. Alta. 2015. "Yellow lights for emerging technologies: all-or-none regulatory systems are not adequate for revolutionary innovations." *Science* 349 (6246): 384-385.

Commission, US Atomic Energy. 1954. *In the Matter of J. Robert Oppenheimer: Transcript of Hearing before Personnel Security Board*. Washington: US Government Printing Office.

Esping-Andersen, Gøsta. 1990. *The Three Worlds of Welfare Capitalism*. Princeton, NJ: Princeton University Press.

Francis, Pope. 2015. *Encyclical on Climate Change and Inequality: On Care for Our Common Home*. Introduction by Naomi Oreskes. New York: Melville House.

Galbraith, John Kenneth. 1993[1952]. *American Capitalism: The Concept of Countervailing Power, Classics in Economics Series*. New Brunswick, NJ: Transaction Publishers.

Helliwell, John F., Richard Layard, and Jeffrey Sachs, eds. 2013. *World Happiness Report 2013*. New York: UN Sustainable Development Solutions Network.

Joravsky, David. 1986. *The Lysenko Affair*. Chicago; London: The University of Chicago Press.

Lardy, Nicholas R. 2014. *Markets over Mao: The Rise of Private Business in China*. Washington, DC: Peterson Institute for International Economics.

Marchant, Gary E., Braden R. Allenby, and Joseph R. Herkert, eds. 2011. *The Growing Gap between Emerging Technologies and Legal-ethical Oversight: The Pacing Problem, The International Library of*

*Ethics, law and technology*. Dordrecht; New York: Springer.

Piketty, Thomas. 2014. *Capital in the Twenty-first Century*. Translated by Arthur Goldhammer. Cambridge, MA: The Belknap Press of Harvard University Press.

Schäfer, Wolf. 2010. "Concepts of globalization, globalism and globality and the method of lean globality studies: a critical adjustment." pp. 23-48 in *New Asias: Global Futures of World Regions*, edited by Hyun-Chin Lim, Wolf Schäfer, and Suk-Man Hwang. Seoul: Seoul National University Press.

_______. 2014. "Pangaea II: the project of the global age." pp. 97-122 in *Global Challenges in Asia: New Development Models and Regional Community Building*, edited by Hyun-Chin Lim, Wolf Schäfer, and Suk-Man Hwang. Seoul: Seoul National University Press.

_______, ed. 1983. *Finalization in Science: The Social Orientation of Scientific Progress. Vol. 77, Boston Studies in the Philosophy of Science.* Dordrecht; Boston; Lancaster: D. Reidel.

Simon, Hermann. 1996. *Hidden Champions: Lessons from 500 of the World's Best Unknown Companies*. Boston, MA: Harvard Business School Press.

Smith, Alice Kimball. 1965. *A Peril and a Hope: The Scientists' Movement in America, 1945-47*. Chicago: University of Chicago Press.

_______. 1971. *A Peril and a Hope: The Scientists' Movement in America, 1945-47*. Cambridge, MA: MIT Press.

Weber, Max. 1949[1904]. "'Objectivity' in social science and social policy (1904)." pp. 49-112 in *The Methodology of the Social Sciences*, edited by Edward A. Shils and Henry A. Finch. Glencoe, IL: The Free Press.

Wittgenstein, Ludwig. 1922. *Tractatus Logico-Philosophicus*. Available at people.umass.edu/phil335-klement-2/tlp/tlp.html, accessed 24 Sept. 2015.

Chapter 4

# *A New "Spirit" of Capitalism?: Globalization and Its Impact on the Diffusion of Neoliberal Management Thinking in Germany and the East Asian Economies*

Markus Pohlmann and Hyun-Chin Lim

## Introduction

The discussion about the "spirit of capitalism"[1] is on the one hand a very old one. On the other hand, we do not know very much about the collective mindsets of economic elites that make up this spirit, and its transformation over time (Boltanski and Chiapello, 1999; 2005; Lim and Kim, 2007; Du Gay and Morgan, 2013; Pohlmann, 2014). Although there are some global studies on attitudes of managers, like the Globe Study (House *et al.*, 2004), Insead Studies (Lanvin and Evans, 2013; Witt and Redding, 2014), the studies of the Harvard Business School (Bloom *et al.*, 2012; Nobel, 2012), and the IBM Studies (IBM, 2011), indicating that there is a convergence of perceptions at work, generalizable findings on the adoption of concepts by top managers are not yet available.

The mainstream globalization literature is nevertheless quite clear in its general assumptions about the effects of globalization (Castells, 1996; Beck, 1997; Münch, 2009; Carroll, 2010). Basically, two strong assumptions underpin the argument that globalization of the economy and enterprises affects the "spirit of capitalism" and its carrier groups. These are:

> 1. The spiritual construction of the modern economy today is said to be founded in a new way upon neoliberalism, understood as a form of radical market orientation in economic thinking (Willke, 2003; Crouch, 2011; Streeck, 2013).
> 2. It is assumed, that an emerging global economic elite acts as pacemakers of this new neoliberal spirit in the world (Castells, 1996; Sklair, 2001; Carroll, 2010), using new management concepts and techniques (Boltanski and Chiapello, 2005; Schmidt-Wellenburg, 2009; Crouch, 2011).

The empirical findings, to be discussed below, will provide proof to support or challenge these two general assumptions.

The research project was funded mainly by the German Research Association and supported by the Asia Research Foundation Grant funded by the Seoul National University Asia Center (#SNUAC-2014-009). It was carried out at the Max Weber Institute at Heidelberg University in cooperation with Seoul National University and Sungkyunkwan University.[2] It focused on the level of top management (CEOs of the biggest manufacturing companies in eleven countries[3]) and sought to break down their collective mind sets towards neoliberal management thinking. The aim of the research is to explore the "spiritual construction (or underpinnings)" of the modern economy by analysing the collective knowledge, the norms and values that it is based upon. Drawing upon the theory of the "capitalist spirit," the project concentrated on two of its three major components, which according to Max Weber are the rationales in economic thinking and organizational action (leaving out for the purpose of this article, Weber's third rationale, the conduct of life).

In this article, the research results on German managers and their collective mindsets will be central, but these findings will also be compared with the findings related to East Asian economies. In Germany, altogether 82 interviews were carried out with two generations of top managers in the biggest industrial companies, while in Korea, Japan, and China taken together, there were 66 top manager interviews from East Asia.

The article starts off with an introduction into the theoretical foundations (2), and follows this by asking how globally recruited and experienced top managers in Germany and East Asia are (3). The article then questions the assumption that they spread ideas of neoliberal management thinking (4) and ends by summing up the findings in some concluding remarks (5).

## Theoretical Foundations

For its theoretical approach, the research project uses the historic findings of Max Weber but merely as a starting point (Pohlmann, 2002; 2005) to ask if a new historical formation of the capitalist spirit is emerging. In line with Weber — and in marked contrast to Boltanski and Chiapello (2005) — the general assumption of the project is that modern capitalism generates the norms and values for its own reproduction (Weber, 1989: 37). Modern

**Table 4.1** Theoretical Frame and Steps of Analysis

| Question | Mechanism | Indicators | Steps of Analysis |
|---|---|---|---|
| Which Companies and Actors? | Competition and Selection | Global recruitment of CEOs in the Top 100 Industrial Companies | Life course analysis of the CEOs of the Top 100 Manufacturing Companies |
| Which Collective Mindsets? | Diffusion, Socialization and Internalization | Rationales of the Neoliberal Management Thinking | Analysis of the Collective Mindsets of Two Generations of Top-Managers |

Capitalism is supposed to be largely autonomous in its self-reproduction through the following mechanisms (Schluchter, 1996; Pohlmann, 2002): (1) the competition and selection of corporations and personnel, (2) the diffusion of ideas and concepts, and (3) the socialization of central actors and the internalization of rationales (Weber, 1989: 204). These mechanisms served as the basis for the lead research questions, indicators, and analytical stages (Table 4.1).

From the perspective of the research project, this already provides an answer to the question raised by Boltanski and Chiapello (2005) about how capitalism can motivate its personnel to commit themselves at work (see also Willmot, 2013: 108-110). However, without carrying out interviews, and relying merely on management literature, this is not easy to pinpoint (Pohlmann, 2014). Nevertheless, the study of Boltanski and Chiapello is very useful in its task of exploring the new historical formation of the capitalist spirit (Pohlmann, 2014: 13-14).

For Weber (1989), this emergence of a historical formation can be located at the levels of economic action, organization, and life maxims. As mentioned before, we concentrate just on the first

**Table 4.2** Rationales of Capitalism and the Challenge to Act Accordingly

| Rationales | Challenges | Selected Indicators |
|---|---|---|
| Economic action | How shall I act in a specific economic setting? | Financial Market Orientations |
| Organizational activities | How shall I lead the company and employees? | Leadership Style |

two rationales (Table 4.2).

Thus, the research project investigates the collective routines and scripts that channel top managers' interpretations as well as their search for solutions to common objective problems that they encounter in their profession. The main thrust of this approach is also derived from Weber who was interested in habitual ideas and principles that composed the spirit of capitalism. He distinguished between the teachings and dogma that constitute the "objective spirit" and the internalized ideas, maxims, and practices that form the "subjective spirit". Oftentimes the latter part of the capitalist spirit is habitualized, routinized and largely taken for granted. This is due to the fact that — according to Alfred Schütz (1982; Schütz and Luckmann, 1994), who developed Weber's ideas further — the contents are replenished from a stock of collective knowledge. The concept of "collective mindsets" therefore contends that routines and scripts (as important parts of the collective mindsets in use) are not just the product of individual actor's intentions, but a social product of their respective culture and embedded in various processes of typification or institutionalization (Schütz, 1982; Schütz and Luckmann, 1994). Thus, the research project is not only interested in the analysis of carrier groups of the new capitalist spirit, but seeks additionally to answer the question: how strongly do their collective scripts reflect principles of neoliberal management thinking?

## Methodology

How exactly are the two assumptions of the mainstream globalization literature to be tested? First of all, a selection was made of the most advanced economies in two of the most prominent economic world regions: Korea, Japan, and China in East Asia, Germany in Europe. Second, within these countries, the CEOs of the Top 100 industrial enterprises were targeted. Industrial companies were the focus as they remain very important in the "real economy"[4] and because they ought to be frontrunners in the adoption of (neoliberal) management techniques. These have been big companies from different industrial branches like carmakers, chemical industries, ship-building, construction and so on.

Third, in a mixed methods-design a variety of research methods were used to analyse the rise of global elites and the "spiritual construction" of industrial capitalism, in order to test two basic assumptions of the globalization literature:

> The "Global Elites" Assumption: By carrying out a standardized life-course analysis of CEOs leading the Top 100 Industrial Companies in each country (using online sources, data bases and CVs), altogether 104 cases in Germany and 371 in Korea, Japan and China, the aim was to find out whether people with a similar educational or international background are selected for these top positions.
>
> The "One Spirit" Assumption: By carrying out 82 in-depth in-

> terviews with top CEOs in Germany and 66 CEO-interviews in East Asian economies a comparison was made of the underlying structures of collective knowledge, norms and values that managerial action is based upon across two generations of top managers.[5]

Relying on the data of our standardized life course analysis, the interview sample was selected using a proportional quota sampling method related to age, sex, education, and international activities of the CEOs (see Table 4.A.1 in Appendix). To select a probability sample is not possible in this field of research because you cannot randomly select interviewees out of the target population of CEOs from the Top100 industrial companies. To reach a qualitative representativeness of the sample, proportional quota sampling seemed therefore to be the best solution. The interviews in Germany were carried out between 2007 and 2009, mostly before the global financial crisis, and between 2013 and 2014. The interviews in East Asia were conducted between 2012 and 2014.

In the selection of interviewees, an age cohort design was implemented, comparing three age groups: CEOs and Ex-CEOs born between 1930 and 1944, between 1945 and 1954 and CEOs born between 1955 and 1964 (see Table 4.A.2 in Appendix). The purpose of this age group comparison was to find out if there is an age cohort effect on the characteristics of the collective mindsets in use and to assess the changes in collective mindsets, although the project could not use longitudinal data. The analysis of collective mindsets (or social interpretation patterns) is a well-established approach in Germany and Europe, related to the hermeneutical tradition of the sociology of knowledge (Reichertz, 2004: 2005).

**Table 4.3** Number of Interviews with the CEOs[6]

| Number of Interviews | CEOs in office | Retired CEOs | Total |
|---|---|---|---|
| Germany | 29 | 53 | 82 |
| South Korea | 13 | 12 | 25 |
| Japan | 12 | 8 | 20 |
| China | 18 | 3 | 21 |
| Other Countries | 82 | 41 | 123 |
| Total | 154 | 117 | 271 |

Using the term "collective mindsets" (the term "Social Interpretation Pattern" is also used), the perspective of socially constructed knowledge is applied (Creswell, 2003: 8). The analysis of collective mindsets (ACM) involves reconstructing the collective frames, habits, and scripts that organize the production of knowledge and attitudes in a social group, culture or society. These tell us how to interpret the world, what is typical, significant, and relevant. In the classical perspective, the ACM deals with collective representations, as Durkheim called it (Durkheim, 1967: 78f.) or with the derivations that could be traced back to certain residues, that Pareto had in mind (Pareto, 1962). Thus, the ACM is primarily interested in the knowledge frames that help members of a specific group, culture or society deal with social problems (Oevermann, 2001). These frames, habits, and scripts are part of a collective inventory of knowledge, inherited through culture, and collectively reproduced or changed (Schütz and Luckmann, 1994; Schütz, 1982). They are enacted by members of a specific group, culture or society but do not always become a conscious or reflected part of their individual knowledge. In a sociological perspective, collective mindsets are pertinent for three questions: What is the problem, how shall we solve it, and what are good and bad solutions? Thus, each collective mindset has a cognitive, a normative and an evaluative dimension, which is to be reconstructed by using the analysis of collective mindsets (ACM)-method (see table 4.A.3 in Appendix). The manifested patterns of argumentation that are articulated by our interviewees[7] are traced back to the dominant knowledge frame. This method was originally conceptualised by Oevermann (2001), and developed further by Ullrich (1999) and Sachweh (2010), and was applied in an international research design under the guidance of native speakers.

## Global Elites as Pacemakers?

A fierce competition for desirable jobs with high income and reputation is said to be taking place, as well as a "war of talents" between nations and between companies to hire the "best brains" (Appadurai, 1998: 15; Dreher, 2003: 18; Chalamwong, 2005: 488). Taking the assumptions of the mainstream globalization literature as starting points, there are three approaches in the scientific debate on global or transnational elites that strongly uphold this idea:

a) The global elites approach (Castells, 1996; Beck, 1997; Münch, 2009 etc.), that entails the idea that global elites are able to produce their goods where costs are minimal, settle and work where life is most comfortable, and pay taxes where the rates are lowest (Beck, 1997: 17). "Elites are cosmopolitan, people are local" as Castells (1996: 414) puts it.
b) The transnational capitalist class approach (Sklair, 2001; Robinson, 2004; 2012; Carroll, 2010 etc.), that tries to show

> that corporate executives (Sklair, 2001: 21) have become more transnational and that the rising number of transnational interlockers indicates the emergence of a new transnational class (Carroll, 2010: 20).
> c) The boundary-less career approach (Sullivan and Arthur, 2006; Thomas and Inken, 2007 etc.) states, that the individual career management (opposed to the career development by the organization) has become more important and leads to greater transnational career mobility (Sullivan and Arthur, 2006: 22).

In each of these approaches, top managers are the personified "avant garde" of globalization. To test this hypothesis, the research project used several indicators. At first, it was asked how many top managers were born and brought up abroad. Second, the companies that these managers were working for were classified in order to find out how many of the foreign-born managers work for domestic companies or for the foreign affiliates of multinational companies. It was also checked how many of the foreign-born managers were recruited from international markets or from inside the mother company as expatriates. Third, weaker forms of internationalization in German and East Asian companies were delineated in terms of whether top managers had studied abroad or spent a significant part of their career working abroad. According to the indicators, the research project classified as international or transnational careers only those with upward or downward career mobility abroad that occurred as part of an international assignment and not as part of career development within the domestic mother company.

## German Top-Managers as Global Elites?

With respect to the CEOs of Germany's top-30 DAX-companies, things seem quite encouraging for supporters of the global-elite-thesis. The analysis of CEOs of the 2012 DAX-top-30-companies accounted for 9 top-managers of a foreign nationality (Table 4.4) and thus a rate of 29%. This quote of slightly more than a quarter will be confirmed, when the origin of all 189 executive board members of the top-30-DAX-companies is taken into account. In other words, the share of executive boards of a foreign origin amounts to 26.5%. Shares are relatively high due to the fusion activities of global companies.

However, things begin to look different when one goes beyond the DAX-top-30 and takes the 100 biggest industrial companies into account too. The rate went down to 16% of the top managers, and declined further when all companies in Germany were taken into account, by using the representative German general social survey (Mikrozensus).

Out of the 16 CEOs that were born and who grew up abroad, in Germany's Top 100 industrial companies only 8 worked for companies that were actually based in Germany. The other 8 CEOs worked for big foreign enterprises. In seven cases, these managers were sent by the multinational companies to run a local subsid-

**Table 4.4** CEOs Born Abroad in Germany

| 2011/2012 | Born abroad (N) |
|---|---|
| Dax 30 CEOs | 29.0% (9) |
| Dax 30 Executive Board | 26.5% (51) |
| Top 100 CEOs Industry | 16.0% (16) |
| All CEOs of Firms in Germany | 8.3% (65,000) |

iary. Thus the rate of 'global' managers is rather low with respect to industrial enterprises in Germany. It is not global elites but those with a home-national background that dominates.

This empirically founded rejection of the strong global-elites-thesis with respect to Germany does not however, mean that there are no globalization effects on companies and on the recruitment and career patterns of managers. Careers have indeed become more international, as we shall see below.

Using reliable data from a big press archive in Germany (the Munzinger archive), and combining it with the interview data, it becomes obvious, that — by comparing the cohorts — the importance of stays abroad has increased (Table 4.5; see also Diehl and Dixon, 2005: 715-716).

With the younger cohort born between 1950 and 1969 the number increases from 31% to more than half of all industrial managers. In particular, the share of managers who have worked abroad has more than doubled. The increase in sending of managers abroad, a kind of enforced 'brain circulation,' makes up the crucial effect of globalization. While global elites are still not globally recruited very often they do increasingly have experience of foreign universities or affiliate firms.

**Table 4.5** Stays Abroad (≥ 1 Year) of German Top Managers by Age Groups

| Cohort | Cohort 1930-1949 | Cohort 1950-1969 |
|---|---|---|
| Activities abroad | N=106 | N=75 |
| Study abroad≥1 year | 20% | 25% |
| Work abroad≥1year | 17% | 42% |
| Activities abroad total | 31% | 53% |

Source: Munzinger Archiv (German press archive).

## Global Elites in East Asia?

The research findings for other countries indicate that Germany is not an exceptional case. In East Asian countries, it was found that altogether 23 CEOs out of 371 were born abroad. This share of 6% is largely due to the Chinese policies of opening up the economy to big transnational companies (TNCs) in order to capitalize on their knowledge. There are in fact, only two CEOs in the Top 100 manufacturing companies that are employed by a domestic company. Most CEOs born and brought up abroad not only worked for a foreign affiliate firm of a multinational company, but were mostly expatriates i.e. they were sent to this country as a challenge in their career development from within their mother company. Only two CEOs out of 371, which is a share of roughly 1%, were recruited internationally (see Table 4.6).

Thus, the results concerning East Asian economies confirm the findings from the German case. The share of internationally recruited CEOs is even lower. If one looks at the other economies in the research project's sample, only in Australia and Switzerland are there higher shares of internationally recruited top managers.

**Table 4.6** Number of CEOs Born/Grown Up Abroad in East Asian Economies

| Countries (n) | Foreign born CEOs (N) | Foreign born CEOs in domestic companies (N) | Foreign born CEOs in TNCs (N) | Expatriates* (N) |
|---|---|---|---|---|
| China (146) | 9% (14) | 0% (0) | 9% (14) | 8% (12) |
| Japan (104) | 4% (4) | 1% (1) | 3% (3) | 2% (2) |
| South Korea (121) | 4% (5) | 0.8% (1) | 3% (4) | 3% (4) |
| Total (371) | 6.1% (23) | 0.5% (2) | 5.6% (21) | 4.8% (18) |

* referring to those CEOs, who work for a foreign affiliate company and have been sent by the mother company for a determined period of time on the CEO position.

Altogether, the shares are too low to provide an empirical foundation for the global elites assumption. At least, it has to be rejected for the CEOs of the biggest industrial companies.

The same pattern of an enforced brain circulation as the primary globalization effect — with the exception of China — is also found in East Asian economies. Taking a closer look at the stays abroad that lasted one year and longer, in Korea a strong cohort effect is detectable, although it must be noted that there is a smaller number of CEOs in the age group between 40 and 49 years. The younger the age cohort, the higher the shares of CEOs who have worked and/ or studied abroad and thus internationalized their careers[8] (see Table 4.7).

In the case of Japanese top managers,[9] there are rather low rates concerning education mobility, but the same cohort effect concerning the number of work assignments abroad.

While the strong globalization hypothesis cannot be sustained, the weaker one of an enforced brain circulation during an

**Table 4.7** Stays Abroad (≥ 1 Year) of Korean Top Managers by Age Groups

| Age Groups (N) | 40-49 years (10) | 50-59 years (63) | 60 + years (45) | Total (119) |
|---|---|---|---|---|
| Study abroad (≥ 1 Year) | 90% | 21% | 16% | 25% |
| Work abroad (≥ 1 Year) | 50% | 38% | 35% | 38% |

**Table 4.8** Stays Abroad (≥ 1 Year) of Japanese Top Managers by Age Groups

| Age Groups (N) | 40-49 years (2) | 50-59 years (28) | 60+ years(73) | Total (103) |
|---|---|---|---|---|
| Study abroad (≥1Year) | 0% | 11% | 11% | 11% |
| Work abroad (≥1Year) | 100% | 39% | 16% | 24% |

insider career at the mother company does find strong support in the data drawn from a life course analysis. If all 1,302 cases from the CEOs of the 11 countries are taken into account, the strong cohort effect is significant and can be confirmed.

## A New Neoliberal Spirit of Capitalism?

If no global economic elite is emerging and no significant global recruitment pattern is taking place then what about the transformation of collective mindsets towards a new neoliberal spirit of capitalism? The recent literature on neoliberalism shares the assumption that a spread of neoliberal ideas and a strong tendency of convergence towards neoliberal management thinking is occurring in the centre regions of the world economy (Boltanski and Chiapello, 2005; Crouch, 2011: 92; Streeck, 2013: 45-46, 58-59). Although numerous studies have already made the case for divergence or 'path-dependency' in models of management and business systems (Whitley, 1999; Hall and Soskice, 2001; Amable, 2003, for welfare state institutions see also Rieger and Leibfried, 2004), "the convergence literature is the longest- established viewpoint" (Clegg, 2012). For the cases of Germany and Japan, Streeck and Yamamura have examined whether the global forces of Anglo-American capitalism is giving rise to a single, homogeneous capitalist system (Streeck and Yamamura, 2003).

The understanding of Neoliberalism nowadays is about the — more or less radical — establishment of market coordination inside firms, inside economies and in the transformation of the state sector and other sectors towards the domination of market rationales

(Willke, 2003: 11-15). A new neoliberalism, originating in the US, seems to be on its triumphal march across the world (Streeck and Yamamura, 2003; Willke, 2003: 11-15). The consequences have so far been seen in the erosion and drawback of the welfare state, the privatization of statist enterprises and in the deregulation of financial markets (Crouch, 2011; Streeck, 2013). But aside these general assumptions, the new neoliberal make-up of the capitalist spirit in the economy remains rather underdetermined (Willke, 2003: 11-15; Schmidt-Wellenburg, 2009). It is often stated that top managers are promoters of these new neoliberal ideas but so far, no systematic empirical proof of this has been generated (Pohlmann, 2014: 14). To examine this assumption using valid qualitative interview data is the purpose of this chapter.

In order to test empirically the spread in neoliberal values and neoliberal management thinking, the project focused on an analysis of management concepts in the last three decades (Schmidt-Wellenburg, 2009: 325-335). For the purpose of this article, two important features of neoliberal management thinking have been selected: a) a financial market driven economic thinking (a financial market mindset); b) a neoliberal management mindset with

**Table 4.9** The New Neoliberal Management Thinking: The Indicators

| The Financial Market Mindset |
|---|
| • Understanding of Enterprises as Financial Market Investments<br>• Shareholder Value Orientation and Market Capitalization<br>• Market Principles in the Global Value Chain |
| **The Neoliberal Management Mindset** |
| • Understanding of Enterprises as Networks of Profit Centers<br>• Indicator Systems and Benchmarks<br>• Output Oriented, Market Indicator Driven Leadership (Results-Only Work Environment) |

market coordination inside the firm and an output driven leadership style (see Schmidt-Wellenburg, 2009: 327). These features make up the most important parts of the neoliberal management thinking and are accompanied by various management concepts that are said to be influential all around the world (see Schmidt-Wellenburg, 2009: 325-335).

## The Financial Market Mindset amongst German Managers

In the interviews conducted not many German managers welcomed the financial market driven economy. Without any exception, for all the German managers, it was quite clear that the "German Model" had greatly changed during the last decades and that a number of companies had been exposed to the (ir)rationalities of financial markets. Only 1 out of 65 professional managers mentioned the opportunities and openings that the financial markets offered to their companies but all others were ambivalent or mostly (50 out of 65) not in favour of a financial market-driven economy. The 17 entrepreneurs from the big family run company groups in Germany all welcomed the fact that they were not exposed to financial markets rationales in any way. Thus, the challenge of how to act in a specific economic setting and make profits for their firms was not answered — neither before nor after the global financial crisis — with a strong reference to the financial market- driven economy.

In answering the questions, how strong the influence of the financial market system is and how CEOs act to meet the challenges of a financial market system, the dominant collective mindset articulated by 77% of the 65 professional managers (not including the 17 entrepreneurs of the family run firms) concerning the financial market-driven economy was a defensive "playing the system"-mindset. This can be understood as a collective script that advocates following the formal rules and procedures of the financial system in order to outfox the system for the sake of the firm's survival and growth. Its underlying logic was quite apparent and consisted of the following components: (1) The system is changing towards a financial market-driven economy; (2) The shareholder pressure is rising as well as the capabilities of fund managers to regulate; (3) This is not good for the company and its long term strategies; (4) The owners or shareholders no longer act in the interests of the company only the managers do; (5) Thus, they have to do the windows dressing carefully and play the system very hard to outfox it!

This defensive "playing the system" mindset is strongly influenced by the financial market-driven economy, but is not essentially about using financial markets to solve economic problems. Rather, it is more about defending the company against its shareholders and the irrationalities of the financial markets, in particular its short-termism. The quarterly reports provide the indicators for all analysts and rating-agencies. That is why the arguments against the financial market-driven economy have been sharp and decisive already before the global financial crisis and became even more negative and defensive straight after. The underlying norm is to protect the company's interests against shareholders who try to realize quick gains and move on to the next hot stock. "Of course, the shareholder, particularly the institutional investors have rising power and influence concerning the strategies of the company. In my perspective, this is not only critical, because we are externally controlled, but also, because it may not be the best of all for the company and its long term strategies" (German CEO in office, Argentina, 2013, translated from German by authors).[10]

However, this is not the whole story. An offensive financial market mindset can be found in Germany amongst a minority of younger CEOs, 3 out of the 25 CEOs in office, from the age group born between 1955 and 1964. The offensive mindset can be defined as using the financial system in order to push the firm, through an infusion of capital and by getting rid of the old boys network of Rhenian Capitalism (Albert, 1993). In this case, the financial market-driven economy is understood as an advantage for the firm in terms of economic efficiency, investor relations, and profitability.

## The Neoliberal Management Mindset: German Top Managers on Leadership

Paternalism as a leadership style is dead in German enterprises today. Delegation is the keyword in the collective mindsets on leadership. For more than 90% of the 82 managers and entrepreneurs it is now natural, that delegation is a mechanism of distributing responsibilities and realizing a higher degree of participation. The concept of delegation is understood as combining the transfer of responsibility and of decision-making power to one or more employees. Usually, delegation in German big business is connected with changes in the labour organization, the introduction of new forms of communication, participation, and employee shares. The concept of delegation is nevertheless articulated in an ambivalent manner by two thirds of the 82 managers and entrepreneurs. On the one hand, it is seen as a way for the company to capitalize on the knowledge of high skilled people and professionals. On the other hand, too much delegation is judged as risky, leading to a loss of control over the strategic guidance of the company's activities. "Your challenges concerning leadership are sometimes black and white. This is the boss, he has to decide. If you don't decide it yourself, you're not just loosing face, but you're losing also your followers" (German CEO in office, Brazil, 2013, translated from German by authors). That is why output oriented, market oriented indicator systems, benchmarks and performance evaluations come in to the picture. At least for the CEOs born between 1955 and 1964, the use of these indicator systems as a strategic framing of decision autonomy, comes very naturally. "I would say, today you're in need of a mixture between delegation, checklist indicators and centralized decisions. In our company, the crash barriers are clearly defined by indicator systems, but inside these barriers, we delegate and the people have decision power. We're doing a kind of checks and balances" (German CEO in office, Germany, 2008, translated from German by authors).

The old-fashioned "talk to the people and listen"-mindset is a collective knowledge form that is mostly used by a significant group (21 out of 53) of the retired CEOs from the age cohort born between 1930 and 1944 in Germany. In order to have direct information and communication, non-hierarchical target groups need to be established. The concept of delegation is not about the transfer of decision-making power and responsibilities, but about the establishment of a communication pattern that is bottom-up.

The new output driven leadership-mindset is not only articulated by the cohort of CEOs born between 1955 and 1964, but also by some of the age cohort of German top managers born between 1930 and 1944. The concept of output-driven leadership style is based on an evaluation of units by indicator systems and benchmarks that help to reduce direct interventions. A smaller group of retired CEOs and entrepreneurs (7 out of the 53 Ex-CEOs born between 1930 and 1944) worked with a system to evaluate their employees' individual performance and organized participation according to the measured performance. The better your performance, the greater the degree to which decision-making power is transferred to you. At the level of work organization, many of the Top 100 industrial companies in Germany like Volkswagen or BMW established indicator and benchmark-systems along with the implementation of profit centers. The purpose is to define output goals for these units, leaving it up to them to decide how to reach these output goals. The better your performance and your contribution to the profitability of the company, the faster you will be promoted and the greater your freedom to decide. This fits perfectly with the neoliberal management mindset.

One third of the German top managers, especially the few female entrepreneurs in the sample and 12 out of 25 of the cohort born between 1955 and 1964 use a collective mindset to describe their leadership role, which in the research project has been termed the "team coach-mindset". It is understood as a conceptualization of the leaders' role not as supervisor, but as consultant of a professional team, which is in need of support, advice, and empowerment, but not of command anymore. In this mindset, all directive or authoritative elements of guidance are negatively attributed. The coaching perspective is dominant: giving people hints, supporting and empowering them. The attribution of "self optimization" capabilities as well as the possibilities for professionals to decide on their own is the backbone of this new leadership role model, one that fits the neoliberal self-governance theory of leadership (Bröckling, 2005). It has become radically anti-hierarchical and anti-paternalistic.

## The Collective Mindsets of Top Managers in East Asia

The CEO interviews in South Korea (N=25), Japan (N=20) and China (N= 21) were carried out in 2012 and 2013, after the global financial crisis, which had no strong impact on the South Korean and Chinese economies. However, the collective mindsets of Korean top managers were strongly affected by a period effect, which was related to the Asian Financial Crisis in 1997/1998. Those managers of Korean big business conglomerates, who survived the Korean economy crash in the late 1990s, were strongly in favour of the renewed Korean family run business model. It kept the advantages of a fast and highly flexible decision making system, very often still 'top down', but became very careful concerning the risks of the financial markets. Till today, the big business groups are almost impossible to be taken over from outside. "But actually this kind of ownership-based business group is proven. It proved to be very effective in the long-term strategy. ... You know, that's why, it was possible to win the race, because Korean ownership-based business is very consistent, very concentrated ..." (Korean Chairman and CEO in office, South Korea, 2013). Thus, for 20 out of 24 Korean CEOs of big business groups in Korea, the financial market-driven economy seemed not to be a real alternative to the Korean model. For the other four CEOs, not the financial market itself but the financial transparency in such a system was welcomed.

Unlike the Koreans, the 20 Japanese top-managers acknowledged that the financial market-oriented system has gained power and that it is now widespread in Japan. However, in the collective mindsets in use, it is the Western system that does not fit the Japanese way of doing business. Most Japanese managers, with the exception of two cases, did not argue in favour of the finance market-driven economy, but rather contrasted it with the advantages of the Japanese system, which they complained was already partly lost. Amongst the 20 Top Manager interviewees, the dominant mindset was opposed to *kabunushi henchô shugi* (Lopsided Shareholder Interest), preferring rather a capitalism of common good (*kôeki shihon shugi*). 17 out of 20 CEOs said that balancing the interests among stockholder, employees, banks, and community is most important. For 9 out of 11 CEOs of the age cohort born between 1930 and 1944, it was quite clear, that the financial market driven system is a Western system, and that it is opposed to the original Japanese system, which is to be developed further.

In China where, since the end of the nineties, institutional investors gained importance, the collective knowledge forms that are dominantly in use (15 out of 21 interviewees) articulate a conservative playing-the-system mindset for the sake of a long-term rationality in running the business. Despite the cultural differences, it is almost the same pattern of management thinking that we found in most German companies. Although a lot of the Chinese big businesses used some of the opportunities that the financial mar-

**Table 4.10** The Financial Market Mindset of Top Managers in Selected Countries

| Collective Mindsets | Other Cultural Frames | Financial Market Mindset |
|---|---|---|
| Germany | Defensive Playing the System-Mindset | Offensive Financial Market Mindset |
| Korea | Korean Business Model-Mindset | Against financial markets |
| Japan | Capitalism of Common Goods-Mindset | Against financial markets |
| China | Conservative playing the system-Mindset | Against the short-termism of financial markets |

kets offered, they conveyed that they have been trying very hard to protect their companies against the short-termism of a financial market-driven economy. Typical for this mindset are statements like the following: "In the long run, we don't accept any institutional investors. They are focussing on their interests, not on ours" (Chinese CEO in office, China, 2013, translated from Chinese by authors). Altogether, the project's findings indicate that the collective mindsets of most top managers in East Asia are not neoliberal (see Table 4.11), but shaped by other cultural frames derived from the business systems in which they have been socialized.

Concerning the use of management concepts, the Korean big business conglomerate has become very modern. A lot of trendy concepts have been introduced especially after the Asian financial crisis. Nevertheless, the collective mindsets of top managers in office remain very much linked to some basic ideas of leadership that do not rely on Western concepts of an output-driven leadership style unlike a lot of German managers. The dominant knowledge form with regards leadership is still a management of give and take networks mindset. "Leadership" was for 19 out of 24 Korean CEOs translated into the responsibility of the supervisor who personally takes care of the employee's well being. This is the case even with

**Table 4.11** The Neoliberal Management Thinking of Top Managers in Selected Countries

| Collective Mindsets | Other Cultural Frames | Neoliberal Management Thinking |
|---|---|---|
| Germany | Listen and talk-mindset | Output-driven leadership-Mindset, Team Coaching-mindset |
| Korea | Management of Give and Take Networks-Mindset | Not found |
| Japan | Representing the group-Mindset | Not found |
| China | Motivate your employees-Mindset | Not found |

the cohort of younger managers born between 1955 and 1964 and is often related to a, "we are all family" ideal. Fast decision-making and if necessary, a top-down system was natural for these managers. Only five Korean top managers argued strongly in favour of delegation and participation. Korean top managers as well as CEOs with an international assignment working in Korea for a multinational company are well aware that the Korean culture is a strong culture, one that permeates all management concepts implemented by the firm. Very often, the collective mindsets in use reduce these concepts to artificial forms that are very neat and professional, but which are in fact, an act of window dressing for the company. "I skipped all the seniority based levels, I mean, the whole hierarchical system. ... There were just the team managers left and then the others, all plain managers. ... All became pretty much flat. But you know, although I eradicate all those hierarchical systems, they know, who the senior is and who not. But at least it helped to communicate more freely" (Korean CEO in office, South Korea, 2013).

The topic of "leadership" seemed not very familiar to a lot of Japanese top-managers. It was very difficult to identify any consistent argumentation patterns about leadership. As some of them pointed out themselves, this might come from the Japanese education system and the Japanese society, with its stronger emphasis on the group rather than on a small number of 'superior' leaders. 18 out of the 20 CEOs agreed that communication with employees based on opinions from the bottom, are valuable. According to this collective mindset of "representing the group," this could lead to creativity, employee participation and responsibility, reform and strategy building. This mindset can be understood as a role model for CEOs, which includes that all decision-making power is left to the group of co-managers and the obligation of the CEO is to represent the group of fellow managers, colleagues and employees of the company properly. It is part of the typical Japanese decision making process, which is called *Ringiseido,* a rotation system for CEO recruitment, that offers — according to seniority, performance and status — the highest position to top managers three years before their retirement. Within the system, deliberations and decisions among the managers at all levels below the executives should come first. The executive decision, therefore, comes last.

The introduction of management concepts in Chinese state or private enterprises is very much influenced by the West. It is common, that new management concepts are introduced by the Chinese government and administration with the purpose of taking over and learning from Western management thinking. For example, lean production, total quality management, and lean management have been implemented in the last two decades. In addition, in recent years risk and performance management are new concepts implemented by many big state enterprises. For roughly 17 out of 21 CEOs of statist and private enterprises, a "learn from the best, but still lagging behind"-mindset is at work. It is strongly correlated with the catch-up ambitions of their companies. Leadership is understood as a task to improve the enterprise culture and the motivation of the employees. In 10 out of 21 cases this "motivate your employees-mindset" is combined with a new bottom-up philosophy of decision-making and participation of the employees. "I'm the CEO. But I don't have to think about the objectives of the development of our company. This is done by our employees, bottom up. I leave it to the department heads, and the department heads to the senior managers. We collect ideas bottom up and discuss in the CEO commission meeting what is feasible and good for the development of the company" (Chinese President and CEO in office, China, 2013, translated from Chinese by authors). So far, however, neither indicator systems (except for the measurement of performance) nor an output-driven leadership style are revealed as mindsets and management techniques in the Chinese interviews.

## Conclusions

The results concerning the two hypotheses of the mainstream globalization literature are quite clear. Not only for Germany, but also for the East Asian economies, the global elites-assumption for the corporate industrial sector has to be rejected. The competition and selection of high skilled personnel did not lead to a high number of globally recruited personnel at the top management level. Mostly, these managers were sent abroad for an international assignment as part of their career path in the mother company at home. There are jet setters and million-milers, but no job hoppers with transnational careers. The effect of globalization can therefore be depicted as "globalization light" in terms of management careers, one that supports "brain circulation" but does not establish a new world class of economic elites in the corporate industrial sector. Why is this the case? On the one hand, economists tell us that the returns on mutual investments are higher for high skilled personnel as well as for the companies when they stay with each other (Williamson, 1975: 75; Lindbeck and Snower, 1988; Bertold and Fehn, 1995). On the other hand, sociologists know, that it is trust, loyalty and a deep understanding of the unwritten rules of the company that are the reasons why insiders at that level are preferred (Stroh and Reilly, 1998; Kotthoff, 2006; Pohlmann, 2009). Insiders are also not so eager to sell, split up or wind up parts of the company like outsiders sometimes are (Lucier *et al.*, 2007). If insiders are preferred in big industrial companies of the leading world regions why should the potential top manager go abroad for a longer period of time, running the high risk of falling behind in the career track within his/ her home country and mother company?

Concerning the second hypothesis about the diffusion and internalization of neoliberal management thinking, the findings indicate that the claim cannot be sustained, at least for East Asian economies. Of course, our findings are related to collective mindsets, the knowledge inventory of top managers, and thus does not deal with the organizational measures inside the companies. Nonetheless, the idea that there is a global diffusion of neoliberal management thinking can be denied. First of all, it was found, that at the corporate level, the neoliberal financial market mindset is not spreading across the world. In Western countries, such as Germany, the dominant mindset is a defensive "playing the system" view. Most top managers are in favour of a long-term strategy to protect the interests of their firms by outfoxing the financial market system. In East Asian companies, most top managers argue against a financial market-driven economy, preferring their own indigenous way to run the business (as in Korea and Japan) or a long-term approach to doing business like in China. Thus, our findings indicate, that the Korean and the Japanese business systems are, at the level of collective mindsets of top managers, still different from the shareholder-centered American corporate governance system (Itami, 2000; 2002). For China, Li, Xinchun pointed out, in his study of 4,256 Chinese entrepreneurs and top managers, there are only rare cases of Chinese firms using the stock markets for financing their corporate strategies because the risk of losing control is estimated to be too high (Li, 2011: 76-79).

The results point to an almost identical pattern with regards neoliberal management thinking on leadership. In Germany the basic understanding of leadership changed a lot and a radical delegative approach is most common today. This is confirmed by other studies on the leadership culture in Germany (Leipprand, 2012; Busch *et al.*, 2013). The new collective mindsets of neoliberal management thinking are, in a significant number of big German manufacturing companies, connected with the organizational restructuring of firms towards the establishment of profit centers, benchmarks, and indicator systems. Again, this was not the case in most Korean and Japanese business conglomerates. Although these companies have established a lot of very modern features of labour organization and management concepts, there was no indication of an output-driven leadership style — one that is not just related to individual performance measures, but to benchmarks and indicator systems for the business units — represented in the collective mindsets of most top managers. In China, where the use of Western management concepts is very common, the collective mindsets regarding leadership were mostly dominated by the idea of motivating people and were not influenced by neoliberal management thinking. This is also confirmed by the study of 4,225 entrepreneurs and top managers by Xu *et al.* in 2011, who showed that motivation and delegation are the dominant approaches towards leadership by managers in Chinese enterprises (Xu *et al.*, 2012: 97-102).

The results indicate that neoliberal management thinking, as expressed by Western management thinkers, has had some impact on the collective mindsets of German top managers, but has not reached the collective knowledge stock of managers in East Asian economies. All these companies have become very modern for instance, in the make-up of their labour organisations and concerning the take-over of management concepts. However, their interpretation frames remain culturally rooted and usually do not make use of neoliberal management thinking.

How does one explain such findings? First of all, collective mindsets as knowledge forms are deeply rooted in culture and therefore do not change easily in a short period of time (Hall and Soskice, 2001). This needs to be taken into account by all mainstream theories and theorists of globalization and the transformation of neoliberalism. According to the findings, it is more useful to stick to a 'varieties of capitalism' approach, one that takes into account the unwritten institutional rules, cognitive frames and belief systems (Streeck and Yamamura, 2001; Whitley, 1999; 2009).

From a sociological perspective, institutions not only prevail because of the advantages that firms have in using national institutional settings and rules (Hall and Soskice, 2001) but also because they became habitualized through internalization and socialization processes.

Second, with regards the financial market mindset, it is not quite clear why managers should be in favour of the financial market-driven economy. Managers are supposed to control and calculate, to be in command of the firm's strategy. In the "monkey circus" of financial markets, this would not be possible any more, as many managers told us in the interviews. When the owners, shareholders, and principals are no longer interested in the survival and expansion of the company group, only top managers are left to protect the company. Thus, the professional role of top managers as organizational men or women, who have mostly climbed the career ladder in one company group, is more of a barrier to the spread of a neoliberal mindset at the corporate level in the real economy.

Third, vis-a-vis the financial markets, all entrepreneurs and managers in the selected countries experienced severe financial crises, leading to the breakdown, winding up and bankruptcy of a lot of big business conglomerates. As a result, a strong period effect is at work, leading to the articulation of collective mindsets that are not in favour of financial markets.

Fourth, concerning the neoliberal management mind set and the takeover of neoliberal management techniques, new institutional theory is correct to point out that organizations very often take over what is modern and the flavour of the year, without applying it to the degree where operations and procedures are substantially changed. Window dressing, outfoxing the system, hidden agendas and unwritten rules are all very common features used by new institutional theory (Meyer and Rowan, 1977; DiMaggio and Powell, 1991).

The neoliberal management thinking is of course only a small cog in the big wheel of neoliberalism. This article was not about the broad picture of neoliberalism (Lim and Jang, 2006), about the neoliberal strategies and ideologies in transforming the states. However, the findings make clear that top managers are not the switchmen they were expected to be, accelerating the trend towards a financial market-driven economy. Furthermore, the collective mindsets across countries are not merging or converging and it must be emphasized that these collective mindsets cannot simply be deduced from the management literature. A deep empirical investigation is crucial to explore and demonstrate how collective mindsets are far more resilient and culturally rooted than the mainstream of globalization literature claims.

## *Notes*

1. Sombart (1902: 319-320) introduced in 1902 the concept of a "spirit of capitalism (Geist des Kapitalismus)." Max Weber (1989) took it over and developed it further.

2. We want to thank Prof. Jonghoe Yang, Prof. Jonghee Lee, Dr. Jaok Kwon, Dr. Sanghui Nam, and Yuanyuan Liu for the excellent support we had in carrying out this research project.

3. These countries are: Argentina, Australia, Austria, Brazil, China, Germany, India, Japan, South Korea, Switzerland, and US.

4. In Germany, almost half of the Top 100 companies (46%) are industrial (including manufacturing, energy, construction business), in Korea 60%, in Japan 41%, and in China 38% of the biggest companies in 2012.

5. The research project compares the top managers in office during the eighties/ nineties, and partly still are (born 1930-1949) and the CEOs of big enterprises who are currently in office (born 1950-1969).

6. Retired CEOs are those who have given up their CEO position in the respec-

tive Top 100 company group. Mostly, these retired CEOs are working as CEOs for other firms or as directors of the board etc.

7. This allowed the project to count how many interviewees articulated a particular pattern.

8. Regarding the general discussion on the recruitment of power elites in South Korea, refer to the research such as Choi (1993), Dong (1995) and Kim (2005). For the historical background of South Korean power elites, refer to the discussion by Kong (2000).

9. For the recruitment of elites in Japan, refer to the research of Mannari (1974), Cutts (1997). For recent research, please see Watanabe and Schmidt (2004) and Schmidt (2005).

10. All quotations are referenced regarding nationality, position and status of the interviewee, the location of the interview and the year in which the interview was carried out. We do not display any further information in order to preserve the anonymity of our interviewees.

## References


Albert, Michel. 1993. *Capitalism against Capitalism*. London: Whurr Publishers.

Amable, Bruno. 2003. *The Diversity of Modern Capitalism*. Oxford: Oxford University Press.

Appadurai, Arjun. 1998. "Globale ethnische Räume: Bemerkungen und Fragen zur Entwicklung einer transnationalen Anthropologie" (Global Ethnic Spaces: Comments and Questions Regarding the Development of a Transnational Anthropology). pp. 11-39 in *Perspektiven der Weltgesellschaft* (Perspectives of world society), edited by Ulrich Beck. Frankfurt/M.: Suhrkamp.

Beck, Ullrich. 1997. *Was ist Globalisierung? Irrtümer des Globalismus - Antworten auf Globalisierung* (What is Globalization? Fallacies of Globalism - Answers to Globalization). Frankfurt/M.: Suhrkamp.

Bertold, Norbert and Rainer Fehn. 1995. "Neuere Entwicklungen in der Arbeitsmarkttheorie" (Recent Developments in the Labor Market Theory). *Wirtschaftswissenschaftliches Studium* (Economic Sciences Study) 24(3): 110-117.

Bloom, Nikolas, Genakos Christos, Sadun Raffaella, and John Van Reenen. 2012. "Management Practices across Firms and Countries." *Academy of Management Perspectives* 26(1): 12-33.

Boltanski, Luc, and Ève Chiapello. 1999. *Le Nouvel esprit du capitalisme* (The New Spirit of Capitalism). Paris: Gallimard.

________. 2005. "The New Spirit of Capitalism." *International Journal of Politics, Culture and Society* 18: 161-188.

Bröckling, Ullrich. 2005. "Gendering the Enterprising Self: Subjectification Programs and Gender Differences in Guides to Success." *Scandinavian Journal of Social Theory* 6 (2): 7-25.

Busch, Rainer, Robert McMahon, Alexander Unger, Christian May, and Ya-Cheng Wang. 2013. "A Comparison of Leadership Styles between Chinese and German Managers of Chinese Companies in Germany." *Chinese Management Review* 16(2): 1-17.

Carroll, William K. 2010. *The Making of a Transnational Capitalist Class: Corporate Power in the 21st Century*. London: Zed.

Castells, Manuel. 1996. *The Rise of the Network Society: The Information Age: Economy, Society, and Culture*. Oxford; Malden, MA: Blackwell.

Chalamwong, Yongyuth. 2005. "The Migration of Highly Skilled Asian Workers to OECD Member Countries and its Effects on Economic Development in East Asia." pp. 487-526 in *Policy Coherence Towards East Asia, Development Challenges für OECD Countries, Development Center Studies*, edited by Kiichiro Fukasaku, Masahiro Kawai, Michael G. Plummer, and Alexandra Trzeciak-Duval. Paris: OECD.

Choi, Jang-Jip. 1993. "Political Cleavages in South Korea." pp. 13-50 in *State and Society in Contemporary Korea*, edited by Hagen Koo. Stanford: Stanford University Press.

Clegg, Steward R. 2012. "Management, Global Models." in *The Wiley-Blackwell Encyclopedia of Globalization*, edited by George Ritzer. Oxford: Blackwell Publishing Ltd.

Creswell, John W. 2003. *Research Design: Qualitative, Quantitative and Mixed Method Approaches*. 2nd edition. California: Sage.

Crouch, Collin. 2011. *The Strange Non-death of Neo-liberalism*. Cambridge: Polity.

Cutts, Robert. 1997. *An Empire of Schools: Japan's Universities and Molding of a National Power Elite*. Armonk: M.E. Sharpe.

Diehl, Claudia and David Dixon. 2005. "Zieht es die Besten fort? Ausmaß und Formen der Abwanderung deutscher Hochqualifizierter in die USA" (Taking It away the Best?: Extent and Forms of Migration of Highly Qualified German in the USA). *Kölner Zeitschrift für Soziologie und Sozialpsychologie* (Cologne Journal of Sociology and Social Psychology) 57: 714-734.

DiMaggio, Paul J. and Walter W. Powell. 1991. *The New Institutionalism in Organizational Analysis*. Chicago: University of Chicago Press.

Dong, Wonmo. 1995. "Regional Cleavage in South Korean Politics." *Korea Observer* 26(2): 1-26.

Dreher, Sabine. 2003. "Vom Wohlfahrtsstaat zum Wettbewerbsstaat? Die Bedeutung der Migration für die Globalisierungsdebatte" (From Welfare State to Competition State? The Importance of Migration for the Globalization Debate). pp. 13-32 in *Migration im*

*Wettbewerbsstaat* (Migration in the Competition State), edited by Uwe Hunger and Bernhard Santel. Opladen: Leske+Budrich.

Du Gay, Paul and Glenn Morgan. 2013. *New Spirits of Capitalism?: Crises, Justifications, and Dynamics.* Oxford: Oxford University Press.

Durkheim, Emile. 1967. "Individuelle und kollektive Vorstellungen" (individual and collective representations). pp. 45-83 in *Soziologie und Philosophie* (Sociology and Philosophy). Frankfurt/M.: Suhrkamp: Ö.

Hall, Peter A. and David W. Soskice. 2001. *Varieties of Capitalism: The Institutional Foundations of Comparative Advantage.* Oxford: Oxford University Press.

House, Robert J., Paul J. Hanges, Mansour Javidan, Peter W. Dorfman, and Vipin Gupta, eds. 2004. *Culture, Leadership, and Organizations: The GLOBE Study of 62 Societies.* Thousand Oaks: Sage.

IBM. 2011. "Capitalising On Complexity: Insights from the Global CEO Study." IBM.

Itami, Hiroyuki. 2000. *Nihonkei Corporate Governance* (Japanese Corporate Governance). Nihon Keizai Sinbun.

_______. 2002. *Jinponsyugi Kigyo: kawarukeiei kawaranugenri* (Humanitarian Corporate: Changing and Unchanging Principals). Nihon Keizai Shinbu.

Kim, Yong-Hak. 2005. *Social Networks within Korea: With a Special Reference to Regional Ties.* Berkeley: University of Berkeley Press.

Kong, Je-wook. 2000. "Han-gook Jeonjaeng-gwa jaebeol-ui Hyeong-seong" (The Korean War and the Emergence of the Chaebol). *Gyeongjewa Sahoe* (Economy and Society) 46: 54-87.

Kotthoff, Hermann. 2006. "Überflüssige Loyalität in großbetrieblichen Sozialbeziehungen der Modellwechsel von Anerkennungsmustern." pp. 225-239 in *Das Problem der Exklusion: Ausgegrenzte, Entbehrliche, Überflüssige* (The Problem of Exclusion), edited by Heinz Bude and Andreas Willisch. Hamburg: Verlag Hamburger Edition.

Lanvin, Bruno and Paul A. L. Evans. 2013. *The Global Talent Competitiveness Index 2013.* Singapore: INSEAD.

Leipprand, Tobias. 2012. *Jeder für sich und keiner fürs Ganze?: Warum wir ein neues Führungsverständnis in Politik, Wirtschaft, Wissenschaft und Gesellschaft brauchen* (All for Themselves and None for All?: Why do we need a new understanding of leadership across government, business, academia, and civil society). WZB, SNV: Berlin.

Li, Xinchun. 2011. "The Financial Market and the Development of Chinese Enterprises: State of the Art, Prospects, Challenges, and Solutions: 2011 Report on the Development of Chinese Entrepreneurs." *Management World* 6: 76-90.

Lim, Hyun-Chin and Jin-Ho Jang. 2006. "Neo-liberalism in Post-crisis South Korea: Social Conditions and Outcomes." *Journal of Contemporary Asia* 36(2): 442-463.

Lim, Hyun-Chin and Kyung-Dong Kim. 2007. *East Meets West: Civilizational Encounters and the Spirit of Capitalism in East Asia.* Leiden: Brill.

Lindbeck, Assar and Dennis Snower. 1988. *The Insider-Outsider Theory of Employment and Unemployment.* Cambridge, MA: MIT Press.

Lucier, Chuck, Steven Wheeler, and Rolf Habbel. 2007. "The Era of the Inclusive Leader." *strategy+business* 47.

Mannari, Hiroshi. 1974. *The Japanese Business Leaders.* Tokyo: University of Tokyo Press.

Meyer, John W. and Brian Rowan. 1977. "Institutionalized Organizations: Formal Structure as Myth and Ceremony." *American Journal of Sociology* 83(2): 340-363.

Münch, Richard. 2009. *Globale Eliten, lokale Autoritäten: Bildung und Wissenschaft unter dem Regime von PISA, McKinsey & Co.* Frankfurt/M.: Suhrkamp.

Nobel, Carmen. 2012. "Measuring the Efficacy of the World's Managers." *Working Knowledge.* Boston: Harvard Business School. <http://hbswk.hbs.edu/item/6918.html.>

Oevermann, Ulrich. 2001. "Die Struktur sozialer Deutungsmuster: Versuch einer Aktualisierung" (The Structure of Social Interpretation Patterns: An attempt at a review). *Sozialer Sinn* 2(1): 35-81.

Pareto, Vilfredo. 1962. *Vilfredo Paretos System der allgemeinen Soziologie* (Vilfredo Pareto's System of General Sociology). Stuttgart: Ferdinand Enke.

Pohlmann, Markus. 2002. *Der Kapitalismus in Ostasien: Südkoreas und*

*Taiwans Wege ins Zentrum der Weltwirtschaft* (The Capitalism in East Asia). Münster: Westfälisches Dampfboot.

_______. 2005. "Die neue Kulturtheorie und der Streit um Werte" (The New Culture Theory and the Case of Value). *Soziologische Revue* (Sociology Review) 28(1): 3-14.

_______. 2009. "Globale ökonomische Eliten? Eine Globalisierungsthese auf dem Prüfstand der Empirie" (Global Economic Elites?: The Globalization-Hypothesis and Its Empirical Proof). *Kölner Zeitschrift für Soziologie und Sozialpsychologie* 61: 513-534.

_______. 2014. "Der Geist des Kapitalismus und seine Trägerschichten." in *Globalisierung als Autokapitalismus? Prüfstandberichte zum Zustand eines Entwicklungsmodells,* edited by Philipp Hessinger and Markus Pohlmann. Wiesbaden: VSA.

Reichertz, Jo. 2004. "Abduction, Deduction and Induction in Qualitative Research." pp. 159-165 in *A Companion to Qualitative Research,* edited by Uwe Flick, Ernst von Kardoff, and Ines Steinke. London: Sage Publishing.

_______. 2005. Prämissen einer hermeneutisch wissenssoziologischen Polizeiforschung. *Historical Social Research/Historische Sozialforschung* 30(1): 227-256.

Rieger, E. and S. Leibfried. 2004. *Kultur versus Globalisierung: Sozialpolitische Theologie in Konfuzianismus und Christentum* (Vol. 2243). Frankfurt/M.: Suhrkamp.

Robinson, William I. 2004. *A Theory of Global Capitalism: Production, Class and State in a Transnational World.* Baltimore: Johns Hopkins University Press.

_______. 2012. "Global Capitalism Theory and the Emergence of Transnational Elites." *Critical Sociology* 38(3): 349-363.

Sachweh, Patrick. 2010. *Deutungsmuster sozialer Ungleichheit: Wahrnehmung und Legitimation gesellschaftlicher Privilegierung und Benachteiligung* (Interpretation Patterns of Social Inequality: Perception and Legitimacy of Social Privilege and Disadvantage). Frankfurt/M.: Campus.

Schluchter, Wolfgang. 1996. *Unversöhnte Moderne* (Unreconciled Modernity). Frankfurt/M.: Suhrkamp.

Schmidt, Carmen. 2005. "Japan's Circle of Power: Legitimacy and Integration of a National Power." *ASIEN* 96: 46-67.

Schmidt-Wellenburg, Christian. 2009. "Die neoliberale Gouvernementalität des Unternehmens: Management und Managementberatung zu Beginn des 21. Jahrhunderts" (The Neo-Liberal Governmentality of the Firm: Management and Management Consulting at the Beginning of the 21st Century). *Zeitschrift für Soziologie* (Magazine of Sociology) 38(4): 320-341.

Schütz, Alfred. 1982. *Das Problem der Relevanz* (The Problem of Relevance). Frankfurt/M.: Suhrkamp.

Schütz, Alfred and Thomas Luckmann. 1994. *Strukturen der Lebenswelt* (Structure of Living Environment). Vol. 1. Frankfurt/M.: Suhrkamp.

Sklair, Leslie. 2001. *The Transnational Capitalist Class.* Oxford: Blackwell.

Sombart, Werner. 1902. *Der moderne Kapitalismus* (The Modern Capitalism). Vol. 1. Leipzig: Duncker und Humblot.

Streeck, Wolfgang. 2013. *Gekaufte Zeit: Die vertagte Krise des demokratischen Kapitalismus* (Purchased Time: The Adjourned Crisis of Democratic Capitalism). Berlin: Suhrkamp.

Streeck, Wolfgang and Kozo Yamamura, eds. 2001. *The Origins of Nonliberal Capitalism: Germany and Japan in Comparison.* Ithaca, NY: Cornell University Press.

________, eds. 2003. *The End of Diversity?: Prospects for German and Japanese Capitalism.* Ithaca, NY: Cornell University Press.

Stroh, Linda K. and Anne H. Reilly. 1998. "Zählt für Manager noch Treue zur Firma? Was ist dran an dem Vorwurf, Manager seien heutzutage selbstsüchtige Opportunisten, denen es nur um das eigene Wohl geht?" (Counts for Managers not Loyal to the Company?: Is there any truth to the accusation that managers are nowadays selfish opportunists who care only about their own well?). *Harvard Business Manager* 20: 9-15.

Sullivan, Sherry E. and Michael B. Arthur. 2006. "The evolution of the boundaryless career concept: Examining physical and psychological mobility." *Journal of Vocational Behavior* 69(1): 19-29.

Thomas, David C. and Kerr Inkson. 2007. "Careers across cultures." pp.

451-470 in *Handbook of Career Studies*, edited by Hugh Gunz and Maury Peiperl. Los Angeles: SAGE.

Ullrich, Carsten G. 1999. "Deutungsmusteranalyse und diskursives Interview." (Interpretation pattern analysis and discursive interview). *Zeitschrift für Soziologie* (Magazine for Sociology) 28(6): 429-447.

Watanabe, Masao and Carmen Schmidt. 2004. "Die wirtschaftliche Elite Japans: Rekrutierungsmuster und Netzwerkbeziehungen" (The economic elite of Japan: recruitment patterns and network relations). *JAPAN aktuell*: 56-66.

Weber, Max. 1989. *Gesammelte Aufsätze zur Religionssoziologie I* (Collected Essays on the Sociology of Religion I). Tübingen: Mohr.

Whitley, Richard. 1999. *Divergent Capitalisms: The Social Structuring and Change of Business Systems*. Oxford: Oxford University Press.

________. 2009. *Business Systems in East Asia: Firms, Markets and Societies*. Los Angeles: SAGE.

Williamson, Oliver E. 1975. *Markets and Hierarchies: Analysis and Antitrust Implications*. New York: Free Press.

Willke, Gerhard. 2003. *Neoliberalismus* (Neoliberalism). Frankfurt/M.; New York: Campus.

Willmot, Hugh. 2013. "Spirited Away: When Political Economy Becomes Culturalized." pp. 98-123 in *New Spirits of Capitalism?: Crises, Justifications, and Dynamics*, edited by Paul Du Gay and Glenn Morgan. Oxford: Oxford University Press.

Witt, Michael A. and Gordon Redding, eds. 2014. *The Oxford Handbook of Asian Business Systems*. Oxford: Oxford University Press.

Xu, Shuying, Lan Li, Hui Wang, Siqin Peng, Dahai Hao, Zhoulan Han, Hongyu Zhang, and Yunfeng Wang. 2012. "Entrepreneurial Perspectives on Human Nature, Management and Performance: 2012 Report on the Development of Chinese Enterprises." *Management World* 6: 96-100.

# Appendix

**Table 4.A.1** Proportional Quota Sampling

| | Age (years) | Female CEOs (%) | Tertiary Education (%) | Natural / Engineering (%) | Study Abroad (%) | Worked Abroad (%) |
|---|---|---|---|---|---|---|
| Germany Top 100 | 53 | 0 | 95 | 62 | 42 | 63 |
| Germany Interviews | 54.5 | 2,5 | 97 | 54 | 32 | 51 |
| Korea Top 100 | 60.7 | 0 | 99 | 51 | 25 | 38 |
| Korea Interviews | 60.4 | 0 | 100 | 38 | 29 | 54 |
| Japan Top 100 | 64.6 | 0 | 100 | 54 | 12 | 24 |
| Japan Interviews | 63.5 | 0 | 100 | 50 | 20 | 70 |
| China Top 100 | 57.4 | 4.8 | 95 | 67.9 | 8.2 | 12.3 |
| China Interviews | 57.3 | 5 | 70 | 43.4 | 0 | 5 |

**Table 4.A.2** Age Cohorts

| Number of Interviews | Age Cohort 1930-1944 | Age Cohort 1945-1954 | Age Cohort 1955-1964 | Age Cohort 1965-1974 |
|---|---|---|---|---|
| Germany | 45 | 12 | 25 | 0 |
| South Korea | 4 | 17 | 4 | 0 |
| Japan | 11 | 6 | 3 | 0 |
| China | 4 | 10 | 4 | 3 |
| Total | 64 | 45 | 36 | 3 |

**Table 4.A.3** Steps of Analysis in the Interpretation of the Interviews

1. Selection: Sequences related to specific topics were selected according to our research interests but with an open coding;
2. Reformulation: Arguments, explanations, narrations in the sequences were summarized through paraphrasing;
3. Abstraction of meaning: The logical and normative structure was abstracted and interpreted in terms of what was evaluated as good or bad in order to trace it back to the underlying norms behind the judgments;
4. Abstraction of order: The logical and normative order in the flow of arguments, descriptions or narrations was abstracted;
5. Comparison: The chosen sequences in all interviews were compared to falsify, modify and extend the discovered collective mindsets as well as to identify most common, shared and dominant cognitive and normative patterns;
6. Contextualization: The cognitive and normative patterns were related to the social reality of actor constellations, cultures, opportunity structures and institutional constraints, in which they appeared;
7. Identification of Rules: Related to this social reality, the typical rules producing common interpretations and actions that were acknowledged and dominant, were identified;
8. Explanation: Related to the theories in this field of research, it was explained why these rules were reproduced or changed, and what the social consequences of these rules were.

# PART II

## Diversity of Asian Capitalism: China, Japan and Indonesia

Chapter 5

# *Capitalism in China: A Centrally Managed Capitalism (CMC) and Its Future*

Nan Lin

## Introduction

The phenomenal and sustained economic growth of China over the past two decades has raised fundamental issues about whether the system is capitalistic. This issue is significant not only because it offers an opportunity to understand and appreciate the dynamics driving the economic growth of China, but it may also challenge existing theories about the nature and characteristics of capitalism and provide clues about the future evolution of China and capitalism itself. In an earlier essay (Lin, 2008) I proposed that a capitalistic society has emerged in China. Specifically, I made the following arguments. First, I defined capitalism as a set of social institutions that sustain the production, accumulation, and reproduction of capital, and identified these institutions as calculating capitalists, free markets, wage labour, an expansive system, and a strong and supportive state. I explicated existing theories that explain capitalism, ranging from self-interest — the psychological motive (i.e., Smith) and exploitative reproduction — the sociopolitical motive (i.e., Marx), to institutional enticement — the cultural motive (i.e., Weber), and the networking imperative — the social motive (i.e., Braudel, 1977; Wallerstein, 1979). Each theory offers only a partial explanation of capitalism, but collectively they explain how these institutions are coordinated. Based on these conceptual and theoretical articulations, I drew on empirical evidence to support the contention that China today strongly meets these requirements as a capitalist state. This capitalist state, however, exhibits two relatively unique features not usually identified with capitalism, namely, the state itself acts as a capitalist, and economic activities are heavily embedded in social relations (*guanxi*). Each of these features, which are not unique to China, shows its full leverage and sustainability in a capitalistic system that is not transitioning to the liberal capitalism of the West, as some have wished or argued, but may instead be establishing an alternative paradigm of capitalism to be emulated by other state-run capitalistic countries.

In this essay I further elaborate on the feature of the state as a capitalist. The other feature — embedding economic activities in social relations, or socially embedded capitalism — will be deferred to comprehensive treatments in other essays. I point out that while China continues to develop capitalistic capacities, the party-state has increasingly tightened control of the economy and synchronized the political and economic stratification — a tendency towards a *centrally managed form of capitalism*. Mechanisms and features of China's centrally managed capitalism (CMC) will be articulated. Three principal mechanisms make this politically commanded capitalism feasible: (1) the control of personnel and the incentive and mobility for political attainment; (2) the control and rewards for organizations, including economic corporations; and

(3) the control of capital.

I then speculate that an ideological transformation is underway. This transformation takes two steps. In the first step, the party-state leadership gradually decouples the justification of its dictatorial position from the Marxist ideology of communism and socialism, and couples with the maintenance of economic growth and social order. This shift relieves the party from the burden of proposing mechanisms by which China can move from the primary stage of socialism to the mature stage of socialism. The second step then allows the legitimacy of party rule to be based on indigenous Confucian ideology (i.e., *Xiaokang* and *Datong*) that emphasizes moral institutions, social relations, and eventually democracy. When fully realized, this transformation will have significant and substantive consequences for China and its paradigmatic position in world capitalism.

## The Role of the State in Capitalism

Empirical modern-day capitalism can be traced to the seventeenth-century financial systems of the Netherlands in which the stock market was innovated, global trade was envisioned, and the banking system established. The British adopted and improved these systems and, along with its industrial innovations, created a world empire. The systems were subsequently transported to the US Mead (2009) and others have called the Dutch system version 1.0 of capitalism in about 1620; the British introduced version 2.0 in about 1700; the Americans upgraded to version 3.0 in 1945. Thus the dominant model of capitalism for the past

300 years has been the Dutch-British-American model — liberal capitalism. Since Adam Smith, the theory of a perfect, frictionless market, including financing, has lent a strong ideological support to the superiority of this model (Krugman, 2009). Some scholars have maintained that capitalism only needs a governance system that monitors the 'natural' free market and allows it to function without interference or abuse. Rand (1966), for example, stated that the only function of the government should be the task of protecting citizens' rights. In a capitalist system all human relationships should be voluntary. Variations of capitalism have always existed, including types of welfare capitalism in Europe (see Lin, 2008) where the state's role in the market is recognized and duly exercised. But ideologically (or theoretically), the state has been treated as a supportive player in capitalism, even though the state has played a critical role in the development and maintenance of the Dutch-British-American systems.

Some scholars challenged this theoretical stance by pointing out that various institutions, including the state, played different roles in different phases of the industrializing process. Gerschenkron (1962) argued that historically when the industrialization process was launched in a backward country, the productive and organizational structures of industry that emerged from those processes were considerably different from those in more advanced or mature countries. These differences were largely attributable to the state's application of institutional instruments for which there was little or no counterpart in an established industrial country. He therefore concluded that the extent to which these institutional instrumentations exhibited utility appeared to have varied directly with the degree of backwardness of the countries. The emergence of Japan as a capitalist country offered an important site, outside of Europe and North America, for intensive, close examination of the development process from early backwardness to an industrialized society. In his study of Japan's capital formation during the period 1868-1940, Rosovsky (1961) shows that the state played a prominent role in the process.

It was probably Johnson (1995) who coined the term the 'capitalist developmental state'. Focusing on the institutional arrangements in the development of Japan, he showed that economic development (growth, productivity, and competitiveness) was the priority for state action. The state used a small-scale, elite economic bureaucracy staffed with the best managerial talent available to guide the privatization and marketization processes. The elite bureaucracy (the Ministry of International Trade and Industrialization) employed consultation and cooperation to forge consensus among corporations on goals and information exchange in their innovative development, manufacturing, and competition in the global market. This strong political system allows the bureaucracy to take initiatives and operate effectively. Thus, in the developmental state, the politicians 'reign' and the bureaucrats 'rule' (Onis, 1991). This seminal work confirmed the significance of the state in the early stage of industrialization or at the developmental phase, as discussed by previous scholars, and set the stage for voluminous studies on the developmental state as found in East Asia.

Subsequent studies in Korea (e.g., Amsden, 1992; Cumings, 1987; Lie, 1998) and elsewhere in East Asia (e.g., Taiwan, Singapore, see Deyo, 1987; Evans, 1995; Onis, 1991; Wade, 1990; Wong, 2004) amplified the role of the state in the development of these states and solidified the linkage of the term 'the developmental state' to the development of East Asia. Onis (1991) and Wong (2004) summarized the developmental state as one in which the state must be autonomous and capable. It employs a small elite bureaucracy to tightly coordinate corporations, provide resources, and set national productivity goals. Because of the economic crisis in Asia in the late 1990s, individual states in East Asia had to adapt and adjust their policies, but it is felt that the role of the state has remained largely unchanged (Wong, 2004).

While this rich literature highlights the significant role of the state in emerging capitalism, especially in East Asia, the literature by omission ignores the role of the state in the entire spectrum of capitalism. This omission can lead to an implicit and erroneous inference: the state is only important for emerging capitalism. As I discussed in a previous paper (Lin, 2008), the state has always played a critical role in capitalism historically. Capitalism requires a *state* — a governance institution — that is willing and capable of protecting, regulating, and promoting the coordination and functioning of capital accumulation, the markets, and wage labour. Historical evidence convincingly shows that in order to thrive, capitalism requires a strong national government — *a powerful state.* Analyses of broad historical data on capitalistic development have amply demonstrated that a strong and supportive state is an essential ingredient for all capitalistic systems. Braudel (1977) stressed that capitalism, differing from a mere market system, triumphs only when it becomes identified with a powerful state. He cites the Italian city-states, Holland, and England as examples. The state provides guarantees that players follow the rules of the game. It ensures that capitalists produce and reproduce commodities with acceptable practices of acquiring material resources and compensating labour. Commodities are channelled through distribution and consumption markets transparently and without price fixing, hoarding, or dumping. Also important is the state's role in arbitrating disputes over production, distribution, and consumption markets. While it attempts to be even-handed, the state is ultimately responsible for protecting capitalists so that capital accumulation can proceed (Johnson, 1995).

Polanyi (1944; see also Polanyi *et al.*, 1957) made the essence of the state explicit. He identified the state and the market as the two central pillars of modern capitalism. For Polanyi, these two institutions are interconnected. The state plays a central role in determining the structure of property rights, the quality of financial institutions, and the incentives for capital accumulation, investments, and entrepreneurship (see Heilbroner, 1985 for elaboration). Of particular interest is the arbitration of disputes between capitalists and labour. While in some capitalist states unions are advocates of labour, the state is the ultimate arbitrator. It ensures that labourers never challenge capitalists for rights to the products of their labour and the means of production. A strong state promotes (domestic) capitalism by providing internal production forces with a protective shell from external challenges, and at the same time insists on a free market elsewhere for domestic corporations to secure markets for resources, labour, and consumption globally.

Many sociologists and political scientists have rightly stressed the significance of the state in modern industrialized societies, among them Wallerstein (1979), Evans (1995), Skocpal (1996), Hobson (1997), Weiss (1998), and Evans, Rueschemeyer, and Skocpal (2002). Historically, the US government has not shied away from interfering with the market system to protect or save firms and industries. Some examples include its long-term farm protection policies; rescues of automobile, steel, and airline corporations; international tariffs; and the recent massive bailout of financial institutions. Examining the recent history of the US, Fligstein (2005) pointed out that in the US entrepreneurship and competition matter to the creation of new markets and industry but that they cannot occur without governments and stable social structures to support them. He shows that the US government has directly affected market activities with laws and rules that determine tax policies, govern the use of equity and debt by corporations, regulate employment relations, enforce patents and property rights, and regulate competition or antitrust policy. The government can act as a buyer of products and a provider of research and development funds to firms. It also makes rules that can directly favour certain firms in particular industries, often at the behest of the most powerful actors in those industries. The government, Fligstein points out, has also built up public and private infrastructures that opened up the possibility for new firms and industries to emerge.

This clarification has important implications for understanding the role of the state in economic development. First, the association of the state with a backward or emerging capitalism is unattainable. Theoretically it has been shown that the state remains important beyond the developmental stage, even though its role also varies for different states embedded in differential historical and institutional arrangements. Empirically, many East Asian countries have long been industrialized and yet the state continues to play critical roles in economic development. Second, the role of the state needs re-conceptualization as we study its role in all types of capitalism.

Historically, the varying presence or absence of various institutions (e.g., the relative powerfulness of the monarch, the nobility, the landowners, the merchants, or the peasants) in different societies has contributed to differential roles that the state has played in different capitalist societies (Lachmann, 2000). But at a minimum, a powerful and supportive state is an essential element in a capitalist state. The significance of the state in a capitalist system is prominently displayed when capitalism inevitably brings the economy to the brink of total collapse, due to the ever-present greed and continued desire for expansion and accumulation of capital. Minsky (2008) theorized that in the normal cycle of an economy, when cash flow rises beyond debt, a speculative euphoria develops and borrowing through hedging, speculation, and Ponzi schemes ensue. These speculations eventually bring about a 'Minsky moment' when an accumulation of debt pushes the economy towards a crisis. This inevitable financial fragility and instability can only be avoided if the government steps in to control it through regulation, central bank action, and other mechanisms. The Panic of 1907, the Great Depression, the oil crisis of the late 1970s, and the current world and European financial crises attest to the danger of this instability and the need for intervention from the state(s).

Yet the conventional wisdom of economists and those espousing the developmental state perspective remain: once the crisis is overcome or the development is attained, the state recedes to the background and allows capitalists to resume their expansive activities and accelerating accumulation of capital. The vision of a perfect, frictionless market system soon regains traction when the debt is dealt with (Krugman, 2009). Calls for deregulation soon appear when the crisis is averted and the cycle resumes. Thus we can hypothesize that in 'Western' capitalism (i.e., the liberal capitalist tradition of the Dutch-British-American model), this cycle of stability and crisis, and the up-and-down role of the state are a routine process. Gaining an advantage over other actors in the marketplace supersedes all other considerations. Driven by greed and forever seeking gaps in regulations and normative trade practices to gain advantage, capitalists will inevitably move the system towards another crisis when the state emerges from its 'invisible' role to its role of blatant and outright intervention.[1]

## Forms of State Capitalism

The term 'state capitalism' has been widely used to characterize capitalism in which the state plays a significant and visible role. However, its usage is diffuse, ranging from characterizing state socialism to fascism, to state-firm-union coordination. In the Marxist tradition, state socialism is a system in which the state owns and controls the means of production while wage labour and limited markets function. Thus the state is the sole capitalist. The fascist variety, characterized by Italian Fascism, identifies the authoritarian role of the state in intervention and supervision of big businesses and the economy. In still a third variation of state capitalism, the state manages strategic resources and coordinates closely with large private firms and unions to guide economic growth and development. Thus the degree or variation of state capitalism can be characterized by two dimensions: (1) the extent to which the state owns the means of production; and (2) the extent to which the state dictates or coordinates with big firms (national champions) and unions in the marketplace. When the state is the sole owner of all means of production it is a dictatorial system, exemplified in state socialism (e.g., Cuba, North Korea). For the purpose of this essay I rule out further discussion on systems where capitalism, if it exists at all, is clearly subsumed under the authoritarian state and serves the pleasure of the dictators. Most state capitalistic countries, however, show that the state owns only some but not all means of production. In fact, it is hard to find any state that does not control or supervise certain industrial sectors and valued resources deemed central to the survival of the state. Most states retain control of all or portions of the defence industry, water (rivers, dams, etc.), environmentally essential resources (pollution control and environmental safeties), taxation, mining, and vital infrastructure (major roads, harbours, airports, communications), and so on. Schmidt (2002) identifies three types of capitalism in modern-day Europe: market, managed, and state. She puts modern-day France and, to a lesser extent, Italy in the third category. Even in the market capitalism category (i.e., Britain), however, the state plays a significant role and controls certain resources.

Some scholars have argued that the saliency of state capitalism as a counterparadigm to liberal capitalism has been a recent development. For more than a century, liberal capitalism (i.e., Britain and the US) assumed the political, military, and economic high ground in international markets, exploiting vital resources (e.g., oil) through its powerful corporations from other and less industrialized countries. Only during the second half of the twentieth century did states holding vital resources learn to mount a challenge. Bremmer (2009), for example, argues that state capitalism first took shape during the 1973 oil crisis when the Organization of the Petroleum Exporting Countries (OPEC) countries agreed to cut oil production in response to the US support of Israel in the Yom Kippur War. The world's most important commodity became a geopolitical weapon, giving OPEC governments unprecedented international clout. The oil crisis gave birth to modern oil corporations, which have since been imitated and extended. Today, governments, not private shareholders, own all of the world's largest oil companies and control three-quarters of the world's oil reserves. The 13 largest oil companies in the world, measured by their reserves, are owned and operated by governments — companies such as Saudi Arabia's Saudi Aramco; the National Iranian Oil Company; Petróleos de Venezuela, S.A.; Russia's Gazprom and Rosneft; the China National Petroleum Corporation; Malaysia's Petronas; and Brazil's Petrobras. State-owned companies such as these control more than 75% of global oil reserves and production. According to Bremmer, a second wave of state capitalism began during the 1980s, with the emerging countries controlled by govern- ments with state-centric values and traditions, and newly reformed countries liberated from state socialism. Examples are the rapidly growing economies of the 1990s, including Brazil, China, India, Mexico, Russia, and Turkey. Finally, a third wave of state capitalism resulted from the fast growth of trade surpluses and was marked by the rise of sovereign wealth funds (SWFs). Most of these SWFs are run by government officials and compete and challenge in the global capital market. I will return to the issue of capital accumulation and reproduction by these states later.

These waves cited by Bremmer (2009) are rather arbitrary as

many of the features he identifies had been evolving over longer periods of time and across different political and economic regimes. Nevertheless, they unfailingly point to growing state capitalism as a viable alternative form of capitalism capable of challenging liberal capitalism today. Yet within the diverse range of state capitalism, China stands out and is perhaps alone in its peculiar alignment and synchronization of a party-government-military-economy regime. The nature of this type of state capitalism will be discussed next.

## Centrally Managed Capitalism

The type of state capitalism I wish to discuss here is one in which the state plays an active role as a capitalist (see Lin, 2008). In this system the state exercises much freedom in creating and maintaining enterprises through ownership, holding majority of the shareholdings, and direct control over critical personnel decisions and supply of capital. I call this type of state capitalism centrally managed capitalism. It differs from liberal capitalism (e.g., the Dutch-British-American model), welfare capitalism in which the state controls welfare systems and otherwise supports but does not own large firms (e.g., most European states), or coordinated capitalism where the state works closely with large firms but does not own any directly (e.g., Singapore, Japan, and Korea). The developmental states, for example, are characterized by separation of the state and the economic corporations in personnel, stratification and mobility, and control of capital. They are also characterized by the role of a small, elite bureaucracy. China, on the other hand, shows a total involvement of the state in the economy and complete synchronization of a party-government-military-economy regime.

Centrally managed capitalism is a form of state capitalism that takes on the capitalistic form with the essential elements of capitalism: it promotes calculating capitalists, a free market, wage labour, and an expansive system. Yet the state plays a critical role in every aspect of the economy. The state-owned or affiliated enterprises compete with other enterprises in the marketplace, and its elites enjoy the rewards and benefits largely consistent with other capitalists. However, the elites ultimately answer to the dictates of the state rather than boards of directors, shareholders, or stakeholders. The 'free' market is asymmetric in favour of state-owned and affiliated enterprises in accessing loans and resources (e.g., land, raw materials, and so on) and operating in both domestic and foreign markets. Labour in state-owned and affiliated enterprises has only limited bargaining rights while enjoying security similar to that offered to employees in the bureaucracy. Some state-owned and affiliated enterprises become 'national champions' as the state restricts their competitors and encourages their mergers and acquisitions. Having national champions does not necessarily indicate a monopoly of one dominant enterprise in an industry or a sector. For example, in China the government deliberately allows several (usually two or three) national champions in a single industry (e.g., automobiles, banks, telecommunications) in order to preserve and encourage competition in the marketplace. But how does the state control and manage firms while allowing them to compete in the marketplace? Specifically, how does the state control and manage the top managers of the firms beyond the usual market-oriented rewards and incentives? And how does it control enterprises while allowing them a free hand to compete with one another and with other enterprises both domestically and globally? A closer look at CMC in China reveals the incentive (and punitive) structure that motivates and propels the top managers as well as the enterprises to respond to the demands and commands of the state.

Over the past three decades China has undergone significant economic reforms, adapting to market mechanisms in alignment with global trends. In the early phase of the reform there was conjecture that this movement towards marketization might represent a transitional phase whereby China would gradually move away from the central command structure towards a market structure consistent with conventional understanding of how such a structure would operate (Nee, 1989; 1996). However, the evidence is that China has instead been 'experimenting' with a new model of capitalism. While understanding the utility of capitalism in building capital and creating wealth for the state and the people, the Chinese government is nevertheless determined to maintain its one-party political rule. The argument is that by uniting under the leadership of a responsible party and its apparatus, China is able to advance economically and socially with efficiency and stability. As such a mixed structure has never before existed in theory or practice, China and the party leadership follow the advice of its leader Deng Xiao-ping, who announced to the world in the early 1980s that China would be 'crossing the rivers by touching the stones'.[2] The other side of the river is a wealthy nation; the way to get over the river is to take one step at a time and, once finding a stone to steady oneself, proceed to find another stone. What was left unsaid is that finding the next stone and coordinating the next movement are commanded by the party, and not by free-market mechanisms.

This new form, capitalism under party-state leadership, is an evolving process. Privatization of the labour force, housing, household commodities, and services has gradually been implemented. Individuals, households, and many firms have been allowed to work for profit, accumulate surplus values, and make capital investments (e.g., investments in supplies, technology, education, jobs, real estate, the stock market, and so on) without blatant interference of the state (Nee *et al.*, 2007). Market forces have gradually been introduced into other spheres of society (e.g., travel, leisure, and recreation). Yet this marketization process is largely and carefully managed by the party-state. Through several mechanisms this management and control is strong and self-reinforcing. Here I highlight three principal mechanisms by which the party-state manages capitalism: a reward and control system for personnel; a reward and control system for organizations, including large corporations competing in the marketplace; and a control system of capital.

## Reward and Control of Personnel

### *Party Control of Personnel*

The Central Organization Department is one of the most powerful central party offices. Initially established in 1924 and directed by Mao Ze-dong himself, the department is in charge of recruiting, appointing, evaluating, promoting, and removing thousands of cadres in the party and government offices at the central, regional, and provincial-city levels. This department holds personnel files of cadres in all important organizations in the country, spanning the party, the government, state-controlled or state-affiliated corporations and enterprises, and judges, to mass media, universities, institutions, foundations, political consultative councils, and provincial and city leaders. Candidates of all major appointments are screened by the department. At lower levels, all the way to each agency, office, and corporation/enterprise, the Central Organization Department is represented and embedded in the party office. The office holds personnel files of all employees in the organization. Actual appointments are determined by the top leaders of the party, but candidates undergo careful and thorough screening by the Central Organization Department.

Corporations in the economic sphere are no exception. The party is embedded and occupies a central position in the organization. The 'organizations' extend beyond party-state controlled or affiliated organizations. In many 'private' enterprises [the term usually used is *min-ying* (民營) or 'people's enterprise', not 'private enterprise' *si-ying* (私營); the distinction is subtle but critical] there is a party secretary and a party office. Geely, for example, is a private automobile corporation that recently acquired Volvo. Li Shufu, its founder and CEO, is also reported to be the party secretary of the company. The secretary may nominally be a member of the board of directors or a deputy CEO in the enterprise (or even chairman of the board or the CEO himself/herself) and centrally involved in all critical decisions. Furthermore, the secretary or an Organizational Department cadre supervises the personnel files 人事档案 (*renshi dang-an*). In China every urban working adult has a personnel file that contains detailed family background; education, marriage, work, and party histories; reviews and evaluations by supervisors; as well as criticism or 'black mails' — anonymous accusations of bad behaviour or conduct (Sun, 1992). This confidential file, which is not available to the worker, is kept in the personnel office directly under the supervision of the party secretary. When a worker requests a transfer to another enterprise or work unit, both sending and receiving units must agree and the file is transferred to the other work unit's party office. A receiving work unit cannot accept the worker without the personnel file. Occasionally, though rarely, the personnel file may mysteriously disappear and the worker's career is in limbo (Hille, 2009). If someone is laid off and the personnel file is missing, he would essentially become a 'homeless' worker as no other work unit would hire him. For workers in private corporations, personnel files may not be as critical. For workers in state-owned, controlled, or affiliated corporations, personnel files assume paramount importance for promotion and mobility. For private or foreign corporations, the party either operates openly as an office or through a party-controlled apparatus such as a union.

### *Synchronized Incentives and Mobility in the Political and Economic Arenas*

In China, top-tier stratifications in politics and economics are synchronized. Personnel move freely from the political hierarchy to the state-controlled and state-affiliated economic hierarchy and back, at the command of the party-state. Incentives are of both types: political positions or political capital, and material rewards or economic capital. Ultimately, attainment of political positions supersedes the significance of that in the state-controlled and state-affiliated economic hierarchy. The party-state is ultimately in control of the political and economic spheres and therefore both the political and economic positions and resources. The motivation and goal of actions for elitists is therefore to strive to attain the highest positions in the political hierarchy. In this politically and economically synchronized stratification system positions in enterprises and the marketplace, while having their own rewards, are means or stepping-stones towards the end goal — political attainment.

It should be noted that the political hierarchy runs vertically from the central apparatus in Beijing to local party and government offices. While local government and party officials are agents of the principles of the central party-state and sometimes take advantage of their positions to serve their own interests, it would be a serious mistake to conceive of the local officials as possible counterweights in a gaming situation. The party-state can and does swiftly remove local officials who are deemed disloyal, incompetent, or corrupt. The local governments are given the opportunity to control and manage their owned and controlled enterprises (to be elaborated in a subsequent section). Identical stratifications and reward structures operate at regional and local levels — the political hierarchy is in command of the controlled and affiliated enterprises and elites compete for the top positions in the local party-state. Vertically, local political elites are under the command of the central party-state. Elites at the local level compete for mobility to the central-level political and economic positions.

In this synchronized stratification system, performance in the marketplace is one of the criteria for mobility in the political hierarchy as well. The firm's performance is an important credential for its leading managers to be promoted to positions in the political hierarchy. The top leaders in the political hierarchy are also evaluated and judged by the overall performance of the economy. In this feedback loop, CMC couples politics and economics. The goals for the elites are consistent across the political and economic spheres:

to compete and perform well in the marketplace.

Leading personnel in state organizations and institutions and in the state-owned or affiliated corporations are transferred back and forth between the central government and local and regional governments with ease, as well as between the government bureaucracies and corporations, as such personnel mobility is largely in the hands of the party-state. One example is Guo Shengkun, who in 1998 was moved from serving as vice CEO of the China Colored Metal Industry Corporation, a State Council-owned enterprise, to deputy chief and member of the party executive committee of the National Bureau of Colored Metal Industry, another state-controlled organization. In 2001 Guo was transferred to the corporate world as the CEO and party secretary of China Aluminum Corporation and the chair of the board of directors and CEO of the China Aluminum Share-holding Company Limited. In 2004 he was transferred back to the government side to become the deputy secretary of the party of the Guaguangxi Zhuang Autonomous Region and elevated to party secretary of the region in 2007. Recently Xiao Ye-qing, party secretary and CEO of the China Aluminum Corporation and chairman of the board of directors of the China Aluminum Shareholding Company, was promoted to deputy secretary of the State Department and member of the party committee. Another example is Yun Gongmin, who was moved from his post as deputy secretary of Shanxi Province to vice chairman of the board and deputy party secretary of Shenghua Corporation in 2006, and then transferred to become the CEO and deputy party secretary of China Huadian Corporation in 2008 (Xinhua Net, 2009).

The interpenetration of personnel extends to 'private' corporations as well. Recently a private (*min-ying*) company, Mengniu

Dairy, China's largest milk producer, was involved in a scandal for selling contaminated milk. Its founder and owner, Niu Gensheng, and the company had previously been held up as a shining example of outstanding private enterprise. In 2002 it was hailed by the state as number one among the fastest-growing enterprises ('not on the stock market and not controlled by the state') in the country. In the wake of the scandal, in July 2009 Mengniu was forced to sell a 20% stake to a consortium led by state-owned China National Oils, Foodstuffs and Cereals Corp (Cofco), China's largest importer and exporter of food. Thus the state became the single largest shareholder of the company. Cofco declared that it would not interfere with the management of the company. Two months later, in September 2009, a senior Cofco executive replaced Niu as chairman of Inner Monglia Mengniu, the main operating subsidiary of the company (Anderlini, 2009).

This intertwining between the political and economic spheres also facilitates intergenerational inheritance among the leading cadres at the central and local governments. Instead of escorting their children through government bureaucracies and being accused of nepotism, they can now see their children promoted through corporations. This is especially convenient if the children are talented. Levin Zhu, son of Zhu Rongji, who received a Ph.D. from Wisconsin-Madison, heads the China International Capital Corporation. China Development Bank is run by Chen Yuan, son of Chen Yun, one of the eight pioneering Communists. Jiang Mianheng, son of former president Jiang Zemin, who holds a Ph.D. from Drexel, controls Shanghai Alliance Investment Limited, a government-owned investment company freely competing as a private equity firm. Wen Yunsong (Winston), the son of Wen Jiabao, who holds an MBA from Northwestern, is the founding CEO of New Horizon Capital, one of the most influential private equity firms in China (Financial Times, 2010). Hu Haifeng, son of Hu Jintao, graduated with a bachelor's degree from Northern China Jiatong University and an EMBA degree from Tsinghua University. He chose to develop his career in the corporate world, joining Nuetech, an offshoot corporation from Tsinghua, after graduation. Nuetech claims to be the world's leading company in 'the research and development of X-ray inspection technology'. Hu started his career in the company as assistant to the general manager and, through a series of promotions, quickly became the executive vice president and then the president by 2006 at the age of 35. Later that year Nuetech was awarded the contract to supply securities scanners for all 147 airports in China, earning the company hundreds of millions of Yuan (Chen, 2006). In awarding the contract, China's aviation authority made it clear that Nuetech won the contract strictly due to its superior technology. Its Container/Vehicle Inspection System has been put into operation by Chinese Customs in customs, ports, and railway stations. In 2008, at the age of 37, Hu became the party secretary of Tsinghua Holding Company, which controls more than 30 Tsinghua-affiliated enterprises (Dwnews, 2009). In 2009 Hu left the corporate world and became the Deputy Secretary at Tsinghua University. The intergenerational transfer is not unique to China; most political and economic elites in major (and minor) capitalist countries show such transfer. What is rather unique in China is that this transfer traverses freely between the public and private sectors and between political and economic hierarchies.

## Reward and Control of Organizations

### *Control and Stratification of Organizations*

Political control extends from personnel to the organization itself. Each state-owned, controlled, or affiliated organization carries a rank in the hierarchy of all public organizations. Following the Soviet Union's wartime socialism tradition and continuing from the state socialism era (1949-1978), all state work units have ranks similar and parallel to military units. For example, a top national university carries the rank of a 'division' and a local university a 'regiment'. To a lesser extent, calculable rankings apply to corpora- tions as well, depending on the scope, size, and other criteria. Positions in corporations are likewise assigned ranks. Synchronization of organizations and positions makes it possible to transfer personnel across corporations with ease. CEOs of banks and oil companies are regularly 'rotated' (similar to regional military commanders), not only between organizations in the same sector but also across sectors. Furthermore, transfers occur that cross political and economic boundaries. A manager with a rank of regimental commander in a corporation may thus be promoted to a divisional commander position in the state or local government or institute. The transferability of personnel serves important functions. For one, the ultimate promotions and rewards are the top positions and ranks in the party and the state in Beijing. Therefore, even for corporate CEOs a promotion may mean not only a position of higher rank but also to an organization of higher rank (preferably in the central party or state bureaucracy in Beijing). The loyalty of the corporate executives is ultimately to the party and the state, not the board of directors, shareholders, or stakeholders. Of course, one significant criterion for being promoted is performance in the marketplace. In this manner capitalism is linked to rewards in the political realm as well.

### *Control of National Champions and Large Corporations*

The party-state manages a reward- and-control system over large and important corporations in the economy. The party-state maintains strong control of the top-ranked corporations in most sectors. These corporations include state-owned (e.g., oil companies, banks, steel); statecontrolled (e.g., most large automobile, telecommunication, and transportation industries); and corporations/enterprises that are affiliated with central and/or local governments through capital, personnel, and other relations. While the private sector has grown rapidly in the number of enterprises and individuals employed, the leading corporations (national champions) in most sectors are public. (Some have argued that retailing may be the only sector that so far has minimal central state participation, Anderlini, 2010). According to a rating of the '500 strongest' enterprises in 2009 voted on by the China Enterprise Confederation and the Chinese Enterprise Directors Association, the top enterprises are all national enterprises. The leading 'private' enterprise, Jiangsu Shagong Corp., ranks thirty-fifth.[3] Furthermore, many of the so-called public and nongovernmental enterprises (e.g., Huawei, Lenovo, Haier, Chery) are in fact closely related to state institutions (universities, academies, or local governments). For example, Tengzhong Heavy Industrial Machinery Corporation, a little-known Chendu company, recently bid to buy Hummer from GM (but eventually failed to receive government approval and support). Tengzhong is listed since 2006 as a private enterprise. Tracing its background, it turns out to be a merged corporation from several state-owned (Sichuan Changdian Power) and provincial-owned (Sichuan Huatong Auditing) companies (Financial Times, 2010). The majority shareholder of Legend (the holding company of Lenovo) used to be the Chinese Academy of Sciences. It was recently announced that the CAS has reduced its shares from over 65% to 36%. Legend itself retains 35% of the shares and a new partner, China Oceanwide (a private enterprise, registered in Beijing), took over 29%. Thus Legend has nominally become a private majority holding corporation (Anderlini, 2009). These direct and indirect linkages allow the state and the party to exert control or influence on the strategies and execution of many private as well as public corporations' activities in the marketplace.

## Control of Capital and Trade

### *State Control of Economic Capital*

Another important mechanism of political control of the economic sphere is the party-state's command of the capital. The party-state has direct control of vital economic capital as it controls all the major financial institutions. All major banks are under the control of a vice premier at the State Council. According to a recent report in *the Economist* (2010), about four-fifths of the assets in the banking system are controlled by 17 institutions, whose leaders are all appointed, ranging from the more visible, such as Zhou Xiaochuan of the People's Bank of China, to the vast and powerful China Development Bank, under Chen Yuan (son of Chen Yun, one of the pioneering Communists). Bank chiefs are readily shifted around (e.g., in 2006 Zhang Jianguo, the president of Bank of Communication, became the president of China Construction Bank, ostensibly one of its competitors). As mentioned earlier, the China International Capital Corporation, the most important domestic underwriter, is under the leadership of Levin Zhu, son of Zhu Rongji, a former prime minister. His two former lieutenants, Wu Shangzhi and Fan Fenglei, are now in charge of CDH Investments and Hopu Investment Management, two of the top private-equity firms in China.

China is expanding its SWFs. From an experimental beginning in 2007 with the establishment of the China Investment Corporation with assets of $200 billion, China now has at least three (not including one in Hong Kong: Hong Kong Monetary Authority, with $140 billion in assets) SWFs: The State Administration of Foreign Exchange (with assets of $347 billion), China Investment Corporation ($289 billion), and the National Social Security Fund ($147 billion). Jointly they hold capital assets of $783 billion, far exceeding the top three SWFs in the world (UAE – Abu Dhabi – with $627; Norway with $445; and Saudi Arabia with $432 billion). As Western countries continue to deal with substantial debts, the unimaginable has happened — top Western debt managers travel to China to seek investment, primarily from its SWFs, in their government bonds. Carl Heinz Daube, the head of the debt management agency of Germany, probably the strongest economy in the West, travelled to China and Singapore in March 2010 to seek such investments.

### *Transferability of Capital*

With control of personnel and organizations, there is little wonder that the financial institutions cooperate fully with the directives of the party-state. When China responded to the world financial crisis in 2007-2008, it asked the banks to substantially increase its loans; the banks responded in unison and were much credited for the swift economic recovery. The stimulation package launched by the Chinese government in November 2008 in response to the financial crisis provided an occasion to illustrate how capital is transferred from the state to state-owned, controlled, or affiliated corporations. More than 75% of the stimulation fund ($586 billion) was allocated to infrastructure work, almost all of which was allocated to corporations owned, controlled, or affiliated with the state or local governments (Elegant & Ramzy, 2009). Another avenue of the stimulation package was bank loans. In the first half of 2009, loans amounted to 7.37 trillion Yuan since the government intended to ensure that it met its 8% economic growth target for 2009. State-owned, controlled, and affiliated corporations are again favoured for loans from the banks and the SWF. Such loans come in handy when corporations engage in acquisitions. This accounts in part for the recent rush of Chinese automobile corporations buying foreign companies. In the last 6 months, for example, both Beijing and Shanghai Automotives have bid on shares of Saab. Shanghai Automotive Industry Corporation has also bid on the GM factory in India. These state-owned corporations will continue to acquire more foreign companies. Even privately owned companies rely on state financial institutions for their acquisitions.

### *Flexibility in Investments*

Capital transfer goes both ways. The state receives capital as the owner or shareholder from these corporations. In 2008, 26 % of government revenues came from corporate taxes. It has the flexibility to increase or decrease its form of control or amount of shares as the state controls the board of directors and the top managers. In a crisis, when the state is in need of additional capital and other forms of aid, state-owned, controlled, and affiliated corporations are among the first to 'volunteer' contributions. Within 2 weeks after the earthquake that struck Sichuan in May 2008, these corporations had donated more than US$645 million in cash and goods (McGinnis *et al.*, 2009). Employees in these corporations were asked to donate their share of contributions 'voluntarily'.

The state has little difficulty in expecting cooperation and coordination with local government corporations in investments. When the state decides to make a certain investment, it simply asks the local government to comply.

One outstanding example of the 'good' investment is China's dramatic commitment to developing sustainable energy. Within the last 2 years China has become the leading country in the development of solar power. First Solar, the solar cell builder based in Tempe, Arizona, signed a 10 year agreement with China to build the largest solar field in the world in Inner Mongolia. The project will eventually blanket 25 square miles of Inner Mongolia — slightly larger than the size of Manhattan — with a sea of black, light-absorbing glass. The solar field will dwarf anything in operation in the US or Europe. At 2 gigawatts, or 2 billion watts, the solar plant could pump as much energy into China's grid as two coal-fired plants, enough to light up three million homes. CEO Mike Ahearn told *The Associated Press* before the announcement: 'The Chinese government is further along in its thinking about solar than we've imagined'. It would be impossible to create such a large field in the US since energy policies are made at the state level, Ahearn said. First Solar signed a 'memorandum of understanding' with Wu Bangguo, chairman of the Standing Committee of the Chinese National People's Congress. China has promised to guide First Solar through the approval process and make the project profitable (Kahn, 2009).

Applied Materials, an important US manufacturer of microchips, has ventured into making solar panels. In the past 2 years it has become the world's largest solar panel manufacturer and has built 14 solar panel factories in the world: five in Germany, four in China, one in Spain, one in India, one in Italy, one in Taiwan, and even one in Abu Dhabi. None is located in the US Uncertainty of price and lack of connectivity and regulation on a national basis has made such investment costly and slow. As a result, 'our federal and state subsidies for installing solar systems are largely paying for the cost of importing solar panels made in China, by Chinese workers, using hi-tech manufacturing equipment invented in America', observed Thomas Friedman (Friedman, 2009). In October 2009, Applied Materials opened the world's largest solar research centre in Xian, China.

### *Coordination in Diplomacy and Foreign Trade*

The synchronization between the state and the state-owned, controlled, and affiliated enterprises and the national champions also operates well in foreign trade. Whenever and wherever the Chinese government signs a trade agreement with a foreign country in the developing world, China inevitably commits itself to providing infrastructure construction and natural resource (e.g., oil, gas, and other mines) explorations. Much of the work is then allocated to one or more Chinese enterprises without bidding. These enterprises selected by the Chinese government are inevitably state-owned, controlled, or affiliated or national champions. Some subcontracts may be extended to other local or Chinese enterprises at the discretion of the contracted enterprises (sometimes with the state's own choices). Most contracts stipulate the maximum number of Chinese workers so that some local workers are employed, but the majority of the managerial and technical personnel are Chinese.

This synchronicity has shown no sign of eroding or retreating in the past decade. Given the steady economic growth and accelerating accumulation of capital, China believes it is crossing the river nicely. China's fast and efficient response to the global financial crisis in 2007 and 2008 and results yielded thus far in its two-pronged state-directed approach (i.e., massive stimulations and investment in infrastructure, and massive bank loans) has only served to reinforce this form of CMC and the stone-feeling methodology.

## The CMC in the Marketplace and Its Costs

The CMC of China, while exercising rigorous political control over personnel, organizations, and capital of economic entities, paradoxically offers extensive flexibility to the local governments and firms. Since the late 1970s when reform began, the Chinese government has implemented a decentralization process by which regional and local governments, first in rural areas and later in urban areas, have been delegated fiscal and administrative responsibilities to engage the market (Lin, 1995; Lin and Ye, 1998; Oi,

1992; Walder, 1994). Local governments in turn have sponsored firms, first as collectives and later as stockholding companies and other corporate forms, to compete in the marketplace. Oi (1992; 1995) recognized them as newly configured local-state-sponsored corporate entities (local-state corporatism).

Rather than as temporary or transitional entities, this pyramidal structure of a political authority at the top and market-oriented parts below has become typical in much of the country in the past two decades. In general, the central party-state delegates much fiscal and administrative authority to the regional and local governments (Zhang, 2006). Likewise, governments, central or local, delegate much fiscal and administrative authority to firms. The extent of such delegation varies widely from region to region and between governments and firms. It is pyramidal because the central political authority is largely invisible and seemingly far away in the marketplace where local governments and firms operate. But CMC in substance is more like an octopus; the central authority affords the local governments and firms the flexibility to reach every corner of the market locally, domestically, and globally and expects the firms to be nimble, efficient, and competitive. The firms, as capitalistic entities, secure and accumulate resources, organize resources in the production process, recruit cheap labour, and explore and exploit markets where they can compete advantageously.

We may describe the relationships between the centre and the local and the local and the market as 'fuzzy relationships'. Some of the fuzziness is unintended, as rules of the game have not been developed (Che and Qian, 1998). However, much of the fuzziness is intended so that governments and firms can maintain their flexibility to compete in the marketplace. Also, partly due to the delegation of authority and the fuzziness of relationships, firms show tremendous variations in their organization, 'ownership', shareholders, involvement of foreign companies, etc. Nee and Yang (1999) observed a hybrid form of firms and thought it might be a sign of a transitional economy. But as Meyer and Lu (2005) and others show there may be indefinite forms and boundaries of Chinese firms as the economy in China advances. As a firm grows, it tends to create other firms, to gain leverage in multiple markets (domestic and overseas). Such reproduction of firms may be both lateral — to different markets, and vertical — taking aim at specific sub-markets. These firms can vary in organizational forms, the structure of ownerships, types of stakeholders, etc. Such conglomerated forms and institutions, however, are not unique to China; similar corporate entities can be found in Korea, Taiwan, and the Middle East. Rather than family-led as in those regions, Chinese entities (including state-affiliated business groups, see White *et al.*, 2008) are guided by the political apparatus from the top down and yet organized as dynamic economic firms in the marketplace. This political-top and market-bottom corporate form offers two types of incentives for the local governments and firms. It offers fiscal incentives to the local entities (Jin *et al.*, 2005; Meyer *et al.*, 2002), as profit-making guides the formation and operation of firms. Just as importantly, performance in the marketplace is an important criterion for political promotions for the executives (Li and Zhou, 2005; Zhou, 2007).

The loose coupling and fuzziness of the fiscal and administrative link between the centre and the local governments create opportunities for the local governments to mimic the central party-state hierarchy and its managed capitalism. They also act like capitalists. These local governments organize their own party-state capitalism — locally managed capitalism. Governments and bureaucratic branches seek sources of revenues (e.g., land development) and establish their sponsored or affiliated firms in the marketplace. Firms compete and seek profits and governments extract or share the profits. Firms, likewise, are allowed to establish more firms in multiple markets or sub-markets. Firm executives are evaluated for their economic performances and afforded opportunities to move up to the local party and government's hierarchy of positions. Ultimately and theoretically, the local governments and firms are all part of CMC, under the political command of the central party-state. In reality, the local governments and firms gain a degree of administration and fiscal autonomy and siphon off surplus values or profits to fulfil their own needs and interests.

## Challenges to CMC

In addition to the potential problems detailed above, CMC faces other serious challenges both endogenous to the political-economy system and exogenous to the system. Synchronicity of the state and corporate interests makes it much harder to control and flush out corruption and nepotism. Corruption has become a deep and pervasive problem, penetrating the bureaucracy from the top to the bottom. Recent cases against top party cadres in Guangdong, Zhejiang, and Chongqing as well as various ministries of the central government have demonstrated the seriousness of the matter and the determination of the party to root out corruption. However, revelations regarding the top leaders in the party's Central Disciplinary Investigation Commission as well as top cadres in both the central government and several regional and local governments and parties suggest that the problem has worsened and has penetrated to the core of the party in recent years.

It is widely known that many corporate and government cadres siphoned off money and fled abroad. Take the capital city, Beijing, as an example. Beijing Municipal People's Procuratorate's Office announced in 2008 that the number of party officials fleeing China had reached between 16,000 and 18,000 since the mid-1990s, taking over 800 billion Yuan overseas. The money was misappropriated primarily from major projects such as land development, tax revenue, loans from financial institutions, funds allocated for government expenditures, and national economic programmes. In the past 30 years Beijing Municipal People's Procuratorate prosecuted over 16,000 cases of corruption and bribery (Xinhua Net, 2009). In Chongqing, the newly appointed party secretary, Bao Xilai, initiated a massive campaign against corruption in the municipal government and found deep-rooted corruption and crime even in the core agencies such as the police force.

The party's Central Disciplinary Investigation Commission holds the primary responsibility for upholding party members' behaviour and discipline, and counteracting their corruption. Confronting the problem of cadre corruption, in 2006 it issued regulations 'regarding leading cadres' reporting of their personal significant events' (News Release, 2009). The regular report includes events such as marriages, going abroad for private purposes, spouse and children living abroad, and spouse and children engaging in business abroad. Realizing that there were some serious gaps, the Commission reissued the regulations in September 2009 and added houses owned, investments, and spouse and children's job situations. Furthermore, the Commission focuses on cases of cadres involved in corruption, business and commercial bribing, implications in 'group or collective accidents', and in activities damaging public interests. Such anticorruption measures seem to follow the 'feeling stones to cross the river' approach as well — installing measures as corruption is discovered.

Social stability has also been problematic. The country responded well to the natural disaster of the Sichuan earthquake, but the violent ethnic protests and clashes in Tibet and Xingjian indicate deep-seated ethnic and religious problems that place the party and the state in an awkward position. Following the Stalinist model, China designated Tibet and Xingjian (along with Ningxia, Inner Mongolia, and Guanxi) as autonomous ethnic regions rather than conventional provinces. The ostensible purpose was to respect and sustain the linguistic, cultural, religious, and other values of the dominant minorities. However, the political leadership (party secretary) has always been in the hands of Han cadres (the only exception was a brief stint of Seypidin Eziz in Xinjiang 1973-1978). Ethnic Uighur and Tibetan officials have served as chairmen of the regional governments, a secondary nominal leadership. The Dalai Lama's escape and the exile government in India have allowed international connections for the local resistance. Likewise, Uighur's connections to Uighurstan communities in Kazakhstan, Kyrgyzstan, Mongolia, Uzbekistan, Turkey, and other central Asian countries occasionally evoke the call for an East Turkistan state.

These historical institutions seem difficult to reverse. It would be dangerous for these autonomous regions to revert back to provincial status as the minorities would surely and strongly oppose.

Yet to date the party has shown little confidence in yielding party leadership to minority cadres. In the meantime, massive immigration of Han people into these regions has further aggravated ethnic tensions as the minorities see them as non-natives who intend to infringe on their land and natural resources and take over better jobs and the economy. These Hans, having achieved critical mass, have also become more aggressive in their confrontations with the minorities. It is becoming increasingly difficult to seal off these regions from the outside world as the Internet, camera phones, and other devices record and transmit news of confrontations swiftly and effectively through security to reach the outside world. Protests and violent clashes with authority are not limited to the border regions. Unemployment, land disputes, complaints about local officials' corruption and injustice, ruthless handling of appeals and protests, and numerous other issues have fanned hundreds of thousands of such protests and clashes throughout the country each year.

## Legitimizing CMC: From Marxism to Economic Growth and Social Stability

Confronting these serious challenges, the Communist Party is reaching a fork in the road where it must make choices. A critical and fundamental element in the choices is the ideological basis on which the party legitimizes its dictatorial rule and demands for mass support. From its inception, the ideological guide of the Chinese party-state has been the Marx-Lenin-Mao doctrine of communism and socialism. In the early period of the People's Republic, the Marxist-Leninist Soviet Union ideology guided institutional creation and development. The Soviet model guided every phase of society, ranging from urban-rural segregation and an emphasis on building heavy industry, to rearrangements of educational systems from nursery school to higher education, the work unit as the core in society and for all urban residents, and, most of all, the supremacy of the party. The ideology focused on class struggle in China, rooting out all bourgeois classes and individuals, and on reducing private properties and inequality to the minimum.

This ideology and its implementation culminated in the ultimate societal struggle and catastrophe of the Cultural Revolution in which the ideology became a pretence for all factions who were desperately trying to preserve their survival by reducing and eliminating their (and the peoples') enemies. Deng Xiaoping's initiatives in rural reform were the beginning of pragmatically moving away from this ideology. Deng understood that it would be impossible to do away with the ideology as it would shake the foundation of all institutions and bring a vacancy that invites chaos and disorder. He chose to redirect the ideology, not to another ideology but rather to pragmatism — seeking truth from practice. His famous saying ('crossing the river by touching stones') reflected not only his approach of pulling away from the prevailing but failing ideology, but also his philosophical stance: let us not argue ideologically and let us be guided by what works. What he wanted was a modern China ('the four modernizations') — a China that was rich, self-sustaining, stable, and orderly. Steps in reform slowly did away with the Stalinist institutions (e.g., reforms in schools and higher education, unequal pay, increasing private property and ownership, and democratic attempts — the big-letter wall newspapers, although this failed because it went too far). Even when the reforms were too extreme and the society was on the verge of challenging the official ideology (e.g., the June 4 Tiananmen struggle in 1989), Deng continued to push his pragmatic approach of reform by giving his blessing to the economic developments in the South.

Avoiding confrontation with the official ideology, his successors have continued the pragmatic approach in economic reforms. Institutional reforms have brought about enormous strides in eliminating large portions of inefficient state enterprises. Instead of vacating the economic sphere to a private sector, the party leaders took steps to rebuild public corporations that could compete in the world market, while retaining and strengthening the party's control of the government and the economy. With favourable foreign trade, cheap and massive labour, and an influx of investments and manufacturing factories from Taiwan and Hong Kong, the government devised policies of protecting domestic enterprises by blocking off certain key sectors from foreign corporations and opening up joint ventures where state-controlled and affiliated enterprises could take advantage of foreign capital and learn from foreign management and technology. China survived the Southeast Asian financial crisis of the late 1990s and weathered the world financial crisis of 2007-2008. While other countries suffered, China gained by comparison. The 'trade rather than aid' foreign policy allows China to avoid any political and ideological traps and apply Deng's pragmatism to dealing with other countries.

By all measures, this subtle but important pushing away from the Marxist ideology towards a centrally managed capitalistic programme has been a success. Coupled with the call for social stability ('harmonious society'), the party-state has used these two pillars to justify its centralized authority. Giving the people a share of the growing wealth and a sense of social security, the party-state hopes to gain their approval and support for this party-state dictatorship. Yet these two pillars, economic growth and social security, represent pragmatic programmes — they are operating mechanisms. Their associations with the party-state dictatorship are ideological rather than theoretical or logical derivations. Many countries have attained both economic growth and social stability without a party-state dictatorship. Parting ways with Marxist ideology is historically subversive and organizationally disruptive, yet a transformation of ideology is needed to keep the two pillars on solid theoretical ground and provide justification for the authority of the party-state in CMC without rupturing the party's roots in Marxism. In the following, I identify three ideological paths and speculate that China is exploring one ideology — the indigenous Confucian ideology.

## Transforming Ideology: Towards *Xiaokang* and *Datong*?

China, it seems to me, or CMC, is faced with three possible ideological alternatives: subscribing to the western or the Dutch-British-American capitalism, committing a transition towards the mature stage of socialism, or moving towards an indigenous-based enlightened authoritarianism — *Xiaokang* and *Datong*. The first alternative is risky not only because it is deemed as likely to bring about instability and slow and inefficient responses to changes and opportunities, but it might fatally up-end the one-party state. It would have to come about through violent revolution.

Both the second and third alternatives are viable ideologies in China. In fact, there has been a tendency in official pronouncements and documents to mix the two: the primary stage of socialism, describing the present era, is a stage where productive forces are unleashed to achieve national wealth and prosperity for all and where a harmonious society with fairness and justice is obtained — *Xiaokang*. The following will explore these two ideological alternatives and assess their relative viability.

While the party leadership continues to claim Marxism as its ideological guide and add some indigenous idioms (Deng's pragmatism, Jiang's 'three principles', and an insistence that this is the primary stage of socialism), a new evolution of the ideology has begun to emerge (Lin, 2008). This was first mentioned by Deng in 1979 when he indicated that for China modernization meant *Xiaokang* (see a recent narrative linking *Xiaokang* and *Datong* to Deng Xiaoping's thoughts: Wang, 2003). Over two millennia ago, Confucian scholars compiled and narrated two visions of societal development in the Book of Rites. These two visionary societies both purportedly existed in ancient times. In fact, they were both idealistic societies. In the earliest of times, it was claimed, there was a world of great harmony, *Datong*. In *Datong*, the ultimate way, the world (authority) belongs to the public, where the wise and able are elected, trust and harmony prevail, and men care not only for their kin but for all. After *Datong* vanished, it was purportedly replaced by a more modest society, a society of good living and wealth, *Xiaokang*. In *Xiaokang* the world belongs to the family (authority became inherited), society achieves moderate prosperity by following moral principles (propriety and justice) regulated by institutions, with all individuals claiming their rightful places in the hierarchical society (e.g., emperor-official, father-son, among brothers, and husband-wife relations) and performing their rightful duties for their own benefits. The state defends the society. Wise men, who follow moral principles, are trustworthy, and exercise legal authority are in charge of the state. Those in authority who do not follow these principles can be removed and are viewed by the people as pariahs.

It is clear that in Deng's conception the primary stage of socialism substantially overlaps with *Xiaokang*, where the principal goal is achieving a certain level of overall prosperity while society maintains stability and harmony under the leadership of the party-state (Lin, 2008; Wang, 2003). The significance of this indigenizing socialist ideology cannot be overlooked. *Xiaokang* stresses order, harmony, and respect for authority and concern for all. These principles are consistent with the visions outlined for the primary stage of socialism. At the macro level, they legitimate the authority of the state and the party based not so much on political ideology as on their wise and competent management of society's well-being and peoples' desire for better lives. At the micro level they expect that indigenously valued social relations and morality will promote and sustain harmony.

Deng, however, interpreted *Xiaokang* narrowly, strictly in terms of economic growth and equality. His 1979 vision of *Xiaokang* was attaining a GDP of US$1,000 per capita.[4] In 1990 the 5 year plan added that 'the so-called *Xiaokang* level indicates the elevation of the quality of life from minimal requirement of food and shelter to sufficient comfort in clothing and food' (China.com.cn, 2002). By early 2000 most of the economic and social indicators that Deng had suggested in 1979 as goals for modernization, or *Xiaokang*, had been achieved, with the exception of income equality. Yet *Xiaokang* has remained a focal rhetoric, widely cited in all important official documents and in the 5 year plans. In 2002 Jiang Zemin outlined the plan for the construction of the *Xiaokang* society over the next 20 years: 'We should concentrate efforts to fully construct a still higher level of *Xiaokang* society, so that the economy will be further developed, democracy comprehensive and healthy, science and education more advanced, culture more prosperous, society more harmonious, and people's living richer' (China.com.cn, 2002). Thus *Xiaokang* was extended from mere economic goals to economic, political, sociocultural, and technological goals.

Left unsaid was the fact that the linkage of *Xiaokang* and the primary stage of socialism could imply that both are transformational stages towards the mature stage of socialism. Also left unsaid was the articulation or theorization of the operational mechanism whereby the present form of capitalism can be transformed into socialism in which most, if not all, capital belongs to the state or the public. To justify the rhetorical silence, in February 2007 Wen Jiabao emphasized that China would remain at the primary stage of socialism for generations, perhaps for 100 years (Wen, 2007). The goals for socialism were not only to unleash productive forces, but also to create social fairness and justice in a 'prosperous, strong, democratic, civilized and harmonious modern socialist society' (Xinhua Net, 2007). Thus Deng's economic goals, the releasing of productive forces and the creation of wealth, have now been supplemented by the social and political goals of fairness and justice, and even democracy. With these expanded goals, *Xiaokang* will not be fully attained in 20 years as envisioned by Deng or another 20 years as advocated by Jiang, but rather not for another 100 years. In this long view, the articulation of the transformational mechanism from CMC to 'mature' socialism can likewise be postponed for generations. This postponement, I suggest, indicates more than reluctance on the part of the leadership to deal with a difficult theoretical issue. Rather, it represents a strategic decision to create space and time allowing for a possible ideological transformation. Would *Xiaokang* lead to *Datong* rather than mature socialism? We take a closer look at the political institutions depicted in these two narratives in order to gain some clues.

In *Datong*, 'all under the heaven are shared (authority is not inherited); the wise and the able are elected; and faith and harmony are advocated' (Wang, 2003). It is a system clearly based on democracy in order to achieve harmony. It is a society that is ruled by the wise and the able through elections, and where individuals care not only for their kin but for all; wealth is not hidden by individuals but shared; behaviour is not motivated by the self but by others as well; and all disadvantaged (the childless elderly, the widowed, the orphaned, the handicapped, and the sick) are taken care of. In other words, in this society democracy brings about wise and able leaders and harmonious social relations through generalized trust and norms of reciprocity.

In lieu of such a democratic, trusting, and reciprocal society, *Xiaokang* is a society where 'all under the heaven are for the self' (inheritance and succession rule) and everyone is expected to care for him/herself. Rites, rituals, and norms, however, are institutionalized: 'rituals (I, or propriety) and justice (yi) bind individuals'. Institutions define social relations (between the emperor and officials, between father and sons, among brothers, and between husband and wife), and property (land and communities). All resources and efforts are for oneself, the wise and the brave are esteemed, and the faithful are rewarded. Thus 'strategies are used and military confrontations arise' (Wang, 2003). *Xiaokang* offers six ancient wise emperors (all succeeded by sons) as exemplary because they followed rituals (propriety) and justice in rewarding and punishing their subjects. 'If any emperor does not follow rituals and justice, he can be removed and despised by the people' (*Xiaokang*). *Xiaokang* depicts a social system that is principally authoritarian but allows for the promotion of self-interest. It is a combination of authority and capitalism. Under wise and able leaders, the society is hierarchical and orderly.

We need to remember that these narratives were constructed over 2,000 years ago and are steeped and bound in Chinese history and culture. They are not theoretical in the contemporary and scientific sense. Nevertheless, they provide typologies and identify elements of theories. These narratives indeed suggest that CMC is closer to *Xiaokang* than *Datong*. Authority is recognized, but its legitimacy is based on its upholding of moral principles and institutions and its respect for self-interest. It is under these conditions that wealth is obtained and social order maintained. It is not far-fetched to view such an explication as legitimizing the authority of the Communist Party in Chinese society. Instead of insisting on the fundamental need to retain class struggle as the core principle, it can now be argued that only under the wise and able Communist Party's leadership can China strive for better economic and social well-being.

The Marxist rhetoric remains pervasive in official speeches and documents, but the increasing emphasis and attention paid to

*Xiaokang* as a vision is subtle but important. *Xiaokang* is an indigenous ideology deeply engrained in the Chinese culture, universally admired by the Chinese, and espoused by Deng, a highly esteemed pioneering leader who heralded reform and brought new life to the party and state in China. An ultimate break from Marxism may not be necessary in the near future as the primary stage of socialism and therefore *Xiaokang* may last for generations. In the meantime, the ideological strategy has been to link *Xiaokang* to socialism. Deng was quoted as saying, 'Without socialism, *Xiaokang* cannot be realized in China'. Furthermore, constructing the *Xiaokang* society has been identified as the task of the 'historical mission' of the primary stage of socialism (Wang, 2003).

## The Transforming CMC: Democratization?

Interestingly, China may have already attained the *Xiaokang* scenario. CMC represents a combination of authority and self-interest. A system is principally in place where occupants in most authority positions can be removed if they do not follow moral rules and institutions and if they are despised by the people. By the beginning of the twenty-first century, most of the economic indicators envisioned by Deng had been attained. The only goal yet to be attained is 'common prosperity' (共同富裕, or sharing of prosperity). 'Common prosperity' may be interpreted as the elimination of poverty, the elimination of the income gap, or the sharing of wealth by society. One path to common prosperity is to move from the primary to the mature stage of socialism in which private ownership of property is eliminated. Even if one ignores the impractical reality of appropriating the growing number of private properties and accepts that it would take 'one hundred years' to make the transition, what is the theory or proposed mechanisms guiding such a transition? So far there has been a total lack of substantive discussion on such a theory.

On the other hand, will the system follow the ideological path from *Xiaokang* to *Datong,* as conjectured in the ancient texts? This evolution depends on the development of democracy where authority is not inherited and instead is delegated to the wise and the able by election. It is obvious such a struggle for democracy and *Datong* is a path that is politically treacherous, arduous, and distant. Yet the movement in that direction may be already underway and detectable. Democracy may have been an indigenous notion in utopian societies. It also happens to be one salient element in contemporary capitalism. As articulated elsewhere, democracy is not a necessary causal element for the development of capitalism, but capitalism does enhance the development of democracy (Lin, 2008). Growing capitalism creates wealth among more and more individuals who desire that their voices be heard and demands be met. Markets benefit from moral principles and institutions. Income equality may be an unattainable goal, but reduction of income inequality and poverty is a key ideal for upholding the social order. All these features of capitalism increase the common peoples' desire for direct or indirect participation in deciding who occupies the authority positions. As managers of the CMC, the leadership of the Communist Party has increasingly been under pressure to recognize and meet these demands. It is therefore not surprising that calls for democratic processes can be heard at all levels.

The discussions and debates about democracy all carefully draw on the writings of Deng and link democracy to socialism. For example, in 2004 Hu Jintao pronounced that 'developing democratic socialism is always a goal of our struggle. We have clearly pointed out that if there is no democracy there is no socialism ... Good institutions of democratic socialism guarantee people's rights in democratic elections, democratic decision making, and democratic supervision' (Xinhua Net, 2004). Note the causal implication that democracy is a necessary condition of socialism in this statement. Xie (2008), a former vice president of Renmin University, elaborated on democratic socialism. He stated that Deng's argument that one goal of *Xiaokang*, to have wealth shared by all, reflected the true merit of socialism — not to get rid of wealthy individuals but to elevate those who do not have wealth (i.e., the working class) so that they can attain wealth. Thus, rather than class struggle, which Xie felt deviated from the original and true intent of Marx, democratic socialism advocated eliminating inequality by elevating the wealth of the poor. In March 2008 Wen Jiabao suggested that the Chinese government was prepared to expand 'socialist democracy' under the leadership of the party: 'We will expand people's democracy, improve democratic institutions, diversify its forms and expand its channels and we will carry out democratic elections, decision making, administration, and oversight'. Such reforms would also include strengthening administrative oversight, fighting corruption, and creating a more efficient government that is ruled by law (Associated Press, 2008).

However, counterattacks came swiftly and emphatically. On February 9, 2009, the *People's Daily* published an editorial titled 'China Will Never Adopt the Multiparty System' (People's Daily,

2009). It insisted that the multiparty system in the West is an institution of capitalism that allows capital and political power to be held by the ruling class. The system would also increase social fragmentation and disharmony, the author claimed. Wu Bangguo, chairman of the Standing Committee of the National People's Congress, stated in his report to the Congress meeting on March 9, 2009, that China will never copy 'tricks' from the West: multiple parties taking turns in holding power, separation of powers, or two separate legislative chambers (China.com.cn, 2009).

These counteroffensives from authoritative sources did not suppress the voice for democracy. Within 2 months, in May 2009, Peng and Xin (2009), retired deputy editorial chief and deputy director of public relations of Xinhua, authored an article titled 'The Spirits of May Fourth and the Universal Values' that pointed out that the true spirit of the May Fourth Movement was that people are the masters and that practice follows the truth. Both principles, they observed, were imported. Past mistakes were made because these principles were not followed. They further noted, without identifying the source, that 'some individual' had made the statement about not adopting tricks from the West, but 'others' criticized this person and this statement for committing the same mistake of not allowing democracy and not understanding the truth. They further pointed out that these democratic and open discussions had not been reprimanded by the top leaders. The authors concluded that China may be turning away from the historical mistake of dictatorship and returning to the spirit of May Fourth.

In the latest party congress held in September 2009, the concluding statement advocated that the party must be close to the people 'by blood and flesh.' Among the important decisions made were: promotion of democracy within the party, consolidation of the party at the basic level, and insistence on rooting out corruption. These calls for democracy within the party and in general have seen modest but significant results. As mentioned earlier, the party now demands that all top cadres periodically report assets of all family members and accounts abroad. A web site has been created (http://www.12388.gov.cn) for reporting corruption at the central and local levels. The party is studying a new election procedure to select delegations to its congress — the number of delegations assigned to each province and city, for example, would be proportional to their membership size.

The media has gained leverage in reporting corruption cases and has demanded government transparency. An official truck driver in Shanghai was recently waved down by a person who sought a ride and offered the driver a fee. The driver was then arrested for accepting a bribe. As it turned out, the rider was an agent planted by a local government agency. The driver appealed to the media, which reported the story. The local government soon announced in a press conference that the rider was indeed part of a larger 'fishing' scheme and the incident should not have occurred. In the past, the government would have rarely retracted such a case, let alone in a press conference. In the media this case is held up as a demonstration of governmental transparency.

Grassroots democracy is reflected in various forms of civil society. For example, religious groups continue to grow in number and size. A recent estimate put the number of Christians (Protestants and Catholics) at 100-125 million (probably including household church members). The number of believers in Buddhism, Taoism, Islam, and other faiths has also seen modest to significant growth. In comparison, the Communist Party claims a membership of 74 million. Another rapidly developing grassroots democratic movement is the rising number of home-owners associations in urban cities. Since most housing became privatized in 1994, the Ministry of Construction called for the formation of associations of residential neighbourhood's property owners and occupants; numerous associations have since been formed voluntarily. According to Read (2008), by the end of 2003 there were 4,756 homeowners committees in Shanghai. Many of the associations were inactive or passive; others are subject to the command of neighbourhood committees or property developers. Yet Li (2008) argued that homeowners associations are gradually learning to assert themselves, and the three parties (i.e., the homeowners associations, the neighbourhood committees, and property developers) now engage in power relations. As the homeowners associations gain their independence, learn how to form effective leadership and collectivity, and create networks with resourceful governmental and other agencies as well as other homeowners associations, they will likely become a uniquely powerful organized civil society in urban China.

Village head elections (with multiple candidates), another grass-roots democratic process, began some 20 years ago, probably in the Buyun township in Sichuan (O'Brien and Li, 2000). By now most villages have village committees and most committees elect their members (one estimate put the number at 95%). How the elections are conducted varies greatly. Whether and how the elections can be elevated to levels of townships and counties is still under debate and study within the Communist Party. One thing is clear: the electoral process for finding grass-roots leaders will slowly but surely proceed. Wen Jiabao proclaimed that China would 'resolutely advance in democracy, including direct elections', even though he did not mention possible elections beyond the village level (Fong, 2005).

In short, democratic demands and practices have emerged at all levels of Chinese society. They do meet resistance, either for ideological or self-preservation reasons, but for the past 2 years they have increased in volume and strength. Of particular interest is the increasing volume of discussion on democracy within the party. Some capitalistic and democratic societies (e.g., Japan) have a dominant political party in which multiple factions compete. These within-party factions do not differ substantially on ideology. Rather they may represent social demarcations (e.g., rural versus urban interests, religious groups, professional or occupational groups, regional interests, etc.). Becoming the major faction in a particular election depends on both endogenous (e.g., charismatic leaders, demographic shifts, and mobility) and exogenous (economic conditions, external challenges, and natural or man-made disasters) factors. Given the nature of the party-state status, this process would seem less risky and more viable in the near future for China.

## Conclusion: The Future of Chinese Capitalism

For the past three centuries industrialized states in North America and Western Europe have equipped themselves with political, military, and economic powers and organized large international corporations. Espousing the ideology of liberal capitalism

— free markets and free competition — these states, through their international corporations, have been able to exploit and appropriate resources around the world and accumulate and reproduce capital. The emergence of state capitalism since the 1970s reflects the awareness of third-world countries of the need to preserve and protect their resources from being appropriated by first-world capitalist states. Using the state's control over valued resources, they have been able to resist such external appropriation and build their own large corporations (e.g., national champions). In the 1990s these self-preserving capitalistic states have been joined by post-socialistic states such as China and Russia. Now state capitalism not only affords these states the preservation of valued resources, but also the organization of large and capital- rich corporations (including the SWFs) competing in the world market.

In this essay I have placed China among these state capitalism countries and highlighted one sustaining trend in current Chinese capitalism: the continuing consolidation of state capitalism tightly managed by the party-state (the CMC). The CMC in part reflects the character of state socialism from the past — central command of the economy. But in contrast to the expectation that as China moves towards a capitalistic state the central command institutions will erode, for more than two decades we have witnessed further consolidation of state power over both politics and the economy.

Centrally managed capitalism is not set in stone. I have speculated in this essay that the Communist Party has increasingly justified its dictatorial leadership for the sake of maintaining economic growth and social stability. By arguing that China is at the primary stage of socialism and introducing the indigenous ideology of *Xiaokang,* the party attempts to convince the Chinese people that it is necessary to maintain party authority and to engage in capitalistic measures at the same time. I argue that the party is facing a choice of either articulating the mechanism by which the primary stage of socialism will transition into the mature stage of socialism — turning private capital into public capital — or allowing the process of democracy to unfold as anticipated by *Datong* and capitalism. Having noted the absence of proposals for such a transitional theory of socialism but more calls and enactment of democracy, I speculate a slow but firm infusion of democratic elements will occur at every level.

It is too early to tell how these transformations, indigenizing the ideology and incorporating democratic practices both inside the party and at the grass-roots level, may affect the viability of CMC. The ideal solution for the Communist Party and those in power is a CMC with a democratic character, just as it has acquired a capitalistic character. This may be a risky and treacherous process, but lacking an alternative (i.e., moving towards the mature stage of socialism and eliminating non-public capital), the party must try. If successful, this ultimately transformed CMC can reduce tension with liberal capitalism and provide a more stable paradigm of state capitalism. If it fails, it will bring chaos and upheaval 'under the heaven' (天下大乱), and turn the political and economic order of the world upside down. There is an urgent need for scholars and theoreticians to contemplate whether and how *Datong*, in its modern form, can mix with socialism. In the meantime, the Communist Party will carefully manage the transformation so that it will not bring about the worst scenario — its downfall from power. What we can thus expect is that the party will use its tried-and-true methodology of crossing the river by touching the stones.

## *Notes*

I am grateful for comments and suggestions on earlier versions from Yanjie Bian, David Brady, Qiushi Feng, Joe Galaskiewicz, Choyun Hsu, Lisa Keister, Steve McDonald, Marshall W. Meyer, William Parish, Jordan Siegel, Joon-mo Son, Lijun Song, Edward Tiryankian, Marty Whyte, Yanlong Zhang, and an anonymous reviewer.

1. Excluded from this discussion of the crisis-cycle thesis is the possibility that the state, due to debts, weakened military power and other deficiencies, cannot rescue the financial crisis. Ferguson (2010) argues that imperial collapse may come much more suddenly than many historians imagine and warns that a combination of fiscal deficits and military overstretch might bring about the sudden demise of the US as an empire.

2. All Chinese names mentioned in the article are based on last name first.

3. The nature of Shagang Steel, like most large 'private' enterprises, is ambiguous. Typical among the Su-Nan model firms, the company was originally a collective enterprise under the jurisdiction of the city of Zhang-Jia-Gang. Shen Wen-rong was appointed as the CEO and party secretary in 1984. Through his able leadership the steel company expanded quickly, and in 2002 it reduced the shares of the city (the collective) to 25% while employees (30%) and leaders (45%, including Shen's own share of 17%) became the majority owners. Two years later, Shen further reduced the collective share and increased his own share to 30%. He remains the party secretary as well as the CEO of the company and was quoted as saying, 'Foreign reporters think I do not speak like an entrepreneur, and more like a party member. Well, I am a party member so I speak like a party member'.

4. In 1982 Deng also stated (Selective Works of Deng Xiaoping, vol. 3, p. 64) that 'the so-called goal of *Xiaokang* is to reach a GDP of US$800 by the end of the century'.

## References


Amsden, Alice H. 1992. *Asia's next giant: South Korea and late industrialization*. New York: Oxford University Press.

Anderlini, Jamil. 2009. "Beijing sidelines top dairy executive." *Financial Times*, 4 September. [Last accessed 15 September 2010.] <http://www.ft.com/cms/s/0/ad62c95a- 98e9-11de-aa1b-00144feabdc0.html.>

_______. 2010. "China: The Wild West with razor-thin margins." *Financial Times*, 21 June.

Associated Press. 2008. "Wen Jiaobao says no democracy in PRC for 100 years." 28 February.

Braudel, Fernand. 1977. *Afterthoughts on Material Civilization and Capitalism*. Baltimore, MD: Johns Hopkins University Press.

Bremmer, Ian. 2009. *The End of the Free Market: Who Wins the War between States and Corporations?* New York: Portfolio.

Che, Jiahua and Yingyi Qian. 1998. "Insecure property rights and government ownership of firms." *The Quarterly Journal of Economics* 113(2): 467-496.

Chen, Shu-Ching Jean. 2006. "China's first son keeps low, goes global." *Forbes*, 13 December. [Last accessed 15 September 2010.] <http://www.forbes.com/2006/12/13/hu-haifeng-china-markets-equity-cx_jc_1213autofacescan02.html.>

China.com.cn. 2002. "The origin of Xiao-kang." 30 December 2002. (In Chinese).

_______. 2009. "Wu Bangguo: China will never practice multiple-party rotations, three branches, etc." 9 March. (In Chinese).

Cumings, Bruce. 1987. "The origins and development of the northeast Asian political economy: Industrial sectors, product cycles, and political consequences." pp. 44-83 in *The Political Economy of the New Asian Industrialization*, edited by F. C. Deyo. Ithaca, NY: Cornell University Press.

Deyo, Frederic C., ed. 1987. *The Political Economy of the New Asian Industrialism*. Ithaca, NY: Cornell University Press.

Dwnews. 2009. "Hu Haifeng, Hu Jintao's son, controls near ten billion yuan of Tsing-hua asset." 16 March. (In Chinese).

Elegant, Simon and A. Ramzy. 2009. "China's new deal: Modernizing the Middle Kingdom." *Time,* 1 June. [Last accessed 15 September 2010.] <http://www.time.com/time/magazine/article/0,9171,1900245,00.html.>

Evans, Peter. 1995. *Embedded Autonomy*. Princeton, NJ: Princeton University Press.

Evans, Peter., Dietrich Rueschemeyer, and Theda Skocpal, eds. 2002. *Bringing the State Back in*. New York: Cambridge University Press.

Ferguson, N. 2010. "Complexity and Collapse: Empires on the Edge of Chaos." *Foreign Affairs* 89(2): 18-32.

Financial Times. 2010. "China: To the money born." 29 March. [Last accessed 15 September 2010.] <http://www.ft.com/cms/s/0/e3e51a48-3b5d-11df-b622- 00144feabdc0.html.>

Fligstein, Neil. 2005. "States, markets, and economic growth." pp. 119-143 in *The Economic Sociology of Capitalism,* edited by V. Nee and R. Swedberg. Princeton, NJ: Princeton University Press.

Fong, T.-H. 2005. "China looks to democracy to cure its ills." *Asian Times,* 20 September. [Last accessed 15 September 2010.] <http://www.atimes.com/atimes/China/ GI20Ad01.html.>

Friedman, Thomas L. 2009. "Have a nice day." *New York Times,* 15 September. [Last accessed 15 September 2010.] <http://www.nytimes.com/2009/09/16/opinion/ 16friedman.html.>

Gerschenkron, Alexander. 1962. *Economic Backwardness in Historical Perspective*. Cambridge, MA: Belknap Press of Harvard University Press.

Heilbroner, Robert. 1985. *The Nature and Logic of Capitalism*. New York: W. W. Norton.

Hille, Kathrin. 2009. "Google warned on China plans." *Financial Times,* 5 September. [Last accessed 15 September 2010.] <http://www.ft.com/cms/s/2/310ccbe2-b915-11df- 99be-00144feabdc0.html.>

Hobson, John M. 1997. *The Wealth of States*. Cambridge: Cambridge University Press.

Jin, Hehui, Yingyi Qian, and Barry Weingast. 2005. "Regional decentralization and fiscal incentives: Federalism, Chinese style."

*Journal of Public Economics* 89(9-10): 1719-1742.

Johnson, Chalmers. 1995. *Japan: Who Governs?: The Rise of the Development State*. New York: W. W. Norton.

Kahn, C. 2009. "Chinese solar plant expected to be the biggest Chinese solar plant." *Associated Press*, 8 September. [Last accessed 15 September 2010.] <http:// www.msnbc.msn.com/id/32737729.>

Krugman, Paul. 2009. "How did economists get it so wrong?" *New York Times*, 2 September. [Last accessed 15 September 2010.] <http:// www.nytimes.com/2009/09/06/ magazine/06Economic-t.html.>

Lachmann, Richard. 2000. *Capitalists in Spite of Themselves*. New York: Oxford University Press.

Li, Youmei. 2008. "Community governance: The micro basis of civil society." *Social Sciences in China* 29(1): 132-141.

Li, Hongbin and Li-An Zhou. 2005. "Political turnover and economic performance: The incentive role of personnel control in china." *Journal of Public Economics* 89(10): 1743-1762.

Lie, John. 1998. *Han Unbound: The Political Economy of South Korea*. Stanford, CA: Stanford University Press.

Lin, Nan. 1995. "Local market socialism: Local corporatism in action in rural China." *Theory and Society* 24: 301-354.

_______. 2008. "Emerging Chinese capitalism and its theoretical and global implications." *Social Transformations in Chinese Societies* 3: 13-62.

Lin, Nan and Xiaolan Ye. 1998. "Chinese rural enterprises in transformation: The end of the beginning." *Issues & Studies* 34(11): 1-28.

McGinnis, Ariel, James Pellegrin, Yin Shum, Jason Teo, and Judy Wu. 2009. "The Sichuan Earthquake and the changing landscape of CSR in China." *Lauder Global Business Insight Report 2009: First-Hand Perspectives on the Global Economy*. 9-11.

Mead, Walter R. 2009. "The debt we owe the Dutch." *Newsweek*, 18 April. [Last accessed 15 September 2010.] <http://www. newsweek.com/2009/04/17/the-debt-we-owe-the- dutch.html.>

Meyer, Marshall W. and Xiaohui Lu. 2005. "Managing indefinite boundaries: The strategy and structure of a Chinese business firm."

*Management and Organizational Review* 1(1): 57-86.

Meyer, Marshall W., Yuan Lu, Hailin Lan, and Xiaohui Lu. 2002. "Decentralized enterprise reform: Notes on the transformation of state-owned enterprises." pp. 241-273 in *The Management of Enterprises in the People's Republic of China,* edited by Anne S. Tsui and Chung-Ming Lau. Boston: Kluwer Academic/ Plenum.

Minsky, Hyman. 2008. *Stabilizing an Unstable Economy*. Vol. 1. New York: McGraw-Hill.

Nee, Victor. 1989. "A theory of market transition: From redistribution to markets in state socialism." *American Sociological Review* 54: 663-681.

_______. 1996. "The emergence of a market society: Changing mechanisms of stratification in China." *The American Journal of Sociology* 101(4): 908-949.

Nee, Victor and Chun Yang. 1999. "Path dependent societal transformation: Stratification in hybrid mixed economies." *Theory and Society* 28: 799-834.

Nee, Victor, O. Sonja, and W. Sonia. 2007. "Developmental state and corporate governance in China." *Management and Organization Review* 3(1): 19-53.

News Release. 2009. "Central disciplinary commission." Cadre reporting personal events emphasized. 23 September.

O'Brien, Kevin J. and Lianjiang Li. 2000. "Accommodating 'democracy' in a one-party state: Introducing village elections in china." *The China Quarterly* 162: 465-489.

Oi, Jean. 1992. "Fiscal reform and the economic foundations of local state corporatism in China." *World Politics* 45(1): 99-126.

_______. 1995. "The role of the local state in China's transitional economy." *The China Quarterly* 144: 1134-1149.

Onis, Ziya. 1991. "The logic of the developmental state." *Comparative Politics* 24(1): 109-126.

Peng, D. and Q. Xin. 2009. "May fourth spirit: Universal values." *Yan Huang Chun Qiu,* 11 May.

People's Daily. 2009. "China will not adopt the western multiple party system." 9 February.

Polanyi, Karl. 1944. *The Great Transformation*. Boston: Beacon Press.

Polanyi, Karl, Conrad M. Arensberg, and Harry W. Pearson. 1957. *Trade Market in the Early Empires*. Glencoe, IL: The Free Press.

Rand, Ayn. 1966. *Capitalism: The Unknown Ideal*. New York: The New American Library.

Read, Benjamin L. 2008. "Assessing variation in civil society organizations: China's homeowners associations in comparative perspective." *Comparative Political Studies* 41(9): 1240-1263.

Rosovsky, Henry. 1961. *Capital Formation in Japan 1968-1940*. New York: Free Press.

Schmidt, Vivien A. 2002. *The Future of European Capitalism*. Oxford: Oxford University Press.

Skocpal, Theda. 1996. "Unraveling from above." *The American Prospect* 25(March-April): 20-25.

Sun, L. H. 1992. "China's secret personnel files: A tool of communist control." *The Washington Post*, 17 May.

The Economist. 2010. "China's financial system: Red mist." 4 February. [Last accessed 15 September 2010.] <http://www.economist.com/node/15453014?story_id=15453014.>

Wade, Robert. 1990. *Governing the Market: Economic Theory and the Role of Government in East Asian Industrialization*. Princeton, NJ: Princeton University Press.

Walder, Andrew G. 1994. "Corporate organization and local government property rights." pp. 53-66 in *Changing Political Economies: Privatization in Post-Communist and Reforming Communist States*, edited by V. Milor. Boulder, CO: Lynne Rienner Publishers.

Wallerstein, Immanuel. 1979. *The Capitalist World-Economy*. Cambridge: Cambridge University Press.

Wang, S. 2003. "The thought of well-off society: Deng Xiaoping's transcendence from the thought of general harmony in modern China." *Journal of Tongji University Social Science Section*, December 20.

Weiss, Linda. 1998. *The Myth of Powerless State*. Ithaca, NY: Cornell University Press.

Wen, Jiabao. 2007. "Our Historical Tasks at the Primary Stage of

Socialism and Several Issues Concerning China's Foreign Policy." *People's Daily*, February 27.

White, R. E., Hoskisson, R. E., Yiu, D. W., and Bruton, G. D. 2008. "Employment and market innovation in Chinese business group affiliated firms: The role of group control systems." *Management and Organization Review* 4(2): 225-256.

Wong, Joseph. 2004. "The adaptive developmental state in East Asia." *Journal of East Asian Studies* 4: 345-362.

Xie, T. 2008. "Only democratic socialism can save China." *China Elections and Governance*, 22 January. [Last accessed 15 September 2010.] <http://www.chinaelections. net/newsinfo.asp?newsid=14848.>

Xinhua Net. 2004. "Hu calls for developing Socialist Democracy." 21 September. [Last accessed 15 September 2010.] <http://news.xinhuanet.com/english/2004-09/21/content_2001652.htm.>

_______. 2007. "Our historical tasks at the primary state of socialism and several issues concerning China's foreign policy." 8 March. [Last accessed 15 September 2010.] <http://ug.china-embassy.org/eng/xwdt/t302141.htm.>

_______. 2009. "Central disciplinary power growing." 22 May.

Zhang, Xiaoke. 2006. "Fiscal decentralization and political centralization in China: Implications for growth and inequality." *Journal of Comparative Economics* 34: 713-726.

Zhou, Li-An. 2007. "Governing China's local officials: An analysis of promotion tournament model." *Economic Research Journal* 7(42): 36-50.

Chapter 6

# State Neoliberalism: The Chinese Road to Capitalism in Comparative Perspective

Alvin Y. So and Yin-Wah Chu

Since the advent of the twenty-first century, researchers have acknowledged the strength and vibrancy of the market economy that is emerging in China. The short story is that, despite the country's commitment to socialism (at least in name) and the ruling party's appellation as the Chinese Communist Party, capitalism has flourished, and the ceaseless drive for capital accumulation is unmistakably present in the Chinese economy. As a result, the term capitalism has gained increasing currency in works analyzing China's post-socialist development (Hsing, 1998; Guthrie, 1999; Huang, 2008; McNally, 2011; 2012; Tsai, 2007).

However, most of these works eschew direct comparisons of China with other forms of capitalism found in Japan, Europe and North America. As McNally (2011: 1) points out, part of this omission stems from the fact that the Chinese road to capitalism is highly complex, multifaceted, and by no means completed. There are also considerable conceptual difficulties in placing China in the larger comparative context of "Varieties of Capitalism" (Hall and

Soskice, 2001). Nevertheless, China seems to be producing a new variety of capitalism, albeit a variety that still continues to evolve.

The aim of this paper is to identify the main elements of this new variety of capitalism within the context of the Chinese domestic political economy, thus providing the first step to examine China's emergent capitalism what we label as "*state neoliberalism.*" We first compare the similarities and differences between state neoliberalism in China with other varieties of capitalism in the South, in the West, and in post-socialist Eastern Europe. Then we identify the distinctive characteristics of state neoliberalism, and how it engenders a ceaseless drive of capital accumulation, which propels China from a poor, third world country in the 1970s to an economic powerhouse of the capitalist world-economy in the twenty-first century. At the end of this paper, we will discuss the future prospect for state neoliberalism in China.

## China and Developmental State Capitalism in the South

Like other developmental states in East Asia, China has strong state machinery. The Chinese state is highly autonomous in the sense that it is not "captured" by vested economic interests. The old generation of capitalists was largely destroyed in the Communist Revolution and later in the Cultural Revolution. The nascent capitalist class that has recently emerged in the market reforms of the 1980s and 1990s was too weak and too dependent on the state to pose any challenge. In addition, the Chinese state has the capacity to carry out its developmental plans. Since it owns the banks and controls the financial sector, it has powerful policy tools at its disposal which makes the cooperation of indigenous business more likely: access to cheap credit, protection from external competition, and assisted access to export markets are all levers that the Chinese state can use to ensure business compliance with governmental goals. Since the Chinese corporations have high debt/equity ratio, even the threat of withdrawal of state loans would be serious.

Second, like other developmental states in East Asia, the Chinese state has actively intervened in the economy. The state has become the engine powering capital accumulation. Aside from debt finance and infrastructure construction, the Chinese central state also develops plans for strategic development, decrees prices and regulates the movement of capital, and shares risks and underwrites research and development. At the local level, Jean Oi (1992) coins the term "local state corporatism" to describe how village, county, municipal, and provincial governments use their political authority single-mindedly to promote local capitalist development. In Zouping, for example, local cadres raised the initial capital for new enterprises and closely supervised and assisted in their subsequent growth. Using their political authority they mobilized capital for investment, arranged and allocated credit, and provided market information and technical expertise well in excess of what was initially present in the locality. In the above process, local governments have taken on many characteristics of a business corporation with local state officials acting as the equivalent of a board of directors.

Third, like other developmental states in East Asia, the Chinese state has actively mobilized the ideology of nationalism and defines itself as carrying out a national project to make China strong and powerful. In the post-reform era, China was experiencing an ideological vacuum since the state could no longer be legitimized by Marxism or communism. Thus, nationalism became the state's only hope to get the support of the Chinese masses. The Chinese state seems to believe that the best response is to build a strong sense of national cohesiveness based on cultural heritage and tradition rather than to develop a nationalism based solely on hostility toward the outside world.

Fourth, like other developmental states in East Asia, the Chinese state adopts authoritarian policies to discipline labor, suppress labor protests, and to deactivate civil society in order to maintain a favorable environment to attract foreign investment and to facilitate capital accumulation. It seems authoritarianism is unavoidable in export-led industrialization because labor subordination is an important means to cheapen labor and to make the working class docile. Otherwise, the exports of the East Asian developmental states would not be competitive in the world-economy, and transnational corporations would not relocate their labor-intensive production to East Asia. It is ironic that the Chinese state, with its tightly organized Leninist party-state machinery, has proven to be very effective in co-opting labor activists, dividing the working class, and silencing labor protests.

Finally, like other developmental states in East Asia, China received an influx of capital during its initial phase of capitalist industrialization. During the Cold War era in the 1950s and the1960s, the massive influx of US aid, loans, and contracts greatly helped East Asian states (South Korea, Taiwan) to solve the problem of initial accumulation and had greatly enhanced their states' capacity to promote developmental policies. The US, of course, would not provide similar aid, loans, and contracts to communist China to assist its developmental program after the fading of the Cold War in the 1980s and the 1990s. Fortunately, there was a comparable influx of Chinese diaspora investment to China at the initial phase of transition to provide capital for initial accumulation. Before 1978, Chinese diaspora capitalism thrived in Hong Kong, Taiwan, Singapore, and overseas Chinese communities. After the Chinese state adopted an open door policy for foreign investment, Hong Kong accounted for the bulk of China's foreign investment and foreign trade. In the early 1990s, Hong Kong firms employed over 3 million workers in the Pearl River Delta. By the end of the 1980s, Taiwan became the second largest trading partner and investor for Mainland China. In the 1990s, overseas Chinese entrepreneurs in Southeast Asia have shown a visible interest in conducting trade and investment in China.

Nevertheless, China state developmental capitalism has also shown a significant difference from that of other East Asian states, especially the Chinese developmental state has exhibited a strong tendency towards neoliberalism.

## China and Neoliberal Capitalism in the West

Before the late 1970s, capitalism in the West took the form of what David Harvey (2005) called "*embedded liberalism.*" In order to solve the acute economic and social problems created by the unfettered market during the 1930s depression, the advanced capitalist state had to take a more active role in managing the economy to provide full employment as well as to avoid wide upswings and downswings of the market. In embedded liberalism, the state is taking on more and more roles (like providing more welfare and social services, strengthening workers' trade unions, imposing more regulations on the market, and imposing higher taxes on the capitalist class). Thus, capital was induced to compromise and have a new social contract with the working class, and capital was embedded in a web of social and political constraints and in a new regulatory regime that serve to constraint its "greedy" profit making behavior. After World War II, a variety of liberal, social democratic welfare states emerged in Western Europe and the US that exemplify this embedded liberalism trend.

According to Harvey (2005), "*neoliberalism*" is a new class project through which the capitalist class fights back against the policies of embedded liberalism. On one hand, neoliberal reforms aim to liberalize markets so that the capitalist class fights back against the high taxes and strict regulations of the state as well as the "rigidities" imposed by the state and the trade union on production relations. On the one hand, neoliberal reforms aim to liberalize markets so that members of the capitalist class have more freedom to hire and fire workers and expand their trading and investment within and beyond national boundaries. From the late 1970s onwards, neoliberal reforms have entailed deregulation, privatization, and the marketization of social services. It is also widely agreed that neoliberalism as a philosophy or ideology seeks to downsize or confine the role of the state to that of establishing and expanding markets. Thus Harvey (2005: 7) uses the term "neoliberal state" to refer to "a state apparatus whose fundamental mission was to facilitate conditions for profitable capital accumulation on the part of both domestic and foreign capital."

In the West, neoliberalism emerged in advanced capitalist societies where both the state and the capitalist class were the two most powerful players in their societies. Neoliberalism was a new project prompted by members of the capitalist class who wanted to revamp the unfettered market when confronted by a crisis of capital accumulation in the 1970s. As "neoliberalism" replaces "embedded liberalism," state-market relations shift from a situation of state domination to one of market domination.

The historical context through which neoliberalism emerged in China, however, was totally different from that in the North. China was a state socialist country where property was predominantly owned by the state and the Collective. In addition, China in the early 1970s had just gone through a devastating Cultural Revolution, the primary aim of which was to suppress the capitalist market and to destroy the capitalist class. Thus, the private sector was almost non-existent and the capitalist class was very weak at the onset of the reform. The market institution, therefore, had to be constructed from almost nothing. In this scenario, which agent had the capacity to re-create the market institution in 1970s China in the aftermath of the Cultural Revolution, where anti-capitalist sentiment was still very strong?

Whereas the capitalist class has been the dominant agency for neoliberalism in the West, the communist party-state had to take the driving seat to propel neoliberalism forward in China. During the initial stage of the reforms, the communist party-state did carry out neoliberal policy progressively because in China, as in other countries in capitalist world-system, the impulse to carry out neoliberal reforms was irresistible when the state faced the crisis of capital accumulation in the 1970s and the 1980s. Thus, the Chinese communist party-state started the reforms to reinvent and to liberate the market from the state as well as to re-integrate China into the capitalist world-economy in order to speed up capital accumulation. It was with the above mindset that the Chinese state leaders carried out the following policies during the late 1970s and the 1980s:

### Decollectivization

In the countryside, agricultural communes were dismantled in favor of an individualized "household responsibility system." Peasant families were given plots of land to cultivate, and they were responsible for their own gains and losses. They were also encouraged to sell their products to rural markets, engage in rural industries, and seek work in nearby township enterprises. Township and village enterprises (TVEs) were created out of the former commune assets, and these became centers of entrepreneurialism, flexible labor practices, and open market competition.

### Proletarianization of Peasants

At the same time, the loss of collective social rights in the countryside meant the peasants had to face burdensome user charges for schools, medical care, and the like. Forced to seek work elsewhere after the end of collectivism, rural migrants flooded — illegally and without the right of residency — into the cities to form an immense labor reserve (a "floating population" of indeterminate legal status). China is now in the midst of the largest mass migration the world has ever seen (Chan, 2003). This rural "floating population" is vulnerable to super-exploitation and puts downward pressure on the wages of urban workers (Pun, 1999).

## Marketization Policy to Restore/Expand the Market

A new labor market was introduced to the Chinese economy in the late 1980s, creating a flexible labor force that is responsive to the ups and downs of the market. After a labor market was set up, the state enterprises were no longer required to provide life-long employment and job security to their workers, and were given the autonomy to hire and fire workers in the name of enhancing productivity and efficiency as called upon by neoliberalism.

## Fiscal Decentralization and the Weakening of the Central State

In the mid-1980s provincial, municipality, county, and township governments were subject to a bottom-up revenue-sharing system that required localities to submit only a portion of the revenues to the upper level, and then they were allowed to retain all, or at least most, of the remainder. This fiscal decentralization policy made local states become independent fiscal entities that had the unprecedented right to use the revenue they retained. As a result, fiscal decentralization had considerably weakened the central state's extractive capacity in the early phase of market reforms in the 1980s. The Chinese state was unable to control the extra-budgetary funds of the local governments, and its relative share of tax revenues had decreased to the extent that the Central state has lost effective control over China's economic life (Wang, 1997; Oi, 1992).

## Opening Up and Spatial Differentiation

There was an open-door policy toward foreign investments. It began with the establishment of four special economic zones (SEZs) in 1979, the opening of 14 coastal cities and Hainan Island in 1984, and the extension to three delta areas (Pearl River Delta, Yangtze River Delta, and Yellow River Delta) in 1985. The combination of decentralization and opening up has led to a very uneven pattern of spatial development in China, with rapid economic growth taking place mostly along the eastern coastal sub-regions. These sub-regions were characterized by an "*extrovert*" economy, i.e., their economies were driven by foreign direct investment and export-led industrialization, and their economic growth relied upon their integration with the global commodity chains (Chen, 2005).

Through the above processes of decollectivization and proletarianization, marketization, fiscal decentralization, opening up and spatial differentiation, China was clearly moving toward the neoliberal capitalist model. On the one hand, the state was being downsized and state capacity was being weakened. On the other hand, the private sector and the various (labor, capital, and finance) markets were expanding rapidly and the Chinese economy was quickly reintegrated with the capitalist world-economy.

## China and Neoliberal Reforms in Post-Socialist Eastern Europe

Chinese state neoliberalism also differs from the neoliberal market reforms that took place in post-socialist Eastern Europe, in the following ways. In the first place, market reforms like "shock therapy" and mass privatization undertaken in Eastern Europe had the *goals* of dismantling communism and stripping communists of power and privileges. However, in China, neoliberal market reforms were intended to allow the communist party-state to survive as an instrument of economic development (Walder, 1996).

Furthermore, the *speed of market reforms* was also different. Unlike the "big bang" and "shock therapy" approaches practiced in Eastern Europe, which called for the dismantling of the centrally planned economy and the building up of neoliberal market institutions as quickly as possible; in China there was no rapid leap to free prices, currency convertibility or cutting of state subsidies; nor was there massive privatization and the quick selling off of state enterprises. The neoliberal market reforms in China have been a gradual, adaptive process without a clear blueprint. John McMillan and Barry Naughton (1992) remark that China's market reforms proceeded by trial and error, with frequent mid-course corrections and reversals of policy.

In other words, the Chinese economic reforms were not a completed project settled in the first stage, but an ongoing process with many adjustments, like two steps forward and one step backward, or one step forward and two steps backward. The Chinese reformers are often said to be highly pragmatic: If the market reforms work, they are continued. On the other hand, if the reforms are not working, the communist party-state would quickly delay, modify, or even reverse the reform process. Thus, the Chinese reforms are often highly contradictory, ambiguous, incomplete, and still in the process of transformation. As such, what explain the emergence of a ceaseless drive to capital accumulation, which has transformed China from a poor third world country to an economic powerhouse in the world-economy?

## State Neoliberalism and the Ceaseless Drive of Capital Accumulation

In the late 1970s, market reforms started when the communist party-state initiated a new reward system for the state officials. Mao's prohibition on material incentive was quickly repudiated. Instead, the party-state adopted *"economic development success" as the primary indicator for determining compensation* of local officials. Those leaders of localities or enterprises that performed well economically were given sizeable monetary rewards in recognition of this success (Oi, 1992). That explains why local officials are so eager to initiate new development projects under their jurisdiction; such projects not only bring revenue and jobs to their region, but they themselves would also get handsome merit increases and career advancement in the Chinese bureaucracy.

Thus, the drive to capital accumulation started at the local level, not at the central level. Starting in the early 1980s, large numbers of formally centrally administered state enterprises were transferred to provincial and lower levels of administration (building on the decentralization waves of the Mao era). Local officials were encouraged to try new ways to promote economic development of their locality. They were gave them full authority and a free hand to make market decisions (so-called *administrative decentralization*).

In addition, subordinate governments entered contractual agreements with higher levels specifying the amount of revenue the lower level had to turn over to the next higher level. Local officials were assured that if their local economic projects were successful, they did not need to be remitted the increased revenue to higher levels (as had been the case before), but they could the increased revenue locally to stimulate economic development, supply public goods, and fulfill other purposes (so-called *fiscal decentralization*).

Similar arrangements were adopted for production enterprises in their relations with their supervising levels of government. Furthermore, enterprise responsibilities for pensions and other welfare benefits for their employees and retirees began to be taken over by pooled funds supervised by local governments in a move designed to allow enterprises to concentrate on their core economic activities.

As a consequences of these policy changes, Whyte (2009) points out, local government and enterprises were provided with a relatively secure set of administrative and fiscal arrangements that enabled them to concentrate on pursuing new market opportunities and developing their economies.

However, firms and local governments also knew very well that if they lost money they would no longer be bailed out by higher levels, thus *forcing them to face market competition* in a structure imposing relatively hard budget constraints.

Once administrative and fiscal decentralizations were set up, localities and enterprises that were relatively slow to pursue new market opportunities could readily observe how they were falling behind the prosperity of their neighbors, and the resulting envy stimulated increased effort to copy the successful market-oriented policies and institutions of the front-runners. The combination of financial rewards for local officials for success in economic development and increased public revenues generated by local firms provided powerful incentives to quickly adopt practices suited to operating in the market environment.

Thus Whyte (2009: 381) concludes that "the hectic market competition among local firms and governments unleashed by these changes was a fundamental source of China's new economic dynamism." Making a related point, Gabriella Montinola and her colleagues (1996) suggested that policies of administrative and fiscal decentralization constitute what they called "federalism, Chinese style." They generated not only economic dynamism of capital accumulation but also political protection from intervention by the central government, which rendered the economic reform durable (cf. Cai and Treisman, 2006; Shirk, 1993).

## State Neoliberalism in China: Distinctive Characteristics

Drawing from the above comparative analysis, we now can delineate the following distinctive characteristics of state neoliberalism (which is quite different from other varieties of capitalism in the contemporary world-economy).

At the surface, state neoliberalism seems to be similar to developmental state capitalism in East Asia because it has a strong state which intervenes in the economy to promote export-led industrialization. But in China, the state is the communist party-state; and Chinese capitalism belongs to the genre of "neoliberalism" which calls for the liberalization of the market, the downsizing of the state; and the empowerment of the capitalist class.

Thus, first and most fundamentally, state neoliberalism identifies the *communist party-state as the dominant agent to promote neoliberalism* as part of its strategy to facilitate national development. Apart from launching many standard developmental state supports, the Chinese state endorsed neoliberalism so that an increasing number of commodities were subjected to market principles, workers and natural resources were exposed to ruthless capitalist exploitation, and many state enterprises in the non-strategic sector were privatized. In so doing, China also differed from neoliberal capitalism in the West in that it is the communist party-state, not the capitalists, who initiated the neoliberal turn. Indeed, before the initiation of policy change in state socialist China in 1978, market relations were strongly suppressed by the state, property was predominantly state-owned or collectively owned, market institutions were rudimentary, and a capitalist class was practically nonexistent. The communist party-state laid the groundwork for the emergence of neoliberal capitalism by carving out a space for the emergence of market relations, the birth of a capitalist class, and for a long time played an instrumental role in the imposition of blatant neoliberal practices. Unlike neoliberal capitalism in the West (where capital accumulation serves as the ultimate motive to drive the economy), the constant ebb and flow of neoliberal practices in China was often governed by the communist party-state's overriding concern for its survival and continued leadership.

Second, the Chinese road to capitalism has been distinguished by its *decentralization policies and local initiatives*. Benefiting from the state socialist legacy of localized administration as well as brigade and commune enterprises, local governments and TVEs (township and village enterprises) played a pivotal role in China's capitalist development, especially in its initial phase in the 1980s. Administrative and fiscal decentralization policies had generated both the institutional foundation and immense incentives (and pressures) for these local actors to capture market opportunities. This is why the Chinese local economy was so competitive in the early 1980s even though the communist party-state had yet to institute legal reforms to safeguard private property rights.

The importance of local governments and their interactions with the state center had exerted other far-reaching impacts on China's path of development. First, local support had provided a counterweight to "the conservatives" and allowed China to undertake economic reforms without initiating liberal political reforms, hence enabling China to travel a path distinct from the one followed by the Soviet Union and Eastern Europe.

Inter-local competitions have interacted with central party-state's policies to determine the trajectory of development in local areas. As different localities try out a different way of market activities (like the Donguan model designed to attract foreign capital in the Pearl River Delta, the Suzhou model in the Yangtze River Delta which was based on state investment, and the Wenzhou model in the mountainous area which was well-known in mobilizing local, private capital), it results in a variety of paths toward capitalist development at the subnational level (Shen, 2015). This pattern of local-central relationship has limitation for capitalist development too. For example, in the case of technology upgrading, even though the central government had poured enormous resources into high-tech research and development, it did not result in any breakthrough in *novel-product innovation*. Instead, structural uncertainties interacted with the concerns of local governments, leading the latter to collaborate with foreign enterprises and engage in a lower-level *organization and process innovation* (Breznitz and Murphree, 2011).

This pattern of central-local relationships also provided a specific way for the Chinese communist party-state to deflect social and political conflicts that emerged in the course of capitalist development. Specifically, labor, land, and environmental conflicts were often tackled by local governments and enterprises, with the central government taking the moral high ground and assuming the role of the final (and benevolent) arbitrator when necessary. Protesters tend to blame the corruption and mismanagement of local state officials rather than the neoliberal policy of the central party-state. Thus, the formation of a bifurcated state (local versus central government) has allowed the communist party-state to deflect the core conflicts emerged in the course of neoliberal development (So, 2013).

Third, the notion of state neoliberalism was also coined to highlight the state's continued label itself as the *communist* party-state while pursuing *neoliberal capitalism*. As in most societies, neoliberal practices give rise to all sorts of social conflicts between the dominant groups and the subordinate ones such as workers, peasants, and the middle class. In China, social conflict was complicated by the party-state's gradual and hesitant policy changes. The dispossessions of the workers and peasants have until now been incomplete and peasants have only partially turned into workers (i.e. there has been partial proletarianization). On top of this, the communist party-state continues to declare itself the defender of peasants and workers and, so long as it sustains this façade, it has found it difficult to defend neoliberal policies at the ideological level. As a result, social actors and segments of the state elite whose material and cultural interests were threatened by the neoliberal reforms could well use the inherent contradictions of state-initiated neoliberal reforms to challenge the party-state itself.

Finally, state neoliberalism also points to a different form of entrepreneurship in doing business in China. For a long time, the emerging capitalist class remained weak, needed to take heed of state policies in order to delineate its market strategies, and often depended on the state for survival. In China, entrepreneurship often requires the capitalists to develop a *personalized, clientelistic* relationship with local state managers. Without a good connection with local state managers, the capitalists may find it difficult to protect their business from the predatory practices of the local labor bureau or the local tax bureau. The capitalists also need the support from local state managers to get access to resources (like getting a bank loan, a business permit, a piece of market information, etc.). Xiao (2015) reports that "No matter what you do in China, can you get anywhere without official approvals? With the possible exception of North Korea, China is the hardest place to do business because you can't get permission to operate or access to markets without political ties. This has been especially true over the past two decades or so." Christopher McNally tries to capture this close relationship between local state and business by labeling China as "*guanxi capitalism*." McNally (2011: 3) explains that this political guanxi network between private entrepreneurs and the institutions and agents of the local party-state "bridge the logics of free-wheeling private capital accumulation and authoritarian control in a state-dominated economy."

In sum, we characterized China's road to capitalism as "state neoliberalism," which is distinguished by the following traits:

(1) Centrality of the party-state but decentralization of the local states at the subnational level
(2) Gradualism and a zigzag path of development between statism and market liberalization
(3) The personalized, clientelistic relationship between capitalists and local state managers
(4) Pushing blatant neoliberal practices but still claims itself as a communist party-state.

Obviously, state neoliberalism is a highly contradictory term, and the Chinese road to capitalism is a hybrid of contradictory, constant shifting policies embedded in a set of contradictory institutions that defies any easy characterization.

## Whither the Chinese Road to Capitalism

The fact that the China communist party-state could manage the challenges of capitalist development quite well at the initial phase of its post-socialist transition during 1978-2014 does not mean that the Chinese road to capitalism will be all smooth from now on. After going through aninitial phase of what can be called "*catching up*" over the past forty years, China now has reached a turning point and will move on to a mature phase of what can be called "*rising power*" in the twenty-first century. This mature phase will involve the following set of new challenges.

### The Challenge of Maintaining the Hyper-Growth Rate

China has attained truly remarkable economic growth over the past three decades, but there are signs beginning in the early 2010s that the Chinese economy is slowing down (or de-acceleration), as the global economic recession continues into the 2010s, as China begins to use up its valuable resources, as China's environment is reaching the point of ecological breakdown, as China's population is aging and its workforce shrinking, and as China is unable to achieve novel product innovation and move up to the top of the value-added hierarchy in the commodity chain. China needs an annual 7-8% GDP growth rate in order to provide enough jobs for the new job seekers every year, or it will have to face a lot of grievances and social unrest from the unemployed young generation. But as the Chinese economy matures and as it has exhausted the potential of an export-led industrialization which is dominated by labor-intensive industries, it will be a real challenge for China to continue the 7-8% growth rate for another decade or two.

### The Challenge of Hegemonic Struggle

The global search for raw materials (especially energy), markets, talents, and capital will inevitably bring China into conflict with major world powers. China's investments in Africa, the Middle East, and Latin America have raised many eyebrows in Europe and North America. Hostility with China's neighbors (Japan, Vietnam, and the Philippines) has also intensified over time, which is not helped by the US's policy of pivot toward the Pacific and rebalancing toward Asia. US pundits and politicians have also explored measures to prevent or to delay the rise of China (Shoup, 2015) As China's economy becomes more global, the hegemonic struggles between China and Western powers are bound to become more acute.

One aspect of the hegemonic struggle concerns whether China's rapid capitalist development will suffer from a premature death like that experienced by Japan in the 1980s. Japan was a very promising global power in the 1980s. However, when the country acceded to US pressure to raise its currency at the Plaza Accord in 1985, it went into a decade-long recession and ceased to be an engine to power the capitalist world economy. Trying to avoid Japan's mistake, China has resisted the pressure from the US and other European states to raise its currency value. It remains to be seen whether China can hold its position as the pressure for currency revaluation increases with the deepening of the 2008 global economic crisis and the de-acceleration of its economy.

## The Challenge of Changing Class Structure, the Changing Power Base of the Party-State, and Power Sharing

Rapid economic growth has resulted in the expansion of both the capitalist class and the new middle class. These rising classes will inevitably seek more power and influence, thus challenging the authority of the communist party-state. At the same time, peasants and workers, as the traditional socio-economic base of the communist party-state, have been subjected to increasing exploitation and suppression. Whether the state neoliberal strategies will continue to succeed in deflecting their dissatisfaction and gaining support for the party-state remains to be seen.

More fundamentally, the party-state has so far avoided making any changes to the political structure. Given the growing unrest in civil society and the expansion of the capitalist class and the middle class, the party-state will be under increasing pressure to initiate political restructuring, democratic reforms, and power sharing with other social classes. These changes are likely to involve radical structural changes, arouse acute political conflicts, and entail high stakes. Minxin Pei (2008), for one, is quite pessimistic about the structural transformations as he talks about the possibility of political decay and a possible "trapped transition."

Since we are now entering a period of turbulence in the capitalist world-economy, it is hard to predict whether the rise of China will continue. What we know for sure is that China has now reached a turning point to move from the initial phase of "catching up" to the mature phase of "rising power." How China handles the above new challenges will play a significant role in determining its historic fate in the near future. Furthermore, whatever China's future role might be, the country's bid for global ascendance in the capitalist world-economy will trigger more conflicts, more uncertainties, and more chaos in the twenty-first century.

## *References*

Breznitz, Dan and Michael Murphree. 2011. *Run of the Red Queen: Government, Innovation, Globalization, and Economic Growth in China*. New Haven: Yale University Press.

Cai, Hongbin and Daniel Treisman. 2006. "Did Government Decentralization Cause China's Economic Miracle?" *World Politics* 58: 505-535.

Chan, Kam Wing. 2003. "Migration in China in the Reform Era: Characteristics, Consequences, and Implications". pp. 111-135 in *China's Developmental Miracle: Origins, Transformations, and Challenges*, edited by Alvin Y. So. Armonk, NY: M. E. Sharpe.

Chen Xiangming. 2005. *As Borders Bend: Transnational Spaces on the Pacific Rim*. Lathan: Rowman & Littlefield.

Guthrie, Doug. 1999. *Dragon in a Three-Piece Suit. The Emergence of Capitalism in China*. Princeton: Princeton University Press.

Hall, Peter A. and David W. Soskice, eds. 2001. *Varieties of Capitalism: The Institutional Foundations of Comparative Advantages*. Oxford, UK: Oxford University Press.

Harvey, David. 2005. *A Brief History of Neoliberalism*. New York: Oxford University Press.

Hsing , You-tien. 1998. *Making Capitalism in China*. New York: Oxford.

Huang, Yasheng. 2008. *Capitalism with Chinese Characteristics*. Cambridge: Cambridge University Press.

McMillan, John and Barry Naughton. 1992. "How to Reform a Planned Economy: lessons from China." *Oxford Review of Economic Policy* 8: 781-807.

McNally, Christopher. 2011. "China's Changing Guanxi Capitalism: Private Entrepreneurs between Leninist Control and Relentless Accumulation." *Business and Politics* 13(2): 1-29.

________. 2012. "Sino Capitalism: China's Reemergence and the International Political Economy." *World Politics* 64: 741-776.

Montinola, Gabriella, Yingyi Qian, and Barry Weingast. 1996. "Federalism, Chinese Style: The Political Basis for Economic Success." *World Politics* 48: 50-81.

Oi, Jean. 1992. "Fiscal Reform and the Economic Foundations of Local State Corporatism in China." *World Politics* 45: 99-126.

Pei, Minxin. 2008. *China's Trapped Transition: The Limits of Developmental Autocracy*. Cambridge: Harvard University Press.

Pun, Ngai. 1999. "Becoming Dagongmei: The politics of identity and difference in Reform China." *The China Journal* 42: 1-19.

Shen, Xiaoxiao. 2015. "Institutional Adaptability in Local China: A Comparison of the Wenzhou, Dongguan, and Suzhou Models." Unpublished master thesis submitted to the Division of Social Science at Hong Kong University of Science and Technology.

Shirk, Susan L. 1993. *The Political Logic of Economic Reform in China*. Berkeley: University of California Press.

Shoup, Laurence H. 2015. "The Council on Foreign Relations and the New Grand Strategy towards China." *Monthly Review* 67(4): 12-22.

So, Alvin Y. 2013. *Class and Class Conflict in Post-Socialist China*. Singapore: World Scientific.

Tsai, Kellee. 2007. *Capitalism without Democracy: The Private Sector in Contemporary China*. Ithaca, NY: Cornell University Press.

Walder, Andrew G. 1996. *China's Transitional Economy: Interpreting Its Significance*. Oxford: Oxford University Press.

Wang, Shaoguang. 1997. "China's 1994 Fiscal Reform: An Initial Assessment." *Asian Survey* 37(9): 801-817.

Whyte, Martin King. 2009. "Paradoxes of China's Economic Boom." *Annual Review of Sociology* 35: 371-392.

Xiao, Zhonghua. 2015. "What's the Murderous Intention behind "Don't Let Li Ka-Shing Run Away"?" *China Change*, Sept 19. <http://chinachange.org/author/yaxuecao/Access on Sept 20, 2015.>

Chapter 7

# *The End of the Long Boom?: A Comparative Institutional Analysis of Long-term Growth in China*

Tobias ten Brink

## Introduction

In the last years, speculations about the coming end of the long Chinese boom are on the rise. The objective of this article is to create a nuanced picture of China's growth model. The assumption is that we need to know more about the institutional foundations for long-term growth in order to also properly address the question whether the long boom is about to come to an end.

China's GDP growth has now surpassed every other long national growth period in the history of modernity. However, although the increasing significance of market institutions is by now indisputable, and even if the People's Republic is an essential part of a world economy organised by neoliberal precepts, it retains a specific character. In the following, China's economy is analyzed as a novel, variegated form of state-permeated capitalism. Its activity is based on close, competition-driven operations between various state and domestic business alliances at the national and subnational level, not solely by an all-powerful, centralised steering bureaucracy — a stark contrast to analyses who do not distinguish the contemporary Chinese economy thoroughly from older varieties of state capitalism and developmental states (cf. Bremmer, 2010). Complementing historical "advantages of backwardness" such as an enormous reserve army of labor and productivity gains from the transformation of rural into industrial labor, mutual complementarities between different institutional spheres made for an institutional "fit" and allowed for the establishment of a very dynamic growth regime, especially from the mid-1990s into the 2010s. In addition, China benefited both from favorable coincidences related to economic dynamics in East Asia, including the importance of overseas Chinese, and from an increasing over-accumulation of capital in the North.[1]

Theoretically, this article combines institutionalist insights in Comparative Political Economy (CPE) and International Political Economy (IPE). On the one hand, I highlight the necessity of reflecting on the historical evolution of national capitalisms. On the other, I combine concepts from CPE with IPE, by placing national systems of capitalism in transnational contexts, thereby contributing to overcoming an artificial split within the political economy tradition.

The specifics of Chinese capitalism are explicated in the following way: Section 2 tackles the historical evolution of the Chinese economy, and its selective integration into the world economy. In section 3, an "inter-personal" mode of coordination in the PRC is depicted, based on private-public growth alliances, which worked both in favor of economic growth and societal stability. Section 4 deals with key institutional foundations of China's thriving capitalism. This includes strong state permeation in corporate governance and corporate finance, segmented systems of low cost, yet comparably well-educated labor, increasing innovation efforts, and company access to large domestic markets. The last section deals with both comparative advantages, resulting from an institutional "fit" in China's economy, and possibilities for destabilization of this model. For the sake of a better understanding, I will contrast my findings with other historical types of capitalism — especially liberal, coordinated, and dependent capitalisms (mostly in the Global South, but also inEast Central Europe for instance) as well as developmental states in East Asia.

## Historical Evolution and Global Insertion

An understanding of Chinese capitalism must include its historical evolution and the specific form and timing of its insertion into the global economy. Three phases of gradual reforms can roughly be identified: the period from 1978 to 1989, the period from 1992 to 2002, and from 2003 onwards. It resulted in a "functional fit" of institutions — although in line with theories of institutional change, this did not exist *ex ante*, but was discovered and developed *ex post*. In addition, the success of a selective economic opening of the economy can be demonstrated, largely guided by preferences for autonomous national development, which led to a differentiated matrix of deep integration into global trade and production networks on the one hand, and shallow integration into global capital markets on the other.

The *first phase from 1978 to 1989* resulted in a "trial and error" reform mode which led to a success of experimentation with markets and entrepreneurialism. It also included the opening of the economy towards foreign capital, and i.e. the permission of FDI, not portfolio capital, into selected Chinese spaces. However, there was no deep integration into global capital markets which is why China was among the few economies in the Global South that were not affected by the debt crises of the 1980s.

The *second phase of reform* roughly took place from 1989/1991 to 2002 and was an era of intensified, yet selective liberalization of the domestic economy, path-breaking company reforms that allowed private firms to become serious competitors on domestic markets, and accompanying reforms of the financial sector, in labor relations and in the education and science system. Thickly embedded private capitalists and "red capitalists" became critical factors. Last not least, it was after 1992, when the integration of China into the world economy was seriously accelerated, although it was still a selective integration. While tariffs were reduced, and the government opened some domestic sectors for foreign participation, the Chinese State Council, certain ministries, and local governments held important regulatory capacities at their disposal to regulate this process and to help domestic firms to keep pace with MNCs.

From its beginning, the long boom thus can be partly explained with reference to external factors. Growing foreign direct investments and their attendant export orientation are an important element here. As an investment location, China was in the immediate vicinity of the East Asian growth region and the networks of the overseas Chinese. From the 1990s on, China benefited from another special global economic constellation. Western transnational capital was desperately looking for profitable investment opportunities (Brenner, 2006). To some extent, the initial FDI of overseas Chinese thereby eased the way for the wave of FDI from Western and Japanese transnational capital. Macro-economically, the two engines of the world economy since the mid-1990s, the US and to a lesser extent China, hence achieved growth via two different, complementary and mutually dependent paths. Whereas in the US large chunks of GDP growth consisted of debt-financed consumption rather than investments, the Chinese boom was a mirror image of that in the US. Here, investments continued to grow massively from around 30% of GDP in the early 1990s to nearly 40% after 2000 (Hung, 2008).

The *third phase of reform* from 2002 up until the 2010s demonstrated the persistence, if not strengthening of non-liberal institutional dynamics. The background of a competition-driven form of (local) governance in China should not lead to any premature conclusion that the central state has been growing weaker. In fact it was precisely its instability in the first phase of reform, culminating in the crises of 1989, which lent the central government and the rule of the Party new legitimacy. One precondition of this was the rise in its extractive power: particularly since the tax reforms of 1994, the central state has been able to recentralize resources to a considerable degree. Moreover, in terms of its own modernization, several waves of bureaucratic restructuring led to strong institutions such as the Ministry of Commerce MOFCOM, or the National Development and ReformCommissionNDRC. Among others, Hu Jintao and Wen Jiabao, and later the administration led by Xi Jinping, were utilizing statist instruments to "rebalance the economy". This was due to perceived export dependencies on the one hand, and deficient domestic demand on the other (ten Brink,

2013b). It included the great economic stimulus set up after the global financial crises in 2008. Development planning remained essential to affect reforms in areas such as industrial upgrading, infrastructural construction, science and technology, human resources and education, and social welfare. Nevertheless, this was new-style development planning aimed at planning "with and for markets" (Heilmann, 2011).

As illustrated in the following, these high levels of state-permeation were largely also in the interest of Chinese business, which forged close alliances mostly with local state managers.

## Private-Public Growth Alliances: A Chinese Mode of Coordination

The Chinese economy changed enormously over the last decades, making it difficult at first sight to grasp the actual model of capitalism that emerged. Still, one can find a dominant mode of economic coordination. It worked both in favor of economic growth and societal stability. In particular, the special role of private-public growth alliances at the local level worked as stability "anchors" for the growth dynamic and for weathering significant institutional changes. The Chinese economy is coordinated by closely interwoven private-public alliances, often grounded on informality. This is different from older, bureaucratic state capitalisms, but also from other models of capitalism, which (ideal typically) are coordinated by the market and formal contracts (liberal market economies), formalized networks and associations (coordinated market economies), or hierarchies within multinational enterprises (dependent market economies). I will now introduce the workings of these private-public alliances and thickly embedded private capitalists that in fact go beyond a purely corruptive or rent-seeking setup. Rather, productive "cronyist" reciprocal relations reduce uncertainties in a quickly-changing economic environment.

Most entrepreneurship in China is thickly embedded into the party-state. This has also been a trend for the lower and medium echelons of the private sector (Chen, 2015). Both the party-state elite and businessmen have an interest in close public-private relations. Indeed, the "larger the 'sales revenue' of a firm, the more likely its owner is a Party member," and the more likely that Party organizations exist in their firms (Dickson, 2007: 852). The prevalence of closely interwoven growth alliances reflects a process that can be coined *unity in diversity*. Although China is a heterogeneous country, this dominant form of coordination based on informal and non-transparent personal relations and aligned through the common interest of national economic growth, acted as a pillar of unity and stability. It was largely unchallenged by wider social unrest in the 1990s and 2000s, achieved also via a temporal taming of labor. Moreover, it was flanked by a comparably strong central state able to regulate competition among local alliances and domestic class fractions (see below).

What made these public-private alliances work? Shared social and political backgrounds are often mentioned when looking for factors that make for intra-elite coherence in China (Li, 2010; McNally *et al.*, 2007). Reciprocal *guanxi* networks add to this, stemming from blood ties or friendly turns, and resulting in intra-family "work partition" (e.g., husband as local official, spouse as well-connected entrepreneur) and amities (e.g., cadres who have strong ties to entrepreneurs from their home towns). Furthermore, shared political backgrounds often make for a conviction in the prevalent statist and long-term-oriented developmentalism. Hence, proactive industrial policies and a preference for patient capital have a high status — even among private entrepreneurs. This is exemplified, inter alia, by individual private entrepreneurs caring "about the overall development of the private economic sector and the development of specific industries" (Chen, 2015: 624). It should therefore come as no surprise that even representatives of Chinese "venture capital," mostly known as anti-state in the West, generally accept this dominant constellation. Notably, in contrast to coordinated market economies for instance, economic coordination in China is not mainly provided by formal institutions. Business associations for private entrepreneurs exist and indeed have become more vital and autonomous from the party state over time (Kennedy, 2011), but are less significant when compared to the role of informal, personalized relations between individual entrepreneurs and state managers at different administrational levels.

Regarding special features of China's interpersonal mode of coordination, three stand out: (1) competition pressures between local alliances and managerial capacities of state actors, which also impinge on the problem of corruption, (2) the significance of an enduring strong central state to minimize socio-economic disparities and divisions between capitalist class fractions, and (3) the largely favorable role of foreign capital.

First, Although public-private growth alliances are analyzed here as representing a non-market mode of coordination, these alliances themselves are subject to competition with other alliances. Since subnational administrations in China have assumed the role of local developmental states, they attempt to build settings conducive to success by creating incentives to stimulate economic efficiency in "their" territories (for early evidence, see Walder, 1995). In this process, government officials often act entrepreneurially — and therefore are depicted as "state managers" here. At the same time, competition among state-business alliances is an important corrective against state-capturing and harmful types of corruption: In opposition to most media coverage, the overall setting in China is not predominately patrimonial. Especially local governments in prosperous regions share with their business partners the overall goals of development, upgrading and innovation to such a degree that they reduce (this is not to say they prohibit) forms of corruption detrimental to economic growth. The opportunity to successfully join in local "cronyist" growth alliances makes local politicians take entrepreneurial risks. Likewise, it fosters individual careers in the political system and within the CCP: The system of cadre-evaluation, essential for individual career paths, is mostly based on economic indicators, although some social indicators have been included lately.

Second, While local competition is of utmost importance, it is still largely *competition under hierarchy* in the last instance. With regards to the central state, the government did not just adopt capitalist growth policies and individual entrepreneurialism (ten Brink, 2013a; Yang, 2014). There was and still is another central-state role that is not to be underestimated: the provision of an overarching institutional architecture that accommodates competition among local alliances. One political strategy regularly used by the regime to gradually initiate reform was to introduce change in only a few test areas, followed by a wider introduction of the policy when the test proved successful. Despite the fact that experimentation procedures have been delegated to local authorities, the central administration in Beijing played an indispensable role in universalizing local innovations (Heilmann, 2008). The relative autonomy of the central government, in a way, enabled it to adopt policies that advanced the interests of the entire power elite without degenerating into clientelism. This is reflected in continuing debates among central policymakers and planning experts revolving around how the state could limit clientelism and corruptive groups with vested interests.

Third, Regarding the role of foreign capital, coordination in China has to take the power of international capital into account, but different from dependent market economies and other large emerging economies in which foreign capital is more dominant (Nölke *et al.*, 2015; Schneider, 2013). The economic integration of China did not lead to box domestic firms out of most dynamic manufacturing sectors. Although MNCs play a significant role, they were generally not able to influence coordination to the detriment of Chinese alliances. Rather they have tried to become part of domestic alliances. This in particular holds true for Taiwanese and Hong Kong entrepreneurs, defined as "patriotic capital" in the PRC. Many overseas Chinese have thereby been deeply integrated into the mainland economy. On another level, MNCs were inducing competitive pressures that also prevented strong rent-seeking, at least in coastal area domestic alliances.

All of this does not imply an analysis of China as a smoothly coordinated and governed entity. However, it contributes to an understanding as to why again and again internal tensions and conflicts did not erupt as severely as in 1989 or in other emerging countries, where such alliances for growth could not be forged. As political factions and capital fractions mostly share the fundamental goals of domestic socio-economic stability, a system of checks and balances has mostly kept conflicts under control.

## Key Institutional Domains

This section deals with key institutional spheres of the Chinese economy and how they each fostered growth of large national firms. At the end of each subsection, problems and potentials of destabilization are depicted.

### Corporate Governance

Ownership of Chinese companies is largely concentrated and control of big firms rests with insiders. Matching the rather decentralized structure of the country, different state levels (e.g., central, province and city level) own, control and/or invest into companies. A complicated system of mostly decentralized state ownership with important segments dominated by private property thickly embedded in the (local) political scene has emerged, including competition among state-owned firms and various forms of state involvement in business operations (McNally, 2011; Naughton, 2011). In most sectors, national capital dominates.

Many large Chinese companies are exchange-listed, and usually dominated by state block-holders. In opposition to the Maoist era and previous versions of state capitalism, there is neither a classical top-down control, nor is there a single guiding enterprise model such as *chaebols* and *keiretsu* in South Korea and Japan respectively. Rather, restructured forms of profit-oriented and competition-driven state-controlled enterprises such as China Mobile, Baosteel, or Sinopec have emerged. Additionally, private firms such as Huawei, Midea or Geely and public-private hybrids have also been able to play a significant role in development.

Although regional and sectoral heterogeneity make for an opaque system of corporate governance, the saliency of national control is astonishing. At the "top tier," refurbished SOEs continue to retain their influence, especially in sectors such as petrochemicals, telecommunications or electricity (cf. Pearson, 2011). In the "middle tier" where no natural monopolies and less strategic concerns exist — such as machinery, automobiles, chemicals, electronics as well as in cutting edge environmental, energy and other "emerging industries" — SOEs now coexist with big public-private hybrids and private firms. Nowadays, such large non-state firms are also seen as "national champions". Beneath those two dominant tiers, a great variety of small and medium, mostly private, firms exist.

Because of the strategic role of government, developments in the financial sector object against the notion of a simple adaptation of prevailing Western models. Stock markets in Shanghai and Shenzhen are no liberal markets for corporate control, and shares are only partly traded. There is rather an "insider"-dominated mode of corporate governance, as Chinese listed companies regularly have very big shareholders who are able to control the company without taking into account the influence of other shareholders. Dispersed shareholding is rare, and minority shareholders are typically disadvantaged. The management of major companies is also comparably independent from short-term fluctuations on the stock markets in

China.

Although since the 1990s, MNCs have drastically increased their prominence in the Chinese economy, they do not dominate the economy. With some notable exceptions for instance in the IT industry, which is deeply integrated into global production networks, most industrial sectors are dominated by national state-controlled, hybrid and private capital, and not by foreign multinationals. Additionally, in marked contrast to more dependent capitalisms, there is no clear sharing of tasks between MNCs (e.g., higher technology, complex manufacturing) and local companies (e.g., low-tech, simple manufacturing). Rather, as the case of the IT industry illustrates, even in foreign-dominated industries, large Chinese firms have emerged as competitors for established Western and East Asian firms.

Finally, some potential malfunctions in Chinese corporate governance have to be mentioned, ranging from assumptions about soft budget constraints leading to the support of unproductive state-owned firms, to assumptions of decreasing SOE profitability in recent years (Meissner *et al.*, 2015) and to expectations about foreign competitors increasingly outcompeting domestic Chinese firms (Brandt and Thun, 2010). Certainly, the passionate debate on whether this system is economically reasonable — which liberal authors would generally deny — or whether it is superior in the long run despite economic deficiencies at plant level — which some heterodox economists would emphasize — is far from completed.

## Finance for Investment

Most large companies in China are relatively independent from short-term volatilities on global capital markets as well as from profit expectations by transnational investors. They raise investments mainly by way of internal savings, in addition to loans by national banks, and enjoy preferential support by the state. This promotes a rather strong role for patient capital and accommodates with long term strategies of firms. The effect is to preserve favorable conditions for domestic enterprises over a longer period. In opposition to coordinated market economies (as historically in Germany), domestic banks and capital markets are more state-controlled. In contrast to liberal and dependent capitalisms, state regulation of the credit sector also limits the influence of foreign capital and thereby maintains the concentration of capital particularly within domestic fractions. This setup has served the Chinese growth strategy well in the 2000s in actively allocating capital towards investment in industry, infrastructure, real estate, and increasingly services.

What are the most important sources of investment in the PRC? It is neither the domestic capital markets, although they have burgeoned into the second largest in Asia (Walter and Howie, 2011). Nor are global capital markets of prime importance. The institutional characteristics of both nationally controlled enterprises as well as a rather closed financial system create incentives in which foreign investment and stock market capitalization play a minor role in investment, thus diminishing the pressure emanating from volatilities in global equity and bond markets. Foreign bank share in China never exceeded 2% in the 2000s and after (CBRC, 2012).

The Chinese economy has been integrated into global product markets, yet the financial sector largely was not. Partly because of this peculiar structure, the financial sector has come through the global financial crisis comparatively well.

Instead, national firms primarily use internal funds for their operations. This facilitates autonomous, and often long-term business strategies which would be less possible if firms were to rely more on (foreign) shareholders. Especially the largest domestic firms additionally finance investment via bank credit. Approximately 85% of external loans for very large firms come from the "Big 5" state banks, other commercial banks and city banks (NBS, 2012). Reform policies thereby led to also provide loans for sino-foreign Joint Ventures (e.g., in automobiles) and private firms (e.g., in real estate or IT). The tipping point is no more if SOE or not but rather is a firm profitable and has it capabilities to pay back. (Note that the size and heterogeneity of China makes for a much more complex reality than that covered here).

Again, this was conducive to long-term strategies of many large firms. While short-term loans doubled between 2005 and 2010, long term-loans more than tripled (NBS, 2012: Table 20-2). Beyond lending practices on paper, bank loans to enterprises are in fact often state credit lines, which both make for strategic advantages over global credit markets due to e.g. longer credit maturities and/or lower interest rates. Similarly, this gives state institutions at different state levels a certain "grip" on companies. Furthermore, other direct and indirect state support especially at the local level such as cheap land, informal preferential credits, and tax rebates contributed to very favourable financing conditions. In contrast, smaller firms on the fringe strongly rely on informal sources as they are disadvantaged by prevailing lending policies (see Allen *et al.*, 2011).

All in all, the Chinese investment regime served the national development strategy of supporting domestic growth by any means and of creating "national champions" for industrial development, while also increasing their regional and global influence. However, state-permeation also creates considerable problems. Whereas in Western economies banks sometimes refused to lend money, China still deals with the economic consequences of its highly expansionary credit policy after 2008. As a result, since 2010 problems of bad loans and over-investment emerged that cannot be easily confined. A housing bubble in urban housing markets also exemplifies this (ten Brink, 2013b).

## Labor Relations

In China, state actors arrange for the preservation of a low wage regime, very often though by *not* intervening into business misconduct. Industrial relations are mostly regulated at the firm level, which is very different from a sector-corporatist model. They show parallels to liberal economies, which also feature firm level regulation, yet differences are observable with respect to lower wages, less worker protection and a larger informal sector. This regime was supported, inter alia, by a continuous supply of cheap rural labor power and de facto state preservation of low wages, often through the selective non-enforcement of labor standards which often only sound comprehensive on paper.

China's industrial structure is the product of its gradual transformation into a party-state mediated, class-divided society (Chan,

2015). A low wage regime, based on a segmentation and segregation of the labor force proves to be a key motor of accumulation and made for significant labor cost advantages. Note that Western MNCs producing in China are also very much benefitting from this system. Generally, labor markets are fragmented between a comparatively well-paid segment of core workers on the one side, and a larger segment of subordinated workers on the other (Lüthje *et al.*, 2013). In 2007, only about 50% of all firms had signed contracts with their employees and the rate for migrant workers was even lower (Friedman and Lee, 2010). Although the 2008 Labor Contract Law officially altered this, it is still common for workers to sign short-term contracts of under one year.

On top of this segmented wage organization comes the *segregation* of urban and migrant workers. The household registration system (*hukou*), which ties an individual's social benefits to a particular place — very much to the detriment of migrant workers — "is obviously central to the current system of sustaining super low-cost Chinese labor in the international market" (Chan and Buckingham, 2008: 604). Thus, although there exist fairly sophisticated labor laws by now, its actual implementation is weak. Moreover, the fact that wages are regulated mainly at the firm level stems from a lack of collective and cross-sector regulation of labor and social standards. Chinese trade unions, controlled by the Communist party, do not work strategically at branch or sector level, in order to curb competition between employees.

What is more, Chinese workers were not only comparably cheap, but productive. Increases in productivity thus compensated wage rises during the 2000s. A combination of low wages, heavy capital investment, positive infrastructure and transportation network externalities, new management systems, and investment in human capitalled to a historic increase in labor productivity. Indeed, China has been increasing labor productivity much faster than Brazil, South Africa, India, or any OECD country since the 1990s (Herr, 2011; Leung, 2011). Only since the early 2010s, labor productivity did not outpace the increase in wages anymore.

However, although media commentators are declaring that the era of low-wage labor has come to an end, this has certainly not been a reality for large parts of the workforce in the early 2010s. Thus, besides its economic "efficiency," the Chinese labor system constitutes a very delicate institutional equilibrium.

## Education and Training

The quality of "human capital" and its institutional fit with other segments of the economy are decisive criteria for economic development. When compared to other large emerging countries, China is the most prominent case of the economically efficient provision of human capital (Nölke *et al.*, 2015; note that this "efficiency" also includes a very low level of class mobility: Lin, 2011; Woronov, 2011). It has developed an education system in which the vast majority of the working population now receives a secondary education of 9 years or more. This even accounts for the migrant workforce (Friedman and Lee, 2010: 516). Complementing industrial relations, a fragmentation between small groups of highly qualified labor and a much larger group of less qualified labor with a focus on general skills can be depicted. Well into the 2010s, this complemented demand for mostly medium-skills. In addition, the challenges of rising demand for higher-skilled work were also addressed by political elites, although prevailing incentives by employers and workers thwart this projected transition.

The central government's aim over the 2000s of achieving a 4% education spending of GDP has nearly been achieved. While in dependent capitalisms, dominant MNCs are often not in favour of a generous tax-funded public education and training system, higher education investments led to an advanced school system in China. Although there was a rise of spending across the board, it is most pronounced in higher education. Education and spending on training is to a large degree decentralized, with large regional variations. Importantly, local state-business alliances have become key players in selective and often informally organized support to vocational training. Close relationships with local state institutions lead to the option for firms of picking interns from vocational schools, and to compatible training in areas in which allied companies are operating.

Regarding incentives, the central state strongly aims at upgrading the skill formation system. Yet, this is not always implemented at the local level. The biggest hurdle to stronger employers and employees incentives to upgrade skills significantly is the high turnover rate in Chinese industries. In such fluid labor markets — we find a similarity to liberal market economies here — the complement is a system that continues to focus on general skills because companies are unwilling to invest in advanced apprenticeship programs "imparting industry-specific skills where they have no guarantees that other firms will not simply poach their apprentices without investing on training themselves" (Hall and Soskice, 2001: 30). Although some companies started their own training programmes, however, this is mostly limited to small groups of employees in need of specialized, high-quality skills.

To summarize, the education and training system functionally benefitted the demand for low and medium skills well into the 2010s. Nevertheless, increased efforts by the state are necessary to cover the rising demand for higher skilled labor and to not remain stuck in a low or medium skill equilibrium so prevalent in Latin America (Schneider, 2013). In general, there is more competition for skilled workers and mid-level-management than for lower skilled workers. Enterprises often complain about human resource constraints in higher skilled segments and there is an oversupply of academics vis-à-vis qualified personnel from vocational education. Thus, even though the government has more power than dependent economies to make substantial investment in skill upgrading and business-state alliances may be more concerned about long term developments, the challenge is huge, as exemplified by the lack of business and worker incentives to implement efficient structures of skill upgrading.

## Innovation

Ideal typically, innovations in liberal economies are spread via markets, innovation in coordinated economies is based on intercompany cooperation, and in dependent economies it is based on intra-firm transfer in multinational firms. The Chinese system of innovation represents a state-permeated variety. It includes technology transfer and reverse engineering through, inter alia, a relatively weak, state-tolerated patent rights systems, and domestic, mostly incremental technological innovations through public support and public-private networking in selected sectors.

For a long time, China's innovation activities concentrated

on labor-intensive "imitative innovation"; hence innovation which is new to firms in China but imitative in nature. Innovation was partially achieved through technology and knowledge transfer via FDI or joint ventures. Most studies conclude, however, that technology transfer did not lead to a fundamental progress of domestic innovation capacities (Fu, 2015). This has motivated Chinese state actors to increase its public innovation policy efforts substantially (Breznitz and Murphree, 2011). R&D spending has risen to 2% of GDP recently.

State managers currently play a crucial role in providing the setting for progress in domestic innovation, for instance via tax incentives, procurement policies, standards setting, subsidies, and knowledge transfer via networks. In addition, a "combination of policies forcing technology transfer and China's failure to effectively enforce protection of foreign intellectual property rights (IPR) are also seen by many as strategic moves to give Chinese firms time and access to proprietary intellectual property (IP) in order to develop competitive domestic alternatives" (AmCham, 2011: 64).

There is increasing evidence that China has by now gone beyond imitative innovation and moved into real innovation. Although some authors show unclear causal effects of government innovation funding, it has also been demonstrated that the effectiveness of R&D subsidies has improved (Guan and Yam, 2015). Regarding the quality of "indigenous" innovation, incremental, i.e. improvements of existing technologies in existing markets, often emerging out of customization, and "really new" innovations, i.e. innovations that embody new, yet no radical new technologies, are on the rise. Most innovation is in medium-technology and rather incremental than radical. Their main advantage is at home – fitting with the demand in medium-tech products. Some spin-offs from state-run research institutes are among those firms that were and are innovation leaders in China. Recent works identify particularly positive effects in regions with proactive local states, party organizations, and state-business alliances (cf. Yang, 2014; Butollo and ten Brink, 2015), like the technologically advanced Pearl River and Yangtze River Deltas. Although some firms are still comfortable with adapting foreign innovations for the domestic markets, R&D spending shifted from state authorities to large (state-owned, hybrid, and private) companies since the 2000s. Under increasing competitive pressures, induced partially by MNCs, firms have hence increased their innovation efforts.

All in all, China has developed a rather effective innovation system when compared to other large emerging countries. Its long-term viability, however, is far from guaranteed. Several dysfunctions in the Chinese innovation system create challenges: The weak IPR system is increasingly to the detriment of Chinese firms, indicated by the fact that most Chinese civil IPR litigation now involves Chinese rights holders suing other Chinese; Chinese companies still only benefit to a rather limited degree from public technology transfer when not only advanced regions are observed; the quality of both public innovation capacity building and public research is controversial; and links between the public research system and companies are weak. Thus, several reforms currently aim at improving China's innovation system (Jefferson *et al.*, 2014).

## Domestic Markets

A very large and thriving domestic market is of particular

importance for China's capitalism. In opposition to East Asian developmental states, the domestic markets of China are far bigger. Yet, while Chinese state managers selectively brought competitive pressures home, into the domestic markets, market protection and proactive support of national capital persisted. Although the regulation of the domestic investment regime has been relaxed, various state policies such as subsidies and public procurement facilitate domestic companies (Gruss and ten Brink, 2016; Butollo and ten Brink, 2015). In this setup, indigenous firms developed comparative advantages vis-à-vis foreign companies in the production of "good enough"products which do not require highest levels of technology. The rise of consumerism and increasing demand for intermediate goods, i.e. goods consumed as production inputs ranging from office equipment, computers to motor vehicles and plant and machinery, led domestic firms to successfully occupy large market segments especially in medium-tech and/or medium-range markets.

In the 2000s, Chinese firms on the average sold three to four times more goods on the domestic market than abroad. Given the structure of domestic demand, it implied producing medium-range goods — a segment in which domestic firms enjoy strategic advantages due to their proximity to home markets, knowledge about consumer preferences, and state support. Since the 2000s, medium-range segments of the market emerged as growth drivers. As Gadiesh *et al.* (2007) show, these medium-tech and/or medium-range markets until recently accounted for two thirds of Chinese TV sales, while the premium range, dominated by foreign firms, only accounted for a market share of 13%. In contrast, Western multinationals for a long time failed to sell medium-range products to consumers (see Brandt and Thun, 2010). Next to end consumer demand, the rising demand for intermediate goods has become essential. Due to China's investment boom, domestic manufacturing firms are among the most important producers of intermediate goods. Construction is an equally important activity, which represented the single biggest portion of GDP growth in the late 2000s (NBS, 2010).

All in all, regardless of its relative percentage of GDP, consumption has been growing faster than in any other large economy in absolute terms (Woetzel and Towson, 2015). The size and structure of domestic markets hence is of major significance for understanding long-term growth. However, as China's economy still is based on rather low wages, underdeveloped social welfare systems, and extreme inequality, this must not prevail forever. Are we thus seeing the exhaustion of this system, as recently indicated by rising indebtedness by financial institutions, non-financial corporations such as property developers and private households?

## Summary and Outlook

This article assumes that an analysis of the institutional foundations for long-term growth can also help identifying problems and instabilities that have already or may soon undermine China's growth model. Before moving on to this, I will briefly summarize how institutionalcompatibilities fostered economic growth up until the early 2010s.

The Chinese economy for a long time enjoyed comparative advantages regarding the processing of labor-intensive goods. In the 2000s however, an increasing productiveness in capital-intensive production made China a major player in medium-range technology. Notably, Chinese producers are increasingly able to serve regional and world markets for mass consumption. However, China's thriving domestic market is of greater importance. While for the most part, Chinese firms do not compete with Western MNCs for global market shares in sectors of highest value added production, due to a proactive state and a familiarity with national consumption patterns, Chinese firms have particular advantages on "their" domestic markets. A diversified industrial economy has fostered the rise of competitive national firms in several sectors such as machinery, textiles, white goods, IT, heavy industry and resources. Moreover, as China's institutional architecture was supportive of medium to long-term firm strategies, it was relatively independent from volatilities on global financial markets and policymakers were capable of protecting the economy from short-term fluctuations. Correspondingly, China has survived the global crisis and subsequent instabilities fairly well.

For an understanding of growth dynamics in China, several *domestic institutional compatibilities* are significant. With regard to *corporate governance* and *finance for investment,* Chinese firms can calculate on both preferential national networks of finance for investment and an enduring national control of enterprises through insiders, making long-term strategies practicable. At the same time, close relations with state managers and the latter's pronounced entrepreneurial stance has led firms to count on numerous types of proactive state support and a careful, selective integration of foreign firms into China, thereby enabling technology transfer, but preventing "sell out." Prevalent firm strategies to succeed by forming close, "cronyist" relationships with state managers in that way fit with informality patterns in corporate governance and corporate finance.

With respect to *industrial relations, education/training,* and *innovation capacity building,* a further institutional fit can be observed. Chinese growth since the 2000s is partially based on compatibilities between large low wage sectors with low and medium skill requirements and an education system in which the working population mostly receives a secondary education and some special training. Moreover, the (still comparably) cheap, relatively disciplined, and adequately skilled mass labor force was complemented by an increasing output of higher skilled labourers such as engineers or technicians. This was assisted by rising public expenditure on education. In conjunction with some progress in innovation capacity building, this helped producers to effectively focus on medium-tech production of medium-range goods, in which skill and innovation requirements are not overly sophisticated. At the same time, medium-range supply matched demand: As exemplified above, rising medium-range demand in mass consumer and intermediate products incentivized domestic firms to specialize on it. Moreover, wage increases were prevented from spiraling out of control.

An overarching role for expectational stability and for the reproduction of these compatibilities has been provided by growth alliances between state and business actors, mostly at the local level. This *interpersonal coordination mechanism* mobilized resources and helped in making institutions "fit" over time. Finally, on the central level, the party-state provided further stability despite vast regional heterogeneity and incessant institutional change.

China's political economy thus seems to demonstrate the

advantages of state-permeated capitalism. Nonetheless, the continuity of the long boom is threatened. Rather than being constantly and necessarily stabilized and controlled, the persistence of this growth model is not guaranteed. On the basis of the analysis presented here — apart from cyclical factors — it is now possible to distinguish more clearly which destabilization factors actually are of primary significance and which are not: The notion in Western public discourse for instance that the end of the great global credit boom in the 2000s, prolonged by quantitative easing, flooding emerging economies with cheap financing, will hit China hard, can be qualified. Since China is less dependent on external finance when compared to other emerging economies, it is also less vulnerable from financial outflows. Moreover, even though the threat of export stagnation due to demand stagnation in the West is arguably bigger, my analysis suggests that export stagnation may be or has already been compensated by domestic market growth particularly in medium-range market segments, although export-oriented sectors may indeed face serious problems.

Other destabilization processes arising from China's institutional architecture loom larger. With regard to interpersonal "cronyist" economic coordination for instance, there is evidence that tensions and conflicts between political and capital fractions erupt with increasing frequency, illustrated by serious recentralization efforts of the Xi administration since 2013 to address them. It remains to be seen whether anti-corruption measures only limit harmful types of corruption or also negatively affect "productive" cronyism in local growth alliances, as they might restrict intra-elite economic decision-making in this authoritarian form of capitalism.

Moreover, China's state-permeated corporate governance and

investment systems with an abundant supply of finance tend to produce excessive investment that cannot be easily confined. Even the central government is only partially coping with heavy competition between local growth alliancesand the associated high-risk growth and financial policies from subnational actors leading to bad loans, over-investment and rising local indebtedness. Last not least, the largely unquestioned belief in the CCP's capacity to command key actors in the financial system is increasingly in doubt.

Regarding industrial relations, education, and innovation, worries exists about whether the rising demand for higher skilled labor can indeed be covered — via serious reforms in vocational training for instance. This holds as well true for the question if China can manage to move from imitation to real innovation. While upgrading in skills and innovation capacities might also contain detrimental effects on institutions such as the low wage regime, they may be insufficient with respect to the challenge of foreign firms that produce where they sell (Herrigel, 2014). Foreign competitors already began to modify their strategies for medium-range segments of the Chinese domestic market and became more successful in the last years (Brandt and Thun, 2013). Last not least, trapped between public promises of social justice and the enduring belief in low wages as a competitive advantage, governmental crisis management oscillates between social appeasement and business-oriented restructuring. Proposed improvements in work conditions and social security are more and more seen as being too sluggish, nurturing the likelihood of an increase in social conflicts and a decrease in individual advancement motivations. The Chinese system will be put to the test if one of its key political attributes — the objective of increased prosperity for broad sections of the population and the motivation for individual advancement — is placed in jeopardy.

## *Notes*

1. Those favorable global coincidences, which made for 'transnational compatibilities', are not taken up here in detail. A much broader analysis of the trajectory and current evolution of China's growth model as well as on conceptual tools to analyze Chinese capitalism can be found in: ten Brink, 2013a.

# References

AmCham (American Chamber of Commerce). 2011. *American Business in China*. 2011 White Paper. Beijing: The American Chamber of Commerce.

Allen, Franklin, Jun Qian, Chenying Zhang, and Mengxin Zhao. 2011. *China's Financial System: Opportunities and Challenges*. <http://papers.ssrn.com/sol3/papers.cfm?abstract_id=1945259.>

Brandt, Loren, and Eric Thun. 2010. "The Fight for the Middle: Upgrading, Competition, and Industrial Development in China." *World Development* 38(11): 1555-1574.

_______. 2013. Constructing a Ladder for Growth: Policy, Markets, and Industrial Upgrading in China. Unpublished Manuscript.

Bremmer, Ian. 2010. *The End of the Free Market: Who Wins the War Between States and Corporations?* New York: Portfolio.

Brenner, Robert. 2006. *The Economics of Global Turbulence: The Advanced Capitalist Economies from Long Boom to Long Downturn, 1945-2005*. London: Verso.

Breznitz, Dan, and Michael Murphree. 2011. *Run of the Red Queen: Government, Innovation, Globalization and Economic Growth in China*. New Haven: Yale University Press.

Butollo, Florian, and Tobias ten Brink. 2012. "Challenging the Atomization of Discontent. Patterns of Migrant-Worker Protest in China during the Series of Strikes in 2010." *Critical Asian Studies* 44(3): 419-440.

_______. 2015. "State Policies and Domestic Demand as Drivers of Industrial Upgrading: The Experience of the Chinese LED Lighting Industry." Paper for the annual SASE Conference, London, July 2, 2015.

CBRC (China Banking Regulatory Commission). 2012. *Annual Report 2011*. Beijing. <http://www.cbrc.gov.cn/chinese/files/2013/8FC77357E36D44D2BD8B3C4BE97F965F.pdf.>

Chan, Anita, ed. 2015. *Chinese Workers in Comparative Perspective*. Ithaca and London: ILR Press.

Chan, Anita, and Jonathan Unger. 2009. "A Chinese State Enterprise

Under the Reforms: What Model of Capitalism?" *The China Journal* 62(2): 1-26.

Chan, Kam Wing, and Will Buckingham. 2008. "Is China Abolishing the Hukou System?" *The China Quarterly* 195: 582-606.

Chen, Minglu. 2015. "From Economic Elites to Political Elites: Private entrepreneurs in the People's Political Consultative Conference." *Journal of Contemporary China* 24(94): 613-627.

CLB (China Labour Bulletin). 2014. *Searching for the Union: The workers' movement in China 2011-13*. Hong Kong: China Labour Bulletin.

Dickson, Bruce J. 2007. "Integrating Wealth and Power in China: The Communist Party's Embrace of the Private Sector." *The China Quarterly* 192: 827-854.

Fan, Peilei. 2011. "Innovation, Globalization, and Catch-up of Latecomers: Cases of Chinese Telecom Firms." *Environment and Planning A* 43(4): 830-849.

Friedman, Eli, and Ching Kwan Lee. 2010. "Remaking the World of Chinese Labour: A 30-Year Retrospective." *British Journal of Industrial Relations* 48(3): 507-533.

Fu, Xiaolan. 2015. *China's Path to Innovation*. Cambridge: Cambridge University Press.

Gadiesh, Orit, Philip Leung, and Till Vestring. 2007. *The Battle for China's Good-Enough Market*. Harvard Business Review, September: 80-89.

Gruss, Laura, and Tobias ten Brink. 2016: "The Development of the Chinese Photovoltaic Industry: An Advancing Role for the Central State?" *Journal of Contemporary China* 25(99): 453-466.

Guan, Jian Cheng, and Richard C. M. Yam. 2015. "Effects of Government Financial Incentives in Firms' Innovation performance in China: Evidences from Beijing in the 1990s." *Research Policy* 44(1): 273-282.

Hall, Peter A., and David Soskice, eds. 2001. *Varieties of Capitalism: The Institutional Foundations of Comparative Advantage*. Oxford: Oxford University Press.

Heilmann, Sebastian. 2008. "Policy Experimentation in China's

Economic Rise." *Studies in Comparative International Development* 43(1): 1-26.

_______. 2011. "Making Plans for Markets: Policies for the Long Term in China." *Harvard Asia Quarterly* 13(2): 33-40.

Herr, Hansjörg. 2011. "Perspectives on High Growth and Rising Inequality." pp. 7-27 in *China's Labor Question,* edited by Christoph Scherrer. München, Mering: Rainer Hampp Verlag.

Herrigel, Gary. 2014. "Globalization and the German Production Model." Paper presented at the conference Transformation of the German Model at the IAB, Nürnberg, Germany, February 13-14, 2014.

Hung, Ho-fung. 2008. "Rise of China and the Global Overaccumulation Crisis." *Review of International Political Economy* 15(2): 149-179.

Jefferson, G. H., Jiang, R., and D. L. Tortorice. 2014. *Restructuring China's Research Institutes: Impacts on China's Research Orientation and Productivity* (No. 72).

Kennedy, Scott. 2011. "The Business of Lobbying in China." pp. 113-35 in *Beyond the Middle Kingdom,* edited by Scott Kennedy. Stanford, CA: Stanford University Press.

King, Lawrence P., and Iván Szelényi. 2005. "Post-Communist Economic Systems." pp. 205-229 in *The Handbook of Economic Sociology,* edited by Neil J. Smelser, and Richard Swedberg. Princeton: Princeton University Press.

Lardy, Nicholas R. 2002. *Integrating China into the Global Economy.* Washington, DC: Brookings.

Laurenceson, James and Danielle Rodgers. 2010. "China's Macroeconomic Volatility - How Important is the Business Cycle?" *China Economic Review* 21(2): 324-333.

Leung, Chris. 2011. *China: Inflation and Labor Productivity.* Frankfurt /M.: Deutsche Bank. <http://www.lntmf.com/Uploads/Knowledge-Center/cn_21_February_2011.pdf.>

Li, Cheng. 2010. "China's Communist Party-State: The Structure and Dynamics of Power." pp. 165-191 in *Politics in China: An Introduction,* edited by William A. Joseph. New York: Oxford University Press.

Liefner, I., Brömer, C., and G. Zeng. 2012. "Knowledge absorption of optical technology companies in Shanghai, Pudong." *Applied Geography* 32: 171-184.

Lin, Yi. 2011. "Turning Rurality into Modernity: Suzhi Education in a Suburban Public School of Migrant Children in Xiamen." *The China Quarterly* 206(2): 313-330.

Lüthje, B., S. Luo, and H. Zhang. 2013. *Socio-economic Transformation and Industrial Relations in China*. Frankfurt/M.; New York: Campus.

Lyons, Thomas P. 1990. "Planning and Interprovincial Co-ordination in Maoist China." *The China Quarterly* 121: 36-60.

McNally, Christopher A. 2011. "State Capitalism is Dead! Long Live State Capitalism! Rebalancing China's Political Economy." Paper for the Annual Meeting of the Association of Asian Studies. Honolulu, HI.

McNally, Christopher A. and Teresa Wright. 2010. "Sources of Social Support for China's Current Political Order: The 'Thick Embeddedness' of Private Capital Holders." *Communist and Post-Communist Studies* 43(2): 189-198.

McNally, Christopher A., Hong Guo, and Guangwei Hu. 2007. "Entrepreneurship and Political Guanxi Networks in China's Private Sector." *East-West Center Working Papers: Politics, Governance, and Security Series 19*. Honolulu: East-West Center.

Meissner, Mirjam, Lea Shih, Luisa Kinzius, and Sandra Heep. 2015. *Wie Phönix aus der Asche: Reformen sollen Chinas Staatsunternehmen den Rücken stärken*. MERICS Web Special. <http://www.merics.org/fileadmin/templates/art/aktuelles/SOE_Reform/SOE-ReformWeb-Spezial.pdf.>

Naughton, Barry. 2011. "China's Distinctive System: Can It be a Model for Others?" pp. 67-85 in *In Search of China's Development Model: Beyond the Beijing Consensus*, edited by S. Philip Hsu, Yu-Shan Wu, and Suisheng Zhao. London; New York: Routledge.

NBS (National Bureau of Statistics of China). 2010. *China Statistical Yearbook 2010*. Beijing: China Statistics Press. <http://www.stats.gov.cn/english/statisticaldata/yearlydata/.>

_______. 2012. *China Statistical Yearbook 2010*. Beijing: China Statistics Press. <http://www.stats.gov.cn/english/statisticaldata/yearlydata/.>

Nee, Victor, and Sonja Opper. 2012. *Capitalism from Below: Markets and Institutional Change in China*. Cambridge: Harvard University Press.

Nölke, Andreas, Tobias ten Brink, Christian May, and Simone Claar. 2015. "Domestic Structures, Foreign Economic Policies and Global Economic Order: Implications from the Rise of Large Emerging Economies." *European Journal of International Relations* 21(3): 538-567.

Pearson, Margaret M. 2011. "Variety Within and Without: The Political Economy of Chinese Regulation." pp. 25-43 in *Beyond the Middle Kingdom*, edited by Scott Kennedy. Stanford, CA: Stanford University Press.

Schneider, Ben Ross. 2013. *Hierarchical Capitalism: Business, Labour, and the Challenge of Equitable Development in Latin America*. New York: Cambridge University Press.

Shao, Sijun, Chris Nyland, and Cherrie Jiuhua Zhu. 2011. "Tripartite Consultation: An Emergent Form of Governance Shaping Employment Relations in China." *Industrial Relations Journal* 42(4): 358-574.

ten Brink, Tobias. 2013a. *Chinas Kapitalismus. Entstehung, Verlauf, Paradoxien*. Frankfurt/M.; New York: Campus (English version forthcoming from University of Pennsylvania Press).

_______. 2013b. "Paradoxes of Prosperity in China's New Capitalism." *Journal of Current Chinese Affairs* 42(4): 17-44.

Tsai, Kellee S. 2006. "Adaptive Informal Institutions and Endogenous Institutional Change in China." *World Politics* 59(1): 116-141.

Walder, Andrew G. 1995. "Local Governments as Industrial Firms: An Organizational Analysis of China's Transitional Economy." *American Journal of Sociology* 101(2): 263-301.

Walter, Carl E., and Fraser J. T. Howie. 2011. *Red Capitalism: The Fragile Financial Foundation of China's Extraordinary Rise*. Singapore: John Wiley & Sons.

Woetzel, Jonathan and Jeffrey Towson. 2015. *The One Hour China Consumer Book: Five Short Stories That Explain the Brutal Fight for One Billion Chinese Consumers*. Towson Group, Cayman Islands.

Woronov, Terry E. 2011. "Learning to serve: Urban youth, vocational schools and new class formations in China." *The China Journal* 66: 77-100.

Yang, Chun. 2014. "State-led Technological Innovation of Domestic Firms in Shenzhen, China: Evidence from Liquid Crystal Display (LCD) Industry." *Cities* 38: 1-10.

Yang, Dali L. 2004. *Remaking the Chinese Leviathan: Market Transition and the Politics of Governance in China*. Stanford, CA: Stanford University Press.

Chapter 8

# *Beyond Predatory Productivism?: The Political Economy of Welfare Capitalism in Post-New Order Indonesia*

Andrew Rosser and Maryke van Diermen

## Introduction

In analyzing the nature of welfare capitalism in Indonesia in recent decades, many scholars have drawn on the typology developed by Holliday (2000) in his examination of East Asian welfare regimes (see, for instance, Gough, 2001; Wood and Gough, 2006; Park, 2007; Kuypers, 2014). According to Holliday (2000), East Asian welfare regimes are 'productivist' in nature — that is, characterised by the subordination of social policy to economic policy and the presence of a growth-oriented state. Countries following this model typically invest little in social protection programmes and, to the extent that they do, prioritise provision of welfare to 'productive' elements in society (e.g., formal sector workers, civil servants, military officials) and areas that promote economic growth. Holliday (2000) further distinguished between 'facilitative', 'developmental particularist' and 'developmental universalist' variants of the productivist model (Table 8.1). In the facilitative

Table 8.1. The Productivist World of Welfare Capitalism Extended

| | Social Policy | Social Rights | Stratification Effects | State-market-family relationship | State Type |
|---|---|---|---|---|---|
| Facilitative | Subordinate to economic policy | Minimal | Limited | Market prioritised | Nightwatchman state |
| Developmental-universalist | Subordinate to economic policy | Limited; extensions linked to productive activity | Reinforcement of the position of productive elements | State underpins market and families with some universal programmes | Developmental state |
| Developmental-particularist | Subordinate to economic policy | Minimal; forced individual provision linked to productive activity | Reinforcement of the position of productive elements | State directs social welfare activities of families | Developmental state |
| Predatory-universalist | Subordinate to economic policy | Limited; extensions linked to productive activity | Reinforcement of the position of productive elements | State underpins market and families with some universal programmes | Predatory/ oligarchic state |
| Predatory-particularist | Subordinate to economic policy | Minimal; forced individual provision linked to productive activity | Reinforcement of the position of productive elements | State directs social welfare activities of families | Predatory/ oligarchic state |

Source: Adapted from Holliday (2000)..

regime (e.g., Hong Kong), social policy is committed to facilitating and benefiting economic growth: social rights are minimal, stratification is limited, and the market is prioritized. In the developmental-particularist regime (e.g., Singapore), the state directs individual welfare provision, playing a regulatory role in social policy alongside substantial reliance on the market and families.

There are almost no social rights, with parts of society excluded from social welfare. The provision of welfare is predominantly for the formal sector or employees who make a financial contribution. In developmental universalist regimes (e.g., Japan and Taiwan), the state steps up to create universal welfare programs, at least for productive elements in society. Social rights are more prevalent with efforts made to extend coverage to all citizens. The state plays a more important role in social policy although the market and family still perform the most significant role. Indonesia is generally been considered a strong fit with the productivist model — in particular, the developmental particularist sub-type — and to have remained a strong fit in this respect despite the collapse of the authoritarian 'New Order' regime in 1998 (see Gough, 2001; Park, 2007; Kuypers, 2014).

At the same time, other scholars writing about the nature of welfare capitalism in Indonesia have drawn attention to the way in which the implementation of government social welfare programs has been undermined by corruption and predation and, again, continued to be so despite the fall of the New Order (Aspinall, 2014; Ramesh and Asher, 2000; Ramesh, 2014). In so doing, they have implicitly added an additional dimension to Holliday's typology related to state capacity. In countries such as Japan, South Korea, Singapore, and Taiwan — the countries that are the central focus of the East Asian welfare regimes literature — productivism emerged within the context of 'nightwatchman' or 'developmental' states characterized by high levels of administrative capacity and low levels of corruption (Holliday, 2000; Kwon, 2005). In Indonesia, by contrast, it has emerged within the context of a predatory/oligarchic state that, while still successful in promoting economic growth, has had a much lower level of administrative capacity and higher level of corruption (Robison, 1994; Robison and Hadiz, 2004). Such accounts suggest that Indonesia during both the New Order and post-New Order periods is better described as having a 'predatory particularist' form of welfare capitalism than a 'developmental particularist' one. The extended typology is outlined in Table 8.1.

In the last few years, both these views of welfare capitalism in Indonesia have been challenged by commentary, much of it in the popular media, pointing to the Indonesian government's introduction of new social protection programmes and shift towards universalism in some areas of social policy since the 1997-1998 Asia economic crisis. Such commentary has suggested that Indonesia is in the process of shifting away from productivism and towards the establishment of a welfare state along Anglo-European lines. *The Economist* (2012), for instance, has declared that Indonesia is now 'laying the foundations of a welfare state' while *Time* (2013) has stated that country is 'starting to build' one. James Riady (2013) has argued that the new social protection programmes are a 'game-changer,' a harbinger of 'the new Indonesian welfare state.' In a more cautious analysis, Edward Aspinall and Eve Warburton (2013) have argued that: 'The tentative beginnings of universal social protection, even of an Indonesian welfare state, are now visible.'

This paper suggests that these different visions of Indonesia's welfare capitalism — and the underlying reality that they seek to describe — reflect contradictions within the nature of Indonesian welfare capitalism. Specifically, they reflect contestation between competing political and social forces over the policies and institutions that govern social welfare in Indonesia, the different agendas and interests that underpin this contestation, and the balance of power between these forces. This contestation has meant that the nature of welfare capitalism in Indonesia has been simultaneously shaped by productivist, predatory and progressive agendas, not merely one or the other. The result has been the emergence of a welfare regime that has multiple and contradictory features; while it is predominantly productivist and predatory in nature, it also has significant progressive elements. In this context, we suggest that the aforementioned visions of Indonesian welfare capitalism are not so much incorrect as partial. They are like the parts of the elephant in the parable about the blind men and the elephant: each vision captures a dimension of what is going on but without necessarily presenting the full picture. This paper aims for 'whole-of-elephant' perspective.

In presenting this view, the paper begins by outlining an approach to explaining welfare capitalism that places contestation between competing political and social forces and the balance of power between them at the centre of the analysis. We then identify the competing actors, interests and agendas that have shaped the evolution of welfare capitalism in Indonesia during the New Order and post-New Order periods and examine how shifts in the balance of power between them have influenced relevant policies over time. In the final section of the paper, we present the conclusions.

## Explaining Welfare Capitalism

Much work on the nature of welfare capitalism, particularly in East Asian countries, has focused on assessing whether East Asian forms of welfare capitalism are distinctive from European and North American varieties of welfare capitalism especially as depicted in Esping-Andersen's (1990) seminal book, *The Three Worlds of Welfare Capitalism*. A key question in this work has been whether there is a single model of East Asian welfare capitalism that is common to the region or a variety of models across the region (Wilding, 2008; Kuypers, 2014). This work has yielded a number of typologies of East Asian welfare capitalism, the most prominent of which has been Holliday's (2000) productivist model (see also Gough, 2001; Croissant, 2004; Wood and Gough, 2006; Peng and Wong, 2010). While scholars engaging in this work have in some cases acknowledged that the nature of East Asian welfare capitalism has changed over time, they have in general given little attention to its political and social underpinnings and their implications in terms of the dynamics of change. For the most part, as Hwang (2015) has observed, they have concentrated on policy and institution-based model-building.

To the extent that scholars have examined the political and social underpinnings of welfare capitalism in East Asian countries, they have taken one of two main approaches. The first has argued that the origins of East Asian welfare capitalism lie in the dominance of supposedly 'Asian' — and in particular Confucian — values such as respect for education, filial piety, deference to authority, and the relative importance of family and kinship ties compared to individual needs and wants (Jones, 1993; Goodman *et al.*, 1998). Such values, it has suggested, have informed the strong emphasis in East Asian welfare systems on the role of families in providing social protection and the relatively limited role of the state in this respect, except in relation to education (Peng and Wong, 2010:

657-658). The second approach has suggested that the nature of East Asian welfare capitalism has reflected the dominance of developmental states within the region (Holliday, 2000; Kwon, 2005; Kwon and Holliday, 2007). In this perspective, social welfare policies have been a functionalist response to the imperatives of late industrialization (see also Pierson, 2005) and in particular an economic strategy aimed at promoting industrial competitiveness and rapid economic growth rather than social protection. This view, as Peng and Wong (2010: 658) have observed, suggests such policies were initiated by economic rather than social policy-makers and were intended, not to provide 'social protection or redistribution, but rather to promote economic productivity.'

The problem with both these approaches is that they lack a dialectic element — that is, some mechanism for explaining change over time. The explanatory variables at work in these approaches — the dominance of Asian cultural values, late industrialisation, and the presence of a growth-oriented developmental state — are things that either have not changed in the East Asian context or have changed very slowly. At the same time, however, much recent analysis of East Asian welfare regimes has suggested that there has nevertheless been some — in some cases, significant — change in the nature of these regimes, particularly since the Asian economic crisis in 1997-1998. In one survey, Peng and Wong (2010), for instance, have argued that welfare regimes in countries such as Japan, Korea, and Taiwan have shifted away from productivism and become increasingly universal in nature, in the latter two cases following the Asian crisis. As noted earlier, some analysis of the Indonesian case has pointed to a similar transition (Aspinall, 2014; The Economist, 2012; Time, 2013). Lacking a dialectic element, these approaches have been unable to explain these shifts.

Recent work on the politics of social protection and inclusive development offers a way of bringing a dialectic element back into the analysis (see especially Hickey, 2008; Bender, 2013; Hickey *et al.*, 2015). This work has emphasized the role of contestation between competing actors, interests and agendas in shaping social policy within specific country, institutional and historical contexts. Hickey (2008) and Niño-Zarazúa *et al.* (2012), for instance, have argued that social protection policy-making and implementation in developing countries needs to be understood in terms of way in which the interests of domestic political elites interact with those of global actors and discourses within the context of specific regimes and socio-economic environments. Similarly, Devereux and White (2010) have emphasized contestation between technocratic, rights-based and political agendas and the actors and interests that are embedded in them in their analysis of the politics of social protection in Africa. Bender (2013: 39) has argued that studies of the political economy of social protection should focus on how structural factors such as regime type and economic context interact with other factors such as the role of 'specific interest group and partisan structures within a country or path dependencies.' Finally, Hickey *et al.* (2015) have argued that development policies need to be understood as a 'political settlement' (Khan, 2010) between competing interests including not only domestic political, bureaucratic and corporate elites but also popular forces and international actors.

A recurring theme in these scholars' work is the importance of *domestic* political factors in shaping the nature of social protection regimes. For instance, Devereux and White (2010: 73-74) argue that while some social protection initiatives in sub-Saharan Africa have been donor-driven — reflecting donor commitments to poverty reduction and a desire by donors to 'plant their flags' in initiatives they fund — many have been 'conceptualized, implemented and financed' using entirely domestic resources and driven by domestic political factors, in particular, political elites' desire to enhance their electoral popularity and build patronage networks. Indeed, they argue that domestically-financed and driven social protection initiatives have in general been more successful than donor-driven projects, especially where the latter have been short-term pilots implemented through 'parallel' administrative systems outside government structures (see also Bender, 2013). Hickey (2008) and Niño-Zarazúa *et al.* (2012) also point to the way in which domestic political institutions influence which actors have access to social policy-making processes and on what terms.

Our approach in this paper is broadly consistent with that of these scholars. Like them, we emphasise the role of contestation between competing political actors, interests and agendas in shaping social protection policy and implementation, focusing in particular on the role of domestic actors. We also emphasise the way in which the balance of power between these actors has been mediated by the institutional and socio-economic environment, again focusing on domestic political factors such as changes in political regime and the economic context. More specifically, we emphasise the way in which changes in institutional arrangements and economic context has shifted the balance of power between competing sets of actors by shaping who has access to the policy-making process, the incentives of political elites, and the government's need for new resources. At the same time, however, our approach differs from that of these scholars in one important respect. In analyzing the politics of social protection or inclusive development in developing countries, these scholars have tended to focus on the role of elite actors — especially political and bureaucratic elites and donor organisations — in shaping social protection policy and implementation (Hickey *et al.*, 2015 being a notable exception). We argue that while elite actors have been very important in the Indonesian context, the poor and their NGO allies have also played a significant role in social welfare policy-making and implementation, at least in the post-New Order period (Aspinall, 2014). Rather than being an entirely elite-driven product, Indonesia's social welfare regime during this period has increasingly come to represent a 'political settlement' between elite and subaltern or non-elite elements. We thus need to factor the role and influence of the latter elements into our analysis.

In applying this perspective, we begin by identifying the key actors, interests and agendas that have been involved in struggles to define the nature of welfare capitalism in Indonesia, in particular, *via* social policy.

## Actors, Interests, and Agendas

Broadly speaking, three competing sets of actors, each of which has had a distinct set of interests and policy agenda, have played a role in shaping the nature of welfare capitalism in Indonesia. The first of these has consisted of liberal economic technocrats in government and their supporters within the donor community and other institutions controlling mobile capital.[1] On the technocratic side, key actors in this coalition have included figures such as Radius Prawiro, Bambang Sudibyo, Boediono, Agus Martowardojo, and Sri Mulyani Indrawati, all of whom were cabinet ministers at one time or another.[2] On the mobile capital controller side, key actors have included the International Monetary Fund (IMF) and the World Bank. This coalition has supported state investment in social policy as a way of building the country's human resources, creating a political and social environment conducive to market-oriented economic reform, and, in so doing, contributing to economic growth (Prawiro, 1998: 173-211; 130-134; ADB, 2006; Boediono, 2009: 13, 31, 44). During the New Order, it emphasized the need for social programmes in education and food security given their perceived payoffs in growth terms. But following criticism of international donors in the 1980s and 1990s for promoting structural adjustment programmes in the developing world that had negative social effects, it has increasingly argued for broad social safety nets (World Bank, 2003). At the same time, it has argued that social programmes need to be affordable, cost-effective, and based on evidence about what works and why (Rokx *et al.*, 2009). It has been prepared to cut investment in social programmes if they do not meet these criteria or serve the overriding goal of increased growth. The influence of this agenda has reflected powerful structural pressures on the Indonesian government emanating from budget constraints, the power of mobile capital as a result of its ability to relocate to alternate jurisdictions (Winters, 1996), and the technocrats' direct access to the policy-making process as a result of their positions within the state apparatus.

The second main set of actors has been the predatory military and bureaucratic officials who have occupied the state apparatus (particularly the bureaucracy and parliament) and the domestic and foreign business groups to which they have been connected (in many cases through family and other personal relationships) (Robison, 1986). Members of this coalition have recognized that social programmes are a useful way of promoting economic development through their contribution to human resource development and political and social stability (Hoemardani, 1975; Moertopo, 1981). But they have had a stronger interest in limiting government spending on social policy to free up resources for other areas (e.g., infrastructure, industrial projects, subsidized credit programmes) more central to their business activities (Riady, 2013). To the extent that the government has spent money on social programmes, members of this coalition have had a further interest in the introduction of programmes that privilege military and bureaucratic officials — e.g., by providing them with pension and other benefits, opportunities for corruption, or opportunities to fuel patronage networks and buy electoral votes. In this respect, managers of government-owned service providers such as public schools, universities, hospitals, community health centres and food security agencies — the government bodies most directly responsible for implementing the government's main social programmes — have been key actors (Irawan *et al.*, 2004; Aspinall, 2014). Members of this coalition have exercised influence over social protection and implementation by virtue of their occupation of the state apparatus and consequent direct access to the policy-making process and central role in the implementation of social programmes.

The third main set of actors has been the poor and their allies in the NGO movement. Drawing on notions of human rights and a radical critique of neoliberalism (particularly the privatisation of public services), this set of actors has sought to promote expanded and equitable access to social protection (Irawan *et al.*, 2004; Tjandra, 2014). Although its members have generally been excluded from policy-making and implementation processes, they have had some influence as a result of their ability to access the media and make strategic use of the court system, particularly since Indonesia's transition to a more democratic regime. Key actors in this coalition have included activists at NGOs such as Indonesia Corruption Watch (ICW), the Institute for Policy Research and Advocacy (ELSAM), the Ecosoc Institute, the Peoples Health Council (DKR), the Indonesian Poor People's Union (SRMI), the Jakarta Legal Aid Bureau (LBH Jakarta), the Trade Union Rights Centre (TURC), the Indonesian Consumers Foundation (YLKI), various trade unions, various parents groups, and the numerous poor and marginalized citizens represented by or linked to these organizations.

In the next section, we show how the balance of power between these sets of actors has changed over time as result of the Asian crisis and regime change and the impact that this has in turn had on the nature of social policy and its implementation. We focus in particular on social policy initiatives related to social security (e.g., programmes providing old age pensions, disability pensions, and unemployment benefits), education (e.g., programmes providing access to free education), health (e.g., schemes providing free access to health care), food security (e.g., subsidized rice programmes), community development (e.g., programmes providing access to financing for local development projects), and employment (e.g., work creation/labour market schemes).

## The Political Economy of Welfare Capitalism in Indonesia

Under the New Order, predatory military and bureaucratic officials dominated Indonesian politics along with the business groups to which they were linked. The Indonesian military seized power in a coup in 1965. Thereafter, its leaders emasculated the political parties and the national parliament, gained control over the bureaucracy through the appointment of military officials to senior bureaucratic positions and the introduction of requirements for government bureaucrats to support Golkar (the government electoral vehicle), and subordinated the judiciary to political and bureaucratic authority. At the same time, they re-engaged with the donor community and sought to attract mobile private domestic and foreign capital back into the country through the introduction of economic policy reforms. As part of this process, they gave considerable authority over economic and social policy to a group of liberal technocrats known collectively as the 'Berkeley Mafia' (Robison, 1986; Winters, 1996). By contrast, the poor and NGO elements were prevented from exercising much influence by the imposition of authoritarian controls on their activities (Robison and Hadiz, 2004).

In this environment, the New Order government spent almost nothing on social programmes. It provided no unemployment benefits, old age social pension, disability pension, or work opportunities for the poor through labour market schemes. It invested in public health and education but inconsistently over time and at a much lower level than neighbouring countries. It formally adopted policies of universal free primary education in 1974, universal free primary and junior secondary education in 1994, and free health care for the poor in 1994. But in practice it permitted public education and health facilities to charge user fees, forcing many poor Indonesians to forgo much-needed health treatment, withdraw their children from school, or enroll them in lower quality (but cheaper) private schools. It expanded access to public education and health care in the 1970s and early 1980s when the oil boom generated a massive revenue windfall, constructing thousands of new public schools and health facilities, particularly in isolated parts of the country, and hiring new teachers and health workers to staff them. This contributed to a significant increase in school enrolment rates and improved health service utilization rates. But the government cut spending on education and health sharply following the collapse of international oil prices and the onset of fiscal crisis in the mid-1980s. The limited nature of funding for public education and health saw the private sector play an increasingly important role in the provision of education and health services (World Bank, 1995: 1; Hill, 1996: 206-213).

To the extent that the government did invest significant resources in social protection programmes, it prioritized (1) the needs of military and bureaucratic officials and (2) investments that served to promote economic growth, in particular by ensuring political and social stability. With respect to (1), for instance, it generously subsidized pension and health insurance schemes for military and bureaucratic officials such as TASPEN (the civil servants pension fund), ASABRI (the military pension fund), and ASKES (the civil servants health insurance fund). Participation in these schemes was mandatory for military and civil servants and entailed fixed contributions by members. The schemes provided varying benefits consisting of health and maternity care, old-age benefits, death benefits, savings programs, disability and workplace accident compensation (Ramesh and Asher, 2000: 43). But it established no similar schemes for informal private sector workers[3] and an inadequate one for formal private sector workers. Known as JAMSOSTEK, the latter was a compulsory provident fund providing pension and health insurance financed through member and employer contributions. While this scheme provided some health care benefits to members, it was much less effective as a pension scheme, with only 10% of members receiving any pension benefit. For this reason, some have questioned whether it even qualifies as a form of social protection. The government also imposed requirements for employers to make mandatory severance payments to workers but these were widely flouted (Ramesh, 2014: 43).

With respect to (2), the government invested heavily in subsidies to stabilize the price of rice, the country's dominant staple food. Using these subsidies, the National Logistics Agency (BULOG) bought and sold rice in domestic and international markets, created a buffer stock, and maintained floor and ceiling prices for rice. In so doing, it ensured that rice farmers received reasonable prices for their produce and consumers had reliable access to affordable rice, particularly at times of short supply. This policy was a key part of the government's efforts to encourage agricultural growth and achieve rice self-sufficiency (a long-standing national economic goal) along with subsidisation of agricultural inputs such as fertilizer and the use of high-yielding rice varieties. But it was also driven by concerns that food price instability could lead to social unrest and, in so doing, undermine both the government's survival and the process of economic development. While BULOG's operations provided a general subsidy rather than one targeted at the poor, the government's efforts to stabilize the price of rice can be considered a form of social protection to the extent that it contributed significantly to poverty reduction efforts (Prawiro, 1998; Arifin, 2008; Timmer, 2008).

Overall, then, Indonesia's social policy regime under the New Order adhered broadly to the 'productivist' model of welfare capitalism. In many East Asian states, productivism entailed a strong focus on education and, to a lesser extent, health (Gough, 2001). In New Order Indonesia, as noted above, education and health were not high priorities even if they did attract greater funding than some other areas of social policy — e.g., social security. But in focusing on the interests of supposedly productive elements such as military and bureaucratic officials and investing in food security as a way of promoting economic growth, the New Order adhered broadly to this model. The New Order was also clearly particularist in its orientation to the extent this led to the concentration of social welfare on specific groups: e.g., military and bureaucratic officials, rice farmers and rice consumers. However, Indonesia's social protection regime was also characterized by widespread predation and rent-seeking as evidenced by high levels of corruption within the country's education and health systems (Achmad, 1999: 72-73; Irawan *et al.*, 2004; Rosser, 2012) and BULOG (Crouch, 1978: 280).

The Asian economic crisis and ensuing demise of the New Order regime produced a moderate shift in the balance of power between the various sets of actors mentioned above. Predatory military and bureaucratic officials and their corporate clients were able to maintain instrumental control over the state apparatus despite the transition to a more democratic and decentralised political system by forging new alliances and making use of political parties (Hadiz, 2003: 593). At the same time, the economic crisis enhanced the structural power of donors and other controllers of mobile capital, at least for the period of the crisis and its immediate aftermath, a time during which Indonesia was subject to an IMF rescue package and foreign aid was desperately needed (Robison and Rosser, 1999). Within this context, predatory military and bureaucratic officials, their corporate clients and mobile capital controllers continued to play a significant role in social policy-making and implementation, ensuring that the government's funding of social programmes remained controlled and focused on areas that promoted economic growth and/or served state-based patronage networks.

However, the economic crisis and subsequent collapse of the New Order strengthened the hand of the poor and their NGO allies for five reasons. First, the devastating social impact of the crisis put the government under significant pressure to change its approach to social policy even if so doing negatively affected the interests of predatory military and bureaucratic elites and their corporate allies. Second, democratisation created an incentive for politicians and their political parties to promote policies favouring the poor and marginalised because of their electoral appeal encouraging numerous politicians to employ social programmes as a way of fostering support and gaining votes (Rosser and Wilson, 2012; Rosser and Sulistiyanto, 2013). Third, democratization removed key obstacles to organisation by groups that had previously been excluded from the policy-making process. As part of this trend, the post-New Order period witnessed the establishment of a wide range of new NGO and citizens groups with a dedicated focus on social policy issues or an agenda flexible enough to incorporate such issues. At the same time, some human rights and other NGOs that were established during the New Order became increasingly active in relation to social policy issues as political and legal mobilization around these issues increased. Fourth, democratisation opening up new policy spaces that these could access in order to influence policy. The latter included regular public consultations held by the national parliament as part of legislative processes, a freer media, and the establishment of a (relatively clean and competent) Constitutional Court, enabling them to challenge laws passed by parliament by requesting that they be subject to judicial review.[4] Finally, legal innovations such as citizen law suits, class actions, and legal standing (all of which were rare, if not unheard of, during the New Order period) opened up new avenues for these groups to engage with Indonesia's general courts beyond pre-existing mechanisms such as judicial review of regulations (Rosser and van Diermen, forthcoming).

The result of these shifts was a change in the government's approach to social policy. Initially — in the midst of the Asian crisis when predatory bureaucratic and business elements were at their weakest — the government introduced a series of 'social safety net' schemes supported with finance from the World Bank and Asian Development Bank (ADB) aimed at helping the poor maintain their living standards. Generally referred to as the 'first generation' of social protection programmes, these ran until the early 2000s. At this point, the government began to introduce a 'second generation' of programmes funded largely through cuts to government fuel subsidies (the benefits of which largely accrued to the middle class and business) as the effects of democratization took root. These included redesigned versions of several 'first generation' schemes plus new conditional and unconditional cash transfer schemes (Sumarto and Bazzi, 2011). The most substantial of these programmes in financial terms were School Operational Assistance (BOS), a school grants scheme aimed at providing for free basic education; Temporary Direct Cash Assistance (BLSM), an unconditional cash transfer scheme; Raskin, a programme aimed at providing rice to the poor; Jamkesmas, a health insurance program aimed at providing free health care to the poor and near poor; and the Community Empowerment Programme, a scheme that funds village-level development projects (Rosser and van Diermen, forthcoming).

In 2011, the parliament passed a new law on Social Security Implementing Agencies (BPJS), taking the post-New Order evolution of the country's social protection regime into a third phase. Under this law, the four existing state insurance companies (TASPEN, ASKES, ASABRI and JAMSOSTEK) and Jamkesmas have been merged into 2 state agencies: BPJS Health (which has taken-over the health-related programmes) and BPJS Employment (which has taken-over programmes related to employment including insurance for old age, death, pension, and accidents). BPJS Health started implementation in 2014 and BPJS Employment will commence in 2015. Both BPJS are self-funded through members' premiums with those for poor people being paid by the government. Informal sector workers are also covered but are expected to pay their own premiums. Prior to BPJS, most informal sector workers did not receive any social protection coverage because they were not classified as poor and were thus ineligible for targeted social assistance programmes (such as Raskin or Jamkesmas), although a small number (358,000 in 2011) received assistance through ASKESOS, an income replacement scheme for informal workers (Satriana *et al.*, 2012: 9-11).

Collectively, these changes have marked a transition in the nature of Indonesia's social protection regime away from the particularistic focus of the New Order period towards a more universalist orientation. Military and bureaucratic officials continue to be privileged as formal recipients of social welfare through continued government subsidization of their pension and health schemes. So, too, do rice producers and consumers as a result of the Raskin scheme.[5] But the new programmes have extended social welfare to a much wider range of people than was the case under the New Order and, in particular, the poor. Indonesia's poor now have access — at least in principle, if not always in practice—to funded schemes—in some cases targeted at the poor, in some cases universal in nature — providing for, among things, free basic education, free health care, subsidized rice, community development opportunities, and cash grants to supplement incomes and enhance access to education and health services.

But the introduction of the new social protection programmes has not fundamentally altered the productivist and predatory nature of the country's social protection regime. With predatory officials, corporate elites, technocratic officials and donors remaining the dominant influence on the government's approach to social protection, social policy has remained firmly subordinate to economic policy. For instance, following changes to the 1945 Constitution in 1999-2002 requiring the central and regional governments to allocate at least 20% of their budgets to education, technocratic ministers and business-linked government officials successfully opposed efforts by the national teachers' union and NGOs to force the government to spend beyond this level by excluding teachers' salaries from the relevant calculation (Rosser and Joshi, 2013: 183-184). The technocrats also successfully opposed calls for the government to increase health spending to 5% of the budget after this was made a requirement in the 2009 Health Law (Prianti, 2010). Even though government spending on social protection has increased, it has thus remained low by regional standards. The private sector has accordingly remained a crucial provider of health and education services. In the area of labour law, mandatory severance payments continue to be widely flouted as companies make increased use of casual agency labour (Juliawan, 2010).

Social protection spending has also remained skewed towards areas that contribute to economic growth and benefit productive elements in society. Food security, education, community development and, to a lesser extent, health have remained the main priorities in terms of social spending while social security has continued to be ignored. The post-crisis period has witnessed the introduction of new social pension schemes for the 'neglected elderly' (ASLUT) and the 'severely disabled' (ASODKB). But these have been tiny, providing very limited benefits and covering only a small proportion of the relevant populations (Rosser and van Diermen, forthcoming). Many Indonesian citizens accordingly remain vulnerable and reliant on family and community support.

At the same time, predation and corruption have continued to undermine the implementation of social protection programmes.

Illegal fees for public education and health services remain a prominent concern as does misuse of funds for schemes such as BOS and Jamkesmas (Rosser, 2012; Rosser and Joshi, 2013). Numerous reports have pointed to corruption in Raskin — in particular, incidences of high quality rice being swapped for lower quality rice, rice being sold at higher prices than those set by government with profits being kept by local officials, and/or subsidised rice being sold to the non-poor (SMERU, 2003: 36, 40; 2008: 9-10). The National Program for Community Empowerment (PNPM) has also faced allegations of misused funds and embezzlement (Jakarta Post, 2011; 2014) as has BLSM (Sumarto, 2014). In some programs, the distribution of benefits has been skewed as a result of regional election campaigns.

## Conclusion

This paper has examined the evolution of welfare capitalism in Indonesia from the New Order to the present time. During the New Order period, it has suggested, Indonesia developed a form of welfare capitalism that was both productivist and predatory in nature. While the post-New Order period has witnessed the introduction of a range of new social programmes, the emergence of a substantially more progressive form of welfare capitalism has been constrained by the continued political dominance of predatory military and bureaucratic officials, domestic and foreign business groups, liberal economic technocrats, and controllers of mobile capital — the groups that dominated the New Order. Democratic decentralization has created an electoral incentive for political leaders to introduce pro-poor social policies and opened up spaces for the poor and their allies in the NGO movement to push for such measures as well. But the ruling coalition has retained sufficient political strength to ensure that the government's new social policy initiatives remain limited, focused on areas that contribute to economic growth, and/or subject to capture by predatory networks. Accordingly, we suggest that welfare capitalism in Indonesia has remained predominantly productivist and predatory in nature, as it was under the New Order, notwithstanding the fact that post-New Order governments have taken some important steps in a more progressive direction.

The implication of this analysis is that, if Indonesia is to develop an Anglo-European form of welfare capitalism — particularly along social democratic lines — there will need to be a prior shift in power away from predatory military and bureaucratic officials, domestic and foreign business groups, liberal economic technocrats, and controllers of mobile capital, on the one hand, towards the poor and their NGO supporters, on the other hand. Only then will the political preconditions for change be in place. At present, it seems unlikely that this will occur given the continued grip of the former coalition on the state apparatus, the limited impact of anti-corruption efforts, and the fact that the poor and their NGO allies have not yet been able to establish a left-wing political party with significant electoral support. In this context, the claims of *The Economist* and *Time* that Indonesia is heading inevitably towards the establishment of an Anglo-European style welfare state seem at best premature and at worst overly optimistic. Such a future is not impossible, particularly in the longer term, but nor is it inevitable.

## Notes

1. See Winters (1996) on the notion of 'mobile capital'.

2. Boediono was also Vice-President from 2009-2014.

3. The ASKESOS programme (see later) was initially trialled between 1996 and 1998 but not fully implemented until the 2000s (Ministry of Social Affairs, nd).

4. The Constitutional Court's reputation was tarnished in 2013 when its then chairman was arrested on corruption charges.

5. As Sumarto and Bazzi (2011) note, however, the positive food security effects of Raskin have been offset by a ban on rice imports because the latter has led to increased domestic rice prices.

# *References*

Achmad, Januar. 1999. *Hollow Development: The Politics of Health in Soeharto's Indonesia.* Canberra: Australian National University.

Arifin, Bustanul. 2008. "From Remarkable Success Stories to Troubling Present: The Case of BULOG in Indonesia." pp. 137-165 in *From Parastatal to Private Trade: Lessons from Asian Agriculture,* edited by S. Rashid, A. Gulati, and R. Cummings. Baltimore: Johns Hopkins University Press.

Asian Development Bank (ADB). 2006. *Indonesia: Social Protection Sector Development Program, Performance Evaluation Report.* Manila: Asian Development Bank.

Aspinall, Edward. 2014. "Health Care and Democratization in Indonesia." Democratization, DOI: 10.1080/13510347.2013.873791.

Aspinall, Edward and Eve Warburton. 2013. "A Healthcare Revolution in the Regions." *Inside Indonesia* 111 (Jan-Mar). Retrieved 18 September 2014 from <http://www.insideindonesia.org/current-edition/a-healthcare-revolution-in-the-regions.>

Bender, Katja. 2013. "The Political Economy of Social Protection Reforms in Developing Countries: What is to be Explained and How?" pp. 33-42 in *Social Protection in Developing Countries: Reforming Systems,* edited by Katja Bender, Markus Kaltenborn, and Christian Pfleiderer. London: Routledge.

Boediono. 2009. *Ekonomi Indonesia Mau ke Mana? Kumpulan Esai Ekonomi* (Where is the Economy of Indonesia Going? A Collection of Economic Essays). Jakarta: Gramedia and Freedom Institute.

Croissant, Aurel. 2004. "Changing Welfare Regimes in East and Southeast Asia: Crisis, Change and Challenge." *Social Policy and Administration* 38 (5): 504-524.

Crouch, Harold. 1978. *The Army and Politics in Indonesia.* Ithaca, NY: Cornell University Press.

Devereux, Stephen and Philip White. 2010. "Social Protection in Africa: Evidence, Politics and Rights." *Poverty and Public Policy* 2(3): 53-77.

Esping-Andersen, Gøsta. 1990. *The Three Worlds of Welfare Capitalism*. Cambridge: Polity.

Goodman, Roger, Gordon White, and Huck-ju Kwon. 1998. *The East Asian Welfare Model: Welfare Orientalism and the State*. London: Routledge.

Gough, Ian. 2001. "Globalization and Regional Welfare Regimes: The East Asian Case." *Global Social Policy* 1: 163-189.

Hadiz, Vedi R. 2003. "Reorganizing Political Power in Indonesia: A Reconsideration of So-called 'Democratic Transitions'." *The Pacific Review* 16(4): 591-611.

Hickey, Samuel. 2008. "Conceptualising the Politics of Social Protection in Africa." pp. 247-263 in *Social Protection for the Poor and Poorest: Concepts, Policies and Politics*, edited by Armando Barrientos and David Hulme. London: Palgrave Macmillan.

Hickey, Samuel, K. Sen, and B. Bukenya, eds. 2015. *The Politics of Inclusive Development: Interrogating the Evidence*. Oxford: Oxford University Press.

Hill, Hal. 1996. *The Indonesian Economy Since 1966: Southeast Asia's Emerging Giant*. Cambridge: Cambridge University Press.

Hoemardani, Soedjono. 1975. *Renungan Tentang Pembangunan* (Thoughts about development). Jakarta: Center for Strategic and International Studies.

Holliday, Ian. 2000. "Productivist Welfare Capitalism: Social Policy in East Asia." *Political Studies* 48(4): 706-723.

Hwang, G. 2015. "The Welfare Modelling Business in the East Asian Welfare State Debate." In Z. Irving, M. Fenger, and J. Hudson (eds.), *Social Policy Review 27: Analysis and Debate in Social Policy 2015*. Bristol: Policy Press.

Irawan, Ade, L. Djani Eriyanto, and Agus Sunaryanto. 2004. *Mendagangkan sekolah: Studi kebijakan MBS di DKI Jakarta* (Trading schools: Studies of school-based management policy in DKI Jakarta). Jakarta, Indonesia: Indonesian Corruption Watch.

Jakarta Post. 2011. "Govt to Crack Down on PNPM Fraud." Retrieved October 2014 from <http://www.thejakartapost.com/news/2011/07/12/govt-crack-down-pnpm-fraud.html.>

_______. 2014. “Rooting Out Corruption One Village at a Time.” Retrieved October 2014 from <http://www.thejakartapost.com/news/2014/04/01/rooting-out-corruption-one-village-a-time.html.>

Jones, Catherine, ed. 1993. *New Perspectives on the Welfare State in Europe*. London: Routledge.

Juliawan, Benny. 2010. “Extracting Labor From its Owner: Private Employment Agencies and Labor Market Flexibility in Indonesia.” *Critical Asian Studies* 42(1): 25-52.

Khan, Mushtaq. 2010. “Political Settlements and the Governance of Growth-Enhancing Institutions.” Retrieved 1 October 2015 from <http://eprints.soas.ac.uk/9968/1/Political_Settlements_internet.pdf.>

Kuypers, Sarah. 2014. “The East Asian Welfare Regime: Reality or Fiction.” CSB Working Paper. Univerity of Antwerp.

Kwon, Huck-ju. 2005. “Transforming the Developmental Welfare State in East Asia.” *Development and Change* 36(3): 477-497.

Kwon, Huck-ju and Ian Holliday. 2007. “The Korean Welfare State: A Paradox of Expansion in an Era of Globalisation and Economic Crisis.” *International Journal of Social Welfare* 16: 242-248.

Ministry of Social Affairs. (nd). *Tentang Askesos*. Retrieved 6 October 2014 from <http://simjks.kemsos.go.id/index.php?page=Berita1andKdBerita=5.>

Moertopo, Ali. 1981. *Strategi Pembangunan Nasional* (Strategy for National Development). Jakarta: Center for Strategic and International Studies.

Niño-Zarazúa, Miguel, A. Barrientos, Samuel Hickey, and David Hulme. 2012. “Social Protection in Sub-Saharan Africa: Getting the Politics Right.” *World Development* 40(1): 163-176.

Park, Chan-ung. 2007. “The Divergent Paths of the East Asian Welfare Regimes: The Effects of Production Regimes and Democratization.” *Korean Social Science Journal* 34(1): 39-70.

Peng, Ito and Joseph Wong. 2010. “East Asia.” pp. 656-670 in *The Oxford Handbook of the Welfare State*, edited by F. Castles, S. Leibfried, S. Lewis, H. Obinger, and C. Pierson. Oxford: Oxford

University Press.

Pierson, Chris. 2005. "'Late Industrializers' and the Development of Welfare Regimes." *Acta Politica* 40: 395-418.

Prawiro, Radius. 1998. *Indonesia's Struggle for Economic Development: Pragmatism in Action*. Oxford: Oxford University Press.

Prianti, M. 2010. "Menkeu Tak Setuju Penetapan Batas Minimal Anggaran" (Finance Minister Disagrees with Minimal Budget Allocations). Kontan. Retrieved 22 September 2014 from <http://nasional.kontan.co.id/news/menkeu-tak-setuju-penetapan-batas-minimal-anggaran-1.>

Ramesh, M. 2014. "Social Protection in Indonesia and the Philippines." *Journal of Southeast Asian Economies* 31(1): 40-56.

Ramesh, M. and Mukul Asher. 2000. *Welfare Capitalism in Southeast Asia: Social Security, Health and Education Policies*. London: Macmillan.

Riady, James. 2013. "Jokonomics, Social Welfare and the Future of Indonesia." *Jakarta Globe*. 11 April. Retrieved 8 October from <http://thejakartaglobe.beritasatu.com/opinion/jokonomics-social-welfare-and-the-future-of-indonesia/.>

Ridding, J. 1998. "ILO warns of social unrest in Asia." *Financial Times* 16 April, p. 4.

Robison, Richard. 1986. *Indonesia: The Rise of Capital*. Sydney: Allen and Unwin.

_______. 1994. "Organising the Transition: Indonesian Politics in 1993/94." pp. 49-78 in *Indonesia Assessment 1994: Finance as a Key Sector in Indonesia's Development*, edited by R. McLeod. Canberra; Singapore: Australian National University and Institute of Southeast Asian Studies.

Robison, Richard and Vedi R. Hadiz. 2004. *Reorganising Power in Indonesia: The Politics of Oligarchy in an Age of Markets*. London: Routledge.

Robison, Richard and Andrew Rosser. 1999. "Surviving the Meltdown: Liberal Reform and Political Oligarchy in Indonesia." pp. 171-191 in *Politics and Markets in the Wake of the Asian Crisis*, edited by R. Robison *et al.* Routledge.

Rokx, Claudia, George Schieber, Pandu Harimurti, Ajay Tandon, and Aparnaa Somanathan. 2009. *Health Financing in Indonesia: A Reform Road Map*. Jakarta: World Bank.

Rosser, Andrew. 2012. "Realising Free Health Care for the Poor in Indonesia: The Politics of Illegal Fees." *Journal of Contemporary Asia* 42(2): 255-275.

_______. 2015. "Law and the Realisation of Human Rights: Insights from Indonesia's Education Sector." *Asian Studies Review* 39(2): 194-212.

Rosser, Andrew and Anuradha Joshi. 2013. "From User Fees to Fee Free: The Politics of Realising Universal Free Basic Education in Indonesia." *The Journal of Development Studies* 49(2): 175-189.

Rosser, Andrew and P. Sulistiyanto. 2013. "The Politics of Universal Free Basic Education in Indonesia: Insights from Yogyakarta." *Pacific Affairs* 86(3): 539-560.

Rosser, Andrew and Maryke van Diermen. forthcoming. "Law, Democracy and the Fulfillment of Socio-Economic Rights in Developing Countries: Insights from Indonesia." *Third World Quarterly*.

Rosser, Andrew and Ian Wilson. 2012. "Democratic Decentralisation and Pro-poor Policy Reform in Indonesia: The Politics of Health Insurance for the Poor in Jembrana and Tabanan." *Asian Journal of Social Science* 40(5-6): 608-634.

Satriana, Sinta, Schmitt Valerie, and Muhamad Tauvik. 2012. *Social Protection Assessment Based National Dialogue: Towards a Nationally Defined Social Protection Floor in Indonesia*. Jakarta: International Labour Organization.

SMERU. 2003. *"Rice for Poor Families" (RASKIN): Did the 2002 Program Operate Effectively? Evidence from Bengkulu and Karawang*. Jakarta: SMERU Research Institute.

_______. 2008. *The Effectiveness of the Raskin Program*. Jakarta: SMERU Research Institute.

Sumarto, Mulyadi. 2014. *Perlindungan Sosial dan Klientelisme: Makna Politik Bantuan Tunai Dalam Pemilihan Umum* (Social Protection and Clientelism: The Political Purpose of Cash Transfers in Public

Elections). Yogyakarta: Gadjah Mada University Press.

Sumarto, Sudamo and Samuel Bazzi. 2011. "Social Protection in Indonesia: Past Experiences and Lessons for the Future," in Annual Bank Conference on Development Opportunities (ABCDE) jointly organized by the World Bank and OECD (Vol. 30).

The Economist. 2012. "Asian Welfare States: New Cradles to Graves." 12 September. Retrieved 7 October 2014 from <http://www.economist.com/node/21562210.>

Time. 2013. "The Welfare State Isn't Dead, It Simply Moved to Asia." 1 November. Retrieved September 2014 from <http://world.time.com/2013/11/01/the-welfare-state-isnt-dead-it-simply-moved-to-asia/.>

Timmer, C. 2008. "Postscript: The Debate Over Food Security in 2006—An Update on the Role of BULOG." pp. 165-173 in *From Parastatal to Private Trade: Lessons from Asian Agriculture,* edited by S. Rashid, A. Gulati, and R. Cummings. Baltimore: Johns Hopkins University Press.

Tjandra, Surya. 2014. "The Indonesian Trade Union Movement Under Reformasi." unpublished paper.

Wilding, Paul. 2008. "Is the East Asian Welfare Model Still Productive?" *Journal of Asian Public Policy* 1(1): 18-31.

Winters, Jeffrey. 1996. *Power in Motion: Capital Mobility and the Indonesian State.* Ithaca, NY: Cornell University Press.

Wood, Geof and Ian Gough. 2006. "A Comparative Welfare Regime Approach to Global Social Policy." *World Development* 34(10): 1696-1712.

World Bank. 1995. *Indonesia—Fourth Health Project: Improving Equity and Quality of Care (Staff Appraisal Report).* Washington DC: World Bank.

________. 2003. *Social Risk Management: The World Bank's Approach to Social Protection in a Globalizing World.* Washington DC: World Bank.

# PART III

## Asia Capitalism in Global Context

Chapter 9

# *How Financial Liberalization Transformed the East Asian Development Model*

Hyungkee Kim

## Introduction

Financial liberalization has significantly changed the East Asian development model that emerged in Japan in the 1960s, Korea in the 1970s, and China in the 1980s.[1] Financial liberalization proceeded in the 1980s in Japan and in the 1990s in Korea. China has been cautious about financial liberalization although there was considerable financial market liberalization after the mid-1990s.

Financial liberalization was the most distinctive in the Anglo-American model. By contrast, financial repression was a major ingredient of the East Asian development model.[2] Thus, financial liberalization would be a destructive force for the East Asian development model. This study aims to clarify how financial liberalization has transformed the East Asian development model. It is argued that the East Asian development model has transformed into a hybrid model in which elements of the Anglo-American model have been grafted onto the East Asian development model. Financial liberalization was followed by labor market flexibilization. Hybridization rather than transition has been the result of the transformation.

Financial liberalization introduced elements of shareholder capitalism into the corporate sector. In shareholder capitalism, maximization of the shareholder value becomes a major goal of management. Short-termism inherent in the principles of shareholder capitalism had impacts on corporate governance and labor market. This study analyzes how financial liberalization has changed corporate governance and labor market. Finally, it evaluates how financial liberalization has transformed the East Asian development model in Japan, Korea, and China through changes in the corporate and labor sectors.

## Financial Liberalization in Japan, Korea, and China

### Trends of Financial Liberalization in the East Asian Development Model

Trends of financial liberalization can be identified by some indicators or indices. To show these trends, this study adopts indicators of capital liberalization measured by the Economic Freedom Index that was constructed by Gwartney *et al.* (2012). The financial reform index constructed by Abiad *et al.* (2008) is used as the financial liberalization index. The overall financial reform index include sub-indices of directed credit, credit ceilings, credit controls, entry barriers, banking supervision, privatization, international capital, and securities markets.

Trends of capital liberalization were differentiated clearly in the three countries. As shown in Table 9.1, Korea and China showed the same trend for capital controls until 1995. They had strict capital controls in the 1980s. However, they liberalized capital controls considerably in the 1990s. After the 1997 Asian financial crisis, China again instituted strict capital controls. By contrast, Korea had strict capital controls for a while in the midst of the 1997 financial crisis but liberalized its capital market abruptly in the 2000s. In 2010, Korea had a much more liberalized capital market than that of the US. Japan liberalized its capital market gradually from the 1980s. In the 1990s, the Capital Liberalization Index of Japan was at the same high level as that of the US and was higher in the 2000s. In 2010, the index showed the same low level of capital liberalization as that of the US. Financial liberalization was one of the major causes of Japan's "lost decade." Rapid financial liberalization after 1993 was an immediate cause of the 1997 financial crisis in Korea. By contrast, the Chinese economy was not influenced in particular by the Asian financial crisis in 1997 because it had relatively strict financial regulations. It is remarkable that Korea liberalized capital market abruptly while China and Japan strictly controlled capital market after 2005.

**Table 9.1** Trends of Capital Liberalization in Korea, China, and Japan

| | 1980 | 1985 | 1990 | 1995 | 2000 | 2005 | 2010 | 2011 |
|---|---|---|---|---|---|---|---|---|
| Korea | 0.00 | 2.00 | 5.00 | 5.00 | 0.00 | 1.54 | 7.69 | 6.92 |
| China | 0.00 | 2.00 | 5.00 | 5.00 | 0.77 | 0.77 | 0.00 | 0.00 |
| Japan | 2.00 | 5.00 | 8.00 | 8.00 | 7.69 | 8.46 | 3.85 | 3.85 |
| US | 8.00 | 8.00 | 8.00 | 8.00 | 6.92 | 6.15 | 3.85 | 3.85 |
| Germany | 8.00 | 10.00 | 10.00 | 10.00 | 9.23 | 3.85 | 3.85 | 3.85 |
| Sweden | 2.00 | 5.00 | 10.00 | 10.00 | 5.38 | 3.08 | 3.08 | 3.08 |

Source: Gwartney J., Lawson R., and Hall J. (2012).

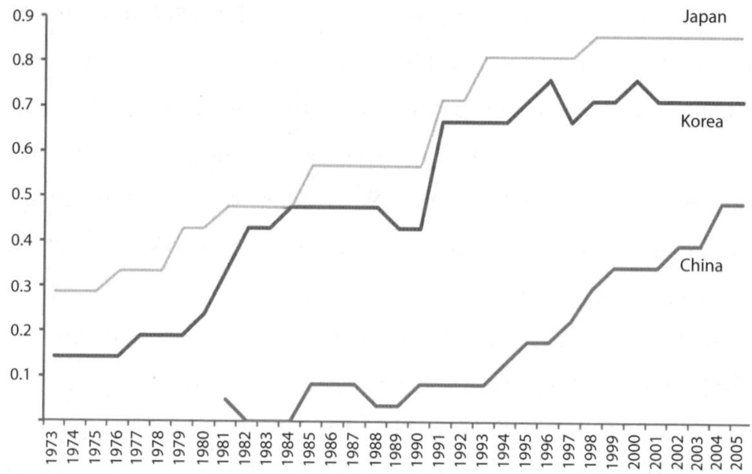


**Figure 9.1** Trends of Financial Liberalization Indices in Japan, Korea, and China
Source: Financial Reform Dataset, 2008, IMF.

The overall extent of financial liberalization can be measured by financial reform indices constructed by the International Monetary Fund (IMF). In this study, a financial reform dataset for 1981-2005 is used for financial liberalization indexes in Japan, Korea, and China. Figure 9.1 shows that there was almost full financial liberalization in the mid-1990s in Japan and Korea.

## Financial "Big Bang" in Japan's model

In Japan, the financial system transitioned from a bank-based to a market-based system. In 1972, the purchase of foreign securities by banks was liberalized, as was outward FDI. A floating exchange-rate regime was introduced and inward FDI was liberalized in 1973. In 1980, transactions of foreign exchange were liberalized. While financial liberalization began in the 1970s, it accelerated in the

1980s, when banks were allowed to enter the securities business. Interest rates were liberalized from 1985. Finally, the "Big Bang" of the capital market was announced in 1996 and the ban on financial holding companies was lifted in 1997. After the Big Bang, foreign investors entered the Japanese stock market (Richter, 2000: 335).

The causes that triggered financial liberalization were twofold: internal demand from the corporate and household sectors and external pressure from foreign investors of the US and EU. Corporate profits accumulated as corporate savings, and the corporate sector emerged as a net saver. Corporations had less need to borrow from banks. Thus, banks demanded financial deregulation so as to develop new business lines. Development of bond markets was spurred by increasing public sector borrowing. As household assets accumulated, there was demand from households for a greater variety of financial products.

Financial liberalization, which brought about overinvestment and speculative investment, was a cause of the asset bubble that developed in the 1980s. Other causes were as follows: easier money conditions following the Plaza Agreement in 1985, overconfidence about the outlook for the Japanese economy, poor credit risk management by banks, and weak prudential regulation (Takahashi, 2012). After the Big Bang, cross-border capital transactions were liberalized and securitization of assets was permitted. Securities were fully liberalized. The establishment of financial holding companies permitted the Japanese economy to be influenced by international finance as foreign investors entered to the Japanese stock market.

Thus, the financial system in Japan transformed significantly from a bank-based system to a market-based system.[3] Corporations became more independent from the banking sector. The proportion of internal financing increased and that of external financing decreased. Of external financing, the portion of bank borrowings drastically declined from 38.9% in the 1960s to 8.9% in the 1980s (Tohyama, 2000). This precipitated the weakening of the main bank system, which supplied stable long-term loans to the industry as well as monitored management of the corporations. However, the transformation of the Japanese financial system was a financial hybridization process in which the main-bank and market-based systems were mixed.

## Rapid Financial Liberalization and Crisis in Korea's Model

Korea introduced a rapid financial liberalization program in 1993 just 4 years before the 1997 financial crisis. This included deregulation of interest rates, abolition of policy loan, granting more managerial autonomy to banks, reducing entry barriers to the financial industry, liberalization of foreign exchange, and opening of capital markets (Chang, 2006: 269). As the non-bank financial intermediaries became deregulated rapidly, they moved outside the ambit of the state's supervision and under the control of the *chaebol*. This sudden domestic financial liberalization left Korea defenseless in the face of massive financial crisis (Woo-Cumings, 2001). Moreover, Korea aggressively removed capital controls on trade financing and short-term borrowings by financial companies. The result of capital market liberalization was excessive short-term foreign debt and a high share of foreign portfolio investment in the domestic securities market, which led to high instability of financial markets.

Financial liberalization in 1993, which institutionalized capital market liberalization, brought about the 1997 financial crisis because it was followed by a sharp increase of short-term foreign debt and massive inflows of short-term international capital or hot money. In the environment of financial liberalization, overinvestment and duplicate investment by the *chaebol* firms in 1994-1997 was precipitated by the abandonment of industrial policy through which the government proactively coordinated investment of the firms. Foreign borrowings of the banking sector amplified the financial crisis. In short, both financial liberalization and the end of industrial policy were the immediate causes of the 1997 financial crisis. Contrary to the argument of the IMF staff (1998), which attributed the 1997 financial crisis in Korea to excessive government intervention in the economy by too strong regulations, the actual causes were too rapid financial liberalization and too weak financial regulations.

After the 1997 financial crisis, the Korean financial system was liberalized decisively according to IMF restructuring programs. Bank laws and finance-related legislation were reformed to strengthen the interests of shareholders. The role of the Bank of Korea was redefined to focus on only price stability rather than enhancing the soundness of bank and financial institutions through price stability. As a result, pro-investment and pro-growth monetary policy retreated in favor of pro-finance monetary policy (Chang, 2006: 273-275). Moreover, capital markets were opened completely. Rapid financial liberalization not only increased the instability of the Korean economic system but also intensified concentration of economic power in the hands of *chaebol* firms. Financial liberalization transformed the Korean financial system from a bank-based to a market-based system, which is one of the major characteristics of the Anglo-American financial system.

## Deliberate Financial Liberalization in China's Model

The Chinese financial system was strictly controlled initially by the state. Even though trade liberalization was pursued rapidly and extensively, financial liberalization was not promoted much. In particular, there was strict regulation of foreign portfolio investment. Sometimes, there has been reversal of financial liberalization. However, there has been a gradual shift toward a more market-oriented system in which capital and stocks markets have begun to play key roles in financial transactions.

The share of the banking sector in financial assets decreased from 83.5% in 1998 to 73.8% in 2009 while the share of investment (insurance, stocks, bonds, and funds) increased from 8.9% to 19.9%. The share of deposits in individual financial assets decreased from 71.8% in 2004 to 64.3% in 2009 while the share of investment increased from 28.2% in 2004 to 35.7% in 2009 (Kang, 2011). With this securitization, there was deregulation in the financial market. The credit market was deregulated significantly from the mid-1990s. The capital market was deregulated considerably in the 1990s.

Interest liberalization began from 1986 when the terms of the lending rate could be determined by mutual agreement between lenders and borrowers. In 1996, the inter-bank offered rate was liberalized. Directed credit was reduced and general guidelines on loans were implemented in 1996. The lending rates on foreign currency and deposit rates on large foreign currency accounts were liberalized in 2000. Foreign financial institutions were permitted to do business in some coastal cities. In 2001, foreign banks were allowed to conduct foreign exchange business (Yan *et al.*, 2011). Hot money began to flow in after 2003 and increased rapidly from 2007. As a result, the volatility of the Chinese economy began to increase. After the 1997 Asian financial crisis, China decisively reversed capital liberalization with strict capital controls.

## Financial Liberalization and Transformation of the East Asian Development Model

### Changes in Corporate Governance: Rise of Shareholder Capitalism

The overall transformation characteristic of the corporate system in the East Asian development model was the introducing principle of shareholder capitalism or the Anglo-American model. Transformation of the Japanese corporate system was more representative than that of Korea or China.

The Japanese corporate system changed during the "lost decade," including reforms to ownership, corporate governance, human resources management, and inter-firm relationships. Several reform measures designed to enhance shareholder value were legislated and implemented in practice in 1997, when the Japanese government initiated a series of reforms of the corporate system, introduction of stock options, establishment of executive officer organization, and legalization of pure holding companies.[4] First,

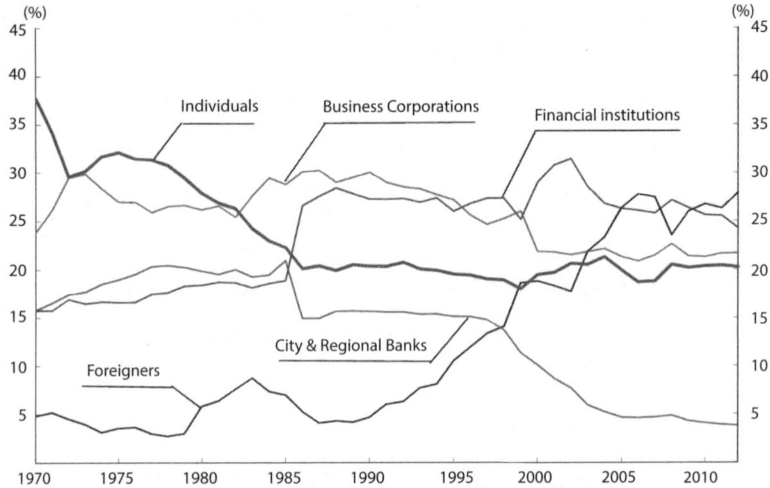


**Figure 9.2** Ownership Structure by Type of Shareholder in Japanese Listed Companies

Source: 2012 Share Ownership Survey, Tokyo Stock Exchange.
Note: 1. Survey has been conducted on a "unit-of-share" basis since a 1985 survey.
2. The market value of financial institutions excludes that of city and regional banks.

change in corporate ownership was a major shift that transformed the corporate system. As shown in Figure 9.2, the proportion of main banks (city and regional banks) in share ownership of list companies decreased sharply from the late 1990s while the proportion of foreign investors increased rapidly from the late 1990s. The proportion of institutional investors (financial institutions) increased from the mid-1980s. From this, it is evident that main-bank ownership weakened decisively. This change in corporate ownership forced managers of firms to adopt the principle of shareholder capitalism, meaning that shareholder sovereignty was strengthened while managerial sovereignty was weakened.

Under the support of institutional reforms, Japanese firms began to combine traditional managerial sovereignty with the emerging element of shareholder capitalism. The pressure to focus on shareholder value and corporate profitability from outside shareholders precipitated a shift from a relationship- and stakeholder-oriented model of corporate governance to a market-based, shareholder-oriented model of corporate governance. In addition, the rise of foreign ownership forced managers to introduce shareholder-oriented corporate governance. Since the late 1990s, shareholders' interests gradually became the center of managerial attention (Colpan *et al.*, 2011). As the holding company system was introduced, the traditional role of main banks in monitoring business management was taken over by holding companies.

Furthermore, there was a change in the *keiretsu* system.[5] Risk-sharing intervention of *keiretsu* to affiliates firms diminished in the lost decades of the 1990s. Foreign investors pressed the managers of firms to sell off shareholdings in affiliates. As modularization in manufacturing proceeded, which required less integration of production stages, the advantages of *keiretsu*-style supply management diminished. Some *keiretsu* firms began to develop arm's-length transactions with affiliated firms. Thus, the Japanese corporate system has been closer to that of the Anglo-American model in terms of inter-firm relationships (Lincoln and Shimotani, 2009). However, there is little evidence to suggest that the dense business networks underpinned by the *keiretsu* have collapsed completely. The enduring long-term and reciprocal business relationships that have tied firms to business groups remain distinctive (Walter and Zhang, 2012: 252).

Korea showed a similar pattern of transformation in its corporate system to that of Japan. Korea's ownership structure of corporations changed significantly. The most prominent changes after the 1997 financial crisis were sharp declines of the shares of gov-

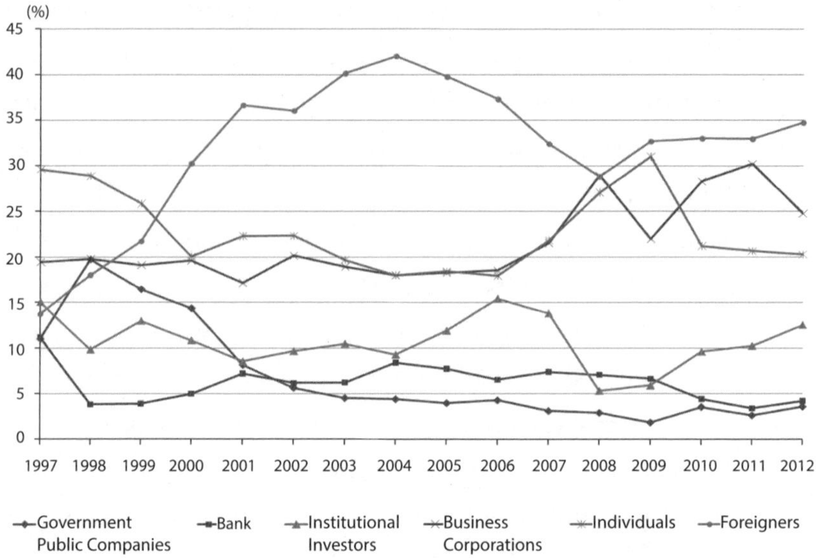


**Figure 9.3** Ownership Structure by Type of Shareholder in Korean Listed Companies
Source: Korea Exchange.

ernment, public companies, and banks and rapid increases of the shares of foreigners as shown in Figure 9.3. Foreign shareholders, including institutional investors, have pressed firms to introduce principle of shareholder capitalism. The 1997 financial crisis gave decisive momentum to the transformation of the Korean corporate system, including the *chaebol* system.[6] The reform of *chaebol* after the 1997 financial crisis included strengthening of minority shareholder rights, introducing outside directorships, and banning circular shareholding. There was an attempt to Americanize corporate governance in Korea(Chang, 2006). This reform contributed to introducing the elements of shareholder capitalism. Even though family ownership in the *chaebol* weakened a little, *chaebol* retained the characteristic of family ownership. The hierarchical sub-contracting relationship between *chaebol* firms and supplier firms has not changed. Thus, after the 1997 crisis, the Korean corporate system transformed from the *chaebol* system to a "*chaebol* system plus shareholder capitalism," with primacy of the former (Kim, 2012).

The Chinese corporate system was also transformed considerably in the marketization and privatization process. There was a separation of ownership from management in the state-owned enterprises (SOEs[7]) by State-Owned Industrial Enterprises Law (SOE Law) in 1988. Based on the ordinance on the Management Mechanism Transformation Act in 1992, independent managerial rights were given to the SOEs (Chen, 2009: 119).[8] Outside directorship was introduced in 2004. In a decentralized economic system, local governments have continued to oversee the implementation of CCP's guiding principles and policies in the SOEs. As the Company Law was introduced in 1993, the maximization of owners' interests became the primary goal of corporate practice (Carney, 2012). It means that an element of shareholder capitalism was introduced in Chinese corporate governance. However, the SOEs were under control of SASAC (State Asset Supervision and Administration Commission). As the proportion of the private and foreign owned enterprises increased, the principle of shareholder capitalism came to be intensified.

In sum, the common characteristic of the transformation of the corporate system in Japan, Korea, and China was the introduction of the principle of shareholder capitalism in corporate governance. The elements of shareholder capitalism merged into the *keiretsu* system in Japan, *chaebol* system in Korea, and SOE system in China. This suggests that a kind of hybridization occurred in the corporate system.

## Changes in the Labor Market: Flexibilization of the Labor Market

According to the hypothesis of institutional complementarity (Amable, 2000; Aoki, 2001; Hall and Soskice, 2001), financial liberalization requires flexibility of labor markets. Marketization and privatization of the public sector, introduction of shareholder capitalism in the corporate system, and liberalization of financial markets in East Asian development model accompanied flexibilization of labor markets.[9] The most dramatic transformation occurred in the Chinese labor market.

From the 1950s to the late 1980s, the Chinese employment system was characterized by lifetime employment. During the re-

**Table 9.2** Share of Contractual Employees in China

(Unit: 10,000 persons, %)

| Year | Total Contractual Employees | Proportion (Total Formal Employees =100) | State-owned Units | Urban Collective Owned Units | Other Ownership Units |
|---|---|---|---|---|---|
| 1984 | 209 | 1.8 | 2.0 | 1.0 | 8.1 |
| 1985 | 409 | 3.3 | 3.7 | 2.2 | 11.4 |
| 1986 | 624 | 4.9 | 5.6 | 2.7 | 14.5 |
| 1987 | 873 | 6.6 | 7.6 | 3.6 | 18.1 |
| 1988 | 1,234 | 9.1 | 10.1 | 5.8 | 20.7 |
| 1989 | 1,468 | 10.7 | 11.8 | 7.0 | 25.1 |
| 1990 | 1,702 | 12.1 | 13.3 | 8.1 | 26.3 |
| 1991 | 1,972 | 13.6 | 14.9 | 8.9 | 28.0 |
| 1992 | 2,541 | 17.2 | 18.9 | 11.0 | 29.8 |
| 1993 | 3,123 | 21.0 | 21.9 | 15.5 | 37.4 |
| 1994 | 3,839 | 25.9 | 26.2 | 20.1 | 45.6 |
| 1995 | 6,096 | 40.9 | 40.1 | 37.4 | 62.8 |

Source: National Bureau of Statistics of China.

form of SOEs, there was a shift from the "iron rice bowl," a word symbolic of lifetime employment in the SOEs before 1978, to contract-work employment. Marketization and privatization of the SOEs in China precipitated flexibilization of the labor market. A lay-off program known as xiagang was introduced. Marketization and privatization of SOEs accompanied large-scale SOE downsizing. About 37 million workers were laid off in the SOE sector from 1998 to 2004 (Aglietta and Bai, 2013: 108-109). The dispatch labor system has become popular in Chinese firms. Among centrally controlled SOEs, about 10% of employees are dispatch workers who are employed temporarily. As Table 9.2 shows, share of contractual employees in total formal employees increased drastically from 1.8% in 1984 to 40.9% in 1995. Even in SOEs, the share was 40.1%.

Thus, there is a tiered employment system in which regular contract workers and non-regular dispatch workers coexist. Because there are no independent labor unions that can bargain collectively with employers, the employment status of workers in China is essentially unstable. Thus, the labor market is highly flexible even though labor legislation, such as the National Labor Law, Labor Contract Law, Trade Union Law, and Labor Dispute Mediation and Arbitration Law, formally guarantee job stability to some extent.

In addition, two historical processes transformed Chinese employment in the past three decades: commodification and casualization. An alliance of interest between the state and capital, both global and domestic, has rendered labor disorganized and individualized (Lee, 2012). The Chinese government attempted to regulate employment relations through a series of labor laws based on the notion of market-oriented, voluntary, and individualist "contract labor." The National Labor Law introduced in 1995 required all employees to sign labor contracts. However, by 2007, only 50% of all enterprises had signed contracts with their employees and the rate among non-state firms was only 20%. Among signed labor contracts, 60-70% were short-term contracts of less than 1 year (Lee, 2012). The New Labor Contract Law revised in 2006 introduced contracts labor without fixed terms alongside those with fixed terms, making employment more stable. Thus, the employment system in China became a three-tier system: non fixed-term contracts, fixed-term contracts, and dispatch work. Casualization of employment can be seen from the huge amount of nongmingong (about 100 millions) in the urban informal sector. The dominant employment trend was reorganization of employment away from manufacturing and the increasing prevalence of temporary and dispatch workers in all sectors of the economy (Lee, 2012).

The Korean labor market was flexibilized rapidly after the 1997 financial crisis. There were two major trends after the crisis: collapse of the internal labor market and increase in the share of non-regular workers. Table 9.3 shows the change in the hiring pattern of major Korean companies[10] after the crisis. There was a drastic decline in the share of hiring new graduates while the share of hiring experienced workers increased rapidly (Kim, 2012). This strongly suggests that internal labor markets in the large firms collapsed. The breakdown of the internal labor market signaled the demise of the convention of long-term employment.

The Protection of Dispatched Workers Act introduced in 1998 opened the path to wide non-regularization of employment. The share of non-regular workers increased after the 1997 financial crisis from 27.4% in 2002 to 34.2% in 2011. Non-regular workers

**Table 9.3** Collapse of Internal Labor Market in Korea after the 1997 Financial Crisis

| | 1996 | 1997 | 1998 | 1999 | 2000 | 2001 | 2002 |
|---|---|---|---|---|---|---|---|
| Hiring of Newly Graduated Students (A) | 7.5 | 5.6 | 3.8 | 4.1 | 4.1 | 2.5 | 1.9 |
| Hiring of Experienced Workers (B) | 4.6 | 4.2 | 4.7 | 11.2 | 14.4 | 9.3 | 8.5 |
| Within a Company (C) | 3.6 | 3 | 4.5 | 10.5 | 4.6 | 3.2 | 6.7 |
| Other (D) | 2.6 | 2.1 | 1.9 | 3.7 | 3.5 | 2.3 | 2.8 |
| Job Accession Rate (E)(Total) | 18.3 | 14.9 | 14.9 | 29.5 | 26.7 | 17.4 | 19.9 |
| (A/E)×100 | 41.0 | 37.6 | 25.5 | 13.9 | 15.4 | 14.4 | 9.5 |
| (B/E)×100 | 25.1 | 28.2 | 31.5 | 38.0 | 53.9 | 64.6 | 42.7 |

Sources: Kim and Jeon (2004).

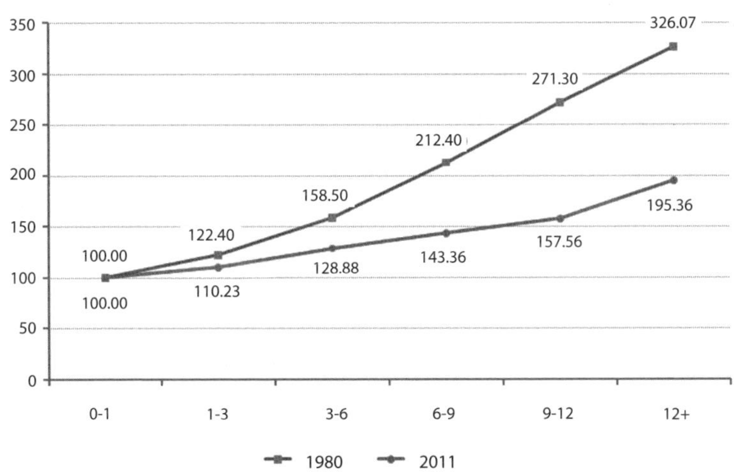


**Figure 9.4** Job Tenure-Earnings Profile in Korea

Sources: Basic Survey on Wage Structure (Raw Data), Ministry of Employment and Labor.

were discriminated against severely compared to regular workers in terms of employment, wages, and social insurance.[11] Labor unions in Korea largely represent and protect the interests of regular workers. Non-regular workers usually cannot become members of enterprise unions, which are organized at the firm level, not at the industry level. The pay-for-performance system, which is a distinctive wage system in the Western model, has been grafted onto the traditional seniority wage system. As pay-for-performance system was introduced, seniority wage system weakened. Seniority wage system has weakened substantially for the period 1980-2011 as shown in Figure 9.4.

In Japan, there was flexibilization of the labor market during the 'lost decade' of the 1990s. There were significant changes in lifetime employment and the seniority wage system, which had been the two major features of Japanese industrial relations. First, lifetime employment has reduced significantly. Reform of labor laws and changes in corporate governance precipitated the demise of lifetime employment. The Labor Dispatching Law legalizing temporary agency labor for specific occupations was introduced in 1985. Revisions of the law in 1996 and 1999 made it easier to use agency labor. The 2003 revision lifted the prohibition on the use of agency labor in the manufacturing industry and extended the maximum employment period of agency workers from 1 year to 3 years. Revision of the Labor Standards Law in 1998 allowed multi-year fixed contracts as an alternative to traditional indefinite contracts.

As corporate governance in Japan moved toward a market-oriented style that pursues the maximization of shareholder value or shareholder-oriented management to achieve short-term performance, lifetime employment began to shrink. Kambayashi and Kato (2011) found through cohort analysis that job retention rates of regular employees fell significantly from the 1987-1997 period to the 1992-2002 period, meaning that job stability of regular employees started to fall from the late 1990s. This tended to be concentrated among female workers and mid-career hires. Male regular employees who were new graduate hires enjoyed traditional lifetime employment. The biggest losers appeared to be female regular employees aged more than 30 years with relatively short tenures in large firms. Hamaaki *et al.* (2010) found a decline in the 5-year job retention rate for educated young workers. There was an inter-generational gap between young workers and middle-aged and older workers in terms of lifetime employment. The widely observed dropout of young workers from the lifetime employment system suggests that it has started to degenerate (Isogai, 2012). The proportion of new graduate hires decreased from 64.1% in 1977 to 52.3% in 2007.[12]

These facts suggest that lifetime employment became limited to a smaller core group of male regular workers. Thus, the proportion of regular employees decreased from 82% in 1991 to 65% in 2012. Meanwhile, the share of non-regular employees increased from 18% to 35%. Non-regularization of employment is one of the major transformation features of the Japanese labor market. Large Japanese firms have relied much more on numerical flexibility than functional flexibility.[13] The impact of the decline in lifetime employment has been greatest among younger cohorts. In 1998, 83% of those aged 15-24 years had regular jobs. By 2006, this had dropped to 54%.

There has been transformation of the seniority wage system also in Japan. As Table 9.4 shows, the proportion of firms that introduced pay-for-tasks, pay-for-ability, and pay-for-performance wage systems increased significantly, meaning that the seniority

**Table 9.4** Transformation of Wage System in Japan

| | 1996 | 1999 | 2004 | 2007 |
|---|---|---|---|---|
| Expand Pay-for-Job | 12.1 | 11.3 | 15.5 | 23.3 |
| Expand Pay-for-Task and Ability | 15.7 | 15.8 | 17.6 | 22.1 |
| Expand Pay-for-Performance | 15.0 | 15.5 | 20.7 | 23.7 |

Sources: Kambayashi and Kato (2011), p 248, Table 7.16 reconstructed.
Note: The numbers represent the percentage of firms that introduced a wage system other than weakening the seniority wage system.

wage system has been in gradual decline. In addition, weakening of the seniority wage system can be confirmed from changes in the job tenure-earnings profile, shown in Figure 9.5. The extent of wage increases by increasing jobtenure significantly decreased for the period 1979-2012.

From the overall trends in the three countries seen in Table 9.5, it is noteworthy that more liberalization of labor markets in terms of hiring and firing was promoted from the late 1990s in Korea and China. China has become closer to the US in terms of hiring and firing regulations. In this sense, the Americanization of the Chinese labor market can be said to be occurring. In Japan, there were not so many changes in hiring and firing regulations in the 1990s. In fact, Japan strengthened regulations on hiring and firing from the late 2000s in the midst of long stagnation. However, there was a decline in lifetime employment and significant non-regularization of employment in Japan in the lost decades. Thus, flexibilization of labor markets in the East Asian developmental model can be summarized as follows: shrinking lifetime jobs, weakening of seniority wage system, and rapid growth of non-regular jobs in Korea and Japan, and a shift from lifetime employment to fixed-term contracts in China.

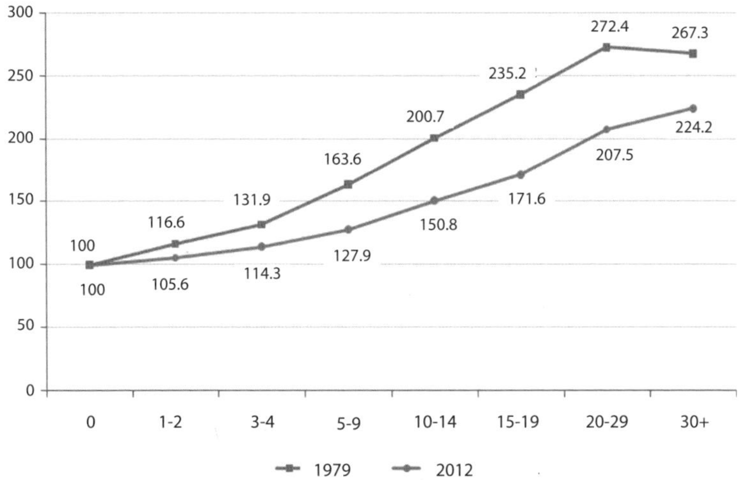


**Figure 9.5** Job Tenure-Earnings Profile in Japan

Sources: Ministry of Welfare and Labor, Wage Census 2012, Wage Survey 1979.

**Table 9.5** Changes in Hiring and Firing Regulations

| | 1990 | 1995 | 2000 | 2005 | 2010 | 2011 |
|---|---|---|---|---|---|---|
| Korea | 3.53 | 3.53 | 4.70 | 4.71 | 3.76 | 3.95 |
| China | 4.30 | 4.30 | 5.10 | 5.27 | 5.45 | 5.47 |
| Japan | 4.82 | 4.82 | 4.18 | 4.62 | 2.97 | 3.04 |
| US | 7.15 | 7.15 | 6.65 | 7.01 | 6.84 | 6.73 |
| Germany | 3.94 | 3.94 | 1.82 | 2.42 | 3.01 | 3.49 |
| Sweden | 3.93 | 3.93 | 2.18 | 1.92 | 2.52 | 3.18 |

Sources: Gwartney J., Lawson R., and Hall J. (2012).

## Transformation of Development Model: Transition or Hybridization?

The transformation of a development model may well be explained by the incrementalinstitutional change approach of Mahoney and Thelen (2010).[14] They identified four mechanisms through which transformation of institutions might occur. "Displacement"occurs when a new model diffuses and displaces the existing model. "Layering" occurs when a new institution coexists with an old institution. "Drift" occurs when rules remain unchanged but existing institutions are neglected by the people. "Conversion" occurs when existing institutions are redeployed for new purposes and goals. While displacement might mean the transition of a development model, conversion and layering might-signal hybridization of a development model. Since the process of transformation includes transition and hybridization, the typology of Mahoney and Thelen (2010) is useful in analyzing the transformation of a development model.

Transformation of a development model may be either transitionto a new model or hybridization within the existing model. When summarizing the changes in the financial, corporate, and labor sectors in Japan, Korea, and China analyzed above, how can we identify the transformation of the East Asian development model? From the analysis above, the transformation of the East Asian development model during the last 2 or 3 decades can be identified as hybridization rather than transition.

Some elements of a liberal market economy, shareholder capitalism, and the Anglo-American model have been introduced to the East Asian model. On the one hand, these elements coexisted alongside the East Asian model ("layering"). On the other hand, they triggered the East Asian model to embrace new goals ("conversion"). In terms of corporate governance, the *keiretsu* system plus shareholder capitalism in Japan, the *chaebol* system plus shareholder capitalism in Korea, and the SOE system plus shareholder capitalism in China were examples of "conversion." In this case, *keiretsu, chaebol,* and SOEs partly pursued the maximization of shareholder value at the expense of other stakeholders, including employees. The results were flexibilization of labor markets, which, in the case of China, accompanied high proportion of contract labor and informalization of employment (nongmingong) and, in the cases of Korea and Japan, accompanied high levels of non-regularization of workers. In some cases, the pay-for-performance wage system was combined with the lifetime employment system. In other cases, shareholdercapitalism-type corporate governance-was combined with lifetime employment. All these show cases of hybridization in the process of transformation.

A good example of hybridization comes from J-type firms. Financial and ownership characteristics of Japanese firms have moved substantially in the direction of market-oriented style in the wake of the banking crisis of 1997. Leading Japanese firms reorganized themselves into hybrid organizational forms by introducing such systems as pay-for-performance wages and market-oriented corporate governance. Here, a new J-type firm has emerged as a hybrid model.

Miyamoto (2007) found four types of Japanese firms: traditional J-type firms (30%) that had lifetime employment and seniority wage systems; A-type firms (18.2%) with shareholder-oriented management that abandoned lifetime employment; new J-type firms (39.7%) that introduced pay-for-performance in order to maintain lifetime employment; and declining J-type firms (12.2%) that abandoned lifetime employment. The new J-type firm is a hybrid firm. Jackson (2009) identified two types of Japanese hybrid firms: type I hybrid firms that combine market-oriented finance and corporate governance with lifetime employment and type II hybrid firms that combine relationship-oriented finance and corporate governance with market-oriented employment and incentive patterns. Type I hybrid firms have become predominant among large Japanese firms (Jackson, 2009). According to these studies, hybrid firms are dominant in Japan. It remains an open question whether new J-type firms can be sustained over the long termas hybrid organizational firms (Isogai, 2012).

Hybridization also occurred in Korean firms in whichthe pay-for-performance wage system was introduced to the existing seniority wage system. There was hybridization of the wage system that weakened the existing seniority wage system.The most distinctive features of hybridization in Korea might be the introduction of elements of shareholder capitalism in the existing *chaebol* system. Even though the *chaebol* system remains dominant in large firms' corporate governance, the new elements of shareholder capitalism are taking root in the existing *chaebol* system. In this hybrid system, it is noteworthy that the conflict between owner management and shareholder rights is arising in the large firms.

In China, the very concept of the SME is a good example of hybridization. This is a kind of a hybrid market economy in which socialist values and policies are combined with a market economy. China's gradual approach to the transition from planned economy to market economy, which is incontrast to the big bang radical transformation of the Soviet Union and Eastern Europe, generated hybrid forms in the corporate, financial, and labor sectors. The seniority wage system is not dominant in Chinese firms because lifetime employment is not prevalent.

When we consider the overall trends of financial market liberalization, changes in corporate governance, and flexibilization of labor markets, we can conclude that hybridization of the coordinated market economy (CME) with the liberal market economy (LME) in Japan, hybridization of the regulated market economy (RME) with the LME in Korea, and hybridization of the socialist market economy (SME) with the LME in China have progressed during the last 2 or 3 decades.

## Conclusion

Financial liberalization was followed by market-based financial system and labor market flexibilization in East Asian development model. The elements of shareholder capitalism were introduced in existing corporate governancein Japan, Korea, and China. Significant changes occurred in the lifetime employment system and seniority wage system. A substantial breakdown of internal labor markets occurred in large firms in Korea and Japan,where the share of non-regular workers increased significantly. In urban China, informal employment increased significantly. The seniority wage system has weakened in Japan. Hybrid wage systems were introduced in Japan, Korea, and China.

From the analysis, it can be argued that the East Asian development model has transformed into a hybrid model in which elements of the Anglo-American model have been grafted onto the East Asian development model. These elements are a market-based financial system, debt securitization, shareholder capitalism, flexible labor market, and pay-for-performance wage system. However, the core of the East Asian model, such as the bank-based financial system, dominance of *keiretsu-chaebol*-SOE, lifetime employment, and the seniority wage system, has not collapsed completely. Hybridization rather than transition has been the result of the transformation.

Hybridization is inherently unstable since two conflicting principles coexist within the same entity. Thus, instability is inherent in the hybridization of the East Asian development model. The East Asian development model may evolve toward a new development model. It remains to be seen whether it will retain the core of its own model or be transformed into a completely new model in the future.

## *Notes*

1 This paper included Japan, Korea, and China in the East Asian development model. The reason why we chose these three countries was that Japan was the creator of the East Asian Development Model and Korea showed a typical East Asian Development Model and China has adopted the East Asian Development Model with its own version. Moreover, it is because Japanese, Chinese, and Korean economy are three representative economies in the East Asian region, the interdependence of which determines the dynamism of the East Asian economy.

2. The major ingredients of the East Asian development model are as follows: developmental state and industrial policy in state sector, insider-oriented governance and relation-based contracting in corporate sector, bank-based system and financial repression in financial sector, long-term employment and seniority wages system in labor sector, and strategic opening, export promotion, and capital control in foreign sector.

3 Changes in the financial system were due to Japanese corporations becoming internationally competitive and less dependent on the banking sector (Boyer and Yamada, 2002: 85).

4 The ban on holding companies was lifted by an amendment to the Anti-Monopoly Act in 1997. In addition, an outside auditor was required to sit on each board to ensure independent oversight of corporate finances by an amendment to the Commercial Code in 1994. Another amendment in 1997 removed legal strictures on stock options, which was effective in aligning the interests of management with those of shareholders. An amendment to the Commercial Code in 2002 introduced American-style "boards with committees" as a second option alongside the traditional Japanese-style boards with statutory auditors (Colpan *et al.*, 2011).

5 Keirezu that was transformed from prewar zaibatzu is a Japanese type of conglomerates.

6 Chaebol is a Korean type of conglomerates that is similar to Japanese prewar

zaibatzu that had family ownership.

7. SOEs are Chinese type of conglomerates that seems to evolve toward Korean chaebol or Japanese keiretzu.

8. Major independent managerial rights were decision making rights on production, pricing, hiring and firing, compensation, personnel management, and cooperation and takeover.

9. Marketization, privatization, liberalization, and flexiblization were major trends of institutional changes in East Asian development model in last two or three decades.

10. These companies included chaebol firms, firms in financial sector, and public enterprises.

11. In Korea, there are triple discriminations against non-regular workers: employment discrimination, wage discrimination and social insurance discrimination.

12. This calculation was based on the data of employment status appeared in Basic Survey on Employment Structures carried by Bureau of Statistics of Ministry of General Affairs.

13. Numerical flexibility means wage and employment flexibility while functional flexibility means skill upgrading and transfer of workers. Numerical flexibility usually accompanies wage-cuts and lay-offs while functional flexibility does not incur them.

14. There are two approaches to institutional change. One is a variety of capitalism approach based on the concept of institutional complementarity by Hall and Soskice (2001). This involves change with long periods of institutional stability disturbed by a radical breakdown. It is overly functionalist in linking system coherence and stability. Here, changes are brought about primarily through exogenous factors. The other approach is incremental institutional change by Mahoney and Thelen (2010), which focuses on a slow pace of continual deinstitutionalization and reinstitutionalization. It emphasizes endogenous change.

## References

Abiad, Abdul, Enrica Detragiache, and Thierry Tressel. 2008. "A New Database of Financial Reforms." IMF Working Paper.

Aglietta, Michel and Gou Bai. 2013. *China's Development: Capitalism and Empire*. New York: Routledge.

Amable, Bruno. 2000. *The Diversity of Modern Capitalism*. New York: Oxford University Press.

Aoki, Masahiko. 2001. *Toward a Comparative Institutional Analysis*. Cambridge, MA: MIT Press.

Boyer, Robert, Hiroyasu Uemura, and Akinori Isogai, eds. 2012. *Diversity and Transformations of Asian Capitalisms*. New York: Routledge.

Boyer, Robert and Toshio Yamada, eds. 2002. *Japanese Capitalism in Crisis: A Regulationist Interpretation*. Vol. 5. Routledge.

Carney, Richard. 2012. "Political Hierarchy and Finance: The Politics of China's Financial Development." In Walter and Zhang (2012).

Chang, Ha-Joon. 2006. *The East Asian Development Experience: The Miracle, the Crisis and the Future*. New York and Penang: Zed Books and TWN.

Chen, Yun. 2009. *Transition and Development in China: Towards Shared Growth*. Burlington: Ashgate.

Colpan, Asli M., Takashi Hikino, and Toru Yoshikawa. 2011. "Changing Ownership and Governance Innovation: Japanese Enterprises in Transition." In Hiroaki Miyoshi and Yoshifumi Nakata (eds.) (2011).

Gwartney, James, Robert Lawson, and Joshua Hall. 2012. *Economic Freedom of the World*. 2012 Annual Report of World Bank.

Hall, Peter A. and David Soskice. 2001. *Varieties of Capitalism: The Institutional Foundations of Comparative Advantage*. Oxford University Press.

Hamaaki, Junya, Masahiro Hori, Saeko Maeda, and Keiko Murata. 2010. "Is the Japanese Employment System Degenerating?: Evidence from the Basic Survey on Wages Structure." ESRI Discussion Paper 232. Economic and Social Research Institute, Cabinet Office, Tokyo.

IMF Staff. 1998. "The Asian Crisis: Causes and Curses." *Finance and Development* 35(2): 18-21.

Isogai, Akinori. 2012. "The Transformation of the Japanese Corporate System and the Hierarchical Nexus of Institutions." In Robert Boyer, *et al.* (eds.) (2012).

Jackson, Gregory. 2009. "The Japanese firm and its diversity." *Economy and Society* 38(4): 606-629.

Kambayashi, Ryo and Takao Kato. 2011. "The Japanese Employment System after the Bubble Burst: New Evidence." In Koichi Hamada, Anil K. Kashyap, and David E. Weinstein, eds., *Japan's Bubble, Deflation, and Long-term Stagnation.* Cambridge; London: MIT Press.

Kang, Dong Soo, ed. 2011. *Development and Challenges of the Chinese Financial System.* Korea Development Institute.

Kim, Hyungkee. 2006. *The Third Way of Korean Economy.* Hanul Academy (in Korean).

_______. 2012. "The Great Transformation of the Korean Economy since 1962: Processes and Consequences." In Robert Boyer, *et al.* (eds.) (2012).

Kim, T. K. and B. Y. Jeon. 2004. *Restructuring and Industrial Relations.* In Proceedings of International Conference of the Korean Economic Association.

Lee Ching Kwan. 2012. "Durable Subordination: Chinese Labour Regime through a South Korean Lens." In Walter and Zhang (eds.) (2012).

Lincoln, James and Masahiro Shimotani. 2009. "Whither the Keiretzu, Japan's Business Network? How were they structured? What did they do? Why are they gone?" Institute for Research on Labor and Employment, Working Paper Series, University of California, Berkeley.

Mahoney, James and Kathlen Thelen. 2010. *Explaining Institutional Change: Ambiguity, Agency, and Power.* Cambridge University Press.

Miyamoto, M. 2007. "Changes in the Corporate Governance and the Diversity of Japanese Firms: Four Types of HRM." In Japan Institute for Labour Policy and Training (ed.), *Japanese Firms and Employment: The Future of Long-term Employment and Pay for Performance* (in Japanese).

Richter, Frank-Jürgen, ed. 2000. *The East Asian Development Model: Economic Growth, Institutional Failure and the Aftermath of the Crisis*. London: Palgrave Macmillan.

Stiglitz, Joseph E. and Shahid Yusuf, eds. 2001. *Rethinking the East Asian Miracle*. World Bank Publications.

Takahashi, Wataru. 2012. "The Japanese Financial Sector's Transition from High Growth to the Lost Decades." In Hiroaki Miyoshi and Yoshifumi Nakata (eds.), *Have Japanese Firms Changed?: The Lost Decade*. Springer.

Tohyama, Hironori. 2000. "The Capital-Labour Compromise and the Financial System." In Boyer and Yamada (eds.) (2002).

Walter, Andrew and Xiaoke Zhang, eds. 2012. *East Asian Capitalism: Diversity, Continuity and Change*. Oxford: Oxford University Press.

Woo-Cumings. 2001. "Miracle as Prologue: The State and the Reform of the Corporate Sector in Korea." In Stiglitz and Yusuf (eds.), *Rethinking the East Asian Miracle*.

Yan, Isqabel K. and Kenneth S. Chan, and Vinh Q. T. Dang. 2011. *Financial Liberalization and Financing Constraints: Some Evidence from Panel Data of Listed Chinese Firms*. Munich Personal RePEc Archive.

Chapter 10

# The "Renminbi Swap Lines" and the Emergent Role of China as an Emergency Lender: Evidence from Argentina

Rodrigo Luiz Medeiros da Silva

## Introduction and Objectives

The growing weight of the People's Republic of China in the world economy, measured by gross domestic product or trade volume, has intensified a debate on the potential international role of its national currency, the yuan-renminbi. Indeed, the Popular Republic of China has recently become the world's largest economy, after having overtaken Japan in 1999 and the US in 2014.[1] It is also the world's largest exporter, having overtaken Germany in 2009.[2] Considering these milestones in Chinese growing economic influence, the wider use of the yuan-renminbi in international transactions[3] is a predictable phenomenon.

Moreover, backgrounded by this rising importance of Chinese trade and investment flows throughout the Globe, and the inexorable presence of the yuan-renminbi in international forex markets, chief Beijing officials have demarcated currency "internationalization" as a stated goal of policy.

Arguably, the privilege of conducting international transactions in domestic currency embeds measurable economic advantages. First, the transformation of the yuan-renminbi into an internationally accepted currency would free Chinese banks and exporters from the costs of converting currencies and hedging exchange rate exposures. Secondly, issuing a global currency may perhaps be a way of projecting China's financial influence internationally, encouraging Shanghai's financial institutions to branch abroad. It presumably would determine positive externalities and efficiency gains for Chinese firms operating or trading abroad. Thirdly, China's over-reliance on the dollar exposes it excessively to idiosyncrasies of US monetary policy, i.e. to an underlying risk of abrupt reduction of trade finance as a corollary of Federal Reserve's liquidity reversals. The faculty of issuing an internationally accepted substitute to the dollar would reduce such risk. Fourthly, a fully internationalized yuan-renminbi could be a tool to correct the mismatch on China's international balance sheet, between liabilities usually denominated in domestic currency and claims on foreigners, which are typically denominated in major reserve currencies, notably the US dollar. When the value of the US dollar decreases against the yuan-renminbi, the value of China's foreign liabilities increases in dollar terms, while that of its foreign assets remains unaffected. Fifthly, an eventual recognition of the yuan-renminbi as a reserve currency would allow it to be openly added to Central Banks foreign exchange portfolios. If so, Beijing would be able to play a role traditionally monopolized by Washington in unilaterally determining the fate of countries facing exchange gaps. This faculty could be a strategic instrument depending on Chinese willingness to influence the shape and structure of the global economy.

It is thus comprehensible that Chinese policy-makers have set their sights on the promotion of the yuan-renminbi to the level of leading international and reserve currency. To date, however, the yuan-renminbi does not yet rank among the acknowledged "convertible" currencies, nor has Shanghai's status been promoted to a first-class-financial-center. Chinese currency is seldom used invoicing China's imports and exports. Its international circulation is still modest. Foreign governments do not openly hold renminbi-denominated assets as part of their foreign exchange reserves, just as foreign companies do not borrow in Chinese capital markets, etc.

Nonetheless, as Chairman Hu Jintao once conjectured to the Wall Street Journal, making the yuan-renminbi an international currency shall be a "fairly long process."[4] Agreeing with such premise, this paper is a contribution to the analysis of the slow and gradual process on which Beijing has embarked with the goal of converting the yuan-renminbi into an international currency, and in due course turning it into one of the world's main reserve currencies. Specifying our scope, the next section is a brief revision of Beijing's most important measures toward the internationalization of the yuan-renminbi, focusing on a specific class of such initiatives: the "swap lines". It will be followed by a deeper analysis of the 2014 Sino-Argentine "swap" agreement, describing the previous domestic circumstances of Argentina and the over-all impact of the agreement in Argentine forex markets. We shall also lay emphasis on how this channel increased the presence of the yuan-renminbi amid the foreign exchange reserves of the southernmost G-20 country, stabilizing the exchange rate and creating an interesting precedent that endorses a potential *de facto* convertibility of the yuan-renminbi.

## Reviewing Chinese Measures toward an International Yuan-Renminbi

Since the 2008 global financial crisis, China has been actively involved in efforts to internationalize the yuan-renminbi. In this part of our article, we shall outline the most relevant official measures undertaken by Chinese government with such aim. According to Barry Eichengreen, who authored several recent studies on this issue:

> "Chinese officials have a carefully calibrated approach, beginning with authorization for domestic and foreign companies to settle their merchandise transactions in the currency, followed by permitting a limited but growing range of financial transactions to be conducted in it, and culminating in the use of the country's currency in a range of additional financial roles, not least as a form for countries to hold their reserves." (Eichengreen, 2013: 148)

Accepting his chronology, we should highlight that the efforts of currency internationalization started in July 2009, with the launching of a pilot scheme that allowed five Chinese major cities[5] to trade using the yuan-renminbi, whenever the commercial partner was an ASEAN (Association of Southeast Asian Nations) neighbor, or the Special Administrative Regions of Hong Kong and Macau. In 2010, the scheme was expanded to 20 Mainland China provinces, authorizing their firms to settle their trade in domestic currency. Later, permission to denominate trade contracts in yuan-renminbi has been extended to the rest of the country. From a mere 1% of the Chinese foreign trade in the second quarter of 2010, yuan-renminbi trade settlement reached 16.5% by the second quarter of 2013. Together with the growth of yuan-renminbi trade settlement, yuan-renminbi-denominated deposits in the Special Administrative Region of Hong Kong have risen intensely, reaching 10.8% of total deposits at the end of October 2013. (Eichengreen *et al.*, 2012)

In addition, Popular Republic of China's policy for Foreign Direct Investment (FDI) also stimulated the use of the yuan-renminbi. Both the approval process in the use of domestic currency for outward FDI and the actual use of it for inward FDI have been simplified with the Renminbi Outward Direct Investment Scheme (January 2011), as well as the creation of the Renminbi FDI scheme (October 2011). Ever since statistical information was made available in early 2012, renminbi-denominated and -settled FDI has accounted for about a third of the Chinese Mainland's total FDI (Eichengreen and Kawai, 2014).

The People's Republic of China still maintains strict controls on portfolio investment flows. Yet, these controls have been gradually relaxed in recent years to expand the range of investors and the type of financial assets allowable to engage in cross-border transactions using domestic currency. Besides relaxing constraints on inward and outward capital flows, China's official support has fostered the growth of an offshore yuan-renminbi-denominated (*dim sum*) bond market in Hong Kong. The first *dim sum* bond was issued in 2007, by the China Development Bank, seeking funds to finance large infrastructure projects such as the Three Gorges Dam and Shanghai Pudong Airport. Since July 2010, foreign corporations and Chinese financial corporations were allowed to operate in the *dim sum* market. However, it was not until August 2010, when the American corporation McDonald's became the first foreign private company to issue a yuan-renminbi bond in Hong Kong, that this offshore bond market captured international attention. In November 2011, Baosteel Group, a Chinese state-owned steelmaker, became the first non-financial direct issuer of *dim sum* bonds. (Fung *et al.*, 2013) Building an offshore market for yuan-renminbi-denominated bonds was seen by Chinese officers as an instrument to provide alternative investment opportunities for yuan-renminbi deposit holders in Hong Kong, as well as another channel for yuan-renminbi to flow back to the Mainland (Subacchi, 2010).

Through all these efforts, Hong Kong has become the financial hub for offshore yuan-renminbi business. Nonetheless, the issuance of *dim sum* bonds continued to be dominated by Chinese nationals, merely recycling the liquidity generated from cross-border yuan-renminbi trade, which is quite an unusual characteristic taking other offshore markets in perspective.[6] Moreover, the variety and volume of offshore yuan-renminbi assets have remained scarce when compared to China's economic size and commercial weight. After an initial period of rapid growth, the appetite for *dim sum* bonds has cooled, following Chinese decision to speed up the opening of its domestic credit market to foreign finance. In May 2015, more than thirty overseas financial institutions, including HSBC, BNP Paribas and Morgan Stanley, have received regulatory approval to access Mainland China's interbank bond market. In July 2015, supranational organizations as the World Bank, just as sovereign wealth funds, have been granted automatic approval to buy onshore bonds in the Popular Republic. Foreign participation in the onshore bond market is still narrow, but it undeniably has a big potential to grow. In October 2014, the German manufacturer

Daimler became the first non-financial foreign company to issue a so-called "panda bond," a bond issued inside China by a foreign entity, and denominated in yuan-renminbi.[7] Other firms are expected to meet the regulatory requirements and follow this example.[8]

Hence, constraints on capital flows have been eased by Beijing in order to facilitate the foreign access to yuan-denominated finance. However, China is far from counting with a fully open capital account, and it has definitely not embarked on the adventure of full liberalization of exchange markets. Consequently, foreign players cannot so easily access Chinese currency on international markets. Furthermore, the Chinese target of converting the yuan-renminbi into a reserve currency cannot neglect the so-called Triffin dilemma.[9] In other words, China will not avoid managing the conflict between stabling a suitable exchange rate and providing adequate liquidity for the use of its currency internationally. The historical solution for the US was to keep regular Current Account deficits. Contrariwise, China has a remarkable series of Current Account surpluses(Gao and Coffman, 2013).

In brief words, Chinese bureaucrats do visualize the goal of raising yuan-renminbi liquidity in foreign markets, but, on the other hand, they reject a sudden Current Account opening, and do not regard Current Account reversal as a politically acceptable option. They have therefore privileged a gradualist approach toward increasing the international presence of the yuan-renminbi, embracing "swap agreements" as short-term mechanisms to increase the international supply of Chinese currency without significant fluctuations in the pattern Chinese foreign accounts (Eichengreen and Kawai, 2014). In December 2008, the Republic of Korea was the first counterparty to such an agreement, totaling CNY180 bil-

**Table 10.1** "Swap" Lines Maintained by the Popular Republic of China

| | Countries | Signing Year | Signing Month | Swap Amount (RMB billion) |
|---|---|---|---|---|
| 1 | Belarus | 2015 | May | 7 |
| 2 | Malaysia | 2015 | April | 180 |
| 3 | South Africa | 2015 | April | 30 |
| 4 | Australia | 2015 | April | 200 |
| 5 | Armenia | 2015 | March | 1 |
| 6 | Suriname | 2015 | March | 1 |
| 7 | Pakistan | 2014 | December | 10 |
| 8 | Thailand | 2014 | December | 70 |
| 9 | Kazakhstan | 2014 | December | 7 |
| 10 | Hong Kong | 2014 | November | 400 |
| 11 | Canada | 2014 | November | 200 |
| 12 | Qatar | 2014 | November | 35 |
| 13 | Russia | 2014 | October | 150 |
| 14 | South Korea | 2014 | October | 360 |
| 15 | Sri Lanka | 2014 | September | 10 |
| 16 | Mongolia | 2014 | August | 15 |
| 17 | Switzerland | 2014 | July | 150 |
| 18 | Argentina | 2014 | July | 70 |
| 19 | New Zealand | 2014 | April | 25 |
| 20 | EU | 2013 | October | 350 |
| 21 | Iceland | 2013 | September | 3.5 |
| 22 | Albania | 2013 | September | 2 |
| 23 | Hungary | 2013 | September | 10 |
| 24 | UK | 2013 | June | 200 |
| 25 | Brazil | 2013 | June | 190 |
| 26 | Singapore | 2013 | March | 300 |
| 27 | Ukraine | 2012 | June | 15 |
| 28 | Turkey | 2012 | February | 10 |
| 29 | UAE | 2012 | January | 35 |
| 30 | Uzbekistan | 2011 | April | 0.7 |
| 31 | Indonesia | 2009 | March | 100 |
| Total | | | – | 3,137.2 |

Source: People's Bank of China press releases. The ordinary validity of the "swap" agreements is three years. Some countries have renewed or expanded their initial swap lines with China. Whenever an agreement has been renewed or expanded, just the most recent version is included here.

lion, with a maturity of three years. Prior to its expiration in 2011, the agreement was renewed, doubling the amount of the swap to CNY360 billion.

After South Korea, several other countries have also firmed

"swap lines" with the Popular Republic of China — see the figures shown by Table 10.1. However, aside from Hong Kong, none of countries with which the Popular Bank of China has signed agreements had actually used it to withdraw Chinese currency, at least until a few months ago.

## Case Study: The Sino-Argentine Swap Line

By irrigating small African Republics with dollar- or renminbi-denominated capitals, Chinese officers may certainly play a more active role in assuring Chinese geopolitical interests in underdeveloped resource-rich regions.[10] Given the known volatility of commodities prices, exporters of raw materials are typically prone to face cyclical exchange shortage followed by insolvency crises. Such structural financial fragility opens periodical gaps for the increase of Chinese influence over unindustrialized countries. However, the goal of universal acceptance as a reserve currency presupposes a significant circulation of Chinese currency, as well as the presence of yuan-renminbi denominated assets, including Central Bank reserves, in regions that play a far more preeminent role in global economy. Taking this defy into consideration, semi-industrialized resource-rich countries may well constitute experimental zones to amplify the visibility of Chinese monetary ambitions.

The rest of this paper aims to analyze the circumstances and major consequences of the "swap agreement" established between China and Argentina, one of G-20's smallest economies. We shall argue that by withdrawing its "swap line" with China as a sort of emergency loan, Argentina has become a pilot experience of yuan-renminbi accumulation in Central Bank's reserves. We will also show that by adding Chinese currency to foreign exchange reserves, the Argentine government indeed managed to stabilize the exchange rate. By doing so, it has experimentally verified that yuan-renminbi inflows are indeed capable of reestablishing liquidity conditions in an economy threatened by financial collapse.

In order to understand the circumstances under which Argentina came to need an emergency loan from China, we should retell a story that begins close to the turn of the Millennium. Following the Russian financial crisis of 1998 and the Brazilian real devaluation of 1999, Argentina's economy immerged into a severe Balance of Payments crisis. The international wave of financial panic resounded domestically, indeed announcing an imminent exchange maxi-devaluation — the outcome of an enhanced foreign awareness of its preexisting external deficit. Efforts to stabilize price expectations by preserving a currency peg to the US dollar were unsuccessful in reversing capital flight. Monetary and fiscal constriction, though backed by IMF loans of tens of billions of dollars, did not either succeed in re-anchoring expectations. In December of 2001, facing a widening "strong currency" gap, the government defaulted on its foreign debt. Weeks later, the currency peg to the dollar was also abandoned. The sovereign debt default and the exchange maxi-devaluation gave rise to a profound financial crisis, as banks did not possess enough convertible currency reserves to honor at once the mass of dollars deposited in the domestic financial system.

The economic prospects could hardly be worse at that juncture. A sort of downward spiral seemed to have engulfed Argentina. But counterintuitively, a rapid GDP recovery started by the second quarter of 2002, persisting up until the global economic slowdown of 2008. With the economy steered by a substantial improvement of its terms of trade, Argentina's real domestic income recovered its pre-crisis level by the first quarter of 2005. From its minimum value of 2002, GDP would simply double before 2013. Needless to say, the sudden reversal of Argentina's terms of change is hardly explainable without the effect of Chinese emergency on commodity markets.[11]

It is opportune to notice that Argentina achieved this unforeseen economic resurgence in spite of the financial constraints produced by its condition of insolvent country, which strongly limited borrowing from international financial markets over those years. Following the default of 2001 and the rejection by a minority of creditors to accept the terms of the restructuring proposals of 2005 and 2010, the conflict concerning the defaulted debit advanced to a judicial arena, since "vulture funds" acquired unpaid bonds expecting to receive their face value after suing Argentina abroad. Under such atmosphere of uncertainty, the international borrowing markets remained reluctant in granting additional funding.

Simultaneously, the country received relatively little Foreign Direct Investment (FDI), perhaps due to a predominantly negative international press reporting, always focusing its relatively high inflation instead of its growth records, or alternatively because the recovery was typically dismissed as a fleeting "commodity boom," driven by contingent high prices for its agricultural exports. Since the very beginning of Argentina's unexpected recovery, many economists, economic journalists, and financial operators have automatically predicted a second "dip" of its economy, as soon as the favorable trend of commodity prices ended. Even if their pessimism proved to be rather exaggerated, as the GDP continued to grow steadily at least until 2013, the foundations of Argentine prosperity have indeed remained vulnerable to any terms-of-trade reversal. In the absence of financial liquidity offered by occasional foreign loans, and without reliance on regular entry of Foreign Direct Investment, the political economy of growth was dependent on a combination of Fiscal and Current Account surpluses. In other words, the economic equilibrium hinged upon the country's own capacity of saving for foreign debt amortization, since the creditors did not automatically grant the refinancing.

The fulfilment of these two structural preconditions for economic growth under foreign insolvency marked President Néstor Kirchner's successful administration (2003-2007), but Argentina's performance in both accounts gradually deteriorated after 2008. The panorama in early 2015 combines Fiscal and Current Account deficits, and foreign reserves fell to a dangerous level. It remains the case that foreign financial lines are not yet open to Argentina. The alternative is to rely upon speculative capitals captured by the emission of bonds promising a very large premium.

Our aim in the next sections is to characterize such situation of exchange scarcity, combined to the absence of financial tools to accommodate external shocks, and then review the unusual strategies adopted by Argentina in its pursuit of means of payment. In other words, we intend to show that the economy has again reached a crossroads. Subsequently, we intend to answer a fundamental question: How did Argentina manage to dispose of a minimum internal supply of foreign exchange throughout 2014, yet with ever- increasing Fiscal and Balance of Payment deficits? Our hypothesis is simple: from the second semester of 2014 and thenceforth, following a Chinese diplomatic initiative that established a generous yuan-peso "swap line," Argentina has been granted the opportunity of exchanging its unconvertible domestic currency into an easily exchangeable foreign one. The inflow of yuan-renminbi thus explains that the country has avoided a severe exchange devaluation.

To characterize Argentina's fragility and test our hypothesis concerning the sudden yuan-renminbi inflows, we propose: (1) To detail the recent trends of Argentine Fiscal and Balance of Payments accounts, thereby the country's present external vulnerability; (2) To examine how the so-called "holdout problem," an international juridical controversy on its past debt restructurings, boosted Argentina's susceptibility towards speculative attacks, enhancing a pre-existing exposure; (3) To quantify the net evolution of Argentine Foreign Exchange Reserves throughout 2014, showing its relative stability, and the decisive contribution of an unusual yuan-renminbi accumulation in avoiding its "melting away"; (4) To examine the evolution of Argentina's Foreign Exchange Rate throughout 2014, demonstrating its relative stability after the contribution of yuan-renminbi inflows.

## A Fiscal and Balance of Payments Trends in Recent Argentina: 2008-2014

As Figure 10.1 indicates, the Argentine Current Account Balance displays a persistent deterioration trend since 2006. The same worsening trend characterizes the evolution of Argentina's Primary Budget Balance.[12] The reasons for this fiscal deterioration are intricate, and a deeper analysis of Argentina's fiscal reality lies beyond the scope of this paper. In what concerns the deteriorating Current Account Balance of Argentina, the fundamental reason is the reduction of Trade Balance surpluses, which declined from 17 to only 7 billion dollars between 2009 and 2014 — notwithstanding the roughly constant level of exports between 2011 and 2013. Figure 10.2 displays the recent figures for Argentine exports, imports and Trade Balance, highlighting the declining trend of foreign trade surplus.

A fading trade surplus is not necessarily an immediate problem for the domestic exchange liquidity, since a complex range of net inflows determines the level of reserves.[13] However, the pattern of Argentine Nonfactor Services Balance is traditionally negative, although totaling just a small value when compared to trade results. The pattern of Factor Services Balance is also negative and its results are far more expressive. At the same time, the behavior of Financial and Capitals Accounts reveals highly volatile results, without clear trends. As such, the global result of Argentine Balance of Payments depends highly on the Trade Balance.

The net variation of Central Bank's reserves — capturing all these accounts and the fading commercial surpluses — was thus positive from 2003 to 2010, turning progressively negative from 2011 to 2013. Nevertheless, breaking this adverse evolution, the year of 2014 marks an unexpected inflection. The Current Account remained negative, but a small accumulation of reserves did occur after a triennium of losses. Figure 10.3 displays the figures for the net accumulation of reserves since the year 2000, including the intriguing amelioration occurred in 2014. This case study is supposed to illuminate the reasons behind this reversal.

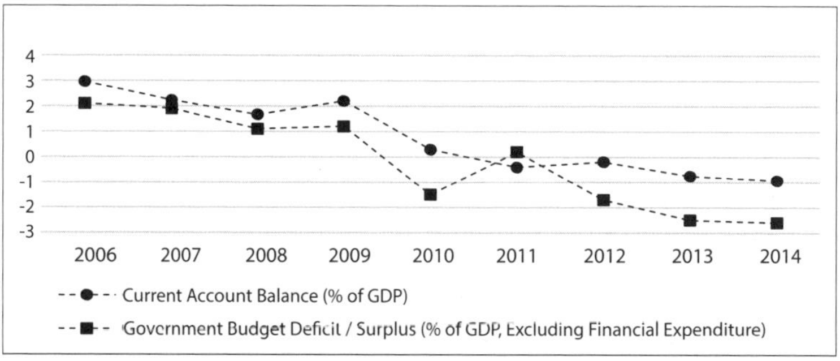


**Figure 10.1** Argentina's Fiscal and Current Account Results

Sources: World Bank and Argentine Central Bank.

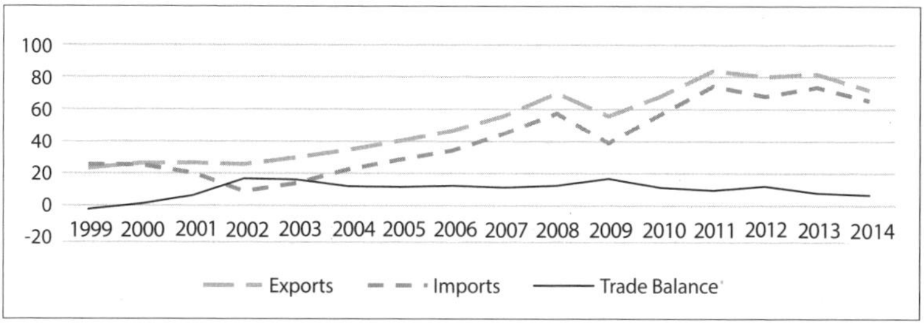


**Figure 10.2** Argentine Exports, Imports and Trade Balance (In billions of current US$)

Source: Argentine National Statistical Office (INDEC).

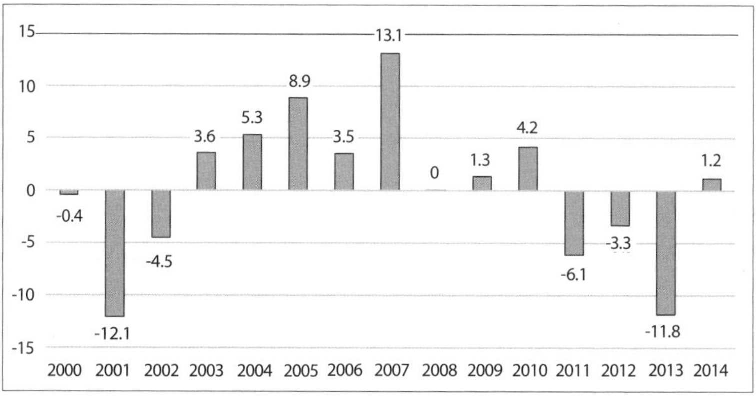


**Figure 10.3** Net Variation of Foreign Reserves (In billions of current US$)

Source: Argentine National Statistical Office (INDEC).

## The "Holdout Question": Buenos Aires' Finances at a Crossroads

In the triennium between 2008 and 2010, the net loss of exchange reserves has gradually incited devaluations of the peso against the dollar. Such devaluations intensified after 2011, partially responding to the exacerbation of speculative activity, as more and more residents decided to keep their savings in dollars instead of local currency. Completing the scenario, in 2014 an exogenous shock inflamed devaluation bets against the peso.

Investors have long labeled the Argentine sovereign bonds "speculative assets." In view of that, most creditors of the country's defaulted debt, assuming sporadic losses as mere corollary of gambling, have promptly considered reducing their expected gains in order to avoid a complete nonpayment. Hence, many owners of defaulted bonds have promptly resold their assets to "vulture funds," which acquired them for an insignificant fraction of their face value, in order to prosecute the Argentine government in foreign courts, and perhaps receive the integral repayment in a distant and unpredictable date. Later, in 2005 and 2010, Argentina offered discounted repayment conditions to all bondholders, in an attempt to normalize the country's international financial involvement. Yet dealing with a panicky exchange market, these initiatives managed to restructure about 90% of its defaulted foreign debt through heavily discounted bond exchanges. However, such repayment conditions did not attract investors that acquired the bonds as purely speculative assets, and therefore insisted in the higher profits of full-repayment, no matter if they would have to postpone their gains.

On June 16, 2014, the US Supreme Court rejected Argentina's last appeal in a controversy with a group of bondholders, led by units of New York hedge funds Elliot Management and Aurelius Capital. The immediate full-repayment of their defaulted bonds was mandated and Argentina's foreign assets, especially funds deposited in official current accounts, could easily be blocked by judicial order in case of non-compliance. The full payment of the non-restructured fraction of the debt would create a precedent that would have to be extended to the entire stock of restructured bonds. The discounted payment deal embedded a "Rights Upon Future Offers" (RUFO) clause, written into the restructured bond contracts. In other words, paying to the "holdouts" would neutralize the effects of the debt restructurings of 2005 and 2010, bringing the country into a new "technical default," since its foreign reserves are clearly insufficient to face this sudden onus.

Given the circumstances, two policy choices remained. (1) To pay the holdout creditors accepting their conditions, defaulting on the other bonds. (2) To disobey the judicial order to pay the holdouts, signaling to other creditors that Argentina would try to honor the restructured bonds, though any disbursements in the US would be in any case subject to precautionary attachment[14] under judicial order. Both options would involve a new moratorium.

Theoretically, any new financial discontinuity would have acute consequences for the fragile equilibrium of Argentine currency market, since the country has experienced significant Current Account deficits, hence requiring permanent capital inflows. The RUFO clause expired only on January 1 2015, and therefore the second semester of 2014 was marked by potential currency gaps in Buenos Aires, which could effortlessly detonate a chaotic speculative run against the Argentine peso.

## Balance of Payment and the Net Evolution of Foreign Reserves

The medium-run evolution of Argentine foreign accounts, particularly with the emergence of the "holdout" dilemma, did indicate that the devaluation of Argentine currency would accelerate by the end of 2014, inasmuch as the level of exchange reserves seemed prone to decline at ever increasing rates. Yet, as we pointed out earlier, the negative prospects of forex reserves did not materialize. Completing the figures offered by Figure 10.3, Figure 10.4 shows the monthly data for these reserves. It is clear that a certain relief did take place after March 2014, and such recovery has accelerated throughout the last trimester of the same year.

This first wave of reserves accumulation, during the second trimester, is almost entirely explained by the compensation deal concerning the expropriation of YPF, Argentina's renationalized Oil Company. According to it, Argentina agreed to pay US$5 billion to Repsol as a recompense for its expropriation of 51% of the company's shares. In order to do so, the Republic of Argentina issued an equivalent amount of sovereign bonds.[15] As a result, there was a once-for-all addition to the Financial Account of about US$ 1.5 billion.[16] Figure 10.5 compares the trimestral accumulation of reserves, the Current and the Financial Accounts.

As for the second wave, during the fourth trimester of 2014, the significant Financial Account surplus that boosted the level of reserves can only be understood in the framework of the emergent Sino-Argentine relationship. As we pointed out earlier, in June 2014, Argentina and China have signed a currency "swap" deal, establishing that up to 70 billion yuan-renminbi (about US$11.4billion)

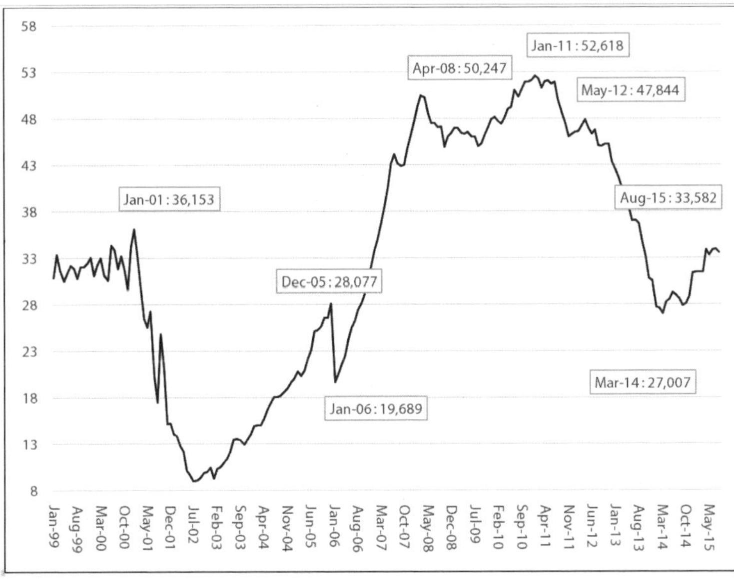


**Figure 10.4** Total Forex Reserves of Argentine Central Bank (In US$ billions)

Source: Argentine Central Bank.

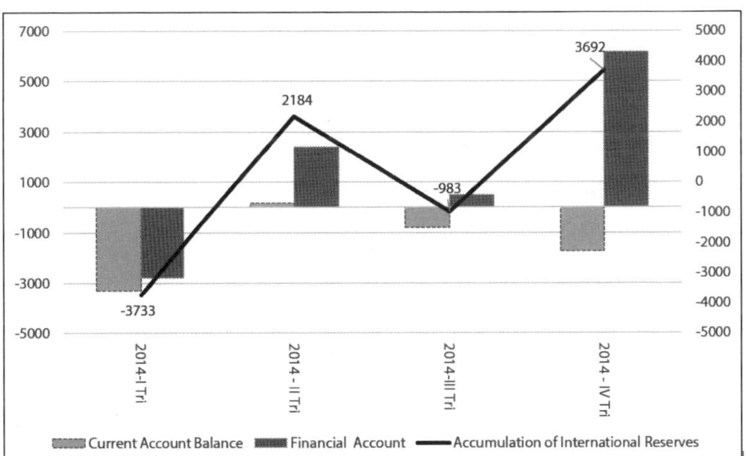


**Figure 10.5** Selected Accounts of Argentine Balance of Payments

Source: Argentine Central Bank.

can be easily exchanged for Argentine pesos, which must be deposited in China within a period of 12 months after Argentina has withdrawn Chinese currency. Being more specific, should the Argentine Central Bank request any yuan-renminbi amount from its counterpart in Beijing, the terms of the deal allow the country to send pesos in exchange, and the loan would be payable in 12 months with an interest rate of between 7 and 8%.

According to what was publicized by the Argentine press, after signing the "debt swap," Argentina registered cash injections of 5 billion yuan-renminbi in October, 3 billion in November, and a similar amount in December. As an evidence of these injections, Figure 10.6 shows that a significant accumulation of non-convertible currency did follow the recovery of forex reserves during the last semester of 2014. Reaching 21% of total exchange reserves in May 2015, these resources have been registered in the Argentine Central Banks's Budget as "currencies not belonging to the SDR basket" (in Spanish, *Monedas fuera de la canasta de DEG.*)[17] As Figure 10.7 indicates, the accumulation of this type of non-convertible reserves is the true responsible for the upturn of Argentina's reserves after September 2014.

In what comes to a sum totaling no more than a few billion dollars, yuan-renminbi can be easily exchanged into "convertible currencies" in Hong Kong, Singapore or London. Hence, it would have been feasible for Argentina to have such sum converted into dollars or euros, in advance of transferring it to Buenos Aires. However, the Argentine Central Bank did not exchange the values withdrawn in China. As we argued earlier in this text, it is presumable that China would favor the simple adding of its currency to Argentina's Central Bank Budget, since it would mean a relevant

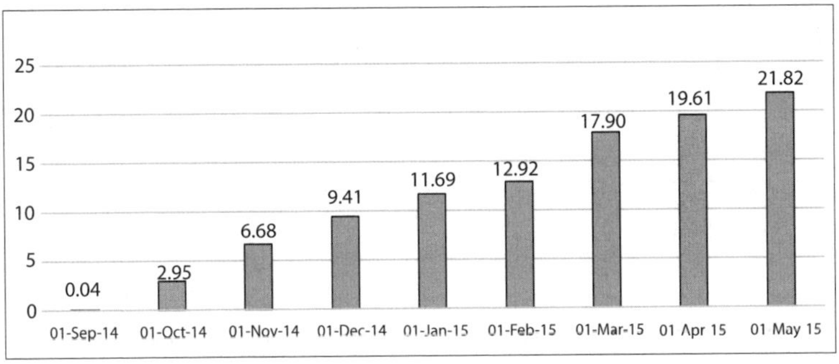


**Figure 10.6** Share of Non-convertible Currencies in Total Argentine Reserves (in %)

Source: Argentine Central Bank.

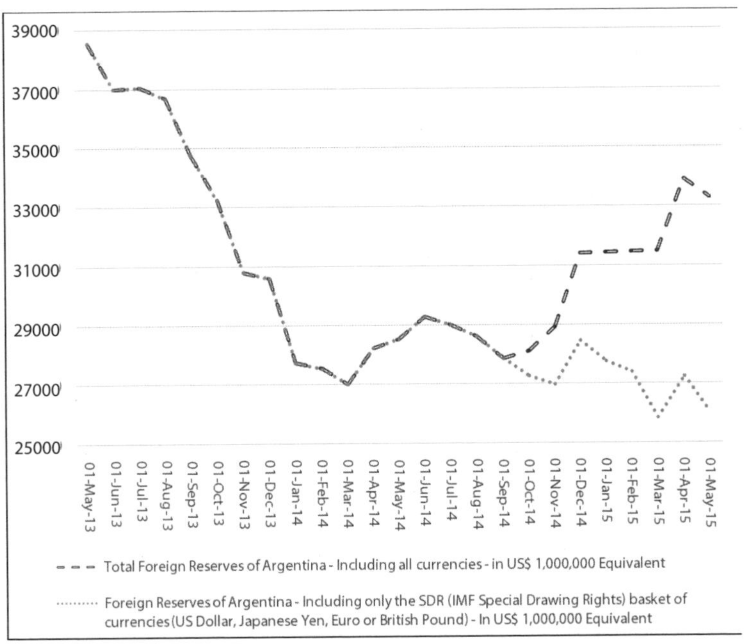


**Figure 10.7** Evolution of Argentine Foreign Reserves: With and Without the Recent Inflow of Yuan-Renminbi

Source: Argentine Central Bank.

precedent of yuan-renminbi accumulation by a G-20 country. However, the precise terms of the diplomatic negotiations concerning the Argentine "swap" are so far unknown. Other tangible concerns, involving the high cost of converting yuan-renminbi and later reconverting it, may be the true explanation.

## The Evolution of Argentina's Foreign Exchange Rate in 2014

Following the short-run stabilization of Argentine Foreign Reserves, the exchange rate remained roughly stable in Argentina throughout 2014. There has been a significant devaluation of the Argentine peso against the dollar in January 2014, but all through the subsequent months, only minor devaluations occurred. In what comes to the Brazilian real- peso exchange rate — a significant figure since Brazil is Argentina's main commercial partner —, much of the devaluation occurred in January had already been reverted

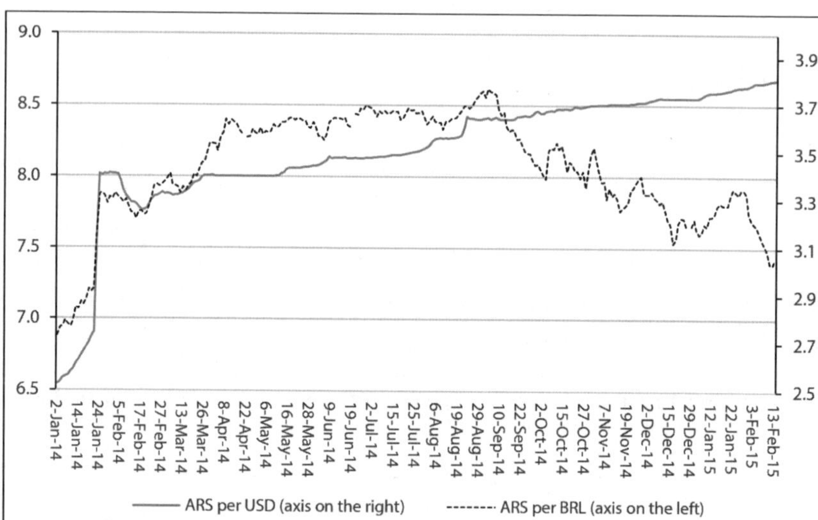


**Figure 10.8** Official Exchange Rates [Jan 02, 2014 - Feb 13, 2015 Pesos (ARS) per Dollar (US$) and Real (BRL)]

Source: Offical Exchange Rates, Argentine Central Bank.

by December. Figure 10.8 shows the dollar-peso and the real-peso exchange rates between January 2014 and February 2015.

## Concluding Remarks

At the beginning of 2014, Argentina seemed to be on the way of an "exchange collapse." The probability of a maxi devaluation of the Peso increased alongside the first semester, climaxing with the mid-year "holdout" crisis. Six months after those events, however, the Argentine exchange Armageddon is yet to come. Just one month after the US Supreme Court's decision favoring the "vulture funds" Elliot Management and Aurelius Capital, Argentina's President Cristina Fernandez and China's President Xi Jinping, raised a glass to one other, proposing a toast to new horizons, during a dinner at the presidential palace in Buenos Aires. "Our two countries find themselves at a historic crossroads," declared President Xi to Vice President Boudou that night. "We have just marked 10 years in the strategic association between Argentina and China and the time has come to open new horizons," he told lawmakers through a translator. Three months later, a new Chinese Ambassador to Argentina would take office. Yang Wanming would soon reaffirm to the local press his Government's commitment in finding a solution to the "holdout crisis." What are these new Sino-Argentinian horizons? This paper is a preliminary effort in understanding the new role of China as a global emergency lender.

Two unprecedented facts arise from the recent Sino-Argentine monetary relations. First, China has deliberately acted as a counterweight to the US mandate over Latin America, the so-called Monroe Doctrine. It has used its national currency in order grant an emergency loan that reverted a situation of short-run exchange scarcity created by a New York judge. Second, and certainly more important, it defied the primacy of the US dollar as the only universal antidote for Balance of Payments rescue from a structural default. After all, this experimental operation has worked. With or without the IMF recognition, with or without American blessing, the yuan-renminbi has indeed functioned, at least by now, as a perfect similar of any convertible currency when added to Argentine reserves. So far, its *de facto* exchangeability in international markets has been enough to contain an imminent devaluation of the Argentine peso.

It is a tremendous novelty for countries exposed to an imminent risk of exchange gap, which may henceforth benefit from the opportunity of bargaining borrowing conditions between two superpowers, thereby widening their autonomy in conducing the strategies for foreign adjustment. In the near future, we should presume that Beijing will receive as many salvation appeals as Washington in such cases, and the conditionings of rescue packages will conceivably reflect Chinese emerging geopolitical interests.

The Argentine precedent is also the sign of a new age in global monetary relations, indicating severe and multifaceted implications for all countries, and the imminent obsolescence of our current International Monetary System. By the end of this year, the International Monetary Fund will decide whether the yuan-renminbi will join the euro, the Japanese yen, the British pound, and the US dollar in the basket of currencies that determines the value of its international reserve asset, the Special Drawing Right (SDR). Chinese diplomacy is pushing hard for the renminbi's inclusion. Nevertheless, the story told here indicates that the emergency of the yuan-renminbi as an international reserve currency will continue to be enforced by China with or without IMF's support.

## Notes

1. According to International Monetary Fund's values for the Gross Domestic Product (GDP) based on the Purchasing Power Parity (PPP) methodology, not on official exchange rates.

2. According to World Trade Organization statistics.

3. Transferences explained by both commercial and financial purposes, besides the ones undertaken by central banks and other official institutions.

4. Q & A with Hu Jintao, Wall Street Journal, January 18, 2011.

5. Guangzhou, Shenzhen, Shanghai, Zhuhai and Dongguan.

6. According to a study released in 2011, about 80% of yuan-renminbi offshore bond issuers in either financial or non-financial sectors were of Chinese nationality, while 30-60% of issuers in other offshore markets are nationals of the country of issue (McCauley, 2011).

7. The International Finance Corporation and the Asian Development Bank issued the first two "Panda" bonds in 2005.

8. See: Noble (2015).

9. See: Triffin (1966).

10. See: Chan-Fishel and Lawson (2007).

11. See: Gallagher and Porzecanski (2009).

12. The primary budget balance equals the government budget balance before interest payments.

13. Comprising also services, capitals, etc.

14. When funds are held by the judiciary to prevent someone from disposing of it.

15. Repsol received a package of dollar-denominated sovereign bonds: Bonar 24, Bonar X and Discount 33.

16. Analyzing the components of the Financial Account, the Non-financial Public Sector produced then a US$ 4.5 billion surplus, just as the repatriation of Repsol's assets caused a deficit in the Non-Financial Private Sector of no more than US$ 3.410 billion. This difference is the main reason behind the Financial Account surplus.

17. The basket of SDR, IMF Special Drawing Rights, comprises the US Dollar, the Japanese Yen, the Euro and the British Pound.

## *References*

Chan-Fishel, Michelle, and Roxanne Lawson. 2007. "Quid pro quo? China's investment-for- resource swaps in Africa." *Development* 50(3): 63-68.

Eichengreen, Barry. 2013. "ADB Distinguished Lecture Renminbi Internationalization: Tempest in a Teapot?" *Asian Development Review* 30(1): 148-164.

Eichengreen, Barry and Masahiro Kawai. 2014. "Issues for renminbi internationalization: an overview." ADBI Working Paper Series 454: 1-20.

Fung, Hung-Gay, Derrick Tzau, Jot Yau. 2013. "A Global Chinese Renminbi Bond Market: The Dim Sum Bond Market." pp. 51-67 in *International Financial Markets,* edited by Hung Gay Fung and Yiuman Tse. Bingley: Emerald Group Publishing Limited.

Gallagher, Kevin P., Roberto Porzecanski. 2009. "China and the Latin America commodities boom: a critical assessment." PERI Working Papers 192: 1-27.

Gao, Yuning, D. Maris Coffman. 2013. "Renminbi internationalization as a response to the global imbalance." *Journal of Chinese Economic and Business Studies* 11(2): 139-151.

McCauley, Robert N. 2011. "Renminbi internationalization and China's financial development." *BIS Quarterly Review,* December, pp. 41-56.

Noble, Josh. 2015. "Appetite wanes for dim sum bonds as entree to renminbi investment." Special Report for the Financial Times, July 29.

Subacchi, Paola. 2010. *One Currency, Two Systems: China's Renminbi Strategy.* London: Royal Institute of International Affairs.

Triffin, Robert. 1966. *The World Money Maze: National Currencies in International Payments.* New Haven, CT: Yale University Press.

Chapter 11

# *East Asia's Inter- and Intra-Regional Trade Networks and Changing Roles in Global Mobile Phone Value Chains*

Joonkoo Lee and Hyun-Chin Lim

## Introduction

The rise of global value chains (GVCs), a fragmented, cross-national production system, illuminates the increasing interconnection and interdependence in the global economy (Dicken, 2011; Gereffi, 2005). A production process that transforms a range of inputs into outputs for the market is now divided into a series of narrow tasks and dispersed beyond a single firm or country through offshoring and outsourcing (Arndt and Kierzkowski, 2001; Krugman *et al.*, 1995; Timmer *et al.*, 2014). Firms are increasingly engaged in the global economy by assuming a specialized role at a specific production stage in a GVC. Many developing countries are also pursuing export and employment growth by promoting GVC participation as a new mode of industrial upgrading, with an anticipation that an initial entry to a GVCs as a simply assembly specialist can be leveraged for further upgrading to higher value-added activities, such as full-packaged production and own brand manufacturing (OECD *et al.*, 2014; WTO and IDE-JETRO, 2011).

In this decentralized production system with a sophisticated international division of labor, the roles played by countries and firms can be diversified as they position themselves in different parts of the chain even in the same GVC. Countries may be similar in term of export intensity, but their positions in the GVC can be different as one focuses on exporting end products while others specialize in intermediate goods such as parts and components. In order to capture such difference in the mode of GVC integration, Lee *et al.* (2016) provides a framework to differentiate a country's position in GVCs in terms of global orientation and value chain specialization. And, using an example of mobile phone GVCs in East Asia, it shows that while China, Japan, Korea and Taiwan are all strong in the GVCs, their roles are quite different. For instance, both Korea and Taiwan rely heavily on exports, but Korean firms perform better in exporting mobile phones with their own brands, while Taiwanese firms excel in contract manufacturing for foreign brands as specialized suppliers. This highlights the existence of multiple entry points for a GVC participation. Countries and firms can take different paths for upgrading, and competition and environmental changes may force them to move from one to another position in GVCs.

Building on Lee *et al.* (2016)'s framework, this paper takes a step forward to analyze regions' and countries' changing roles in GVCs. It modifies and extends the framework, particularly, to accommodate international trade data, i.e., statistics from the UN Comtrade dataset, which provides detailed annual export and import statistics for virtually all the countries and territories in the world at the most disaggregated product level, i.e., six-digit

Harmonized Standards (HS) codes. By linking the framework with international comparable trade data, this paper analyzes the differentiation of regions' and countries' roles in international trade networks, specifically inter- and inter-regional trade networks. Focusing on a post-crisis period, 2007-2013, our analysis illuminates how the structure and dynamics of GVCs have changed in the aftermath of the global economic crisis of 2007-2008 (Cattaneo *et al.*, 2010; Gereffi, 2014).

This paper examines the changing pattern of international trade in the mobile phone GVCs, and, specifically, the role of East Asia in inter- and intra-regional trade networks, and the divergent positions of East Asian countries in this high-tech sector. East Asia has been playing an important role in the mobile phone industry. By the late 1990s, the industry was dominated by advanced industrialized countries in North America and Western Europe (Steinbock, 2005). Over the next two decades, however, the geography of mobile phone production dramatically shifted to East Asia and emerging economies like Mexico, Brazil and Hungary. And it has changed the trade patterns of the mobile phone GVCs as new countries joined the production networks of mobile phones as the final product as well as mobile phone parts as intermediate goods (Lee and Gereffi, 2013; Yeung *et al.*, 2006). And, as countries move up and down in the GVCs, not only inter-regional trade networks but also the intra-regional division of labor among East Asian countries have also changed. Thus, this paper examines how the roles of major exporting and importing countries have changed and the inter- and intra-regional trade patterns have evolved, focusing on diverging and emerging positions among East Asian economies in the GVCs.

The paper is organized as follows. The next section discusses theoretical backgrounds pertaining international trade networks and divergent integration in GVCs and introduce an extended framework to understand the difference. Then, findings from three sets of analysis are presented: (1) the key exporting and importing trends of mobile phones and parts, and the changing positions of major trading countries in the mobile phone GVCs; (2) interregional trade patterns of mobile phones and parts; (3) intra-Asia trade networks and their changes over the period. The paper concludes with a discussion of the implications of the findings in terms of convergence and divergence of global integration in East Asia.

## International Trade and Divergence in GVC Integration

As barriers for international trade and investment lowered, the global economy has become increasingly interconnected and interdependent (Dicken, 2011; Mittelman, 1996). One of the key features of economic globalization over the last few decades was that production has been fragmented into a series of narrow tasks and dispersed through offshoring and outsourcing beyond a single firm or country and across regions (Arndt and Kierzkowski, 2001; Krugman, 1995; Timmer *et al.*, 2014). As a result, many manufacturing goods are produced through a complex inter-firm network that cuts across national boundaries, or so-called "global value chains" (GVCs) (Gereffi, 2005; Gereffi *et al.*, 2005). More intermediate goods like parts and component are internationally traded in multiple times for further processing before reaching the final stage of assembly. The international division of labor has become more sophisticated to the level of trading tasks, instead of final goods (Sturgeon and Memedović, 2011; WTO and IDE-JETRO, 2011).

In this fragmented production system with an elaborated division of labor, countries and firms can play distinctive roles even in the same value chain (Lee *et al.*, 2016); some focus on one or two production steps like simple assembly for exports while others assumes a much broader range of manufacturing tasks, or full-packaged production (Neidik and Gereffi, 2006). Some firms may specialize in research and design (R&D) and marketing while leaving the midstream of their value chains like assembly to contract suppliers, whereas others choose to vertically integrate most of their value chains vertically. It implies that there can be multiple entry points through which countries and firms can participate in GVCs, and they also can change their positions within the chains to increase their economic and social gains from the participation as they economically upgrade, or move from lower to higher value-added nodes of value chains (Gereffi, 1999; Humphrey and Schmitz, 2004). At the same, it highlights that old distinctions like export orientation versus import substitution are insufficient to distinguish different ways in which countries and firms are integrated and positioned in the network of global production.

In an effort to address the shortcoming, Lee *et al.* (2016) propose a more sophisticated framework to understand a country's mode of global integration and its role in GVCs based on two dimensions: the degree of global orientation and the type of value chain specialization. The former distinguishes the extent of a country's engagement in exports vis-à-vis supplying the domestic market. The latter differentiates a country's role in GVCs according to the value chain activities it is mainly engaged in, e.g., up-stream (e.g., R&D and product design), mid-stream (e.g., assembly) and down-stream (e.g., branding). By juxtaposing the two dimensions, the framework shows multiple possible roles that can co-exist the single GVC. They are illustrated with the example of four East Asian countries and their engagement in the mobile phone GVC. It finds that while China, Japan, Korea and Taiwan are strong in the high-tech sector, the roles of these countries in the GVC are not quite the same. For instance, Korea and Taiwan have been successful in competing in global markets, but Korea firms like Samsung and LG perform well with their own branded products whereas the Taiwanese focus on contract manufacturing for brand producers like Apple as specialized suppliers.

This paper extends the framework in a way to allow to compare a much greater number of countries and their GVC roles with internationally comparable quantitative data, i.e., international trade statistics. International trade is one of the major ways, along with foreign direct investment (FDI), for countries to engage in the global economy, and the rise of GVCs highlights that not only final goods but also increasingly raw materials and intermediate goods are traded internationally often to be put together in another country. Thus, to understand a country's mode of integration in GVCs, it is critical to analyze the country's position and role in the trade network and their change.

An extended framework is illustrated in Figure 11.1 to linking a trade pattern with the role in a GVC. The two most distinctive roles in GVCs are, first, producing and exporting parts and component that are used for the final assembly; and, second, producing and exporting the end product. By juxtaposing trade patterns in

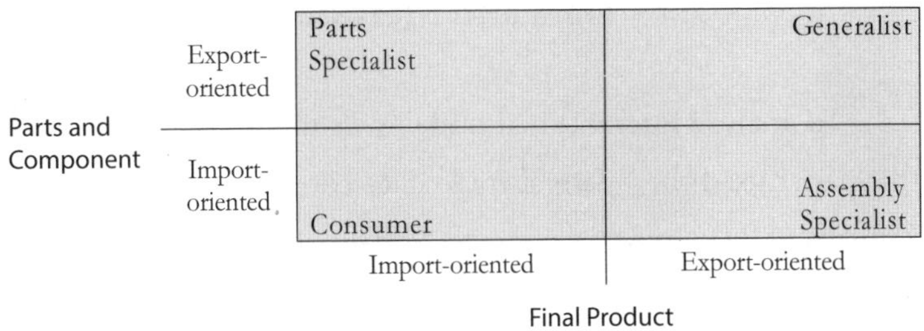


**Figure 11.1** Trade Patterns and Roles in GVCs: A Framework Parts and Component
Source: Authors.

these two roles, the four distinctive role-positions are identified. First, when a country is strong in exporting both parts and the end product, it can be considered as a *generalist* (upper-right). Second, a country can excel in one of the activities, either exporting parts, or be a *parts specialist* (upper-left), or putting parts together into a final product, or be an *assembly specialist* (lower-right). If a country is in a position to import both the final product and the parts, it is likely to rely on imported phones at the same time importing parts necessary for repair and we can call it a *consumer* (lower-left).

With this framework, we can examine how countries are positioned in different parts of the GVC and which role they play. Similar questions can be asked at the levels of inter-regional and intra-Asian trade networks. Each region play a different part in the global trade network, and countries may play a different role within the region from what they do in the global network.

We can also understand the change of not only trade network structure as well as countries' roles therein by comparing them in two different periods.

## Data and Methods

To analyze international trade flows in mobile phone GVCs, this paper used the bilateral trade data compiled from the United Nations (UN) Comtrade dataset (http://comtrade.un.org), one of the most extensive database of international goods trade from 1962.

To identify the product categories for the mobile phone and the parts used for it, the paper used Harmonized Standards (HS) codes at the six-digit level, the most disaggregated level with internationally comparable product classification. For mobile phones, HS 2007 classification code 8517.12 ("telephones for cellular networks or other wireless networks") was used along with its 2002 classification code 8525.20 ("transmission apparatus for radio-telephony incorporating reception apparatus"). For mobile phone parts, HS code 8517.70 is used.[1] To measure the amount of bilateral trade (nominal value in US dollars), the paper used trade data reported by the importing country since import data are usually considered more accurate than data reported by exporting countries (Escaith, 2011).

The analysis covers a post-crisis period from 2007 to 2013, focusing on the effect of the global financial crisis and the ensuring recession. Included to the analysis are all the countries that reported their imports in the aforementioned product categories at least once during the seven-year span.[2] To analyze intra- and inter-regional trade flows as well as trade between and within developed and developing economies, the countries are aggregated by geography and income level. The regional and income-level aggregations follows the World Bank country classification.[3]

## International Trade of Mobile Phones and Parts

The world's exports of mobile phones nearly doubled in 2007-2013, from $131 to $230 billion, despite a dip in 2009 caused by the global economic crisis. During the period, China consolidated its position as the leader of the world exports as its share climbed up from 35% to nearly 60%, as shown in Figure 11.2. East Asia has also strengthened its position as the top exporting region; its share in the world's exports increased from 59% to 78% in the period as a result of strong performance by China as well as other key exporters like Korea and Vietnam. The three countries together represented 74% of the world mobile phone exports in 2013, indicating a high level of regional and country-level concentration in mobile phone exports, as shown in Table 11.1. The share of the top ten exporters steadily increased from 84% to 90% in 2007-2013.

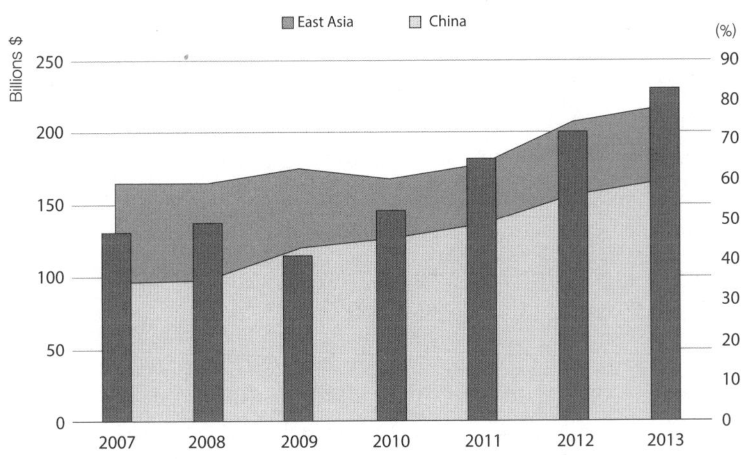


**Figure 11.2** The World's Mobile Phone Exports (value), 2007-2013

Source: Compiled from UN Comtrade.

By contrast, other regions and many former major exporting countries suffered; e.g., Europe lost its share by 16% and Latin America's share also dropped to 2% from 5% in the seven-year period. The European countries that used to be the major mobile phone producers and exporters dropped out, to name a few, Finland, Germany, and Hungary. Even in Asia, Malaysia and Singapore are no longer on the leaderboard, while Vietnam only emerged as the leading exporters in the last few years, indicating the fast changing landscape of mobile phone exports. Table 11.1 shows the change of the leading exporting countries over the period.

On the import side, the US is the largest importer of mobile phones, representing 22% of the world's imports in 2013. Other top importers include Hong Kong (11%), Japan (7%), Germany (5%) and UK (5%), as shown in Table 11.2. By region, Europe is the largest importing region (33%) with major importing coun-

**Table 11.1** The World's Leading Mobile Phone Exporting Countries, 2007-2013

| 2007 | | 2009 | | 2011 | | 2013 | |
|---|---|---|---|---|---|---|---|
| China | 35% | China | 43% | China | 49% | China | 60% |
| Korea | 16% | Korea | 16% | Korea | 9% | Vietnam | 9% |
| Finland | 7% | Mexico | 7% | Taiwan | 7% | Korea | 7% |
| Hungary | 7% | Hungary | 6% | Mexico | 5% | Netherlands | 4% |
| Germany | 5% | Taiwan | 4% | Hungary | 5% | Taiwan | 3% |
| Malaysia | 4% | Finland | 3% | Vietnam | 3% | Mexico | 2% |
| Mexico | 3% | US | 3% | Netherlands | 2% | US | 2% |
| US | 3% | India | 2% | US | 2% | Germany | 1% |
| Taiwan | 3% | UK | 2% | UK | 2% | India | 1% |
| Singapore | 2% | Canada | 2% | Ireland | 2% | Hungary | 1% |
| Others | 16% | Others | 13% | Others | 14% | Others | 10% |

Note: East Asian countries are shaded.
Source: Compiled from UN Comtrade.

tries like Germany, UK and France, although the region's share decreased from 40% to 33% in 2007-2013. It is followed by East Asia (29%) and North America (24%), whose shares increased from 19% and 21% respectively in 2007. The developed economy market (particularly OECD countries) is still the major importer, accounting for 82% of the world imports, compared to developing country markets (18%).

One notable change over the last several years was the rise of Japan as the world's third largest importer; the country, which used to be one of the major exporters of many advanced electronics goods, now imports much more than exports mobile phones ($16.5 billion in imports; $514 million in exports). Japan's imports more than tripled in 2010-2013, which is mostly attributed to the rising popularity of foreign brand phones like iPhones as well as growing outsourcing by Japanese mobile phone brands to China

**Table 11.2** The World's Leading Mobile Phone Importing Countries, 2007-2013

| 2007 | | 2009 | | 2011 | | 2013 | |
|---|---|---|---|---|---|---|---|
| US | 20% | US | 30% | US | 23% | US | 22% |
| Hong Kong | 7% | Hong Kong | 8% | Hong Kong | 9% | Hong Kong | 11% |
| Germany | 5% | France | 4% | UK | 6% | Japan | 7% |
| UK | 5% | Germany | 4% | Japan | 5% | Germany | 5% |
| Singapore | 5% | Mexico | 3% | Germany | 5% | UK | 5% |
| Russia | 4% | Singapore | 3% | Singapore | 3% | Mexico | 3% |
| Mexico | 3% | India | 3% | India | 3% | France | 3% |
| Netherlands | 3% | Japan | 3% | France | 3% | India | 3% |
| France | 3% | Italy | 3% | Mexico | 3% | Singapore | 3% |
| India | 3% | Spain | 2% | Canada | 2% | Saudi Arabia | 2% |
| Others | 41% | Others | 38% | Others | 37% | Others | 37% |

Note: East Asian countries are shaded; UK import data are unavailable for 2009.
Source: Compiled from UN Comtrade.

(Euromonitor International 2012). In 2013, China represented 88% of Japan's mobile phone imports.

Meanwhile, the international trade of parts and components for mobile phones also steadily increased in 2007-2013, from $59 billion to $119 billion, despite a dip in 2009 (see Figure 11.3). Similar in mobile phones, East Asian countries performed strongly in mobile phone parts; four out of the top five exporters in 2013 were Asian countries, i.e., China (57%), Korea (14%), Japan (3%), and Taiwan (3%), and the US was only non-Asian among the top five, as shown in Table 11.3. The major Asian exporters expanded their world share — China (+22%), Korea (+6%), Vietnam (+1.3%) and Taiwan (+0.2%), whereas many non-Asian countries that used to be strong in mobile phone parts production suffered the loss of their world market share, e.g., the US (-3%), Mexico (-3%), Germany (-3%), Canada (-3%) and Finland (-2%).

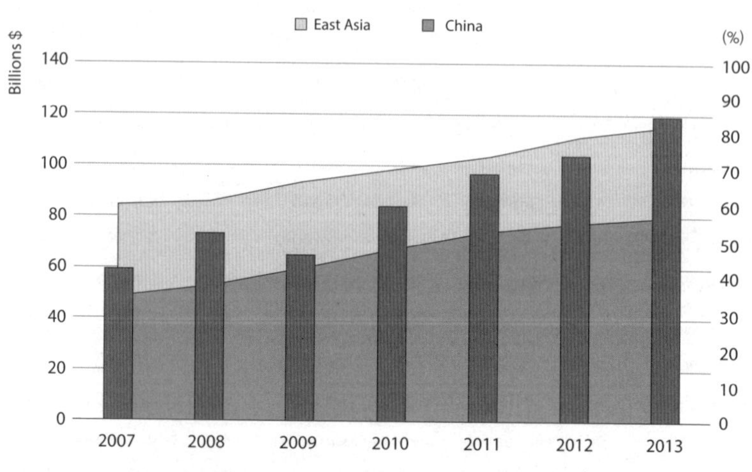


**Figure 11.3** The World's Mobile Phone Parts Exports (value), 2007-2013

Source: Compiled from UN Comtrade.

Regional performance reflects the rise of East Asia as well. East Asia expanded their share in the world's mobile phone parts exports from 62% to 82%, while both Europe and North America experienced a drastic decline of their share. At the same time, concentration has increased in parts exports; the leading ten exporting countries accounted for 88% of the world's exports in 2013, up from 76% in 2007.

The fact that a similar pattern was found in mobile phone trade suggests that the international trade of mobile phone parts is linked to that of the final product, meaning that the change of mobile phone exports affects that of parts as well. The case of Finland is illustrative; the home country of former Nokia (now acquired by Microsoft) lost its world's export share by 7% as its finish good exports decreased $9 billion to less than $1 billion in 2007-2013. During the same period, the country's parts exports also experienced a drop from 3.4% to less than 1% of the world's share.

**Table 11.3** The World's Leading Exporting Countries of Mobile Phone Parts, 2007-2013

| 2007 | | 2009 | | 2011 | | 2013 | |
|---|---|---|---|---|---|---|---|
| China | 35% | China | 43% | China | 53% | China | 57% |
| Korea | 7% | Korea | 7% | Korea | 8% | Korea | 14% |
| US | 6% | Japan | 6% | US | 4% | Japan | 3% |
| Japan | 6% | US | 6% | Japan | 4% | Taiwan | 3% |
| Mexico | 5% | Mexico | 4% | Malaysia | 3% | US | 3% |
| Malaysia | 5% | Malaysia | 4% | Taiwan | 3% | Malaysia | 2% |
| Germany | 4% | Sweden | 3% | Sweden | 3% | Mexico | 2% |
| Canada | 3% | Taiwan | 3% | Mexico | 3% | Sweden | 1% |
| Finland | 3% | Thailand | 3% | Thailand | 2% | Vietnam | 1% |
| Thailand | 3% | Germany | 2% | Germany | 2% | Thailand | 1% |
| Others | 24% | Others | 20% | Others | 16% | Others | 12% |

Note: East Asian countries are shaded.
Source: Compiled from UN Comtrade.

On the import side, China and Hong Kong are the leading. These two, combined, represented 55% of the world's mobile phone parts imports in 2013, up by 38% from 2007. Vietnam has emerged as the third largest importer as it quickly became a major hub of mobile phone production. The US is still an important importer but its share significantly declined from 14% to 5% of the world's imports in 2007-2013. Other major mobile phone producing countries filled the bottom of the leaderboard, including Mexico, Korea, Japan, Brazil (all 3%) and India (2%). These eight leading importers accounted for 80% of the world's mobile phone parts imports, suggesting a high degree of concentration in the import market as well. By region, East Asia accounted for 70% of the world imports as it consolidated its position of the global factory for the mobile phone. And, more mobile phone parts are imported to developing countries. In 2013, 52% of parts products were imported by developing countries, up from 26% in 2007, indicating

**Table 11.4** The World's Leading Importing Countries of Mobile Phone Parts, 2007-2013

| 2007 | | 2009 | | 2011 | | 2013 | |
|---|---|---|---|---|---|---|---|
| China | 23% | China | 22% | China | 25% | China | 33% |
| Hong Kong | 15% | Hong Kong | 17% | Hong Kong | 19% | Hong Kong | 22% |
| US | 14% | US | 9% | US | 6% | Vietnam | 6% |
| Japan | 6% | Mexico | 6% | Mexico | 5% | US | 5% |
| Netherlands | 4% | Japan | 5% | Hungary | 4% | Mexico | 3% |
| Germany | 4% | India | 4% | Japan | 3% | Korea | 3% |
| Finland | 4% | Korea | 4% | Korea | 3% | Japan | 3% |
| Sweden | 4% | Netherlands | 3% | India | 3% | Brazil | 2% |
| Korea | 3% | Germany | 3% | Netherlands | 3% | India | 2% |
| Singapore | 3% | Hungary | 3% | Brazil | 2% | Netherlands | 2% |
| Others | 20% | Others | 24% | Others | 26% | Others | 18% |

Note: East Asian countries are shaded.
Source: Compiled from UN Comtrade.

the rise of developing countries as the center of mobile phone production.

Overall, our analysis illustrates the increasing role of East Asian exporters in the world's mobile phone trade, particularly the consolidation of China's position and the fast rise of Vietnam as the leading exporters of mobile phones. China's role as both the largest exporter and importer of mobile phone parts, along with other East Asian countries, has also increased significantly in the trade of mobile phone parts.

## Countries' Changing Positions in the Mobile Phone GVC

To examine countries' positions in the mobile phone GVCs based on the framework outlined above, we analyzed their trade performance in terms of trade balances in mobile phones and parts. To reduce the complexity of analysis, our analysis was limited to 25 major trading countries that were listed to the top ten largest exporting or importing countries at least for one year between 2007 and 2013 in mobile phones or parts.[4] In 2013, they accounted for 92% of the world's mobile phone exports, 80% of the imports, and 93% and 91% of the world's mobile phone parts exports and imports, respectively.

For the sake of brevity, trade positions are presented only for two years, 2008 and 2013, in Figure 11.4 (2008 in triangle and 2013 in square). The horizontal and vertical axes represent trade balance (in US$ billion) respectively in mobile phones and parts. As a country is located in the upper right corner, it is positioned as a generalist, marking a trade surplus both in the end product and parts. Those in the lower left corner are generally considered as a consumer that rely on imports for both items. The upper right and lower left corners are occupied by specialists but in different value chain positions: parts production and assembly.

As shown in Figure 11.4, most of the countries are populated in the crowded center (zoomed in Figure 11.5), indicating the relatively small size of their trade balances compared to those of four countries whose positions are discernable. China is clearly located in the generalist position, which was strengthened in 2008-2013 as their trade surplus increased in both the final good and components. Korea also moved within the generalist territory. Its mobile phone exports suffered but it managed to keep the balance in the black, and its trade surplus in components significantly improved. Both the US and Hong Kong are located in the consumer position.

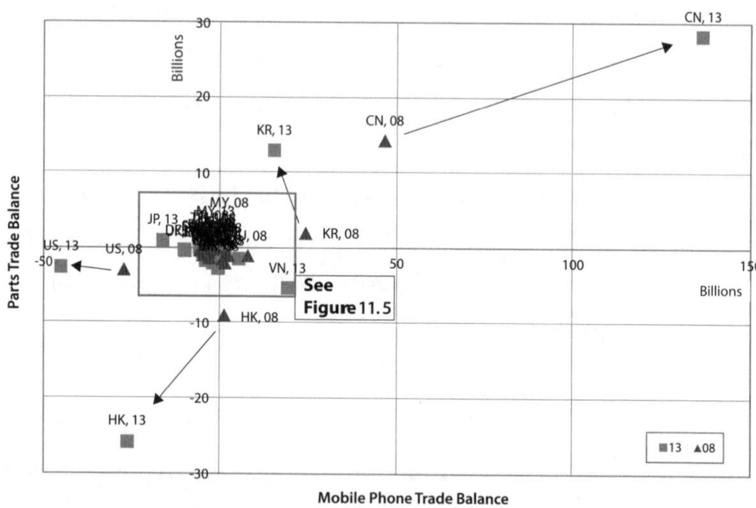


**Figure 11.4** Mobile Phones and Parts Trade Positions, 2008 and 2013
Source: Compiled from UN Comtrade.

For the US, it was mainly due to a rising deficit in the final good while for Hong Kong, it was attributed to a trade deficit in both the final good and components, mainly in its trade with mainland China (see below).

In Figure 11.5, we zoomed in the center area crowded by many other countries. Their positional change in 2008-2013 is less moderate given a relatively small amount of their trade surplus or deficit compared to those of the four big trading partners. Overall, the left side is more crowded than the right side, suggesting many are mostly the importers of mobile phones. But as for component trade, they are distributed relatively evenly between the surplus and the deficit area while value differences among them are much smaller compared to mobile phone trade (see the scale of the axes). Yet, two Asian countries are notable here; Japan's trade surplus improved in components while its deficit in the mobile phone in-

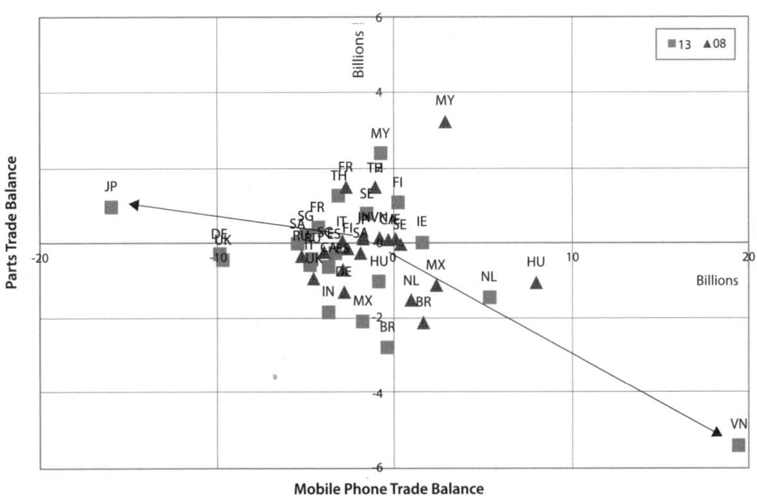


**Figure 11.5** Mobile Phones and Parts Trade Positions (part), 2008 and 2013
Source: Compiled from UN Comtrade.

creased significantly, as noted above, as the country imported more mobile phones, mainly from China (see Table 11.2). Vietnam moved in a different direction; its mobile phone exports increased considerably, increasing its trade surplus, but the country also imported more parts, strengthening a specialist position in final assembly.

A further closer examination shows several distinctive patterns of position changes. In Figure 11.6, each panel highlights some of the movements.

(1) *Generalist path*: China and Korea are the two notable examples. The two countries clearly strengthened their surplus positions in both parts and final product trade [see Figure 11.6.a].

(2) *Assembly Specialist path*: Vietnam is the most obvious and the only case. The country rapidly expanded its surplus in mobile phone trade with a considerable increase in component imports, indicating the country's mobile phone exports are largely based on imported parts [see Figure 11.6.a].

(3) *Path out from Assembly Specialist*: Some countries that used be in the assembly specialist position recently suffered the decline of their mobile phone exports. Hungary and Mexico are the examples. They both reduced a trade deficit in components in 2011-2013, but that was accompanied by a much greater decline of a trade surplus in mobile phones. In fact, the two countries' trade balance went into the red in both mobile phones and components in 2013, putting them now in the consumer position [see Figure 11.6.b].

(4) *Parts Specialist path*: Countries like Malaysia and Thailand are not particularly strong in mobile phone trade but maintain a surplus in components trade. Sweden and Singapore also moved

into the area of Parts Specialist while their deficit extended in mobile phone trade [see Figure 11.6.b]. Japan also increased its surplus in components, but the growth of its deficit in mobile phone was much greater than any other countries in this category (see Figure 11.5).

(5) *Consumer path*: Many advanced industrial countries formerly known as the major exporters of mobile phones are now in this category as firms in the countries suffer in global markets or outsource their production to overseas. The US is one of them, as shown above. The others include Germany, Canada and UK [see Figure 11.6.c]. Hong Kong is also in this category, but it moved in the different direction because its deficit in parts declined much drastically (see Figure 11.4).

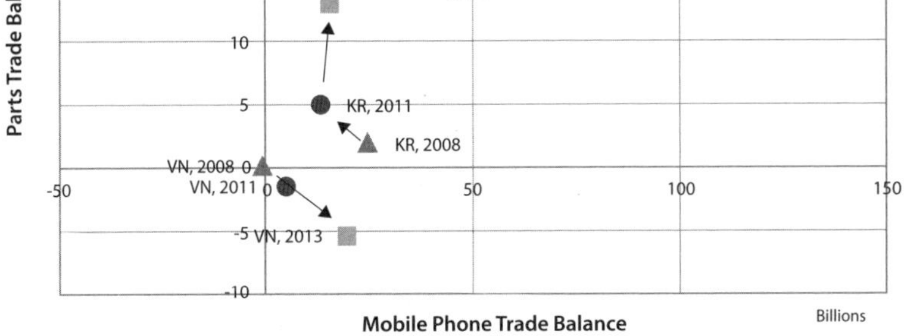


**Figure 11.6.a** Trade Position Changes of Major Trading Countries (part), 2008-2013: China, Korea and Vietnam

Note: Scales are different in the charts; Malaysia's trade balance in 2009 is used, instead of 2008.
Source: Compiled from UN Comtrade..

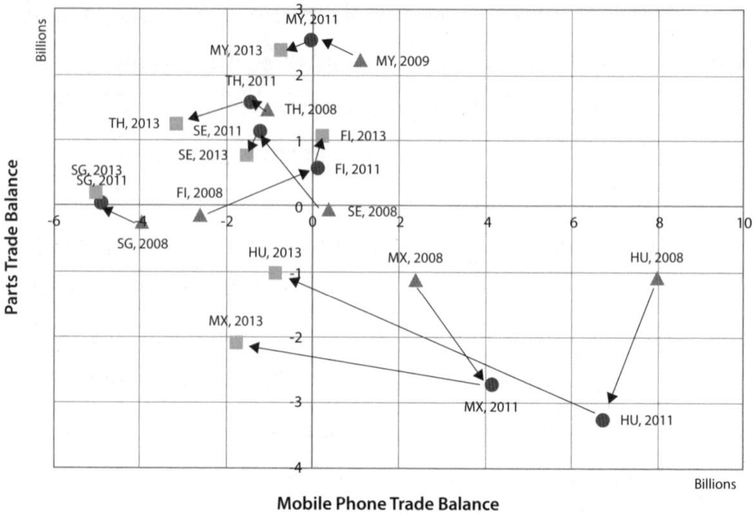


**Figure 11.6.b** Trade Position Changes of Major Trading Countries (part), 2008-2013: Finland, Hungary, Malaysia, Mexico, Singapore, Sweden and Thailand

Note: Scales are different in the charts; Malaysia's trade balance in 2009 is used, instead of 2008.
Source: Compiled from UN Comtrade.

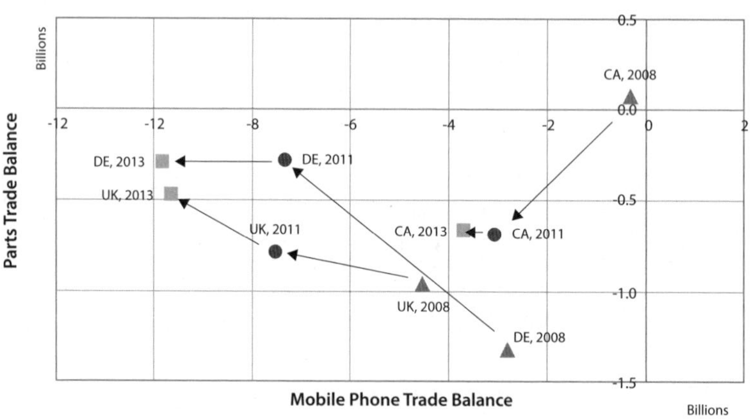


**Figure 11.6.c** Trade Position Changes of Major Trading Countries (part), 2008-2013: Canada, Germany and UK

Note: Scales are different in the charts; Malaysia's trade balance in 2009 is used, instead of 2008.
Source: Compiled from UN Comtrade.

In sum, our analysis shows that the major trading countries are positioned in different segments in the mobile phone GVC. And their positions have changed over the last several years in different directions. China and Korea have consolidated their generalist position, so has Vietnam as an assembly specialist. In contrast, Mexico and Hungary have shifted to the consumer position. A few countries have entered the parts specialist area, while others have moved to the consumer domain.

## Inter- and Intra-Reginal Trade Networks of Mobile Phones and Parts

Our analysis of regional trade flows shows how the rise of East Asia as the center of mobile phone and parts production affected the patterns of inter-regional trade as well as intra-regional trade in other regions.

The changes in the regional trade flows of the mobile phone between 2007 and 2013 are illustrated in Figure 11.7. First, intra-regional trade grew strongly in East Asia, from $21 billion to $55 billion, and from 16% to 24% of the world's mobile phone trade in value. This is attributed to the rise of the region as the center of production as well as consumption. Second, East Asia's exports to all the other six world-regions amounted to more than a half of the world trade (54% of the world trade in 2013). Taken together, East Asia's intra- and inter-regional trade accounted for 82% of the world trade in 2013, up from 62% in 2007, illustrating the rising importance of the region in the mobile phone GVC. Third, as imports from East Asia played a bigger role in mobile phone GVCs,

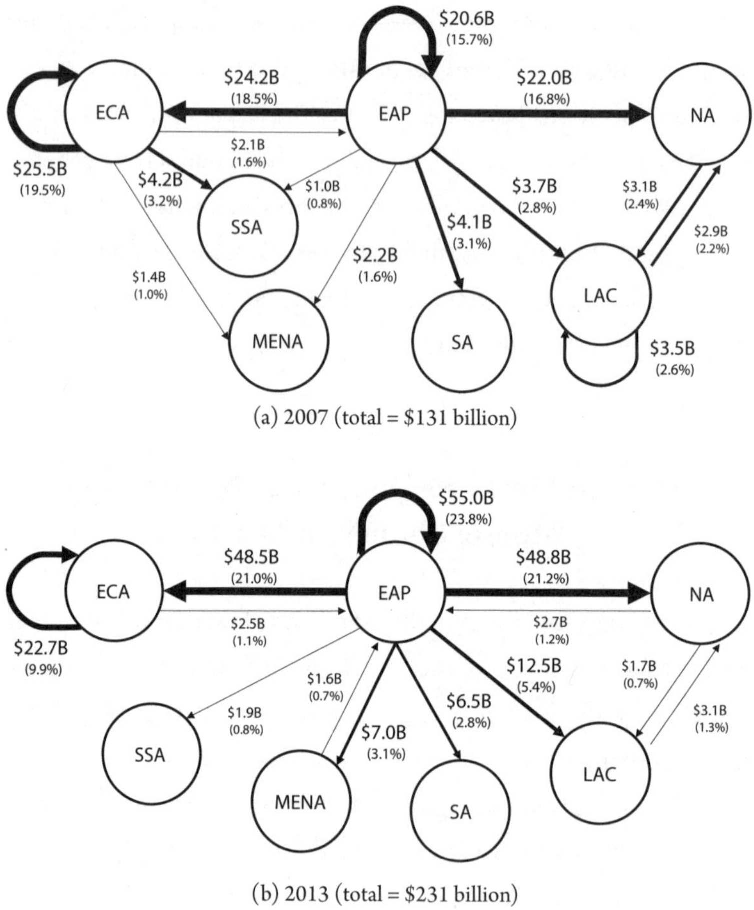


**Figure 11.7** Inter-Regional Trade Network of Mobile Phones, 2007 and 2013

Note: Appeared are the trade linkages only with more than 0.5% of the world trade.
Source: Compiled from UN Comtrade.

intra-regional trade in other regions has declined; intra-European trade decreased from $25 billion to $22 billion, now 10% of the world trade, and trade within Latin America also declined $3.5 billion to $0.5 billion in 2007-2013. Europe's exports to other regions like Sub-Saharan Africa (SSA) and Middle East and North Africa

(MENA) also decreased as the latter shifted to imports from East Asia, mostly China. Similarly, inter-American trade linkage also weakened as both regions more relied on imports from East Asia.

Our findings from mobile phone parts trade show some similarities with those from mobile phones, such as the growing importance of East Asia and its intra-regional trade. At the same time, there are some differences, such as the stagnation of exports from East Asia to Europe and North America. The key findings, as shown in Figure 11.8, are as follows.

First, intra-regional trade within East Asia increase significantly to $76 billion, 64% of the world's mobile phone parts trade in 2013. Second, while in mobile phone trade, the rise of East Asia increased the region's exports to Europe and North America (see above), it had a different effect in parts trade, i.e., stagnating part exports between East Asia and these regions where mobile phone manufacturing is declining. It also suggests that the most of the recent growth in East Asia's part trade was attributed to trade among East Asian countries. Third, intra-regional parts trade declined in Europe and North America; for example, Intra-European trade shrunk by $2 billion in 2007-2013. This is likely related to the decline of mobile phone manufacturing and the rise of offshore outsourcing to East Asia and Latin America in these regions. Finally, exports from East Asia rose significantly to Latin America, South Asia and even MENA. Exports to Latin America also increased from North America and Europe. This suggests that the growth of mobile phone manufacturing in the countries like Brazil in Latin America and India in South Asia, which facilitated the trade linkage of these rising production regions with East Asia and to a less degree with Europe and North America. It is also likely to reflect the

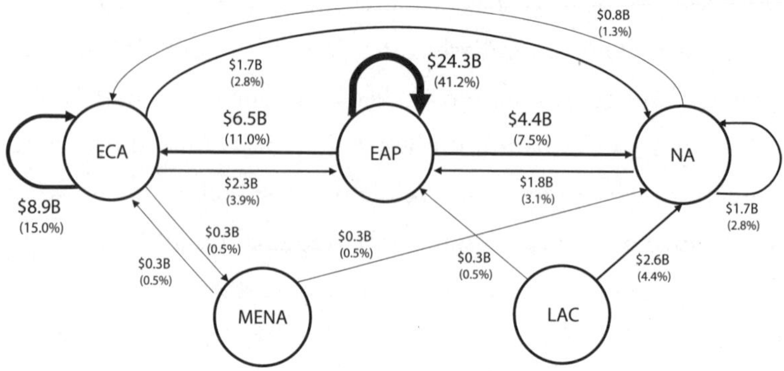


(a) 2007 (total = $59 billion)

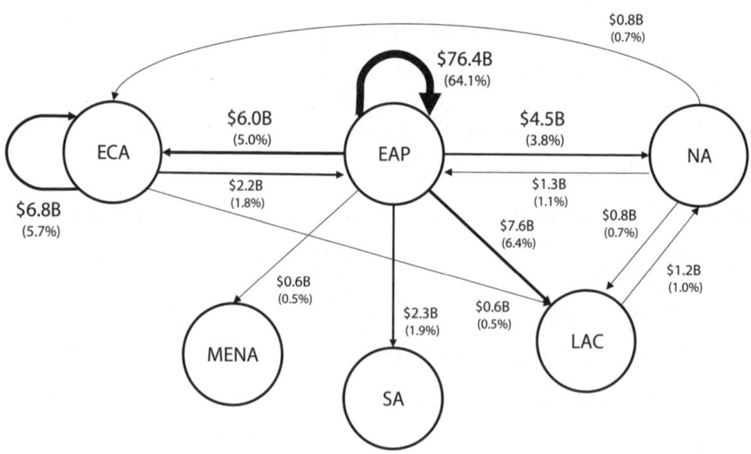


(b) 2013 (total = $119 billion)

**Figure 11.8** Inter-Regional Trade Network of Mobile Phone Parts, 2007 and 2013

Note: Appeared are the trade linkages only with more than 0.5% of the world trade.
Source: Compiled from UN Comtrade.

growing investment of East Asian firms like Samsung in countries like Brazil and India (Kim, 2012), which facilitated the exports from East Asia to these countries.

## Intra-Asian Trade Networks of Mobile Phones and Parts

The previous analyses have shown the importance of East Asia in the global trade of mobile phones and parts and the growing significance of trade within East Asia and with other Asian countries, particularly South Asia. The final part of our analysis in this paper, therefore, focused on the dynamic of intra-Asian trade.[5] Mobile phone trade within Asia rose from $26 billion to $65 billion in 2007-2009 and its share in the world's total mobile phone trade increased from 20% to 28%. In mobile phone parts, trade among Asian countries more than tripled, from $26 billion to $81 billion in the same period. The share of the intra-regional trade in the world's parts trade rose from 43% to 68%, indicating that intra-Asian trade has been intensified more in parts than the final good. Figure 11.9 shows the changing pattern of mobile phone trade between Asian countries from 2007 and 2013. Only the bilateral trade linkages whose value exceeds 1% of intra-regional trade in a given year are represented in the diagram.

In 2007, the largest trade linkage in this trade network was China's exports to Hong Kong (21%), followed by China's exports to Singapore (14%) and India (10%). Including these, China's export linkages to other Asian countries amounted to 58% in 2007. There were other notable intra-regional exporters. For example, Korea exported to China, Japan and Malaysia (7.4% of the total flow), and Malaysia to Singapore, Hong Kong and Japan (8%). Also, Singapore's exports to China amounted to 3.7%. In this sense, China was by far the largest exporter in the intra-regional trade network but a few other exporters also played a significant role.

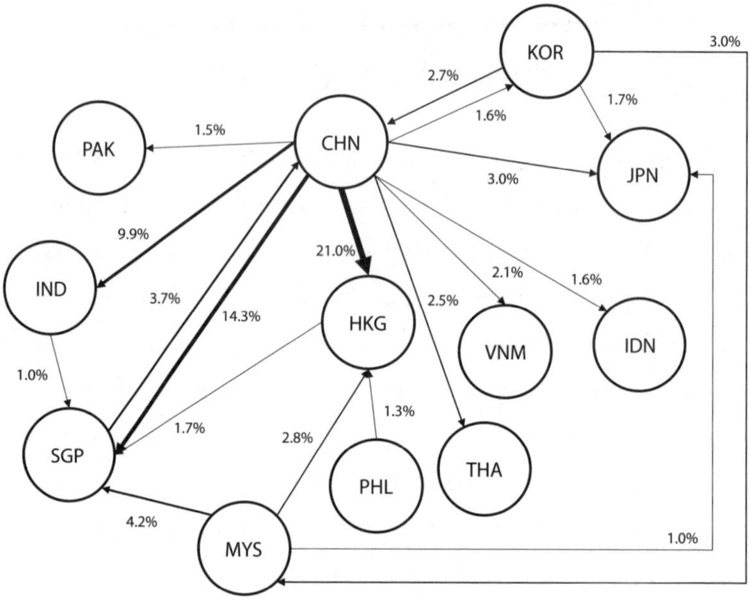


(a) 2007 (total = $26.2 billion)

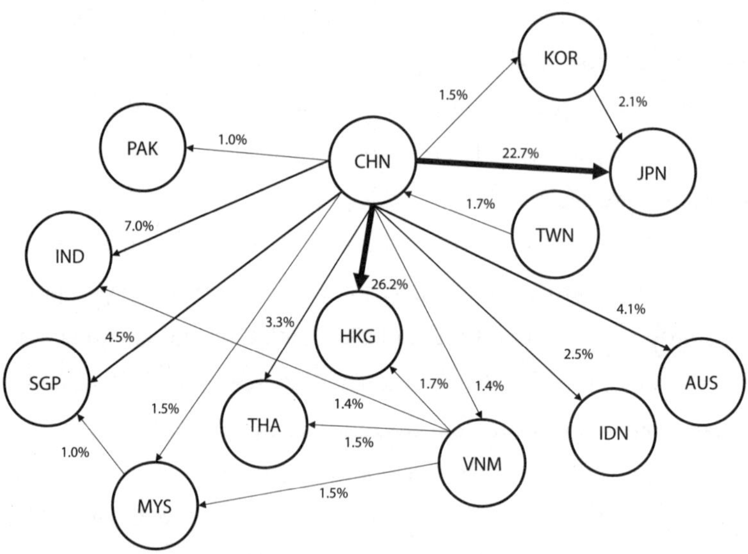


(b) 2013 (total = $64.6 billion)

**Figure 11.9** Intra-Asian Trade Network of Mobile Phones, 2007 and 2013

Note: Appeared are the trade linkages only exceeding 1% of the intra-Asia trade.

Source: Compiled from UN Comtrade.

The trade flow in 2013 shows that such multi-polarity has significantly declined. While China's exports to other Asian countries has risen to 76% of the total intra-regional trade, the role played by countries like Korea, Malaysia and Singapore has dwindled. The only export tie that was still meaningful in 2013 were Korea's exports to Japan (2%) and Malaysia's to Singapore (1%). Two notable new developments are: first, China's exports to Japan considerably increased, and now the trade link accounted for 23% of all the intra-regional trade. As noted above, it is likely attributable to the growing popularity in Japan of foreign mobile phones (mostly produced in China) as well as Japanese firms' rising offshore outsourcing of phone production. The other key development is the rise of Vietnam as the exports to multiple countries. While its share was much smaller (7%) compared to China's, the country has developed export linkages to countries like India, Thailand and Malaysia as well as Hong Kong. As a result, the 2013 trade flows shows that one big (China) and one smaller (Vietnam) exporters play a key role in the intra-Asian trade of mobile phones.

The intra-Asian trade patterns of mobile phone parts shows another interesting dynamics. As shown in Figure 11.10, the largest trade linkage in 2013 was China's reimports (mostly through Hong Kong). The share of the reimports increased from 23% to 29% of the total intra-Asian trade of mobile phone parts over the period.[6] And China's exports to Hong Kong remains the second biggest linkage, accounting for 27% in 2013. This shows the important role of the China-Hong Kong linkage in the trade network. Also, our analysis shows the intensity of trade among Korea, Japan and China. In 2007, the three countries exports and imports mobile phone parts with one another, accounting for 12% of intra-Asian

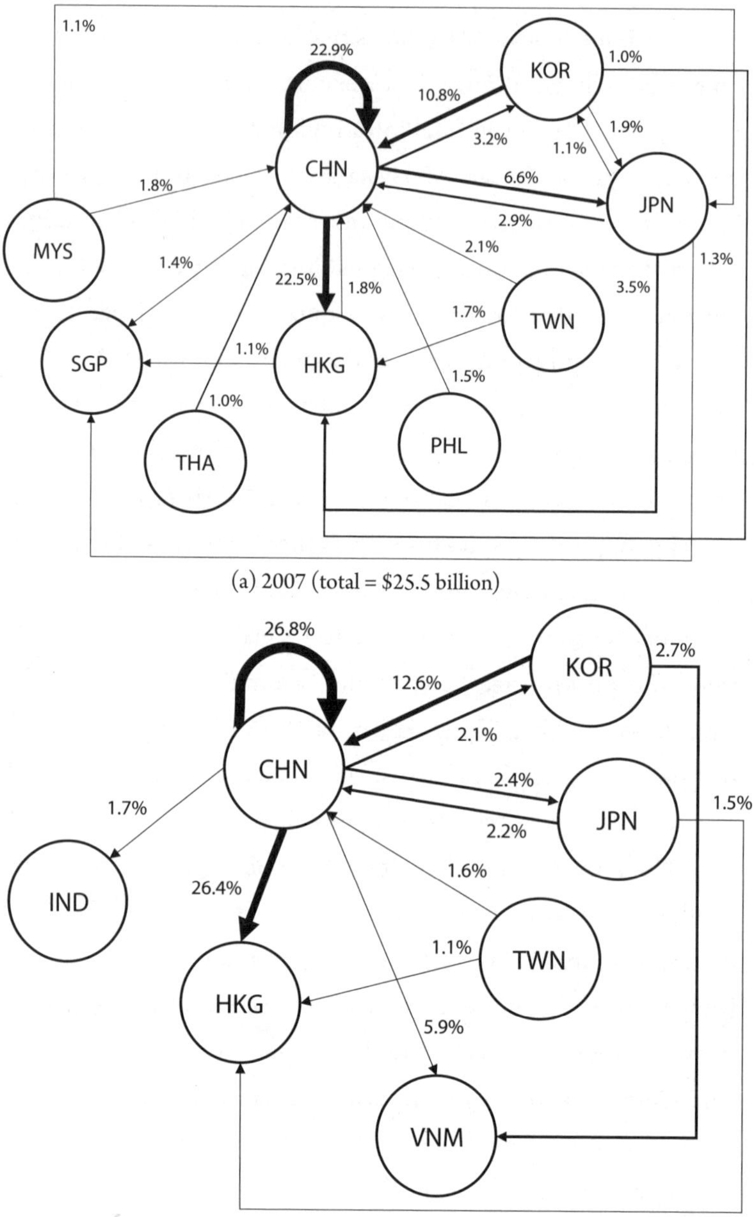


(a) 2007 (total = $25.5 billion)



(b) 2013 (total = $81.4 billion)

**Figure 11.10** Intra-Asian Trade Network of Mobile Phone Parts, 2007 and 2013

Note: Appeared are the trade linkages only with more than 1% of the intra-Asia trade.
Source: Compiled from UN Comtrade.

parts trade. In 2013, the Korea-Japan linkage became insignificant, but the two countries' ties with China were still important.

On a broader scale, a more interesting picture arose in China's changing trade relations with other Asian countries. In 2007, China was mainly the importer of parts from other Asian countries, Korea (11% of the total intra-regional trade), Japan (3%) and Taiwan (2%) as well as from Malaysia (1.8%), Hong Kong (1.8%), the Philippines (1.5%), and Thailand (1%). In turn, China exports parts for mobile phones to Japan (6.6%) and Korea (3.2%), where many global mobile brands are headquartered. In 2013, China's import partners were reduced to Korea (13%), Japan (2%) and Taiwan (2%). By contrast, China's export partners became diversified, now including Vietnam (6%) and India (2%) as well as Korea and Japan.

This suggests that China's domestic parts production increased significantly during the period, whether due to the relocation of foreign parts producers to China, or Chinese firms' replacement of imported parts by domestically produced ones through firm-level upgrading, or both. At the same time, now China is able to exports parts to Vietnam and India, the countries where mobile phone assembly is rising fast.

## Conclusions

The paper has examined the shifting positions of countries and the changing patterns of inter-regional and intra-regional trade in the mobile phone GVCs, focusing on the role of East Asia and diverging positions of East Asian countries in the trade networks.

It highlights that major exporting and importing countries were located in different positions in GVCs and some of them experienced a significant shift in their GVCs position during the post-crisis period. Also, the paper illuminates that inter- and intra-regional trade networks in mobile phones and parts have changed and the changes in mobile phones are, to some extent, related to those in parts trade networks.

The paper confirm the importance of a sophisticated framework to analyze countries' different positions in GVCs and the convergence and divergence of the positions. And, combining it with international trade data, it presents a general analytical framework that can be used for many other sector or value chains with publicly available international trade statistics.

The framework takes into account both exports and imports by using trade balance measures and also two key segments in GVCs, i.e., final goods and intermediate goods. Since trade statistics are available for each year and product categories are much disaggregated, such analysis can provide an up-to-date picture of countries' positions in GVCs for much detailed product groups or sectors, compared to other alternatives like international input-output tables, which have a considerable time lag until the data become available only at a broader industry level.

While the findings of the paper affirms some of earlier findings on the changes in the mobile phone GVCs, such as a growing consolidation of mobile phone production in East Asia and China, they provides a more detailed view of the changes not only in the manufacturing of final goods but also intermediate goods trade. Also, more interesting dynamics emerged through our trade position analysis. Vietnam's rise as the world's second largest mobile phone exporters was accompanied by the country's growing imports of parts and components, deepening its trajectory for the assembly specialist based on imported intermediate goods. This is a similar path took by Mexico in 2008-2011, but declining mobile phone exports later moved the country to the consumer position. Such a transition was shared by another major production hub, Hungary, which experienced a shift of production away from Europe to East Asia. In addition, our analysis shows that some of Asian countries like Japan, Malaysia, and Singapore have moved to the parts specialist position as more assembly production migrated from these countries to China and Vietnam, implying a different impact of production migration on a country's GVC position.

Our regional-level analysis sheds light on an interesting interaction between inter- and intra-regional trades. Mobile phone trade within a region has become less significant outside East Asia as the region bolstered a cross-regional trade linkage with East Asia, as shown in the decline of intra-regional trade in Europe and Latin America as well as inter-American trade, suggesting a replacement effect of intra-regional trade by inter-regional trade with East Asia. A similar effect is noticeable in parts trade; for example, the intra-regional trade of mobile phone parts declined in Latin America while imports from East Asia considerably increased. These changes are likely to be affected by not only trade but also investment relationships; for example, a growing investment by Asian firms such as Samsung, LG and Foxconn in Latin America has likely led to the growth of parts imports from East Asia. This raises the question whether regionalized production in these regions have a future in the face of a growing concentration of mobile phone GVCs in Asia.

Finally, our analysis affirms the importance of the China-

Hong Kong tie in mobile phone trade networks within Asia. China's leading role in the networks is prominent in both the final product and the parts. At the same time, it shows that Vietnam has begun to develop its own exporting network, partly supported by imported parts from China and Korea as well as by foreign investment from Korea as well as Singapore and Malaysia. It also illuminates the possibility of China's upgrading in parts production as it moved from importers to exporters to major emerging production hubs like Vietnam and India. To further understand the dynamics, we need to examine the unit value of imports and exports to see if there was any value increase or decrease in China's parts trade. At the same time, we need to combine trade analysis with an analysis of FDI statistics to better understand an interaction between GVC trade and investment activities.

## *Notes*

1. A separate category for the mobile phone, 8517.12, was first established in the HS 2007 classification codes. Countries began to classify the mobile phone according to the new HS codes in different years and until then, the mobile phones were included to HS 2002 code 8525.20, which also included other types of non-cellular wireless phones, such as code-less phones. HS 8517.70 was first introduced in the HS 2007 codes for parts for mobile phones.

2. In the UN Comtrade dataset, the data of trade with Taiwan are unavailable, despite its strong position in the mobile phone industry. However, countries to export to or import from Taiwan include it to the partner category of "Other Asia, not else specified" (code 490). According to the UN International Trade Statistics Knowledgebase, in reality, only trade of Taiwan is included under the code, except for several countries that include in this category all of their trade with unidentified Asian countries (http://unstats.un.org/unsd/tradekb/Knowledgebase/Taiwan- Province-of-China-Trade-data). Thus, in the paper, we consider all the trade included for the code as Taiwan's trade.

3. The world are divided by geography to seven regions, i.e., East Asia and Pacific (East Asia hereafter) ; South Asia; Europe and Central Asia (Europe hereafter); Middle East and North Africa (MENA); Sub-Saharan Africa (SSA); North America; Latin America and the Caribbean (Latin America hereafter). By income level, coun-

tries are grouped into developed countries (high-income OECD countries; high-income non-OECD countries) and developing countries (low income countries; upper-middle income countries; lower-middle income countries). For more on the classification, see http://data.worldbank.org/about/country-and-lending-groups (July 2015).

4. The countries include: Brazil, Canada, China, Finland, France, Germany, Hong Kong, Hungary, India, Ireland, Italy, Japan, Malaysia, Mexico, Netherlands, Korea, Russia, Saudi Arabia, Singapore, Spain, Sweden, Thailand, UK, US, and Vietnam. Taiwan was not included in this part of analysis because its trade balance cannot be calculated because Taiwan does not report its import to the UN Comtrade dataset.

5. In this part of analysis are included the countries in the following two geographic categories: East Asia and Pacific and South Asia. Also, trade to/from the category of "Other Asia, not elsewhere specified" is considered as Taiwan's.

6. More than 90% of China's reimports are produced in China, exported to Hong Kong, where many MNCs' distribution centers are located, and then re-imported in China, mostly to Guangdong province to be used as inward processing materials (http://www.trademap.org/stFAQ.aspx).

## *References*


Arndt, Sven W. and Henryk Kierzkowski, eds. 2001. *Fragmentation: New Production Patterns in the World Economy*. Oxford: Oxford University Press.

Cattaneo, Olivier, Gary Gereffi and Cornelia Staritz, eds. 2010. *Global Value Chains in a Postcrisis World: A Development Perspective*. Washington, DC: World Bank.

Dicken, Peter. 2011. *Global Shift: Mapping the Changing Contours of the World Economy*. New York: Guilford Press.

Escaith, Hubert. 2011. "Understanding International Trade Statistics." *International Trade Statistics 2011*. World Trade Organization, Geneva, pp. 4-5.

Euromonitor International. 2012. "Mobile Phones in Japan." Euromonitor International.

Gereffi, Gary. 1999. "International Trade and Industrial Upgrading in the Apparel Commodity Chains." *Journal of International Economics* 48(1): 37-70.

_______. 2005. "The Global Economy: Organization, Governance, and Development." pp. 160-182 in *The Handbook of Economic Sociology*, edited by N. J. Smelser and R. Swedberg. 2nd edition. Princeton, NJ: Princeton University Press.

_______. 2014. "Global Value Chains in a Post-Washington Consensus World." *Review of International Political Economy* 21(1): 9-37.

Gereffi, Gary, John Humphrey, and Timothy Sturgeon. 2005. "The Governance of Global Value Chains." *Review of International Political Economy* 12(1): 78-104.

Humphrey, John and Hubert Schmitz. 2004. "Chain Governance and Upgrading: Taking Stock." pp. 349-381 in *Local Enterprises in the Global Economy: Issues of Governance and Upgrading*, edited by H. Schmitz. Cheltenham, UK: Edward Elgar.

Kim, Hyun-seok. 2012. "Samsung Electronics Restructuring Oveaseas Mobile Phone Production Facilities, Closing Shenzhen Plants and Increasing Capacity in Vietnam and India." *Hankyung Daily*, 20 March. <http://www.hankyung.com/news/app/newsview.

php?aid=2012032075781.>

Krugman, Paul, Richard N. Cooper, and T. N. Srinivasan. 1995. "Growing World Trade: Causes and Consequences." *Brookings Papers on Economic Activity*, 1995(1): 327-377.

Lee, Joonkoo and Gary Gereffi. 2013. "The Co-Evolution of Concentration in Mobile Phone Global Value Chains and Its Impact on Social Upgrading in Developing Countries." Capturing the Gains Working Paper 2013/25, University of Manchester. <http://www.capturingthegains.org/publications/workingpapers/wp_201325.htm.>

Lee, Joonkoo, Jong-Cheol Kim, and Jinho Lim. 2016. "Globalization and Divergent Paths of Industrial Development: Mobile Phone Manufacturing in China, Japan, South Korea and Taiwan." *Journal of Contemporary Asia* 46(2): 222-246.

Mittelman, James H., ed. 1996. *Globalization: Critical Reflections*. Boulder, Colo.: Lynne Rienner Publishers.

Neidik, Binnur and Gary Gereffi. 2006. "Explaining Turkey's Emergence and Sustained Competitiveness as a Full-Package Suppliers of Apparel." *Environment and Planning A* 38(12): 2285-2303.

OECD, WTO and World Bank. 2014. "Global Value Chains: Challenges, Opportunities, and Implications for Policy." Report prepared for submission to the G20 Trade Ministers Meeting, Sydney, Australia, 19 July.

Steinbock, Dan. 2005. *The Mobile Revolution: The Making of Mobile Services Worldwide*. London; Sterling, VA: Kogan Page Publishers.

Sturgeon, Timothy J. and Olga Memedović. 2011. *Mapping Global Value Chains: Intermediate Goods Trade and Structural Change in the World Economy*. United Nations Industrial Development Organization.

Timmer, Marcel P., Abdul Azeez Erumban, Bart Los, Robert Stehrer, and Gaaitzen J. de Vries. 2014. "Slicing up Global Value Chains." *Journal of Economic Perspectives* 28(2): 99-118.

WTO and IDE-JETRO. 2011. "Trade Patterns and Global Value Chains in East Asia: From Trade in Goods to Trade in Tasks." World Trade

Organization and Institute of Developing Economies, Geneva and Tokyo. <http://www.wto.org/english/res_e/publications_e/stat_tradepat_globvalchains_e.htm.>

Yeung, Henry Wai-chung, Weidong Liu, and Peter Dicken. 2006. "Transnational Corporations and Network Effects of a Local Manufacturing Cluster in Mobile Telecommunications Equipment in China." *World Development* 34(3): 520-540.

Chapter 12

# *Development Cooperation and the Legacy of the Developmental State: Government Initiative and State-Business Partnership in Korean Development Cooperation with Mozambique and Rwanda*

Thomas Kalinowski and Minjoung Park

## Introduction

Korea's path from a poor agricultural country in the 1960s to an industrial powerhouse and OECD membership in 1996 was too a large degree shaped by a strong developmental state. The debate on how much remains of this old Korean developmental state has been going on at least since the Asian financial crisis of 1997/98. First, this debate was dominated by case studies that investigated the effect of reforms promoted by or imposed upon Korea by external pressure such as IMF structural adjustment.[1] Changes were discussed in the context of a struggle between the Korean state-led development model and a "Wall Street-Treasury-IMF Complex" (Veneroso and Wade, 1998). Then the debate on the (Western) "varieties of capitalism" facilitated by Hall and Soskice (2001) introduced very useful concepts of path dependency and institutional complementarity that helped explaining a lack of convergence to one form of "best practice" capitalism. Ultimately, studies of comparative capitalism that originated in the observations of US-American and European advanced capitalist models extended beyond their Western comfort zone and included Japan (Streeck and Yamamura, 2001) and state-led Asian capitalism (Coates, 2002). The foundation of the SASE Network on Asian Capitalism in 2011 was a signal that the study of "Asian capitalism" (Storz et al., 2013; Walter and Zhang, 2012) had finally been fully acknowledged by the mainstream of comparative capitalism research.

Another major step forward in the research on comparative capitalism was an improved understanding of institutional change. Originally studies of comparative capitalism focused on institutional complementarity, highlighted path dependency and even divergence of capitalist models. Soon this static institutionalist model was criticized for a lacking conceptualization of change in the comparative capitalism approach. Particularly by looking at (US style) neoliberal reforms implemented in Europe and Japan critics highlighted the aspect of path dependent change and even gradual transformation (Vitols, 2003; Yamamura and Streeck, 2003). While distinct models of capitalism do show a path dependency in the broader sense but that established institutions could change and even transform gradually through institutional displacement, layering, drift, conversion or exhaustion (Streeck and Thelen, 2005). In this context institutions are usually very broadly defined as formal and informal settlements that are shaping the interaction between actors within a society or in Hodgson's words as "systems of established and prevalent social rules that structure social interactions" (Hodgson, 2006: 2).

This paper builds on above introduced concepts of path dependency and change to understand recent changes in Korean state-led capitalism. At the same time the paper extends the investigation of path dependency and change into new fields. Unlike most studies of comparative capitalism we do not follow established institution of the Korean developmental state in traditional areas such as industrial policy, economic planning, technology, financial regulation etc. Instead we are interested in investigating how these institutions and practices extend to new policy fields such as development cooperation. We want to find out how much of the Korean state-led model of capitalism can still be found in the new policy field of development cooperation. We argue that central elements of the Korean developmental state that have lost relevance in Korean domestic policies and are severely criticized within Korea continue to play an important role in shaping Korean development cooperation.

To describe this extension of established institutions into a new arena we want to propose a new term of institutional retreat. Institutional retreat means that institutions that became anachronistic and dysfunctional in their established areas are retreating to other policy fields. Institutional retreat is similar to what Thelen called institutional conversion where "institutions are not so much amended or allowed to decay as they are *redirected to new goals, functions, or purposes*." (Streeck and Thelen, 2005: 26, italics in original) The difference is that in the case of institutional retreat goals, functions and purpose of institutions remain largely the same but merely the policy field has changed. The elements of the developmental state we found in the field of development cooperation still have the same goal of expanding industries and facilitating investment but these goals are now pursued not domestically but internationally. In some sense development cooperation can be described as an "international extension of the national industrial and mercantilist policies that were the essence of Korea's development strategy in the past." (Kalinowski and Cho, 2012: 243) At the same time institutional retreat can also be distinguished from institutional spill-over in which successful institutions are extended from one policy field to the next because retreat implies that the institutions have become less successful in their original area and in order to survive have to retreat into a new area. Most importantly, actors, interests and ideologies connected to institutions that are pushed out of their traditional fields are now finding new niches in which their specifically structured relationships can survive. In Korea, developmental cooperation could be such an area of retreat in which elements of the old developmental state survive and even thrive.[2]

Most literature on Korean development cooperation (DC) focused on the evaluation of aid, the lessons that can be learned from Korea as a recipient country and the knowledge from Korean development that can be transferred to the developing world (Kim et al., 2013). This paper has a different focus. It is less concerned with the lessons that can be theoretically learned from Korea's role as a recipient country for Korean development cooperation policies today but what shapes these policies in reality. We are less interested in what developing countries can learn from the Korean development experience (which is a lot) but we want to find out how Korean DC is influenced by the legacy of the Korean developmental state. With development cooperation in this paper we mean not just official development assistance (ODA) but also includes more broadly foreign investment that are aimed at developing the economic capacity of a developing country for example as part of a public private partnership (PPP).

Before we investigate two cases studies of Korean cooperation with the developing world more closely, we need to define what we mean with developmental state in the context of this article. When we think about the Korean developmental state we think primarily of two aspects. First, the classic dictum of Chalmers Johnson (1982; 1995) about state autonomy and nationalist state-led development and second, Peter Evans concept of "embedded autonomy" (Evans, 1995) focusing on the strong partnership and collusion between an authoritarian state and large business conglomerates (Kim, 1997). Within Korea both elements of the developmental state have become under serious pressure since the beginning of democratization in the late 1980s and economic globalization particularly since the Asian financial crisis of 1997/98. Korean global business conglomerates (*chaebol*) have emancipated themselves from government leadership and guidance. Under the old developmental state the *chaebol* implemented government-led investment and employment plans and in turn received support and protection from the state. Today, Korea's *chaebol* are globally operating businesses with massive assets and their own research facilities depending far less on government support and protection than in the past. Consequently the *chaebol* are reluctant when the Korean government wants them to support their national plans for investment and job creation. At the same time, the process of democratization since 1987 has created a democratic civil society that is criticizing authoritarian politics and exposing collusion between state and businesses. Fundamentally, it is this dual emancipation of corporate globalization and domestic democratization (as well as the occasional setbacks within these broad trends) that has been shaping Korea's recent development and is shaping Korean development in the foreseeable future. If these two central elements of the developmental state are under pressure within Korea, how much of them can be found in Korean development cooperation today?

In this paper we are showing that both elements of the developmental state — government leadership and state-business collusion — play an important role in how Korean development cooperation is conducted. Unlike in countries with a long history of outward foreign investment in the developing world, Korea's external economic relationship with the global South is largely state-led. The government actively uses development cooperation to secure access to resources and open markets for Korean business conglomerates. To put it simple, while at the domestic level market competition, civil society activism and parliamentary oversight have weakened the traditional developmental state it has found a new playground in the field of development cooperation. Of course, Korea is not a special case in that it uses development cooperation to advance national economic and political goals. All countries do that in one or the other way. The difference is only in what kind of national interests are promoted and in which way. In Korea the national interest in development cooperation in Korea is structured along the lines of the old state-business development alliance established during the times of the developmental state. Unlike European countries and the US that have a long standing relationship with the developing world including in many cases a colonial or semi-colonial legacy Korea is a newcomer in many developing country and thus has to be more aggressive. Unlike established players Korean companies need the active supporting role of the government to penetrate markets in the developing world and invest in an unfamiliar and highly risky environment. In some sense, the old dictum of Gerschenkron (1962) that the later a country develops the more state involvement is necessary also holds for the globalization of economies. The later a country globalizes and starts to export and invest abroad the more state involvement is necessary to facilitate this process. Development cooperation is part of this process of economic globalization.

In this paper we want to introduce two cases of development cooperation that illustrate the legacy of the developmental state in Korea's relationship with the developing world: Mozambique and Rwanda. In both countries we can observe that development cooperation consisted of a joint effort of increasing ODA and expansion of foreign direct investment and trade. In both cases the initiatives for the increased cooperation came from the Korean government and not from private businesses. In the case of Mozambique development aid was the door opener for the investment of Korean state owned company KOGAS in a large gas field as well as a gas liquefaction project. In Rwanda, development aid helped to pave the way for a major government contract for a privatized business conglomerate Korea Telecom to improve the countries IT infrastructure. Both projects were state-led and characterized by the close cooperation between government agencies and businesses.[3]

It is important to note that this paper primarily aims at a better understanding of the way Korean development policies are conducted. It is not the purpose of this paper and much too early to offer a comprehensive evaluation of these policies. From our perspective it seems that Korean development cooperation is by no means per se less or more successful than development cooperation conducted by established donors. Indeed the record of Western development cooperation is mixed at best (Easterly, 2006) and there are many promises in Korea's role as a bridge between the developing and developed countries (Kalinowski, 2010). From our two case studies it seems that despite the similarities the benefits and problems of Korean development cooperation seem to depend primarily on the concrete projects and how exactly they are conducted.

## First Case: State-Led Development Coopration and "Resource Diplomacy" in Mozambique

The first case study of Korean engagement in Mozambique is an excellent example to show how Korean development cooperation and economic relations with the developing world are shaped by the legacy of the Korean developmental state. During the times of the old developmental state in Korea government planning and industrial policies "governed the market" (Wade, 2004) and facilitated the growth and domestic market expansion of large business conglomerates. Current development cooperation policies have similar goals but instead of facilitating domestic investment now the focus is on facilitating foreign investment and the global expansion of domestic businesses. The government leads and facilitates the expansion of national businesses into new difficult markets and helps them quickly expand market share by socializing risks of investments. Compared to other destinations of Korean investments like the US or Europe, Africa is still regarded as a high risk market to Korean business. Therefore, the state acts as a risk manager using ODA and especially concessional loans. This has set it apart from the traditional donors and provides a different kind of role in the field of development cooperation. The case of DC with Mozambique shows the state leadership and direct involvement in facilitating foreign direct investment.

Mozambique is a country with abundant resources of natural gas, crude oil as well as other minerals and became a target country in Korea's "resource diplomacy" to secure access to natural resources for the Korean economy. The relations with Mozambique are a good example to illustrate the state-led strategy in which development cooperation in general is used to incite and in this case even initiate Korean overseas investment. In 2010, the country was named a strategic partner in development cooperation and since then aid to the country is steadily increasing (see Figure 12.1). Until 2010 Korea's ODA to Mozambique was concentrated only on grants and amounted to less than 1 million per year. Since the country has been selected as a strategic partner country the volume of its ODA has been scaled up dramatically and particularly through concessional loans. In 2013, Korea's bilateral aid to Mozambique was US$ 57.08 million. Among them, only 3.58 million were provided as grant. US$ 53.5 million were provided as concessional loans through the Export-Import Bank of Korea (Korean Eximbank, hereafter) to build infrastructure. In 2014, Mozambique became the largest recipient of the Korean Economic Development Cooperation Fund (EDCF) in Africa, 8th in all 48 ECDF recipient countries (Korea Eximbank, 2015b).

The naming as a strategic partner and the massive increase of

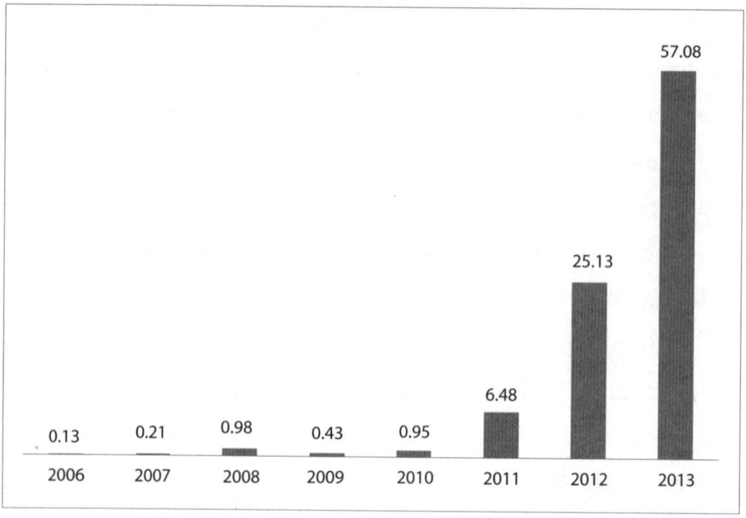


**Figure 12.1** Korea's bilateral aid to Mozambique, 2006-2013 (million US$)
Source: ODA Statistics, Korea Eximbank (2015b).

development aid facilitated another form of development cooperation between the two countries. In 2011, Korea's state owned Korea Gas Corporation (KOGAS) invested in major gas liquefaction projects in Mozambique. Since then, gas reserves of 1.8 billion tons have been confirmed off the Eastern coast of Mozambique. KOGAS 10% stake in the exploration is equivalent to Korea's nationwide demand of more than five years making the case a rare success story in Korea's resource diplomacy projects that have largely failed to meet expectations (Shin, 2012). Mozambique plans to build four LNG units with a total capacity of 20 million metric tons a year by 2018, making it the largest LNG export site after Ras Laffan in Qatar. The Korea Eximbank confirmed that the discovery of a natural gas field has given added boost to bilateral talks on economic cooperation and to the local presence of Korean companies (Korea Eximbank, 2015a). Based on the gas exploration in

Area 4, KOGAS plans to build a floating liquefied natural gas plant (FLNG) off the coast of Mozambique in cooperation with Korea's big three shipbuilding companies, Hyundai, Samsung, Daewoo. The intensified economic exchange is also reflected in the bilateral trade that has shown a fivefold increase from $25 million in 2007 to $110 million 2012 (Korea Eximbank, 2015a).

The economic engagement of KOGAS had a high political priority which can be seen by Prime Minister Kim Hwang-sik's official visit to Mozambique in 2012 to strengthen ties between the two countries. In 2013, the newly elected President Park Geun-hye held talks with visiting President Armando Guebuzza of Mozambique and discussed ways to expand resources development cooperation by offering Korea's economic development expertise. The case of Mozambique shows a typical characteristic of the 'package deals' offered by the Korean state including intensified political and economic relationships facilitated with projects of development cooperation. The involvement of the Korean state in such arrangements acts as an important reassuring factor for state-owned and private firms that would otherwise never be willing to take the risk in advancing into volatiles markets in the developing world. Unlike European and American companies that have long been established in African markets, Korean newcomers only have a chance within such an integrated strategy with active state involvement.

The recent emphasis on Mozambique in Korea's ODA program seems to be intended to gain greater access to the nations' natural resources. The impact of Korean ODA in Mozambique's development is hard to measure since its volume is amounted only 0.3% of Mozambique's total ODA flow in 2013. Korea's development efforts might support technical advance and infrastructure development for Mozambique. Given that the natural gas sector attracts the majority of Korean investment, yet, Korea's economic approach to Mozambique on the basis of searching for raw materials can be detrimental to its economic development, often causing a greater dependency on mega-projects in the extractive industries and the energy sectors which might harm governance and efficiency. Some argues that although mega-projects have a positive effect on the economy they do not create many jobs, but instead lead to enrichment of the happy few, while many people remained unemployed. Also as environmental NGOs argue that the rich ecology may be negatively affected by gas production in the area resulted in a loss of income to local artisanal fishermen due to fish stock deaths and migration (Folley, 2011).

## Second Case: Extending into New Markets in Rwanda through Public Private Partnership

In Mozambique the government not just took the lead through diplomatic activities and development cooperation but also indirectly carried out the foreign investment through a state-owned company. The case of Rwanda is different. The state also initiated the intensified relationship but the economic investment was conducted by the previously state-owned but now privatized business conglomerate Korea Telecom. The case of Rwanda thus illustrates the close cooperation between state and private business in development cooperation.

Korea's engagement in Rwanda began in the mid-2000s and gradually intensified as can be seen in Figure 12.2. Until 2013,

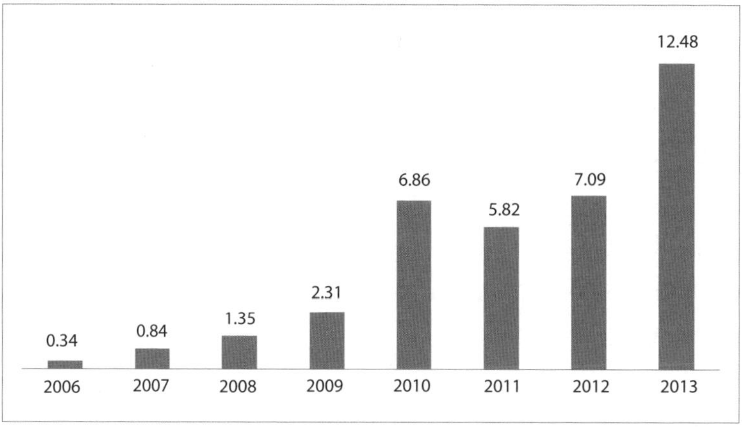


**Figure 12.2** Korea's bilateral aid to Rwanda, 2006–2013 (million US$)
Source: ODA Statistics, Korea Eximbank (2015b).

Korea's ODA to Rwanda was concentrated only to grants, the total volume of Korea's grant aid is amounted US$ 38.06 million so far (Korea Eximbank, 2015b). Most of grants aid has been focused to technical cooperation, especially in the field of ICT. KOICA has implemented a number of grants project for strengthening the growth and development of the ICT industry in Rwanda including the dispatches of ICT technicians.

The Korean state has placed a significant emphasis on ICTs within its development cooperation program since the beginning. The ICT sector is a strong component of both the Korean economy overall and also of Korean exports, a quarter of total goods exports in Korea is ICT goods exports, amounted to approximately US$ 170 billion in 2013 (Kim et al., 2014). Hence, ICT forms one of the seven strategic components of Korean ODA in order to find new consumption markets abroad. The portion of Korea's ODA in ICT is much larger than in any other OECD DAC member countries. From 1990 to 2010, 15% of the Korea's total ODA was spent for ICT sector, compared to less than 1% for the OECD DAC average. Most of this ODA is provided as loans and most of them are going to middle or upper middle income countries (Kim et al., 2014). This focus on ICT reflects not only Korea's own comparative advantage but also the significant need for ICT investments in the developing world. Korean assistance in the field of ICT led to a diffusion of ICTs in the recipient countries and brought ICT-related benefits to those nations.

In case of Rwanda, Korea's support for ICT aid has been closely linked with KT's involvement in the Rwanda's ICT industry. In 2007, Korea Telecom (KT) signed a contract with the Rwandan government for wireless high-speed internet project. KT is the largest telecommunication business in Korea and a formerly state-owned company that was privatized in 2002. Since then KT has evolved from a telecom company to the 9th largest business conglomerate in Korea that is active in many areas including fixed line and mobile telephony, internet services, digital television, credit card, entertainment, education, real estate, infrastructure, sports and software.

In 2008, KT signed a contract to build a national backbone network to connect the Rwandan capital city of Kigali with 30 other major cities for a contract value of US$ 38 million. This turnkey project involved the construction of a national fiber optic cable network, transmission network and internet network as well as equipment supply, engineering construction and operator training and training to be completed by November 2009 (Darracq and Neville, 2014). During this stage Rwanda registered one of the highest internet user growth rates in Africa at 8,900% compared with the continent's growth rate of 2,450%, and the world's average rate of 444% (Nirit, 2014). According to the Rwanda Development Board, almost every one in four public sector entities, ministries, agencies, provinces and districts as well as about a third in the private sector had a web presence (Republic of Rwanda, 2013). Based on the mutual trust built during the previous 4-year project, the Government of Rwanda and KT agreed to form a joint venture company, Olleh Rwanda Networks, in June of 2013 to deploy a high speed broadband network to cover 95% of the population in three years (Darracq and Neville, 2014). In November 2014, Olleh Rwanda Networks launched the 4G LTE, high speed internet that supports over five times data capacity of up to 100 Mbps speeds (Mugisha and Mwai, 2014). In September of 2014, the second joint venture company between the Government of Rwanda and KT, Africa Olleh Services Ltd. was established to accelerate deployment of IT infrastructure and to develop and operate online services. This second company is in charge of the country's cloud services capability, as a system integrator and provider of IT solutions to the broader market across the region. It started the delivery of the first of many projects of the Rwandan government that it was assigned in accordance with the shareholder's agreement. Currently 2,500 km of fiber optic have been laid throughout the country with nine regional links to neighboring countries (3 links to Uganda, One link to Tanzania, 3 links to Burundi and 2 links to Democratic Republic of Congo) to facilitate cross-border data traffic and trade (Mugisha and Mwai, 2014). The Government of Rwanda says with the launch of 4G LTE it wants to increase ICT's contribution to GDP to 4% in 2014 up from 3% 2013 (AfDB/OECD/UNDP, 2014).

Unlike in the case of Mozambique were the Korean government was initiator, facilitator and investor the Korean government played largely the role as a facilitator and broker between the Rwandan government and KT. President Paul Kagame was invited to Korea three times in 2008, 2011, 2014 and one of the main agendas for State Summit with Korean Presidents was ICT investment from Korea. Rwanda opened its embassy in Seoul in 2009 and KOICA send a large number of KOICA volunteers to Africa. Even when Lee Suk-Chae, KT chairman who was under investigation by the Prosecutor's Office for professional negligence, paid a visit to Rwanda to participate in the Transform Africa Summit 2013, the exceptional overseas trip since the search-and-seizure warrant has been issued. The event was sponsored jointly by KT and the Rwandan government, attended by the summits of 12 African nations as well as high-ranking officials of the International Telecommunication Union (ITU) and the World Bank to discuss ways to develop African economies through the active use of ICT tools (Jun 2013). The Minister of Foreign Affairs made a special request to the Prosecution Service to allow Lee's attendance at the event.

There is no doubt that the Rwandan case is much more promising for Korea's engagement with the developing world based on mutual benefit. An important positive aspect and in difference to the case of Mozambique there was a large degree of ownership by the Rwandan government. The cooperation with Korean donors and the contract with KT was part of a Rwandan national development strategy since 2000. The Rwandan government has attributed the ICT projects and planned an improvement of information infrastructure, which would create jobs, support social progress and propel economic growth through the extensive investment in ICT sector. KT's partnership on ICT development in Rwanda well supports Rwanda's long-term developmental goals, embedded in its Vision 2020, to transform Rwanda from a low-income agriculture-based economy to a knowledge-based and service-oriented economy by 2020. Thanks to PPP projects with KT, Rwanda became the first African country to launch a wireless broadband facility (MOFAT, 2011). With the leading position in ICT infrastructure in the African continent, Rwanda launched a grand scheme to become an IT hub in Central Africa. The PPP model of the Government of Rwanda and KT, through the form of establishing joint venture companies is expected to be a role model for building broadband in developing countries as representing a hope that it is possible to leapfrog into the digital age.

Today KT's engagement can generally be considered a success story in which the close cooperation between the Korean company and a private company was able to gain access to the African IT market and beat established Western rivals such as British Telecom (BT). However, the Korean ICT projects have also been criticized that the developmental focus has been on the ICT consumption side, not the ICT production side. According to Heeks (2006), the former refers to the use of technology in applications like e-commerce and e-government; the latter to the creation of hardware, software and other components of the ICT infrastructure. More importantly, most of Korea's ODA to ICT involve tied aid. It is Korean firms that are contracted to build the tele-centers, the e-government systems, and so forth. Recipient national firms are excluded from participation. Therefore, in reality, Korea's ICT development projects make much less contribution than they could to economic development and the development of new livelihoods in the recipient countries. At worst, then, firms, communities and individuals in the developing countries are being seen as objects to serve the consumption of goods and services produced in Korea — a mere extension of the commercial focus of existing Korean exporters. Some argue that far from being a "new wave" of donor activity, Korea's ICT projects may instead resemble more of a throwback to activities of Western donors in the 1970s and 1980s. In those years, there was a strong linkage between aid and trade agencies in government. Aid projects were specifically used as a means to "shift kit" for western ICT firms; sometimes kits that were rather outdated (Odedra, 1993).

## Conclusions

The case studies of Korean cooperation with Mozambique and Rwanda have strengthened our original hypothesis that Korean economic relations with the developing world are primarily state-led and dominated by close cooperation between state and businesses. In this sense the two central elements of the Korean developmental state have survived by retreating into the field of development cooperation. As we have seen, the strong state involvement can be largely explained by the underdeveloped ability of Korean businesses to invest in new and risky environments abroad. While Korean businesses have freed themselves from the protection and support of the state within Korea they still need its support for the extension of their business to the developing world. We called this kind of transformation institutional relocation or institutional retreat in the sense that the specifically structured relationship between state and businesses that were weakened in their original policy area retreated to a new and much more limited policy niche.

A second aspect that enabled this institutional retreat is the lack of democratic scrutiny and civil society criticism in fields such as development cooperation at least compared to other areas of state-business relationships. Foreign policies generally are bias towards the executive and in addition development aid is rightly seen as an obligation of Korea being part of the global community. These positive goals have partly shielded the policy area of development cooperation from criticism. At the same time, the expansion of Korean businesses to the developing world is seen as beneficial for Korea as such. Thus, government-business collusion remains much less scrutinized in the field of development cooperation compared to the domestic level where it is primarily seen not as beneficial but as a problem. There might even be feedback loops in the sense that businesses criticize domestic activities to fight corruption because they are hurting the business of Korean companies abroad (Hwang, 2014). Most likely civil society scrutiny of development cooperation will increase as Korea's global role grows and more and more Koreans become interested in issues of the global South.

Another finding of this research is that the two studied cases differ quite substantially in the closeness of the cooperation between state and business, the type of the project and the expected outcome. In the case of Mozambique the project has been conducted by a state owned company. The government in Mozambique, the Korean government, a Korean state owned company together with other foreign investors made a classic closed door deal that is ensured to enrich investors and a few government officials in Mozambique while the effects on the development in Mozambique will be small or even negative due to the resource course effect. There was no civil society involvement or democratic oversight in Mozambique while the public in Korea concentrated on the benefits for Korea in this rare case of a (from Korean perspective) successful case of resource diplomacy.

In the case of Rwanda on the other hand the state cooperated with a privately owned business conglomerate in securing contracts for IT infrastructure projects. Development aid was used to incite Korean foreign investment and advance opportunities of a Korean private company and this form of using aid to advance economic interest might not be fully compatible with OECD-DAC rules. At the same time Korean investments in Rwanda will most likely have positive effects for Rwanda which means that state-business collusion can have positive aspects if it is embedded in a clear development plan and national ownership of the recipient country.

It was not the purpose of this paper to offer a comprehensive evaluation of Korean development cooperation but to try to understand why Korean development cooperation is conducted in the way it is done. Indeed our hunch is that the outcome of Korean development cooperation will be very mixed and not necessarily inferior to that of established donors. From out case studies it seems that the purpose of the development and investment project itself (resource extraction versus IT infrastructure) and the existence of sound national development plans in the recipient country are more important than detailed rules of aid effectiveness or untying aid from foreign economic policies. Nevertheless the Korea the strategy of strong state-business cooperation in the interaction with the developing world clashes with global standards and "best practices" of development cooperation that are formulated by the OECD-DAC. These rules highlight the need to untie official development assistance from commercial interests and industrial policies as well as a preference for grants as opposed to concessional loans.

Finally, this paper helps to understand why it is difficult for new donors like Korea but also bigger players such as China and Japan to follow global rules set by established Western donors. Their difficulties do not primarily come from a simple political decision to follow their "national interests" but we also have to take into account the domestic institutional path dependencies and the legacies of the East Asian state-led development model. All countries follow what they perceive to be their national interests. The difference is that the national interests of new donors such as Korea and China are different from those of established donors and thus not compatible with the global standards set by traditional Western players. Of course, this incompatibility is not an excuse for not following global rules, particularly if countries have subscribed to them like in the case of Japan and Korea as members of the OECD-DAC. There might be, however, the need to rethink of at least some of the global rules and take into account some of the experiences of new donors like the ones described in this paper. Indeed, one practical conclusion of this paper could be that issues of grants versus loans and untied versus tied aid might be less relevant then the purpose of the project and the governance capacity and ownership of the recipient country. Another implication concerns the debate on the role of PPP in development projects.

Much more research is needed to gain a better understanding of Korean development cooperation in the context of continuity and change of the Korean political economy and the legacy of the developmental state. Two research strategies seem to be particularly promising. First, we need more detailed case studies on how exactly Korean development cooperation is conducted. We need more studies on successful and failed projects to understand the mechanisms of state-business collaboration and how they affect the outcome. Second, we need more comprehensive academic evaluations of Korean development projects that go beyond the checklists and criteria of development agencies and that take into account the context of development cooperation not just in the donor country but in the recipient country as well.

## *Notes*

1 These include many important contributions different academic traditions (Pirie, 2005; Weiss, 2000; Weiss, 1999; Stubbs, 2009) as well as some of my own early work (Kalinowski, 2009; Kalinowski, 2008).

2. Another example of institutional retreat from a completely different context could be the institution of performance based pay that had quite disastrous effects in the field of banking in the time leading to the global financial crisis of 2008/09 is now extending into new areas such as the pay for CEOs of manufacturing companies or the salary of academic scholars. While excessive bonuses are now increasingly criticized and regulated in the financial sector they have extended into new areas without meeting similar critique and resistance.

3. There are many other examples where institutions, structures and even actors of the old Korean developmental state resurfaced in the field of development cooperation. One of the most actively promoted projects of development cooperation and knowledge sharing of is a relic from Korean development that was believed to be long forgotten: the new village (saemaul) movement under military dictator Park Chung Hee in the 1970s that aimed at developing rural communities. A lot of the actors involved in the original new village movement have now become promoters of the similar project in the developing world particularly since Park Geun-hye, the daughter of President Park Chung Hee was elected president in 2012.

# References

AfDB/OECD/UNDP. 2014. *African Economic Outlook: Rwanda 2014: Global Value Chains and Africa's Industrialisation*. Paris: OECD.

Coates, David. 2002. *Models of Capitalism: Debating Strengths and Weaknesses*. Cheltenham, UK; Northampton, MA: Edward Elgar Pub.

Darracq, Vincent and Daragh Neville. 2014. *South Korea's Engagement in Sub-Saharan Africa: Fortune, Fuel and Frontier Markets*. London: Chatham House.

Easterly, William Russell. 2006. *The White Man's Burden: Why the West's Efforts to Aid the Rest Have Done So Much Ill and So Little Good*. New York: Penguin Press.

Evans, Peter. 1995. *Embedded Autonomy: States and Industrial Transformation*. Princeton: Princeton University Press.

Folley, Rob. 2011. "Korea's ODA to Africa: Strategic or Humanitarian?" *SAIS US-KOREA 2010 Yearbook*, 83-94. Johns Hopkins University.

Gerschenkron, Alexander. 1962. *Economic Backwardness in Historical Perspective*. Cambridge, MA: Belknap Press of Harvard University Press.

Hall, Peter A. and David W. Soskice. 2001. *Varieties of Capitalism: The Institutional Foundations of Comparative Advantage*. Oxford; New York: Oxford University Press.

Heeks, Richard. 2006. *Implementing and Managing Egovernment: An International Text*. London: SAGE.

Hodgson, Geoffrey M. 2006. "What Are Institutions?" *Journal of Economic Issues* 40: 1-25.

Hwang, Jung-il. 2014. "Four-River Fines Dog Korean Companies Abroad." *Korea Jungang Daily*, 24 November.

Johnson, Chalmers A. 1982. *Miti and the Japanese Miracle: The Growth of Industrial Policy, 1925-1975*. Stanford: Stanford University Press.

_______. 1995. *Japan, Who Governs?: The Rise of the Developmental State*. New York: Norton.

Jun, Sel lee. 2013. "KT Chairman to Participate in 'Transform Africa Summit' in Rwanda." *The Korea Economic Daily*. 29 October.

Kalinowski, Thomas. 2008. "Korea's Recovery since the 1997/98 Financial Crisis: The Last Stage of the Developmental State." *New Political Economy* 13: 447-462.

_______. 2009. "The Politics of Market Reforms: Korea's Path from Chaebol Republic to Market Democracy and Back." *Contemporary Politics* 15: 287-304.

_______. 2010. "Can Korea Be a Bridge between Developing and Developed Countries in the G20 and Beyond?" In T. Fues and P. Wolff (eds.), *G20 and Global Development: How Can the New Summit Architecture Promote Pro-Poor Growth and Sustainability?* Bonn: DIE-GDI.

Kalinowski, Thomas and Hyekyung Cho. 2012. "Korea's Search for a Global Role between Hard Economic Interests and Soft Power." *European Journal of Development Research* 24: 242-260.

Kim, Eun Mee. 1997. *Big Business, Strong State : Collusion and Conflict in South Korean Development, 1960-1990*. Albany, NY: State University of New York Press.

Kim, Eun Mee, Pil Ho Kim, and Jinkyung Kim. 2013. "From Development to Development Cooperation: Foreign Aid, Country Ownership, and the Developmental State in South Korea." *The Pacific Review* 26: 313-336.

Kim, Jongil, Jung-min Kim, and Dong-geun Kang. 2014. *International Cooperation for Ict Sector Development in Vietnam*. Korea Institute for International Economic Policy .

Korea Eximbank. 2015a. *Mozambique Credit Rating Report 2015*. Seoul: Korea Eximbank.

_______. 2015b. Oda Statistics. Seoul: Korea Eximbank.

MOFAT. 2011. *Rwanda Profile*. Kigali: Embassy of the Republic of Korea in Rwanda.

Mugisha, Ivan R. and Collin S. Mwai. 2014. "4G Internet Launched". *The New Times*. 12 November.

Nirit, Ben-Ari. 2014. Big Dreams for Rwanda's Ict Sector [Online]. UN.

Odedra, Mayuri S., ed. 1993. *Enforcement of Foreign Techonology on Africa: Its Effect on Society, Culture, and Utilisation of Information Technology*. Cambridge: Intellect Press.

Pirie, Ian. 2005. "The New Korean State." *New Political Economy* 10(1): 25-42.

Republic of Rwanda. 2013. *National Broadband Policy for Rwanda*. Kigali: RITA.

Shin, Hyon-hee. 2012. "KOGAS Finds More Gas in Mozambique Field." *The Korea Herald*. 15 February.

Storz, Cornelia, Bruno Amable, Steven Casper, and Sebastien Lechevalier. 2013. "Bringing Asia into the Comparative Capitalism Perspective." *Socio-Economic Review* 11: 217-232.

Streeck, Wolfgang and Kathleen Ann Thelen. 2005. *Beyond Continuity: Institutional Change in Advanced Political Economies*. Oxford; New York: Oxford University Press.

Streeck, Wolfgang and Kozo Yamamura. 2001. *The Origins of Nonliberal Capitalism: Germany and Japan in Comparison*. Ithaca: Cornell University Press.

Stubbs, Richard. 2009. "What Ever Happened to the East Asian Developmental State? The Unfolding Debate." *The Pacific Review* 22: 1-22.

Veneroso, Frank and Robert Wade. 1998. "The Asian Crisis: The High Debt Model Versus the Wall Street-Treasury-Imf Complex." *New Left Review* I: 3-23.

Vitols, Sigurt. 2003. "From Banks to Markets: The Political Economy of Liberalization of the German and Japanese Financial Systems." pp. 240-260 in *The End of Diversity? Prospects for German and Japanese Capitalism,* edited by K. Yamamura and W. Streeck. Ithaca: Cornell University Press.

Wade, Robert H. 2004. *Governing the Market : Economic Theory and the Role of Government in East Asian Industrialization*. Princeton, NJ: Princeton University Press.

Walter, Andrew and Xiaoke Zhang. 2012. *East Asian Capitalism: Diversity, Continuity, and Change*. Oxford University Press.

Weiss, Linda. 1999. "State Power and the Asian Crisis." *New Political Economy* 4(3): 317-342.

_______. 2000. "Developmental States in Transition: Adapting, Dismantling, Innovating, Not 'Normalizing.'" *The Pacific Review* 13:

21-55.

Yamamura, Kozo and Wolfgang Streeck, eds. 2003. *The End of Diversity? Prospects for German and Japanese Capitalism*. Ithaca: Cornell University Press.

# *Exploring 21st Century Capitalisms and Asia: The Impact of Financialization*

Glenn Morgan

## Introduction

The study of institutions is increasingly dominated by discussions of change; how and why forms of capitalism are changing, particularly in the light of the impact of globalization, neo-liberalism and the 2008 Global Financial Crisis e.g. (Schmidt and Thatcher, 2013; Morgan and Whitley, 2012; Thelen, 2014; Streeck, 2014) and specifically on East Asia (Walter and Zhang, 2012: Whitley and Zhang, 2016). Mostly these discussions focus on particular national contexts and the impact on them of both internal and external changes. Rarely do they focus on the interdependencies between national capitalisms and even more rarely do these accounts examine interdependencies across regional contexts, e.g. between forms of western capitalism and forms of Asian capitalism. In this paper, I take the view that in order to understand these changes, it is necessary to undertake just such analysis and see how Western and Asian forms of capitalism are interacting in the current period. In so far as this interaction is examined in the comparative capitalisms context, it is primarily from the point of view of global production networks and how, why and with what effects the emergence of these networks is related to national and local institutions and processes of change within them. However in this paper, I examine the interactions from a different perspective. In particular, I focus on the concept of financialization. As many authors have pointed out (Van der Zwan, 2013), this concept has been used at a variety of levels — institutions, firms, states, financial institutions, individuals — to explain a fundamental shift in the nature of capitalism in the late 20th and early 21st centuries (Froud *et al.*, 2006; Martin, 2002; Carruthers, 2015; Engelen *et al*, 2011; Krippner, 2005). However it is noticeable that unlike global production networks where the nature of Asian forms of capitalism is a central part of the explanation for their growth, development and restructuring, the debate about financialization proceeds with very limited reference to Asia. This reflects in part the sense that still surrounds the concept — that it is primarily related to shifts in liberal market economies, particularly the US and the UK. Recent research both on other European countries and on the impact of the 2008 financial crisis leading into the Euro-crisis (see for example Alvarez, 2015; Engelen and Konings, 2010; also the contributions to the Special Issue of Socio-Economic Review July 2015) has shown how financialization is a process that is tying together Western economies in new and unexpected ways. Thus various forms of financialization are penetrating into not just liberal market economies but also more coordinated forms of capitalism. Unpicking where and how this occurs depends on detailed analysis of institutional legacies, political contingencies and the impact of global economic movements yet the point is clear. Financialization is not just about the US and the UK. Similarly it is not just about the US and Europe. We can expect that it will also figure in various ways in Asian forms of capitalism (see Guillen, 2015 for one of the few efforts to link all these parts of the global system together). This paper is an effort to consider in what ways financialization is emerging in Asian capitalism, how this connects it to processes of financialization in Western forms of capitalism and what the consequences of these interactions might be. The paper firstly describes financialization as it has emerged Western economies and how it has led to a restructuring in Western forms of capitalism. It emphasizes that financialization is a political process that builds a particular dynamic of capitalist development by facilitating the creation of coalitions of powerful actors that transform long standing institutions and create a new pattern of norms for states, firms, markets and individuals to abide by. There can be multiple forms of adaptation and resistance but an overwhelming logic of transformation continues, surviving even such setbacks as the 2008 Global financial crisis. The second part of the paper then asks what, if anything, the growth of this powerful coalition of interests and institutions linking European and US forms of capitalism together means for Asian forms of capitalism. Firstly are these trends independent of Asian forms of capitalism or are they somehow connected? If so, in what ways and with what consequences? Secondly are these trends towards financialization also appearing in Asian forms of capitalism and if so in what ways and with what impact on institutions, firms, states and individual actors?

## Financialization and Capitalism

Financialization remains a rather diffuse and elusive concept. This is in part because in academic literature it has been defined in a number of ways ranging from macro theories of the changing nature of society and the economy (Krippner, 2005; 2011), through firm-level accounts of the increased focus on short-term financial returns for shareholders (Froud *et al*, 2006) and through to the idea of the financialization of everyday life and individual identity as a result of the web of credit and debt in consumer societies (Martin, 2002). The approach taken here is that financialization can exist across a number of different levels; at each level it acts to dissolve previous norms and practices though the degree to which it achieves this and becomes dominant varies. Its success in this respect is partially dependent on the degree to which similar changes are occurring at other levels. In this sense there is a process analogous to what is described as 'institutional complementarity' in the varieties of capitalism literature (Hall and Soskice, 2001), i.e. if financialization has become more dominant at one level, this will fit with and produce stronger returns if it also exists at another level.

What are these levels of financialization and what resistances do these processes encounter? The first level is economy as a whole and the sources of profitability in the economy. The rise of first Japan, later Korea and more recently China, Vietnam etc. and other sources of cheap labour has undermined the profitability of many forms of manufacturing in the developed West. Whilst some more complex manufacturing remains, much has been outsourced to these alternative locations. Even in those manufacturing industries which remain, competition between firms from the developed economies as well as emerging has made it more difficult to create long-term sustainable advantage and stable profitability. This has led to a shift to services in many of the developed economies and in particular within the US and the UK a shift towards a focus on financial services. This is reflected not just in a growing banking sector but also in the way in which companies based in manufacture have extended themselves into financial services, often at first by providing credit to consumers for the purchase of their goods but gradually into more complex forms of finance. Selling financial products to households, corporations and to other financial institutions has for a variety of reasons become more profitable for many Western companies than selling goods and manufactures. Thus financialization at one level refers to this shift between sectors and across the economy as a whole so that finance becomes the dominant driver of economic growth as seen in the US and the UK in the 2000s up to the 2008 crisis.

A central driver in this process has been the extension of the financial markets based on shareholder value driven models of the firm (Davis, 2009; Froud *et al.*, 2000) where the concerns of senior managers became increasingly focused on generating short-term gains for shareholders in return for reward packages that were linked to this performance. From the 1980s, more activist policies on the part of shareholders drove a more powerful disciplinary regime over the actions of managers. Failure to produce returns would result in shareholder dissatisfaction which would emerge in falling share prices and the threat of takeover. The growth of the market for corporate control was primarily driven from within the financial system; there needed to be financial institutions capable of bringing together large scale loan capital at low enough interest rates to make the risks worthwhile. Favourable tax and legal regimes for these sorts of activities reinforced the emergence of such processes. Where profitability for manufactured goods was becoming increasingly difficult because of global competition, activities in the financial markets offered an alternative or additional source of profitability as rapid shifts in share price could be engineered by takeover bids bringing short term rewards to existing shareholders and managers. In terms of firm strategy, the result was that managers became increasingly focused on returning profits to shareholders, particularly through share buy back arrangements instead of retaining and investing in growth. Share buybacks were ways to push up the stock price that again advantaged existing shareholders and senior managers in stock option schemes. Thus senior managers increasingly turned to the bond markets to fund growth as interest rates were low and capital easily available (Lazonick and O'Sullivan, 2000; Lazonick, 2009).

The growth of shareholder driven firms impacts on the third level of financialization which is the growth of financial markets and these markets became increasingly powerful and influential in policy making pressing for forms of financial market deregulation and articulating and pressing for a low tax regime both in terms of personal taxation but also in terms of corporate taxes (Froud *et al.*, 2006; Froud *et al.*, 2007; Morgan and Sturdy, 2000). The Bretton Woods settlement aimed to place finance in a constrained position by regulating capital movements across national boundaries and within nation-states limiting the sorts of businesses and the sorts of structures which the banking sector could take on. As these controls were taken off and new financial markets invented and constructed, a massive expansion occurred. Whilst the US and the UK were central to these developments, by the 1990s, French and German banks, in particular but also other European banks were internationalizing in order to participate in the earnings potential of these markets. As rules about financial markets and institutions changed in key markets like the US and the UK, these firms spread across the world creating a series of inter-connected 'world cities' (Taylor and Walker, 2001) through which capital flowed supported by a vast array of services, such as law firms, accountants, consultants, advisers, regulators etc.. These markets expanded as financial surpluses grew (in expanding economies such as China, the Middle East, Russia, Brazil) and firms and wealthy individuals from these economies and from the US, Europe, Japan sought new outlets for their wealth. Financial institutions flooded with funds from investors demanding higher returns are incentivized to create new money (by increasing their leverage ratios and through this their lending) and new products. Unlike manufacturing industry where new product development can take years from conception to selling on the market, financial institutions have the capacities to develop new ways of engaging in the market in a matter of months. They can also adjust their offerings overnight once they have the basic contract established so they have no worries about ending up with products unsold and having to manage a massive inventory. From the 1990s through to the 2010s, financial institutions have been adept at developing new products. Derivatives, in particular, designed to protect against various forms of risk have grown exponentially. As well as performing their original function of protecting against risk, such products can also be purchased for purposes of speculation; rather than dispersing risk around the system, risk can become concentrated, e.g. as happened in 2008 (Morgan, 2010; 2012; Lounsbury and Hirsch, 2010; Carruthers, 2015). Ultimately, therefore, the new institutional ensemble that arises from the emergence of finance is one that leads to a high risk economic experimentation where booms and collapses become increasingly endemic (Minsky, 2008).

The concept of financialization, however, does not just describe the growth of the rich, the rise of finance in the economy, the changing nature of firms and the ensuing instabilities. It is also used to analyse wider changes in society and in particular the impact on firstly labour and work conditions and secondly on the state and state financing. In relation to labour, the pressure to maximize shareholder value feeds down into management strategies that seek to match labour requirements more closely to market conditions and to avoid processes of regulation and standardization that set rewards and work conditions through collective organization. This is reflected in Piketty's finding that the share of GDP going to labour has been shrinking in most countries compared to that going to capital (Piketty, 2014). Shareholder driven firms have increasingly looked to develop more diverse ways of managing their labour force; extensive outsourcing to emerging economies, the use of temporary and part-time contracts, the creation of 'self-employed' status for employees as ways of cutting wages and benefits. As work and careers become more precarious, and more individualized and rewards more uneven over the course of a lifetime due to firms restructuring and reducing core labour whilst increasingly employing temporary, part-time, low paid, agency based workers, a trend exacerbated by the growth of service work in retail and personal care (Wren, 2013), financial products become an essential supplement to wages and benefits, from the poorest dependent on loan sharks and payday loans through to home owners dependent on mortgages and credit cards whilst trying to save for pensions, education, health etc.. The result has been that incomes for the working population have been stagnating even in successful economies such as Germany and the US over the last 20 years due to the impact of global competition and the dismantling of labour market protections and regulations. Alongside this, welfare benefits supplied by collectivist schemes at state, occupation or firm level have been progressively eroded and replaced by private savings schemes. Staying out of poverty and maintaining a reasonable standard of living has become ever more demanding, requiring more and more dual wage-earning families.

This has boosted the financial markets in two respects. Firstly in order to purchase large cost items such as housing and cars and to pay for higher education and in the US health costs, individuals have increasingly had to borrow from financial institutions through mortgages, credit cards, and loans, usually at interest rates far higher than the banks themselves borrow at. The higher the risk profile of the borrower, the higher the rates of interest, a process reflected in the growth of pay day lending with interest rates over 1,000% per annum in some extreme cases. At the same time, individuals and families are pressurized to save in order to make themselves eligible for lower interest rate loans as well as so they can meet their own health and old age costs. Financial institutions have developed all sorts of products, though often with highly marginal differences on interest rates or conditions of withdrawal to ensure they gain these savings. The life chances of individuals and families are increasingly wrapped up in how they engage with the financial markets. Financial institutions developed an ever increasing array of pensions and savings products to suck in funds from individual savers pushed by states to become self-reliant in a lengthening old age (Fligstein and Goldstein, 2015).

The same increasingly goes for the state in Western capitalisms. Sovereign debt rose as countries sought to shrink their tax base following the policy recommendations of neo-liberalism whilst being constrained from shrinking their spending as much due to embedded social opposition and the need to respond to the challenges of global competition. As state borrowing in the bond markets expanded in order to support public spending when tax yields decreased due to declining levels of corporate tax take and reductions in higher rates of tax, annual budgets had to be managed increasingly carefully and governments resorted to privatizing former state services to reduce costs. The state divests itself of direct responsibility for the provision of public services, instead contracting these out to the private sector through creating market structures and market prices some of which require a vast panoply of expertise and technology to make them work, e.g. as in the energy market or telecoms. The 2008 Global financial crash exacerbated these processes as tax revenues further collapsed, demands on the welfare bill increased and at the same time states had to rescue their banking systems. States have covered the gaps from the financial markets in the process becoming what Streeck labels as 'debtor states' reliant on the good will of the markets to renew, extend and issue bonds at interest rates which are sustainable (Streeck, 2014).

By the 1980s, finance had grown sufficiently in the US and the UK and the ideological and technological supports for this extension had been established in contrast to the declining legitimacy of Keynesian constraints that key reforms were made such in both the wholesale and the retail financial services markets to enable the sector to expand rapidly (Mirowski, 2002; Peck, 2011; Morgan and Sturdy, 2000; Augar, 2008). As this new institutional complex around finance grew within and across national borders, resistance was limited , particularly as finance extended its presence into everyday life through the processes described earlier e.g. expansion of credit and mortgages, individual share-ownership efforts during phases of privatization and the reduction of collective forms of pension provision (in the state and in occupational/firm based schemes) with individual pension ownership (Lounsbury and Hirsch, 2010). These institutional experiments chimed with the changing nature of governance in big firms. For firms, as described earlier, their goal has become to maximize their financial value through squeezing their assets, borrowing for investment, selling back their shares to push up their price and making as much use as they can of tax opportunities to minimize their contribution to state treasuries. For states, a similar logic began to take hold from the two directions described earlier — borrowing from the financial markets (Krippner, 2011) and contracting out state services.

Clearly the degree of financialization differs across national contexts in Europe and the US; it appears in different forms depending in part on institutional legacies, path dependencies, political coalitions and external conditions. For example, different forms of housing provision and how these fit into the social reproduction of families and intergenerational inheritance clearly affects the degree to which financialization has embedded itself through mortgages (Schwartz and Seabrooke, 2008). Similarly legacies in terms of distinctive corporate governance systems such as the significance of Foundations as owners in the Nordic countries (Thompson and Kaspersen, 2012) or state ownership of minority shareholdings can reduce aspects of shareholder value type activity (Musacchio and Lazzarini, 2013).

Nevertheless in these economies, institutions of the state, welfare, and finance have been reshaped to facilitate the growth of financialization which eats ever more deeply into how actors define themselves and their role in the economy. Corporations focus more on short-term results, juggling their costs including labour in ways to satisfy shareholder demands. States are increasingly subjected to the discipline of financial markets as they borrow (whilst paradoxically at the same time propping them up). In the process, states are privatizing and contracting out as well as reducing the costs of benefits directly. The standard of living and security of families and individuals is increasingly wrapped up in how they manage their finances and in particular the balance between savings and debts at various points in the life cycle with issues of housing, health and pensions increasingly financialized.

## East Asian Capitalism and Financialization

What does the growth of financialization mean for East Asian forms of capitalism? The rest of this paper explores this question drawing on the diverse notion of financialization used in the first section of the paper and drawing analogies and/or connections across countries. Firstly are these trends dependent on Asian forms of capitalism? If so, in what ways? Secondly are these trends having similar impacts in Asia as in Western forms of capitalism?

## Dependent on Asian Forms of Capitalism?

The most obvious form of dependency arises from the way in which China has managed its surplus with the Western economies and particularly the US (Helleiner and Kirshner, 2012; 2014). China has kept much of this surplus in dollar form and has invested it primarily in safe havens such as US Treasury Bills (Schwartz, 2009). This has been described as a major part of the 'wall of money' which has arrived in the Western financial centres from the 1990s and has contributed to keeping interest rates low in the Western economies. Low interest rates in turn have driven 'the search for yield', i.e. the effort of financial institutions and investors to find returns which are above the safe returns from bonds. The result is a further pressure on two forces. First, this reinforces the push for firms to achieve high levels of returns to their investors through share buy-backs etc. Secondly it pushes financial institutions to find assets that can provide higher returns. This is the source of the development of financial derivatives in mortgages; packaging individual mortgages up into securitized bonds based on derivatives and then splitting these packages into various tranches enabled financial institutions to sell products which appeared to deliver higher than average returns whilst being relatively risk free, as credit rating agencies were rating such instruments as very safe with triple A status.

This surplus itself is dependent on the different cost structures of the US and China. Over the last two decades, the ability of Chinese firms to produce cheaply in a large number of mass production industries has led to a concentration of such activities in China and their decline in the West, a process which is ongoing and shifting, both within China (away from the coastal areas towards inland China) and within Asia (with the growing importance of other locations such as Vietnam etc.) (Steinfeld, 2004). The decline of manufacturing jobs in the US and elsewhere is an important factor weakening efforts at collective regulation and thus leading to the stagnation of wages and the decline of full time, long-term employment contracts in favour of temporary and part-time work. As a result of this stagnation, US workers have been driven into dependendence on credit as one way of maintaining their standard of living. Reducing the costs of their bill for providing health care and pension rights for workers as part of meeting Asian competition similarly pushes employees into personal savings for pensions and health. Thus one part of the consequences of the changing competitive position of US capitalism and Asian forms of capitalism is to push the growth of financialization.

This creates a curious dependency between China and the US. As Eichengreen and others have pointed out (Eichengreen, 2010), because so many investors from other countries keep their money in dollars, the dollar acts as a sort of reserve world currency. Nobody wants the dollar to significantly devalue as it would undermine the value of their holdings; they therefore continue to invest in the dollar which receives seigneurage advantages from this. On the other hand, the US government may allow the dollar to devalue in order to improve competitiveness. The printing of money under the quantitative easing process also brings fears of inflation and a possible future reduction in the value of the dollar but to shift assets out of the dollar is only likely to lead to further devaluation. So long as the dollar remains central to international trade and the 'safe' haven at times of volatility, China will have difficulty disentangling itself from the one-sided nature of this relationship (Prasad, 2014). China has indicated its dissatisfaction with this and has begun discussions on the development of a different form of reserve currency in terms of the Special Withdrawing Rights which the IMF has developed as an alternative to the dollar as a 'world currency'. Nevertheless the way the two countries have accommodated to the change in the global division of labour leaves them interdependent and managing potential conflict areas in order not to damage their own interests (Guillen, 2015: ch. 5).

These macro-economic dependencies clearly also affect the terms of trade between currencies and from this trade flows. Most Asian economies use a form of the dollar peg to keep them in line with the US currency and ensure that there is no disruption to trade caused by rapid devaluations. However, under Abe (as discussed below) Japan has engaged in just such a devaluation which has led to fears of a currency war particularly with China where minor adjustments of the value of the remnimbi have been undertaken to combat losing competitiveness. If China's competitiveness does begin to decline and the trade surplus with the US declines, then it may be that the 'wall of money' will decline, contributing to rising interest rates and a form of 'credit crunch' affecting all those companies and individuals that have become overendebted. Another threat is if China starts to liquidate its holdings in US Treasuries because it needs the funds to deal with its own internal problems, e.g. the emerging banking crisis in China due to overlending on unproductive assets in the aftermath of the 2008 Financial crisis and global downturn. Another potential pressure on China is expanding middle class consumption by offering more credit facilities and/or by reducing the pressure to save; this can be done by expanding areas of state provision of welfare (housing, education, health, pensions). Growing state expenditure in this area, however, has implications not only for administration but also for the organization of taxation, both of which are enmeshed in all sorts of complex relationships in contemporary China and would be difficult to reform. Finally a threat to this system lies in the politics of China and if there is any destabilization of the current regime arising from the disparate causes of unrest which bubble under the blanket of repression and control currently exercised by the Chinese Communist Party.

In this sense, financialization in the West is threatened by growing currency wars, the possibility of the decline of Chinese competitiveness and the need of the Communist Party to manage these processes whilst retaining control over the loyalty of the population in part through extending the material rewards of the system (see also Helleiner and Kirshner, 2014). Thus at this macroeconomic level, there is strong interdependency between financialization and Asian, particularly Chinese, capitalism.

## Are Asian Economies Becoming Financialized in the Same Way as Western Capitalisms?

In the earlier discussion, financialization was described in terms of the way in which firms were organized, the centrality of financial markets to the economy, the dependence of the state on the financial markets and the degree to which the lives of individuals were financialized.

### *Firms*

In broad terms the way corporate governance and ownership is organized in Asian capitalisms remains distinct from the shareholder value model of firms in the West. Key practices like the importance of family majority ownership, the existence of business group structures, support from the state appear across many Asian economies (Aguilera and Jackson, 2010; Aguilera *et al.*, 2012). Whilst many firms sell a portion of their shares on stock markets in Asia and in the West, they rarely sell sufficient (or sufficient of the right kind where there are category A and category B shares available, the latter with non-voting rights) to enable a market for corporate control to emerge. Managements in most Asian companies are unlikely to be ousted by external shareholders; the dynamics of conflict within boards will usually be hidden and will occur between family members or between insiders of various sorts. The weakness of external shareholders protects against the sort of short term pressures which are exerted for returns in the West, though it also leads to the possibility of insiders raiding corporate assets and using them for their own purposes, including personal consumption or bribery or to exert political influence as has happened in the Korean case in relation to the leaders of some *chaebols*. It also seems clear that levels of reward for senior executives have not expanded to the same degree as in the US and the UK. The use of stock options, a source of major inequality in the West, is still limited in Japan. Arguing that Asian firms are not financialized along the lines of what has occurred in the US and elsewhere does not mean that they are necessarily more investment focused or less unequal but rather that the constraints under which they operate and the choices they make have not been restructured into a financialization mould.

### *Financial Markets*

It is the case that Western financial institutions have moved into certain parts of Asia and have tried to establish markets for corporate control. Japan, for example, has experienced waves of entry of US banking institutions and whilst there has been a small increase in mergers, these remain usually by mutual consent rather than takeover battles. Private equity and hedge funds have also established themselves in Japan but they remain more like part of the existing investment management community than a radical alternative as they present themselves in the West. Derivatives markets are growing in Asia in terms of currency risk, interest rate risk, credit risk etc. but these markets were not initiators of the products that led to the 2008 crash. Nor were they major buyers of these instruments compared to US and European financial institutions.

### *Financial Institutions and Financial Markets*

Under conditions of financialization, financial institutions and financial markets become more powerful drivers in the economy and source of the most profitable businesses. In Japan and Korea, the financial institutions have generally been subordinate to and supportive of major manufacturing companies, a process reinforced by the way in which the state has managed the banking sector as a source of capital for development. In Korea, a brief period of deregulation in the early 1990s led to an influx of foreign capital that was recycled by the banks loosened from the tight control which previously the state had exercised over them. As a consequence asset prices boomed without being able to develop sustained returns commensurate with the new investment. Once this became clear, foreign capital left and the Korean financial system collapsed. In the reform period to 2000, tighter regulation was placed over the banks (Haggard *et al.*, 2003) at the same time as they were separated more clearly from the state, placing them on a more commercial footing. Meanwhile the state accumulated more foreign reserves to protect itself against the volatility of foreign investment and currency fluctuations. In Japan, a period of financial expansion during the 1980s built on the revaluation of the yen due to Japanese competitiveness and accretion of foreign reserves led to a strengthening of the yen and an asset price boom in the stock market and in property as well as a vast growth of over-priced foreign assets. Japanese firms and individuals borrowed to invest at home and abroad, speculating that prices would continue to rise irrespective of the quality of the underlying asset. When the bubble burst, Japanese banks were left with large debts and holes in their balance sheets due to the failure of the over-valued assets to deliver. For much of the 1990s, these debts were not resolved and Japanese growth stagnated. As a result of these crises and their overhang, neither Japanese nor Korean banks participated much in the expansion of financial products occurring in the US and UK during the alte 1990s and 2000s reducing their exposure to the financialization trends noted earlier. China on the other hand which seemed relatively insulated from these financialization pressures until around 2010 now seems to be heading into a similar credit crisis as post 2008, the government released the banks to make loans easier so that spending on infrastructure could substitute for shrinking demand on the world market for Chinese goods. As in Korea and Japan, this created an asset price boom in which speculation was rife and firms and individuals borrowed in the expectation that prices would continue to move up. However, many of the assets have failed to deliver returns and as a result many banks are having to be propped up by the state. Similarly, prices have been falling on China's stock markets as economic growth has slowed. Individuals and companies which borrowed to speculate as the market was moving up are in increasing difficulties. If they liquidate too quickly, price falls speed up leading to catastrophic losses and bankruptcies. The Chinese government has closed stock exchanges and trading to stop this happening and it has other weapons in its armoury to defend itself, not least its huge foreign exchange reserves but nevertheless, these developments have potential global significance given the role that China plays in the world economy. In conclusion, Asian capitalisms have not purposely grown large independent financial sectors free from state control; mostly the state has framed the way in which finance works and where it has loosened the controls, the results have generally been to lead to credit crises, causing the state to come back into the equation. However, the current situation in China reflects the inability of even such a strong state avoiding crises arising from the expansion of financialization.

### *States and Financialization*

Does Streeck's concept of the debtor state apply in East Asia? Certainly Japan has a high level of borrowing to GDP (226% in 2011) but much of this debt is held by Japanese citizens and not by global financial institutions. It is therefore less subject to the risk that interest rates will be driven higher because overseas financial institutions have begun to reassess risk. This is not to claim that the Japanese state is unaffected by the size of its debt — this is clearly not the case and the difficulties of resolving this revolve around the role of increased taxation (politically unpopular and also a further dampener on the Japanese economy) versus reducing state expenditure either via cutting welfare and education costs or via privatisations or by reducing the sort of 'pork-barrel' politics which has been central to Japanese politics and the dominance of the Liberal Democratic Party for most of the post-war period. Another option being followed by the Abe government is deliberately stoking inflation (so that debt can be repaid more easily) by printing more money resulting in the other advantage of devaluing the Japanese yen and making it more competitive against other currencies such as China, Taiwan and Korea. The potential for currency wars in East Asia is high in these circumstances. Is Japan a 'debtor state'; yes it is and this is affecting state services and leading to more debate on the balance between collective and individual welfare provision but Japan is distinguished from the Western debtor states because most of its debt is held internally and long-term. Korea on the other hand has been careful to avoid debt. Its debt to GDP ratio in 2012 was 33% whereas the US was approaching 90% and the UK 75%, whilst the European countries worst hit by the sovereign debt crisis were over 100% up to 165% in 2012 for Greece. Finally the Chinese state appears a very complex case. The ability of the state to control the external funds generated by the country's expansion and its use of state banks internally mean that an essential part of keeping Chinese capitalism on the road revolves around managing finance. But contrary to the West, it still seems that it is the state that is in the driving seat and it is not being pushed out of that by foreign capital and the forces of financialization emanating from the West.

### *Individuals, Families and Financialization in Asian Capitalisms*

In the Western economies, the collapse of state welfare systems under the pressure of financialization led to an increased interdependence of individuals and families on the credit provision side of finance as well as on the savings side. The expansion of credit also appears to be occurring rapidly in East Asia. According to a survey conducted by the German financial services provider Allianz in 2014, household debt was increasing fastest in the world in China, growing 332% in 2013. Household debt as a % of GDP in Korea was 92.9%, the 10th highest in the world. In terms of total household debt (i.e. unadjusted for population), Japan and China were 2nd and 3rd in the world respectively some way behind the US. On the other hand, China also has a very high savings rate (50.1% in 2013) as does Korea (34.1%) compared to the UK (15.1%) and the US (16.3%). Japan which traditionally had a high savings rate still remains above the Western economies but is gradually declining — from 20% in 2010 to 18.3% in 2013. These figures make clear that the financial sector in these East Asian capitalisms is increasingly becoming entangled with people's lives as these economies make the adjustment to higher expectations about standards of living. This requires much further investigation to assess the degree to which everyday life is becoming financialized in these economies. One aspect which needs particular attention in comparison to Western capitalisms is the role of the family as a source of financial aid and security. High levels of savings in China reflect a general distrust of the state and the banking institutions and a preference for keeping funds amongst the family, although interestingly recent research has shown that for the very richest Chinese access to tax havens via Hong Kong has become an important way to protect one's capital against the state even if this is illegal and increasingly opens one up to the severest punishment.

## Conclusions

Western forms of capitalism have over the last two decades become increasingly financialized. This process has affected firms and their corporate governance and strategy together with their modes of management of labour, financial markets and their expansion linked to the growth of the new financial products, states and their increased dependence on financial markets and individuals, families and households and their dependence on financial markets. This set of processes has changed the institutional framework of Western forms of capitalism to varying degrees with impacts on inequality, security, welfare policy, taxation, innovation and the provision of state services. The paper asked firstly how these processes are connected to developments in Asian capitalisms and secondly whether Asian capitalisms were becoming more financialized. With regard to the first question, Western financialization was seen as highly interdependent with developments in China in two ways. Firstly, the relative competitive position of China and the US based on the forms of labour control and regulation in both countries had led to China building a huge trade surplus with the US and effectively destroying many areas of manufacturing. This weakened the power of US labour to resist the development of shareholder value ideology a key part of financialization. It also meant that China had a surplus of dollars which it had to handle carefully.

China decided to invest large amounts in US Treasury Bills and this recirculation of the surplus into the US financial system was an essential part of creating a low interest rate environment which facilitated increased borrowing, sometimes in order to take on risk that might yield higher returns. So financialization in the West is highly dependent on the stability of China.

Is financialization penetrating into these East Asian forms of capitalism? Overall, the answer seems to be that this is not the case. Financial institutions are not the dominant players and in Japan and Korea have been relatively weak over recent years. State borrowing from the markets is limited in Korea; state borrowing is very high in Japan but predominantly from Japanese citizens rather than the financial markets. In the Chinese case, the government has massive financial resources which it directs internally and externally for its own interests. Whilst there is evidence that this has led to an asset boom in China and huge losses for banks, and that this is creating worries about the instability of the Chinese financial system and the potential knock-on effects of this, this is because the state has over-reached itself not because the financial institutions have independently brought a crisis as could be said about 2008. Perhaps the most interesting aspect of financialization in the Asian case is the expansion of credit and debt to the population as a whole. It would be interesting to understand this further and how it is related to changes in regulation, changes in wages and salaries, changes in state and corporate welfare and changes in expectations, though all of this needs to be considered in a context where the extended family as the financial unit remains much more important than in the West. To what degree might financialization from below drive other changes in the institutionalization of financialization.

## *References*

Aguilera, Ruth V. and Gregory Jackson. 2010. "Comparative and International Corporate Governance." *The Academy of Management Annals* 4(1): 485-556.

Aguilera, Ruth V., L. R. Kabbach de Castro, J. H. Lee, and J. You. 2012. "Corporate Governance in Emerging Markets." pp. 319-344 in *Capitalisms and Capitalism in the Twenty-First Century*. Oxford: Oxford University Press.

Alvarez, Ignacio. 2015. "Financialization, Non-Financial Corporations and Income Inequality: The Case of France." *Socio-Economic Review* 13(3): 449-475.

Augar, Philip. 2008. *The Death of Gentlemanly Capitalism: The Rise and Fall of London's Investment Banks*. London: Penguin.

Carruthers, Bruce. 2015. "Financialization and the Institutional Foundations of the New Capitalism." *Socio-Economic Review* 13(2): 379-398.

Davis, Gerald F. 2009. *Managed by the Markets:How Finance Re-Shaped America*. Oxford: Oxford University Press.

Eichengreen, Barry. 2010. *Exorbitant Privilege: The Rise and Fall of the Dollar and the Future of the International Monetary System*. Oxford: Oxford University Press.

Engelen, Ewald and Martijn Konings. 2010. "Financial Capitalism Resurgent: Comparative Institutionalism and the Challenges of Financialization." pp. 601-624 in *The Oxford Handbook of Comparative Institutional Analysis*, edited by Glenn Morgan *et al.* Oxford: Oxford University Press.

Engelen, Ewald, Ismail Erturk, Julie Froud, Sukhdev Johal, Adam Leaver, Mick Moran, Adriana Nilsson, and Karel Williams. 2011. *After the Great Complacence: Financial Crisis and the Politics of Reform*. Oxford: Oxford University Press.

Fligstein, Neil and Adam Goldstein. 2015. "The Emergence of a Finance Culture in American Households, 1989-2007." *Socio-Economic Review* 13(3): 575-601.

Froud, Julie, C. Haslam, Sukhdev Johal, and Karel Williams. 2000.

"Restructuring for Shareholder Value and Its Implications for Labour." *Cambridge Journal of Economics* 24(6): 771-797.

Froud, Julie, Adam Leaver, and Karel Williams. 2007. "New Actors in a Financialised Economy and the Remaking of Capitalism." *New Political Economy* 12(3): 339-347.

Froud, Julie, Sukhdev Johal, Adam Leaver, and Karel Williams. 2006. *Financialization and Strategy*. London: Routledge.

Guillen, Mauro F. 2015. *The Architecture of Collapse*. Oxford: Oxford University Press.

Haggard, Stephan, Wonhyuk Lim, and Euysung Kim. 2003. *Economic Crisis and Corporate Restructuring in Korea*. Cambridge: Cambridge University Press.

Hall, Peter A. and David Soskice. 2001. *Varieties of Capitalism: The Institutional Foundations of Comparative Advantage*. Oxford: Oxford University Press.

Helleiner, Eric and Jonathan Kirshner. 2012. *The Future of the Dollar*. Ithaca, NY: Cornell University Press.

Helleiner, E. and J. Kirshner. 2014. *The Great Wall of Money*. Ithaca, NY: Cornell University Press.

Krippner, Greta R. 2005. "The Financialization of the American Economy." *Socio-Economic Review* 3(2): 173-208

Krippner, G. R. 2011. *Capitalizing on Crisis*. Cambridge, MA: Harvard University Press.

Lazonick, William. 2009. "The New Economy Business Model and the Crisis of US Capitalism." *Capitalism and Society* 4(2): article 4.

Lazonick, William and Mary O'Sullivan. 2000. "Maximizing Shareholder Value: A New Ideology for Corporate Governance." *Economy and Society* 29(1): 13-35

Lounsbury, Michael and Paul M. Hirsch. 2010. *Markets on Trial: The Economic Sociology of the US Financial Crisis*. Vol. 2. Emerald Group Publishing.

Martin, Randy. 2002. *Financialization of Daily Life*. Philadelphia: Temple University Press.

Minsky, Hyman. 2008. *Stabilizing an Unstable Economy*. Vol. 1. New York: McGraw Hill.

Mirowski, Philip. 2002. *Machine Dreams: Economics Becomes a Cyborg Science*. Cambridge: Cambridge University Press.

Morgan, Glenn. 2010. "Legitimacy in Financial Markets: Credit Default Swaps in the Current Crisis." *Socio-Economic Review* 8(1): 17-45.

_______. 2012. "Reforming OTC Markets." *European Business Organization Law Review* 13: 391-342.

Morgan, Glenn and Andrew Sturdy. 2000. *Beyond Organizational Change*. London: Palgrave MacMillan.

Morgan, Glenn and Richard Whitley. 2012. *Capitalisms and Capitalism in the Twenty-First Century*. Oxford: Oxford University Press.

Musacchio, Aldo and Sergio Lazzarini. 2013. *Leviathan Evolving: New Varieties of State Capitalism in Brazil and Beyond*. Cambridge, MA: Harvard University Press.

Peck, Jamie. 2011. *Constructions of Neoliberal Reason*. Oxford: Oxford University Press.

Piketty, Thomas. 2014. *Capital in the Twenty-First Century*. Harvard: Belknap Press.

Prasad, Eswar S. 2014. *The Dollar Trap Princton*. Princeton, NJ: Princeton University Press.

Schmidt, Vivien A. and Mark Thatcher. 2013. *Resilient Liberalism in Europe's Political Economy*. Cambridge: Cambridge University Press.

Schwartz, Herman M. 2009. *Subprime Nation*. Ithaca, NY: Cornell Univ Press.

Schwartz, Herman M. and Leonard Seabrooke. 2008. "Varieties of Residential Capitalism in the International Political Economy: Old Welfare States and the New Politics of Housing." *Comparative European Politics* 6(3): 237-261.

Steinfeld, Edward S. 2004. "China's Shallow Integration: Networked Production and the New Challenges for Late Industrialization." *World development* 32(11): 1971-1987.

Streeck, Wolfgang. 2014. *Buying Time*. London: Verso.

Taylor, Peter J. and D. R. F. Walker. 2001. "World Cities: a First Multivariate Analysis of Their Service Complexes." *Urban Studies*

38(1): 23-47.

Thelen, Kathleen. 2014. "Varieties of Liberalization and the New Politics of Social Solidarity." Cambridge: Cambridge University Press.

Thompson, Grahame F. and Lars B. Kaspersen. 2012. "The Globalization of the Business Sector in a Small Open Economy: the Case of Denmark and Its Wider Implications." *Socio-Economic Review* 10(4): 627-653.

Van der Zwan, Natascha. 2013. "Making Sense of Financialization." *Socio-Economic Review* 12: 99-129.

Walter, Andrew and Xiaoke Zhang. 2012. *East Asian Capitalism*. Oxford: Oxford University Press.

Whitley, Richard and Xiaoke Zhang, eds. 2016. *Changing East Asian Business Systems*. Oxford: Oxford University Press.

Wren, Anne. 2013. *The Political Economy of the Service Transition*. Oxford: Oxford University Press.

# Biographies

**Hyun-Chin Lim** is Professor Emeritus of Sociology and Founding Director of Asia Center at Seoul National University. He is Member of the National Academy of Sciences, Korea, and serves as the president of Korean Social Science Research Council. He taught and did research at Harvard, Chicago, University of California (San Diego), Duke, Paris Diderot, and Vietnam National University (Hanoi). He was previously the dean of Faculty of Liberal Education, the dean of the College of Social Sciences, and the director of Asia Center, all at Seoul National University. He also served as the president of such professional association as Korean Association of NGO Studies, Korean Sociological Association, and International Development and Cooperation Association. His publications include more than 50 books and over 250 scholarly articles on dependency, development, democracy, and civil society in East Asia and Latin America.

**Jan Nederveen Pieterse** is Mellichamp Professor of Global Studies and Sociology at the University of California, Santa Barbara. He specializes in globalization, development studies and cultural anthropology. He was previously at the University of Illinois Urbana-Champaign, the Institute of Social Studies in The Hague, the University of Cape Coast, Ghana, and the University of Amsterdam. He holds a part-time chair at Maastricht University. He currently focuses on new trends in twenty-first-century globalization and the implications of economic crisis. He is on the editorial board of Clarity Press, the *Journal of Global Studies* and e-global, and is associate editor of the *European Journal of Social Theory, Ethnicities, Third Text* and the *Journal of Social Affairs.*

**Suk-Man Hwang** is Professor of Sociology at Changwon National University. He studied Sociology at Yonsei University, Korea, where he got BA and MA, and received his PhD from University of Illinois at Chicago. After returning to Korea, he worked for the Research Center for the Federation of Korea Trade Unions. He also taught about Asian development at the Schools of Business Studies of the Trinity College, University of Dublin, Ireland. His recent research interest is related to the post-developmental state model in Korea.

**Kyong-Dong Kim** is Professor Emeritus of Seoul National University and Member of the National Academy of Sciences, Korea. He previously taught at North Carolina State University at Raleigh, L'Ecole des Hautes Etudes en Sciences Sociales in Paris, Duke University, Korea Development Institute School of Public Policy and Management, and Korea Advanced Institute of Science and Technology College of Business, and was Fellow of Woodrow Wilson International Center for Scholars, Washington, DC. He published internationally on development, modernization, Confucianism, industrial relations, political sociology, education, in journals and edited books, and was awarded major academic prizes in Korea.

**Wolf Schäfer** is a Professor of History at Stony Brook University and has served twice as interim Dean of International Academic Programs & Services. Educated at the universities of Marburg, Bonn, Kings College London, Munich, and Bremen, he earned an MA in History, International Politics, and Philosophy, followed by a PhD in History of Science and Technology and Social History. He pioneered global history (as an alternative to world history) and founded the Center for Global & Local History (home of the *Long Island History Journal*), as well as the Stony Brook Institute for Global Studies. The author of over eighty articles and ten books, Schäfer also founded the *Globality Studies Journal*, which he edits. His current research seeks to distinguish between functional and dysfunctional management styles in the organization of big science projects in the United States and Germany during World War II.

**Markus Pohlmann** is a full professor in Sociology at the University of Heidelberg, Germany. His major fields of research are Sociology of Organization, Sociology of Management, Economic Sociology, Organizational Deviance and Corruption Studies. He received his diploma in Sociology at the University of Bielefeld. After his PhD he went to the University of Jena in the Eastern Part of Germany as an assistant and associate professor. He stayed several years abroad, doing research in the US, in South Korea, Taiwan, Singapore and Hong Kong. He had conducted a research project on Top Managers and the New Spirit of Capitalism in 11 countries. His recent research is focusing on organizational deviance and active corruption in the US, Germany, Brazil, and China.

**Nan Lin** is The Oscar L. Tang Family Professor of Sociology Emeritus, Duke University. He is an Academician at Academia Sinica, Taiwan and holds an honorary doctorate degree from the National Chengchi University, Taiwan. Previously he was Director of the Asian/Pacific Studies Institute at Duke and Vice President of the American Sociological Association. His research areas include social networks and social capital, economic sociology, social stratification and inequality, and Chinese societies. His recent books include *Social Capital and its Institutional Contingency* (editor with Yangchih Fu and Chih-jou Jay Chen, Routledge, 2014), *Social Capital: Critical Concepts in Social Sciences* (editor, 4 volumes, Routledge, 2011), and *Social Capital: An International Research Program* (editor with Bonnie Erickson, Oxford, 2008).

**Alvin Y. So** is Chair Professor at the Division of Social Science, Hong Kong University of Science and Technology. His research interests include development, social class and social conflict, and East Asian societies. His recent publications include *The Global Rise of China* (co-authored with Yin-Wah Chu, Polity, 2015), and *Class and Class Conflict in Post-Socialist China* (World Scientific, 2013).

**Yin-Wah Chu** is Associate Professor at Department of Sociology, Hong Kong Baptist

University. Her research interests include development, social resistance, and East Asia. She is editor of *Chinese Capitalisms* (Palgrave Macmillan, 2010), *The Asian Developmental State* (Palgrave Macmillan, 2016), co-editor of *East Asia's New Democracies* (Routledge, 2010), and co-author of *The Global Rise of China* (Polity, 2015). She has also published research in Economy and Society, International Journal of Urban and Regional Research, Urban Studies, and Journal of Contemporary Asia.

**Tobias ten Brink** is Professor of Chinese Economy and Society and director of China Global Center at Jacobs University. He was Visiting Professor for International Political Studies at University Witten/Herdecke, Germany, and fellow at the Institute for Social Research, Frankfurt. His research centers on the political economy of China and large emerging economies. Since 2011 he is Network Organizer ("Asian Capitalisms") for the annual SASE-Conferences (Society for the Advancement of Socio-Economics). He has published numerous articles in academic journals, and his books include *Global Political Economy and the Modern State System* (Brill, 2014), which was awarded by the German Publishers & Booksellers Association in the category 'Humanities international,' and *Chinas Kapitalismus. Entstehung, Verlauf, Paradoxien* [China's Capitalism: Emergence, Trajectory, Paradoxes] (Campus, 2013).

**Andrew Rosser** is Professor of Southeast Asian Studies at the University of Melbourne and a political economist who works on development issues in Southeast Asia, especially Indonesia and Timor Leste. He is currently working on a research project focused on law, politics and socioeconomic rights in Indonesia courtesy of an Australian Research Council Future Fellowship. He has worked at the Institute of Development Studies (Sussex), AusAID, the University of Sydney and Murdoch University and acted as a consultant to the World Bank, the UK Department for International Development, the Organisation for Economic Cooperation and Development, Oxfam, UNRISD, UNDP, and the Department of Foreign Affairs and Trade.

**Maryke van Diermen** is a researcher in International development. She is an Indonesian social policy specialist. Her main expertise span the areas of the political economy of policy making, the politics of inclusion, governance, social protection and poverty reduction. She is currently completing her PhD in International Development at the University of Adelaide.

**Hyungkee Kim** teaches political economy and labor economics at Kyungpook National University. He is a member of editorial board of International Critical Thought. His recent research area is economic development model, especially East Asian Development Model. He wrote many books and articles on labor economic problems and economic development. Major books include *New Political Economy* (2001) and *An Alternative Development Model: Beyond Neoliberalism* (2007). His recent articles include "Capitalism after the Great Recession: Agenda for a New Progressive Development Model," *World Review of Political Economy* 1(2)(2010), and "he Great Transformations in the Korean Economy since 1962: Processes and Consequences," in Boyer, Robert et al, eds.(2012), *Diversity and Transformations of Asian Capitalisms.*

**Rodrigo Luiz Medeiros da Silva** received his PhD in Sociology from the University of São Paulo in 2012 and then joined the Latin American Institute of Economics, Society and Politics at Unila (Federal University for Latin American Integration, Brazil), as the Adjunct Professor of International Economics. He also holds Bachelor's and Master's Degrees in Economics. He is involved in researches concerning the evolution of the Capitalist World-System and the impact of its rebalances on peripheral development, and is a member of the group responsible for creating ECLA's Gratuate Programm in Economic Planning.

**Joonkoo Lee** is Assistant Professor of Organization Studies in the School of Business at Hanyang University, Seoul. Before joining Hanyang in 2012, he was a postdoctoral research scholar in the Social Science Research Institute at Duke University and a sector coordinator for the Capturing the Gains research programme. His research interests include globalization and development, global value chains, organization studies, political economy inAsia, and cultural and creative industries. His work has appeared in Proceedings of the National Academy of Sciences, European Planning Studies, *Journal of Supply Chain Management*, and *critical perspectives on international business*.

**Thomas Kalinowski** is an Associate Professor of Political Science at the Graduate School of International Studies, Ewha Womans University in Seoul, Korea. He is teaching International Political Economy, Comparative Political Economy, European Integration, International Organizations and Development. After receiving his PhD from Freie Universität Berlin in 2004, he was a lecturer at Humboldt University Berlin, a postdoctoral fellow at the University of California in Berkeley and a visiting assistant professor at Brown University, Providence. Recent publications include works on financial crisis, financial regulation and bank reform, the IMF, the global role of East Asia, the diversity of capitalism, and the transformation of the East Asian developmental state. Currently Professor Kalinowski is working on a book about the international regulation of finance. You can follow his research at www.researchgate.net/profile/Thomas_Kalinowski.

**Min Joung Park** is a PhD student in the Graduate School of International Studies at Ewha Womans Univertisy. She received the Master of Science in International Development Studies from London School of Economics and Political Science (LSE), UK. She served as a Policy Specialist in the Development Policy Division and African Division at the Ministry of Foreign Affairs, Republic of Korea. Her research interests focus on Korea's foreign policy towards Africa, developmental state, private sector engagement in development.

**Glenn Morgan** is Professor of Management at Bristol University in the UK. He has previously worked at Cardiff Business School, Warwick Business School and Manchester Business School. He has held visiting appointments at Copenhagen Business School, University of Paris 1 (Sorbonne), University of Aix-en-Provence, University of Alberta and WZB, Berlin. In 2014-2015, he was President of the Society for the Advancement of Socio-Economics. Recent edited book publications include *Capitalisms and Capitalism in the 21st century* (Oxford UP, 2012), *Elites on Trial* (Volume in Research on the Sociology of Organziations series, 2015); *The Oxford Handbook of Sociology, Social Theory and Organization Studies* (Oxford UP, 2014), *The Oxford Handbook of Comparative Institutional Analysis* (Oxford UP, 2010). He has published articles in a range of journals including *Socio-Economic Review, Economy and Society, Sociology, Organization Studies, Human Relations*. From 2005 to 2008 he was Chief editor of the journal Organization.

# Index

## C



## D

## H



## I



## J



## K

## L



## M

## N



## O



## P

## X



## Y



## Z